GROWING A NEW ECONOMY

BEYOND CRISIS CAPITALISM & ENVIRONMENTAL DESTRUCTION

Growing a New Economy

Beyond Crisis Capitalism & Environmental Destruction

Roar Bjonnes and Caroline Hargreaves

InnerWorld Publications
San Germán, Puerto Rico
www.innerworldpublications.com

Dedication

Roar wants to dedicate this book to:

My parents, Tor and Ranveig Bjonnes, who taught me that economic and environmental justice is won through struggle, and to my wife, Radhika, for reminding me that despite the struggle, love is all there is.

Caroline wants to dedicate this book to:

The teachers who have paved my path, to deep ecology and living systems, to the sacred feminine, and to Thomas for always keeping it real.

Contents

Introduction

THE DATA IS IN, the experts have spoken. Today's global economy is in deep trouble, both financially and environmentally. The debt, inequality, and environmental crises are troubling signs that our economic system is not working, and many economists and environmentalists believe we are rapidly heading toward a global meltdown, a perfect storm of rising economic inequality, resource depletion, and global warming that threaten life as we know it.

Those same experts have no clear vision for how to fix these problems. This is where our book comes in. *Growing a New Economy* not only summarizes the latest, hard-hitting critiques from the experts; it contains a probing analysis of the data. Most importantly, it offers a compendium of practical solutions: a set of new economic principles and a new economic structure that can prevent the perfect economic and environmental storm from happening. These are solutions that will not only help balance our economy but also save our rapidly deteriorating environment.

Many popular writers on economic and environmental issues believe that a greener capitalism can save the day. While their ideas are well intentioned and sometimes spot on, we are of the opinion that greening capitalism will not be enough to create a new economy—an entirely new approach to economics is necessary. It is time for a new market system where poor countries are empowered to industrialize in a sustainable way; time for a new economic structure with a people- and nature-friendly economy based on economic democracy and environmental responsibility; time to go beyond both old-school capitalism and socialism. This new economic system will integrate the cost of natural capital into our industries and will recycle effluence into affluence. Such a change, coupled with a restructuring of the ownership of the economy—from corporate owners to worker owners—will revolutionize the way our economy works.

In Part One of this book, we analyze the debt, inequality, resource, and environmental crises and demonstrate how they have been caused by an interrelated web of destructive factors, all rooted in the modern economic system. We then analyze these four systemic issues, each describing one aspect of the perfect storm, and show that these problems cannot be solved in isolation—they must be solved in an integrated way.

In Part Two, we delve into the past for empirical evidence on how we were led astray, tracing the history of economic policy from mercantilism to the creation of the European Union to today's growing environmental movement and its green political agenda. We show how past economic policies have led to the current economic and environmental crisis and how history has favored those nations in dominant trading positions. We also describe how the current economic crisis in Europe is a direct result of the monetary policies behind the formation of the EU, and how an economic system built on a weak and unequal foundation is bound to cause destructive ripple effects. Finally, we assess the potential of green economic theory and activism to create coherent economic policies and why these noble efforts have failed to gain ground thus far.

In Part Three, we take a closer look at the current market economy, which dominates the world through international trade, corporate control, and a blind belief in "free markets." While there are several theoretical justifications for today's free markets, the one most economists subscribe to is Neoclassical Economic Theory (NCE), often termed neoliberalism. In this section, we confront this theory head on. We illustrate step-by-step why this blind faith in free markets cannot be justified and why the theoretical logic behind NCE theory is not as sound as economists would have us believe. Indeed, there are fundamental flaws in the very foundation of modern economics, and in this chapter we expose these flaws in great detail.

In Part Four, we look at how we can reform the dominant workings of capitalism and take steps towards solving the immediate crisis. To tackle the debt crisis, for example, we argue that it is people with regular jobs—not banks, speculators, or financiers—who produce and purchase most of the goods in our economy. Therefore, it would be much more productive to bail out the people rather than the banks. We also examine ways of making poor countries richer and more sustainable through measures such as fair trade and sustainable industrial development. By examining how rich countries have climbed the growth ladder, we isolate four policy suggestions for boosting developing economies, while also considering ways to establish social and cultural harmony.

In Part Five, we sum up the reforms we discussed in the previous chapters and attempt to consolidate them into a coherent economic theory. In doing so, we draw upon the concepts developed by P. R. Sarkar in his Progressive Utilization Theory, an alternative vision that transcends both capitalism and socialism, yet incorporates important elements of both. We introduce five fundamental economic principles for growing a new and more balanced economy that will ensure the efficient use of resources, provide the minimum necessities of life for all people, facilitate a more equitable distribution of surplus wealth, and guarantee a better quality of life for all in a thriving, resilient, and sustainable economy.

Even though our book is critical of the way the current economy works, we are hopeful that humanity can create a better economic system. The old economy is outdated and an entirely new economy is already emerging. In fact, it began emerging in the 1940s with Karl Polanyi's groundbreaking conclusion that capitalism tries to "commodify everything" and continued with the consequent development of the "small-is-beautiful" economics of E. F. Schumacher, which inspired a whole new generation of green and progressive economists, and it has culminated in P. R. Sarkar's brilliant insight that a more balanced economy will need a new economic structure in order to blossom and thrive.

With this short overview, we extend our sincere hope that our book will provide the reader with the same optimism we share—that growing a new economy is not only desirable and possible; it is inevitable.

Part I:
The Perfect Storm

We live in a time of overlapping crisis, and we need to connect the dots, because we don't have time to solve each crisis sequentially. We need a movement that addresses all of them.

—Naomi Klein

WHEN A FRIEND ATTENDED a meeting of independent leaders in Oslo, Norway recently, one of the speakers said that most politicians and activists interested in a better economy had "run out of ideas." Sadly, it seems easier to envision the end of the world than to envision an alternative to our economic and environmental troubles. In this book, however, we have not run out of ideas. We have not only attempted to spell out the shortcomings of the capitalist market and the four crises it has created—the financial, inequality, resource, and environmental crises—we have also presented new ideas on how to create a better market in a postcapitalist economy. Before we do that, however, we make the case that these issues can no longer be solved in isolation—they are interrelated and only economic-systems change can solve them.

The latter part of this book consists of new ideas envisioning a new economy. Since the growth of capitalism during the Industrial Revolution, we have largely lived in a divided world—one for the rich and one for the poor. But during the optimistic years of the 1970s, economists promised that modern capitalism would more or less end inequality for good. Capitalism would deliver not only more wealth but also fewer working hours, not only for the few in the richest part of the world but also for those living in the developing countries of Asia, Africa and South America. Now, forty-five years later, the world is still divided. People in wealthy countries still work long hours and have more debt than ever before, and in the developing world people are still poor, often uneducated, and malnourished. As bestselling economist and author Thomas Piketty declares in his seminal book *Capital in the 21st Century*, economic inequality is actually on the increase worldwide.

Few members of the world's privileged business class pay much attention to this inequality, nor to the fact that half the world's population lives in poverty, subsisting on less than $2.50 a day. It is thus unlikely the businessmen riding taxis from the Mumbai airport to the city's business district pay much attention to the plight of this Indian city's millions of poor people. Busy checking emails and phone messages, they are oblivious to the tens of thousands of people living in primitive, two-room homes with five to ten other family members on the other side of the tall fences lining the road. Malnourished and often illiterate, these slum dwellers wash their clothes in toxic water and feel blessed if they are able to scrape together enough money to eat a full meal.

While Europeans drive fancier cars and live in bigger and better houses than a few decades ago, they also have more debt and more stress. Despite Eurocapitalism's lofty promise of reduced working hours, it generally takes both parents working full time to feed, clothe, and house themselves and their children. Despite modern capitalism's promise to deliver more economic balance, more than 80 percent of the world's people live in countries where income inequality is widening.

The world is not only experiencing inequality and debt crises; it is also experiencing a resource crisis and an environmental crisis. Experts in the late 1960s promised that the green revolution, with its better grains and pesticides, would soon feed the world abundantly and safely. But capitalism has also failed us in this area. We have yet to be able to feed the world well. Despite an abundance of food, we have a distribution crisis: the world's vegetables, fruit, fish, meat, milk, and grains are not reaching those who need it the most—the poor. Moreover, our atmosphere, soil, and waters are polluted, most of our fish stocks have been depleted to near extinction rates, and many of our resources are dwindling so fast that one observer noted that we are not only going to experience peak oil, we will soon experience "peak everything." If current economic and environmental trends continue, we will soon be in serious global trouble.

Take recessions in the global economy for instance, which are a common economic problem and have occurred regularly in the past. The present financial tsunami, which started in the United States and is now pounding the world's shores, is markedly different. There seems to be no end in sight. The financial shock waves just keep on coming. While politicians take more and more desperate measures to stem off an economic collapse, the economy continues to perform poorly. It is time to ask ourselves: Have decades of relative prosperity come to an end? Norwegian economist Erik S. Reinert certainly thinks so. In an article in the online newspaper *Nettavisen*, he writes: "This is not just a crisis, but possibly the beginning of the fall of Europe. The question is only whether we will fall completely, like Venice in the past, or only partially, like Amsterdam did, after their days of greatness."[1]

The reason for the grave situation in Europe and the world today is that we are not only facing a financial crisis—we are facing something much bigger, a crisis the likes of which the world has never seen. The reason is this: the financial crisis can only be fully understood in the light of a series of other crises raging across the globe and cascading together in a perfect storm. This perfect storm is made up of four elements, each of which is covered in four different chapters in the first part of this book. They are: the Financial Crisis, the Inequality Crisis, the Resource Crisis, and, perhaps the most globally threatening of all, the Environmental Crisis.

The financial economy has amassed huge amounts of profits, money that has been taken out of the real economy to benefit a small minority of people, the so-called rent seekers—those financial speculators who increase their share of wealth without actually contributing any new wealth to the economy. Chapter One looks at the different options available to deal with the mountain of national and individual debt, and we come to a rather stark but perhaps not surprising conclusion: economic fundamentals today are dubious at best and there is no easy way out.

The only people who think they have an easy answer to the crisis are those economists and politicians who claim we need to do more of the same, more of what caused the various crises in the first place. That those leaders can still get away with proclaiming such failed myths shows we are in great need of new ideas and solutions. Indeed, it is about time we started thinking outside the box. We need to develop a new economy based on new economic fundamentals that are true regardless of time, culture, or natural environment. What emerges then is the idea that economy, culture, technology, and ecology are interrelated—and that this broader economic vision is our best antidote to market globalization. We outline our prescriptions for this new economy toward the end of the book.

Chapter Two deals with inequality and assesses the evidence that shows how the growing inequality in Europe and the rest of the industrialized world is directly linked to the increasing mountain of debt. This chapter discusses the various policy decisions that have led to the growing economic divide, eroded the safety nets of the middle class, rocked the foundation of the welfare state, and swelled the ranks of the poor. That said, inequality is not just a European or American issue—it is a global problem. The concept of global free trade often leads to the opposite: shameless protectionism for the economic superpowers and unfair trade agreements with the developing world. We thus agree with economist Erik S. Reinert that rich countries tend to grow rich and poor countries tend to stay poor.

The Financial Crisis and the Inequality Crisis are both expressions of human-made systems, namely our economic and political structures. Both of these crises are thus within the reach of politicians, activists and economists to reform, restructure or tweak. In other words, most problems in the economic sphere are neither so great nor so complex that they cannot be undone or rectified. That is, unless the economic situation in question is directly dependent on an external, limited natural resource such as oil. All activities in the global ecosystem take place in a vast yet limited environment, which we only partially understand and control. Regardless of society's goals and people's desires, regardless of our economic system, many of our activities are constrained by the limits of this physical universe and its laws—and more specifically, by the natural limits of this planet. If a nonrenewable resource, such as oil, is depleted, it will be depleted forever, and we will have to live with the consequences of that loss. If any of our life-giving natural systems are destroyed—be it a forest, a river, or a mountain—no human or economic power can return that loss. We will have to live with the consequences.

In Chapter Three, we describe the increasing cost of obtaining energy and raw materials, and the physical boundaries we live within on this planet. The chapter looks at the arguments for or against peak oil, and concludes that regardless of one's view on this topic, it is apparent to all that nonrenewable energy will become increasingly costly to extract. Economic performances are directly tied to the kind of natural resources available to us, and nature places certain thresholds on our economy that, when crossed, can cause severe, even irreparable damages.

Just think about the relationship between oil exploration and pollution, between industrial agriculture and rainforest destruction, between deep-water trawling and fish-stock depletion. Economy and ecology are highly interdependent. It is about time we humans, as stewards of this planet, begin to conduct our political and economic activities accordingly. Many politicians, economists and other experts are aware of the interdependence between economy and ecology, but we have yet to create an economy of scale that takes it into account. This book is our humble contribution to this important effort.

Chapter Four proceeds from where Chapter Three ends, looking at the environment from a broader perspective. Not only are we running out of nonrenewable resources, we are systematically destroying the global ecosystems of herbs, fruits, trees, bees, fish, and fresh water, these integrated ecosystems that provide us with free services vital not only to our own survival but to the survival of all life on the planet.

Nowadays, both economic and environmental problems are increasingly global in scope. We are facing monumental problems that are no longer confined to nations or to isolated sectors of the economy or to local ecosystems—our crises are increasingly interrelated, increasingly global in scope. Without thoroughly understanding each of these megacrises and how they are tied together, we will neither be able to grasp the magnitude of the problems that face us, nor find solutions to move forward. And since all our major problems are closely connected, possible solutions must also come forward in an integrated way. That is what the rest of the book is all about. We comb through the history of modern economics; we take a critical look at the environmental movement; we suggest new solutions beyond sustainable capitalism, and finally we present our version of a New Economy. Like the American Capital Institute, we conclude that there is an urgent need for a more holistic economy, an economy beyond both old-school capitalism and socialism. But we go one step further than the esteemed Capital Institute—we outline the growing new economy, an economy that is no longer informed by impractical mathematical formulas but by ecology, ethics, and aesthetics; indeed, by the best values and the deepest knowledge human society has to offer.

Chapter One

The Financial Crisis:
A Question of Life and Debt

It is time to stop listening to what banks say, and start focusing on what they do. We must re-evaluate the distorted political economy of the financial sector, before the excessive power of the few imposes even larger costs on everyone else.

—Daron Acemoglu and Simon Johnson

I CELAND'S PRIME MINISTER, DAVID Oddsson, was a big Ronald Reagan fan. In the true spirit of Reagan's deregulation policies, Oddsson, with the help of the "New Vikings," a group of hard-hitting Icelandic entrepreneurs, started to privatize the nation's three national banks in 1999—a process which was completed by 2003. A brave new world of unregulated markets took over the quiet island. These private banks were neither regulated, monitored, nor guaranteed. The New Vikings entrepreneurs bought up banks in England, Scandinavia and the Netherlands. They also enticed companies, schools and individuals to join the financial bonanza by investing funds. These Icesave accounts promised high interest rates, and in order to deliver as promised, the banks invested in risky loans and other speculative ventures. By 2008, a run on the Icelandic banks sent the economy into a tailspin and three of Iceland's major banks went bankrupt within days of each other. Depositors in the UK and Holland alone lost over 6.7 billion euro overnight.

In a single day of trading, the stock market lost two-thirds of its value. The Icelandic krona, which had been stable against the euro at around ninety kronur per euro since the euro was introduced, fell to 340 against the euro when the trading in the currency was suspended. Unemployment rose from less than 2% in 2007, to 9% in 2009.

This quiet and relatively stable Scandinavian country of only 315,000 people, with one of the highest living standards in the world, was suddenly in a chaotic free fall. In the years prior to the crisis, Iceland, like the rest of Scandinavia, had been an egalitarian society, with relatively few wealthy people at the top and relatively few poor people at the bottom. Most citizens were comfortably middle class. In 2007, Iceland topped the ranking of the Human Development Index (HDI) of the United Nations Development Programme, a set of indicators combining life expectancy, educational attainment, and income into a composite human development index. In other words, Iceland, the land of the Midnight Sun, was both geographically and developmentally on top of the world.

However, with the onset of the financial crisis, the country quickly lost both its confidence and its economy. In a span of a few days, the relatively balanced economy of the past was history. Iceland suddenly owed 750% of its GDP in external debt, 80% of which was owed by the country's banks.

Luckily, the Icelandic government acted quickly. With Viking foresight and determination, and only days before the bankruptcies, the government passed a law that would compensate all domestic depositors in full, but it gave no such guarantees for foreign depositors. The government also imposed currency controls, which, as of this writing, are still in place.

These changes did not take place without political drama, however. Iceland's parliament voted to respectfully pay back the debt. But there was a problem: President Olafur Grimsson refused to sign the bills.

The UK and Holland had to use their own resources to bail out their citizens and tried to force Iceland to pay back the minimum deposit guarantees, a staggering four billion Euros. After several rounds of negotiations, the terms were rejected in public referendums, the first since 1944. The debt owed to outside lenders was equivalent to 296,000 Euros per person, or 1,186,000 Euros for a family of four. The vote was an overwhelming no—93 percent to be exact. The case then went to the European Free Trade Association (EFTA) court, which, on January 23, 2013, ruled in Iceland's favor.

While the main crisis is over, the aftermath of the shock to the small island is not. The lesson of the dangers of financial deregulation is one that Iceland has learned the hard way. Had Iceland been inside the EU, the outcome could have been much more complicated. Due to treaty obligations, Iceland would most likely have had to go bankrupt in order to bail out foreign depositors.

This is how economy professor Brynhildur Davidsdottir sums up the discussions in Iceland during this period of great economic turmoil:

> We realized this was not the economy Icelanders wanted. We had a national dialogue with meetings in every Icelandic town about what kind of economy people want. It was clear that Icelanders don't want an economy that makes a few people wealthy while risking everyone else's well-being. We found that Icelanders want stable, safe, healthy communities, education, health care, and a fair, sustainable economy. [1]

We believe that most people across the globe have a similar wish for the future as the people of Iceland: a fair and sustainable economy. This wish and vision is also the main topic of this book. While the crisis in Iceland was handled with unusual firmness and resolved in the interest of the people rather than the bankers, it was only a warning shot of things to come. And even if the situation in Iceland had been unusiual, the financial problems were not. Similar problems were soon to embroil the whole of Europe.

The Crisis in Greece

Since the construction of the Acropolis around 500 B.C., Greece has had many problems with debt. Dionysius the Elder, elected ruler in 406 B.C., forced all citizens to hand over their coins when his lending options had run out. Then he re-stamped all one-drachma coins as two drachmae coins and repaid the citizens their money at face value. In other words, he returned one coin for every two he had collected. With the balance he had enough money to pay his outstanding debts and even some left over for extra spending. In order to get out of his personal debt crisis, Dionysius devalued the currency. Since his time, currency devaluation has become a last resort for states not able to repay their loans.

In modern times, Greece has also had a recurrent debt problem. To date, it has spent half of its time as a sovereign nation in default of its debts. That is, the country has been unable to make debt payments when they were due. When Greece defaulted in 1826, for example, it spent the next fifty-three years locked out of foreign capital markets.[23]

The current EU crisis reached increasing levels of intensity when, in May 2010, the crisis in Greece erupted. Until that point, the government had not openly disclosed the amount of money it owed to its lenders. The debt, when finally revealed, represented a staggering 304 billion euro, or 143 percent of Gross Domestic Product (GDP), a measure of the total size of a nation's economy. Greece's financial bonds were soon downgraded to junk status by leading international financial agencies, such as Standard and Poor's and Moody's. The world's oldest democracy soon became the first Eurozone country to have its bonds downgraded to a C rating—"imminent default with little prospect for recovery," the worst possible rating short of default. As a result, Greece was effectively frozen out of the private capital market. Greek bonds were viewed as far riskier than bonds issued by other Eurozone countries. Thus, in order to find buyers, the price of Greek bonds plummeted, raising the yield to record highs.

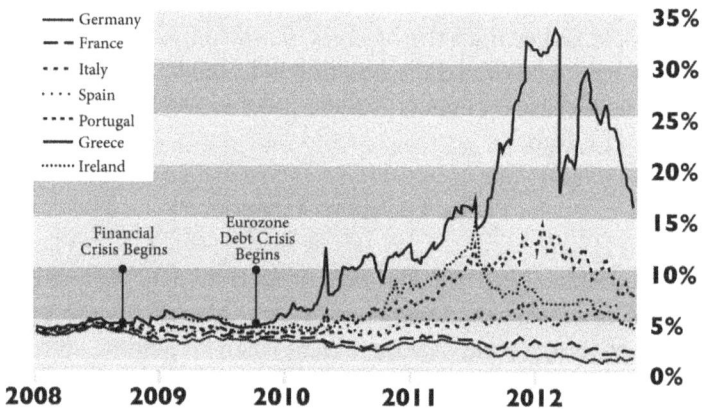

Figure 1. Eurozone, ten-year government bond yields

Faced with an unsustainable debt burden and imminent bankruptcy, Greece approached the EU for a bailout. In return for international bailout funds, the Greek government agreed to a harsh austerity program and labor-market reforms. Since then, pensioners and civil servants have seen a string of pay cuts, and the government has terminated many public employees. Taxes and utility prices have gone up, and investments in infrastructure and other discretionary spending have been reduced drastically. As the government cut down on spending, many people lost their jobs or received reduced salaries and thus were unable to meet their basic needs or to buy the specialty goods they were accustomed to. In return, private companies could no longer produce and sell at the same profitable level as before, and this forced them to institute drastic worker lay-offs— some even went bankrupt. This has reduced the purchasing capacity of people even more, and a downward spiral has hampered growth and crippled the economy. Such economic contractions have devastating effects on millions of people's lives in the form of lost jobs, bankruptcies, and the government's inability to pay out salaries and pensions.

As the conditions worsened, Greek citizens from all walks of life showed their discontent by taking part in anti-austerity protests, riots, and strikes across the country. In February 2013 we witnessed a new wave of demonstrations against Greece's government and its wealthy elite.

The austerity programs and the slowdown in the economy led to increased unemployment. At the time of this writing, the unemployment rate is 31.1 percent, and an astonishing 60 percent of youth under the age of twenty-five are unemployed.[4,5] As a consequence, many young people have moved to the countryside to take up farming, preferring to work and live outside the banking and financial system. While this exodus to the countryside may be good for the sustainability of Greece in the future, these migrations have a negative impact on the economy in the short turn.

The social impact of the sudden economic collapse has also been earth-shattering. For example, social workers and municipal officials in Athens report "that there has been a 25 per cent increase in home-lessness. At the main soup kitchen in Athens, 3,500 people a day come seeking food and clothing, up from about 100 people a day when it first opened 10 years ago."[6]

For those lucky enough to still have jobs, there is no guarantee that they will be paid on time. On a plane trip back from a research visit to Greece, one of us talked with a young Greek woman. Working as a make-up artist in a TV station, she had not received her salary for eight months. When asked how she could afford the airline ticket, she said it had been paid by her mother, who lives abroad. Greeks who still are employed are often having a difficult time. They often do not get paid, and if they complain, someone else will more than gladly take their job.

As the young woman said, "It is better to have a job and get paid late than not to have a job at all."

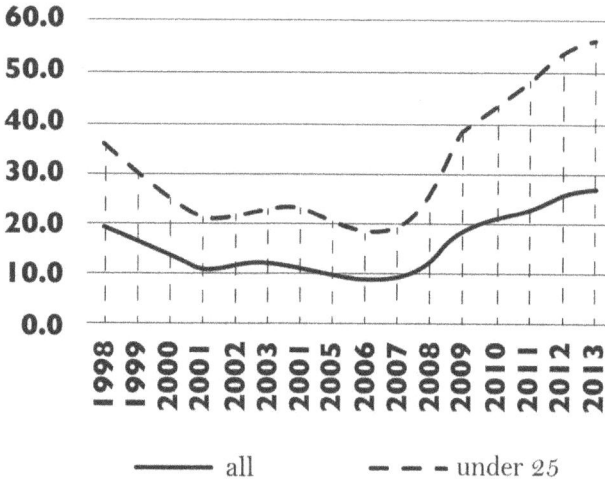

Figure 2 Unemployment rates in Greece

After the first Greek bailout in 2010, a second bailout package was introduced in October 2011 by the European Commission, the European Central Bank, and the International Monetary Fund (IMF), aiming to avoid an uncontrolled default. When Greece received this emergency assistance, very limited amounts went to cover government expenditure on public services. Instead, the vast majority of the funding (85% of the loan installment) went to paying the interest on the country's debt and helping to stabilize the banks.[7] A growing number of Greeks are therefore of the opinion that the bailout is more about saving the banks than about helping the country.

As part of the bailout deals, banks lending money to Greece had to take a 50 percent "haircut;" they were forced to write off half of the loans. This approach had an unintended victim, namely Cyprus, the small island nation in the Mediterranean. Like Ireland and Iceland, Cyprus had also deregulated its banking sector to attract capital and easy financial profits. A large proportion of deposits in Cypriot banks, however, went to purchase Greek government bonds and other loans to prop up the Greek economy. With this restructuring, half of the money Cyprus owed Greece had to be written off, thus effectively bankrupting the Cypriot banking sector. In 2013, Cyprus thus became the first direct casualty of the Greece bailout. This ripple effect is what scares economists and governments the most. The bankruptcy or even the bailout of one country can create a chain reaction, setting off similar economic time bombs in other countries.

So what was the final outcome of all the austerity and bailout measures to try to reduce the Greek debt? Remarkably little was actually accomplished.

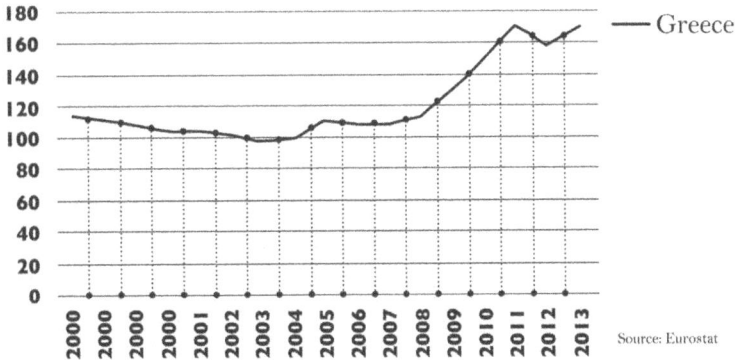

Figure 3 Government debt in Greece as % of GDP

As can be seen in the statistical figures above, the bailouts made a small, short-lived dent in Greece's debt, and the people are still suffering from the ripple effects. In spite of the bailouts, the debt burden has increased—at the time of this writing, it is around 170 percent of GDP. Some commentators, such as Giorgos Kyrtsos, are of the opinion that Greece's only hope is for part of its debt to be forgiven. In a comment to the *Guardian*, he said, "If the economy is to function again and the country is to remain in the Eurozone, it has to be absolved of at least 50% of its debt. Currently, the situation is hopeless…" So far, austerity measures have not improved the economy; they have only brought the economy into deeper trouble, to the point of near collapse.

According to Helena Smith in the *Guardian* in May 2013, "Many believe a clampdown on tax evasion and the perceived privileges of the rich, as well as a successful privatization campaign and foreign direct investment, will be critical to keeping chaos at bay."[8] But even if there is the political will to implement such measures, it is unlikely that they alone will solve the problem. A clampdown on the rich can easily result in capital flight, and both privatization and direct foreign investments have mixed records. Initially, such methods can bring capital into the country; the long-term impact, however, will be to increase the capital flow out of the country. As of this writing, in the spring of 2016, the Greek economy is still in deep trouble: unemployment hovers around 30 percent, and the EU finance ministers are debating the need for another bailout package.

The underlying problem of the Greek economy is related to its low growth in labor productivity. The country is so far behind Germany and other advanced countries that it is unable to compete in EU's common market. Unless this problem is tackled, other measures will do little to improve the long-term prospects for this economically troubled nation. However, labor productivity is not achieved overnight; it has to be built up gradually. And in the current global free market, in the EU and elsewhere, new and fledgling industries that have not yet reached the optimum level of efficiency are effectively destroyed by the competition, especially those in poor countries. Hence, these industries, and the local economies in which they operate, never get the chance to develop to a competitive level. This is a fundamental problem in the current global economy, and we will return to this topic several times in this book.[9]

Beyond the Crisis in Greece

Financial analysts generally do not worry so much about Greece's problems, except as a potential trigger for a larger crisis. The Greek economy is small enough to be bailed out without any catastrophic consequences to the world's financial system. Seen in isolation, Greece could even be left alone to default on its debt and leave the Eurozone without causing too many ripple effects. In retrospect, it would simply have been a Greek crisis, not a Euro crisis.

Unfortunately, the crisis is not limited to Greece. The same problems we find in Greece are also found in several other countries in Southern Europe. The unemployment rates in Spain, for example, are as high as in Greece, with one out of three persons out of work, and two out of three persons below the age of twenty-five out of work.

In November 2012, the European Commission approved a thirty-seven-billion-euro bank bailout for Spain. This bailout went to four banks and was given under strict conditions. One of the immediate results was the layoff of thousands of employees. Moreover, the Spanish economy remains very unstable in the aftermath of the correction in the housing market that followed, and many economists, including Juan Ignacio Sanz, professor of banking at the Esade business school in Barcelona, doubt the Spanish economy will recover any time soon.[10] Spain's economy has been growing slightly in 2015 and 2016, but unemployment is still at 21 percent, only 5 percent lower than during the worst of the crisis. In addition, the country's credit rating has been lowered from A to BBB by the Standard & Poor (S&P), or from High Grade to Lower Medium Grade, the lowest possible investment grade.[11]

While Greece can be bailed out, Spain, the fourth-largest economy in the EU, is too big to fail. There is simply not enough money available to take care of Spain if its economy tumbles.

The financial markets are also worried about Italy, Europe's third-largest economy. Italy has a constant budget deficit, and its debt is now reaching 130 percent of GDP. Then we have Portugal and Ireland, both with massive debt problems and stagnant economies. Just like in Greece, the very austerity programs designed to save these countries are responsible for the economic slowdown that makes complete recovery impossible.

All of these countries are currently very unstable and could easily collapse in the advent of another crisis. Their economic ailments can largely be classified into two groups: fiscal crisis and banking crisis. In a so-called fiscal crisis, the government does not have the capacity to finance activities such as social services. Such a predicament may lead to unrest amongst citizens and discourage potential foreign investors, which has been the case in Greece. The government then borrows money to be able to continue its spending. This is frequently accomplished by raising bonds on the international market.

Among the PIIGS countries (Portugal, Italy, Ireland, Greece, and Spain), Greece, Portugal, and Italy are all experiencing a fiscal crisis. As can be seen below, their public debt as a percentage of GDP is very high. In addition, the external debt, the amount of money the country owes to other countries, is even higher. All the numbers describe debts as a percentage of GDP,[12] that is, a percentage of the market value of all goods and services produced by a nation in one year.

Fiscal Crisis (2011)

- Greece's public debt: 165% (External debt: 220%)
- Portugal's public debt: 103% (External debt: 257%)
- Italy's public debt: 120% (External debt: 161%)

The first of these figures above represents government debt—how much the government owes to investors, banks, etc. The second figure, in parenthesis, represents the external debt, or how much the entire country, including private individuals, companies, and banks, owes to foreign investors, companies and banks.

Besides debt, another type of economic ailment during a banking crisis, takes place when the banking sector is jeopardized, and the government is forced to step in to prop it up through a bailout. This occurred in Iceland in 2008 and is also causing problems in Ireland and Spain:

Bank Bailouts (2011)

- Ireland: 107% (External debt: 1,243%)
- Spain: 68% (External debt: 229%)

In the numbers above, the external debt is far bigger than the government debt. The astounding 1,243% external debt for Ireland is an astronomical figure and the chance of it ever being paid back is absolutely zero. In practical terms, you would have to take the entire national economic output for more than twelve years and give all of it to foreign debtors, without spending anything on food, housing, transport, education, and so on. If the entire population gave all its income to foreign creditors, the country would soon be on the road to economic damnation, so such a scenario is obviously an unrealistic proposition.

Ireland's case is very similar to that of Iceland. The banking sector had been deregulated. Banks took deposits from abroad. When these investments went sour, the banks had no means to repay the deposits, resulting in huge liabilities.

When a country spends more money than it receives in taxes and other income, it has to borrow money. The government keeps spending more than it earns, and if this goes out of hand, we end up with a fiscal crisis. When a fiscal crisis becomes so severe that the government can no longer pay the banks and the bondholders, it quickly turns into a banking crisis. If the government owes money to banks and is unable to pay back the loans or honor its bonds, the banks can face enormous losses and even bankruptcy. This is exactly what occurred in Cyprus.

While the sovereign debt crisis can trigger a banking crisis, the reverse can also be true. When banks need to be bailed out, governments can be forced to step in and hence increase the spending beyond what is sustainable. This is what took place in Iceland, Ireland and Spain.

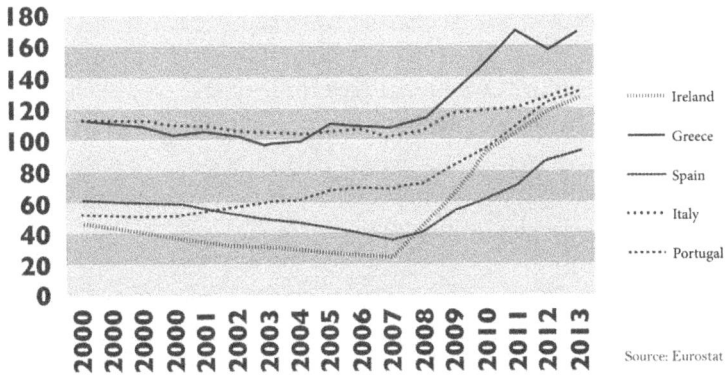

Figure 4 Government debt as % of GDP for Ireland, Greece, Spain, Italy, Portugal

As illustrated above, the debt as a percentage of GDP was low before the financial crisis hit in 2007. Italy, on the other hand, has had constant high deficit levels. Its crisis is purely a fiscal one, with the government consistently spending more than it earns.

The Eurozone countries are facing a difficult and unique situation, indeed unparalleled by world standards. With a common monetary policy decided by the European Central Bank, each individual country is allowed to follow its own fiscal policy. This mismatch gives the member countries the worst of both worlds. While the central bank ensures that the currency cannot be inflated, the individual countries borrow money as if they could get out of their debts by increased inflation.

In order to address the lack of fiscal unity, the German chancellor, Angela Merkel, as a condition for expanding bailout provisions in December 2011, convinced other Eurozone leaders to agree to a fiscal pact. The fiscal pact is officially named the Treaty on Stability, Coordination and Governance (TSCG). It is essentially a balanced-budget requirement. It requires countries to maintain either a budget surplus or at least a maximum structural budget deficit of 0.5 percent of GDP. A key aspect of the fiscal pact is that no country can receive bailout funds from the European Stability Mechanism unless it has ratified the fiscal pact.

As Peter Spiegel explains in the Financial Times:

The need for Ireland and Spain to pump billions into their
banking sector to keep them afloat forced otherwise fiscally
prudent governments into Eurozone bailout programmes with
painful austerity measures that have exacerbated recessions.
(…) Under the June deal, such bailouts would no longer be
the responsibility of national governments but would shift to
the Eurozone rescue fund, the European Stability Mechanism
(ESM), which was given the authority to inject capital directly
into struggling banks. As part of the deal, Ireland was given a
promise of equal treatment with Spain.[13]

But even if the money comes directly from the Eurozone rescue fund, it
will not prevent a prolonged crisis. As we mentioned earlier, while the EU
could conceivably bail out Greece, Portugal, and Ireland, the two other
PIIGS countries, Spain and Italy, are too big to be bailed out. As argued by
economist Nouriel Roubini, "If Spain falls off the cliff, there is not enough
official money in this envelope of European resources to bail out Spain.
Spain is too big to fail on one side—and also too big to be bailed out. Spain
alone has a public debt of €1 trillion, in contrast to Greece's €300 billion in
debt. In addition, Spain also has €1 trillion in private foreign liabilities."[14]
    It is tempting to think that only the countries responsible for mis-
managing their economies, such as Greece and Spain, are facing a debt
crisis. But in reality, even countries with fairly well managed economies,
such as Germany and France, have debt levels approaching 100% of GDP.

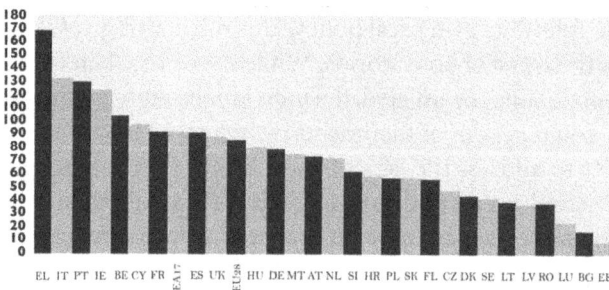

Figure 5 Government debt to GDP ratio, 2013 Q2 in percentage

As the mountain of debt rises, countries like the UK are starting to tighten
their belts. They have imposed austerity measures on their citizens,
and consequently the economy of the entire Eurozone is contracting.

According to the Economist, the EU economy contracted 0.4 percent in 2013.[15]

As argued by financial expert Margaret Bogenrief from ACM Partners, the Eurozone was headed for "deeper, more intense, and much less retractable trouble in 2013. There is no foreseeable way for the region to recover as it exists today in its current form."[16] This economic contraction is most acutely felt by Europeans as a rise in the unemployment rates.

Unemployment in the Eurozone

Unemployment and economic hardships are taking their toll. A recent report for the Red Cross with the thought provoking title 'The Humanitarian Impact of the Economic Crisis in Europe' explains that the situation is causing severe psychological distress: millions of Europeans are living lives of constant insecurity, with little or no hope for the future; there is widespread depression and anxiety. Suicides among women in Greece have doubled. In Italy, 150,000 small businesses had to close down in the last five years. Spain is receiving immediate food relief for the first time. In France, 350,000 people fell below the poverty line between 2008 and 2011. The Slovenian Red Cross reports that in addition to working with the poor and elderly with small pensions, they have registered a new group of people in need: those who have not received their salaries in months.

According to the British newspaper the *Statesman* in April 2013, the unemployment figures in Europe were "the worst they've ever been."[17] How bad? In the Eurozone, unemployment figures were at 12.1%, while only slightly better in the entire EU, at 11.6%. As stated above, Greece's situation was much worse. This otherwise sunny country had an unemployment rate that could darken anyone's mood. The situation was not much rosier in Spain, which had an unemployment rate of 26.6%, with an unemployment rate for those under 25 reaching upward of 59%. These are figures generally only seen during severe economic depressions. Indeed, they are even worse than during the Great Depression of the 1930s. The unemployment rates for a few other countries can be seen in the graphs below. (All the data is from 6.)

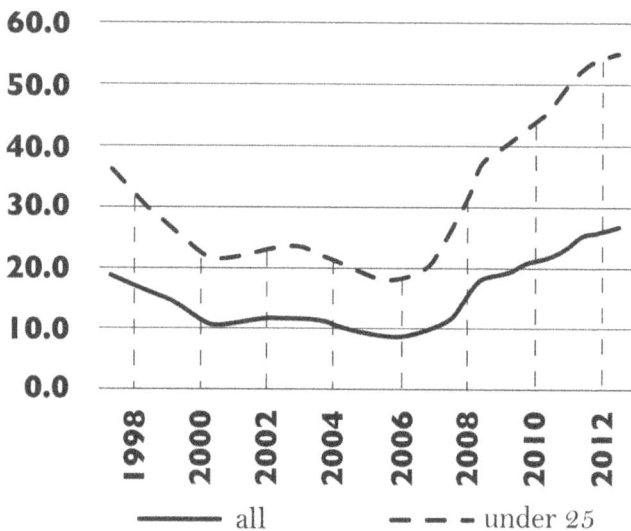

Figure 6 Unemployment, Spain

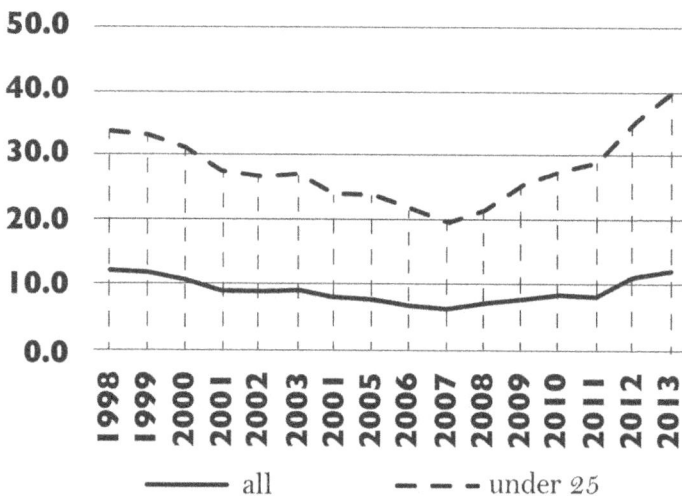

Figure 7 Unemployment, Italy

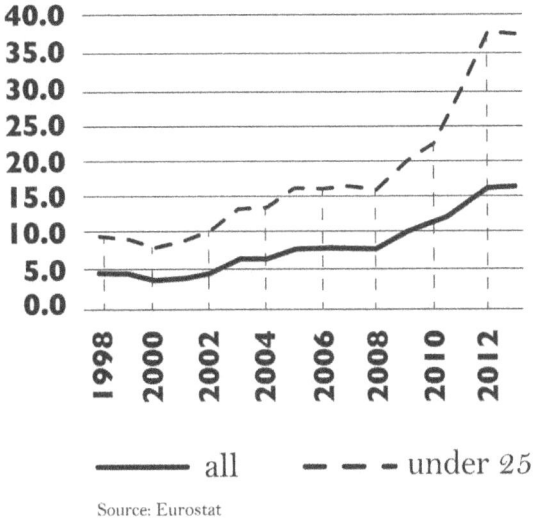

Source: Eurostat

Figure 8 Unemployment, Portugal

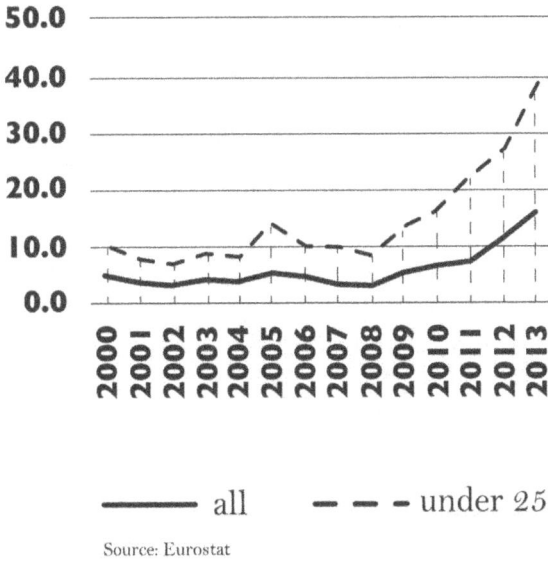

Source: Eurostat

Figure 9 Unemployment, Cyprus

Who benefits from the euro?

With all the difficulties facing the Eurozone, let us look a bit closer at the euro and find out who actually benefits from the common currency. There are naturally some obvious benefits: there is no longer any need to exchange money when you cross the borders, and the transaction costs of doing business are reduced. On the other hand, in many countries, especially in Southern Europe, prices have gone through the roof and the cost of living has dramatically increased.

The introduction of the euro initially benefited the less developed countries, since the cost of lending was drastically reduced. The steering course for interest is set by the central bank, and prior to the introduction of the euro, different central banks often set different interest rates. A higher interest is generally needed to discourage borrowing and protect the currency from devaluation. With the introduction of a single currency, there was now one central bank that set interest rates, and the interest rate was set relatively low compared to many of the rates set for weaker currencies in the past. This meant that countries like Spain and Greece could suddenly borrow money at the same low interest rates as Germany, something unthinkable until the introduction of the euro. Cheap money, however, is a double-edged sword. It encourages borrowing, but if a country borrows too much, it will have difficulty repaying the debt. This is exactly what happened in the Eurozone.

In theory, low interest rates encourage business investments and increase overall productivity, thus fueling an economy's long-term growth. But in Europe this was not the case. In Spain the new money went into expanding the real estate bubbles, and in Greece it encouraged the government to spend more on nonproductive ventures, such as the Olympic Games. Another important factor in a free market is that the amount of productive investments in poorly developed countries are often limited. If they had received investments, new industries in southern Europe would not have had time to grow strong enough to withstand international competition. We will return to this important yet often overlooked topic many times in the book. [18] Government investment to improve infrastructure and education could have been helpful, but without investing in new industries and technology, this would only have had a limited effect.

The low interest rates prompted a borrowing spree, and Greece, Italy and other countries borrowed heavily, thus increasing their indebtedness beyond the country's ability to repay the huge loans. Cheap money creates property booms, since people are tempted to borrow heavily to buy new property for investment purposes or to improve their standard of living. When payments are low and people can afford them, the real estate market expands. This is what took place in Spain and Ireland, where property prices rose drastically. Many people from around Europe bought investment properties in Spain in the hope of striking it rich or to expand their retirement funds, and many companies were enticed to set up shop in Ireland, where tax reforms had reduced corporate taxes to historically low levels.

But like all speculative bubbles, the bubbles in Spain and in Ireland eventually burst. Since banks had lent out money using the properties as collateral, the security to back the loans disappeared once prices dropped. Even if the investors were able to sell their properties, they did not make enough money on these sales to repay the bank loans. Hence the banks also faced huge losses, and the government had to step in to rescue them. Consequently, the incentive of lowered interest rates caused much more harm than good to countless individuals, businesses, banks, and countries. While the euro benefitted poorer countries short-term, only the richest and strongest economies benefited long-term.

In particular, Germany has been a clear winner in this regard. With its growth in labor productivity outstripping other countries in the Eurozone, and a common currency with its neighbors, it easily outcompeted most of the Eurozone nations. As a result, Germany's exports have risen dramatically in the last decade, and continue to grow today. [19]

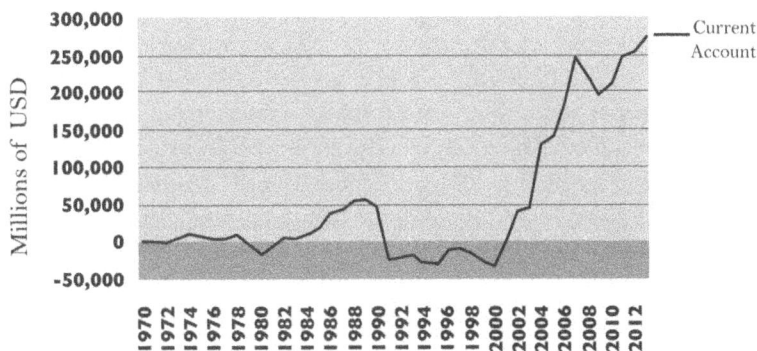

Figure 10 Trade balance, Germany

To better understand Germany's economic position in the Eurozone, we need to take a closer look at its economic development over time. When productivity increases in a country, such as it did in Japan and Germany before the introduction of the euro, that country becomes more competitive; it can lower its prices and it can export more. This strengthens its currency; as a consequence, the lower prices are compensated by a more expensive currency. If the exchange rate is fixed, there is no such "equalizing mechanism" in place. This means that a country whose productivity increases the fastest becomes very well off, and this in turn creates huge trade surpluses. Countries that are not so competitive, on the other hand, will be hit hard and accumulate huge trade deficits. The competitiveness of the PIIGS countries, for example, was reduced in part because unit-labor costs had risen compared to Germany. Without the euro, many of these countries would probably have devalued their national currencies, but being Eurozone members this was not possible. Therefore, the main winner from welcoming the euro into their economy has been Germany, while most of the other countries have been losers.

If Germany had retained the Deutschemark, the automatic strengthening of the currency that took place prior to the introduction of the euro would have continued, thus neutralizing much of the gain from increased labor productivity. As we can see from the graph above, German trade was more or less balanced until 2002, when the euro became fully functional.[20] In other words, the value of its exports was at that time roughly equal to the value of its imports. After the introduction of the euro, Germany exported far more than it imported.

While Germany gained due to the introduction of the euro, the balance of trade of most other Euro members took a nosedive. Greece, Spain and the other PIIGS countries were not the only ones affected. Even France, Europe's second-largest economy, experienced a downturn in the national trade balance. Note in the graphs below how the downturn clearly started at the time of the introduction of the euro. It has taken a severe recession, high unemployment, and painful austerity to adjust the imbalance.

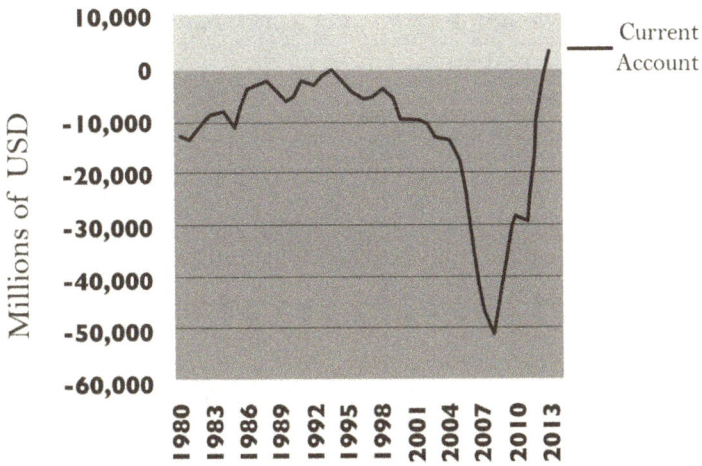

Figure 11 Trade balance, Greece[21]

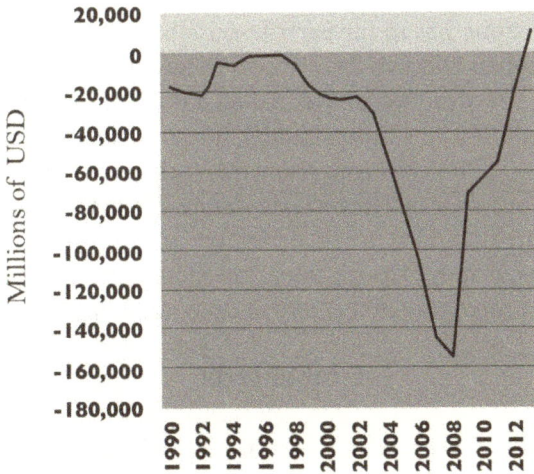

Figure 12 Trade balance, Spain

France, which has not embarked on widespread austerity measures, has not yet recovered its balance of trade after introducing the euro.

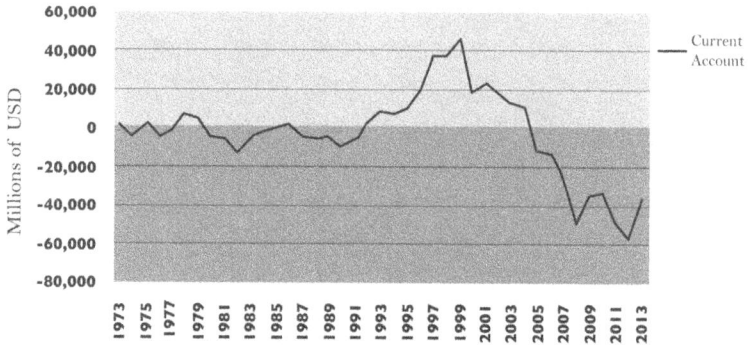

Figure 13 Trade balance, France

In essence, the euro worked against countries with lower productivity; it virtually killed their industries. Countries experiencing problems before joining the Eurozone faced even more hardships after joining the club.

It is therefore not unfair to ask, as did American commentator Roger Cohen in 2010, "Is the euro to the early twenty-first century what the League of Nations was to the early twentieth: a fine idea that became a political orphan and was condemned to unravel?" [22] Other critics of the Eurozone have pointed to past failed monetary unions such as the Scandinavian Monetary Union (SMU), which began in 1872 and ended abruptly in 1924. They effectively argue that such unions are impossible to maintain in the long run without a similar movement toward a stronger, more integrated political union—a nation or an economic federation of states. It looks indeed as if Cohen and these critics are right in their assessment of the future of the euro: it does not look bright.

Global Debt

Debt is not only a European problem; almost all industrialized countries in the world are heavily in debt today, as can be seen in the graph below.

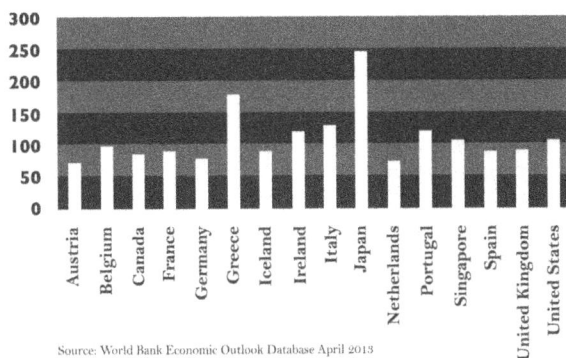

Source: World Bank Economic Outlook Database April 2013

Figure 14 Government debt as% of GDP 2013

The EU and other Western countries are in fact drunk on debt, and like alcoholics, they are struggling to manage the addiction. The market economies of these modern nations have become dependent on the same toxic substance: ever-increasing levels of debt.

The debt levels in the United States are also a cause for concern. While other countries have made attempts to reel in their deficits and balance the budget, no such attempts have been made in the United States. The periodic showdowns in the US Congress over the debt issue, such as the shutdown of the government in late 2013, seem to be more for public consumption and political posturing than a real attempt to reduce the debt. The reason for this is probably that the United States has much less to worry about by running deficits than any other country, due to the unique position of the US dollar. Since the dollar is the world's reserve currency, through which most trade is conducted, the United States never needs to worry about foreign exchange. The American nation can create any amount of this currency and use it to buy any goods it may wish abroad. No other country is in such a unique economic position.

Since the world economy has become totally dependent on ever-increasing levels of debt, some observers claim that the only thing keeping the world from a worldwide recession is the ability of the United States to create almost unlimited amounts of new debt. Still, the growing debt of the United States, even though it is more easily managed than that of any other country, also needs to be brought under control.

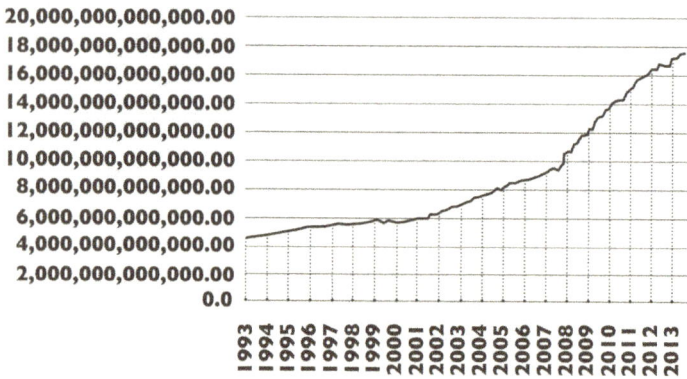

Source: Bureau of Public Debt, United States Department of the Treasury

Figure 15 US public debt

The level of debt in the USA as of mid-2014 was 17.6 trillion US dollars, amounting to 105% of GDP, which is not too different from other industrialized nations. What is remarkable is the rapid growth of the debt. In addition, the United States also has other debts that do not show up in the national accounts. These unfunded liabilities amount to a staggering 124.7 trillion US dollars, or 789% of GDP. [23] The breakdown of these unfunded liabilities is $16.4 trillion in social security, $21.7 trillion in prescription drugs liability, and 86.4% in Medicare liabilities. Since the 1970s, the United States has constantly run a trade deficit, sometimes called a current account deficit.

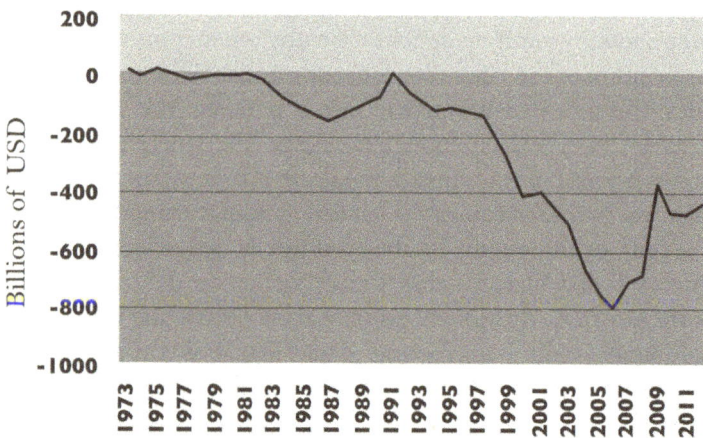

Figure 16 US trade balance

Let us now look at the curious relationship between the trade deficit and the Dow Jones Industrial Average (DJIA)[24].

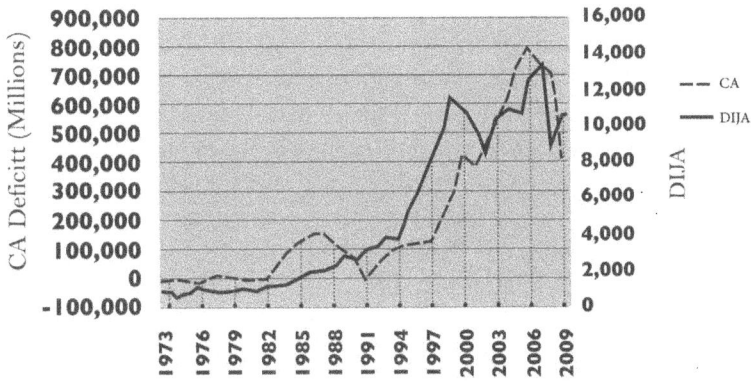

Figure 17 DJIA and current account deficit 1973-2009

As can be seen above, when the trade deficit index moves up, the Dow Jones Industrial Average (DJIA) index follows in tandem, and when the trade deficit is reduced, the DJIA curve responds with a similar downward trend. The most probable reason for these trends is that when the trade deficit goes up, more US dollars are being created and sent overseas. The recipients of these dollars use this capital to invest in the economy, primarily through US treasury bonds and the US stock market. Therefore, when the trade deficit is high, more money is pumped into the US stock market, pushing the DJIA higher, and when the trade deficit goes down, less money goes into the stock market, pushing the DJIA to a lower level. This economic activity creates a false perception— that rise in the stock market is a true indicator of economic health. In fact, it is often the opposite, as well as being an indicator of the rise in economic speculation.

As the debt has increased in the United States, inequality has also risen. While the richest 10 percent have seen their pocketbooks expand, everyone else's has shrunk. Indeed, everyone else has, in relative income, become poorer. In 2012, one in five children below eighteen in the United States lived below the poverty threshold. [25] We will return to this topic in the next chapter.

Debt Reduction Strategies

Governments have traditionally been able to cope with high levels of debt through increased economic growth. With a growing economy the debt becomes smaller in relation to GDP and can be managed up to a certain point. Let us again look at the United States. In the middle of the twentieth century, the United States had a national debt in excess of 100% of GDP, yet it was still able to manage its debt. How? Through continuous economic growth. This time, however, the United States, just like all other heavily indebted Western countries, will not be able to use the same approach. The reason? Continued economic growth is no longer the quick fix it used to be.

During the Second World War, the US national debt was 121% of GDP. This debt was never reduced, and it has kept growing ever since. What saved the government from bankruptcy was the GDP's growth after the war—it grew faster than the debt.

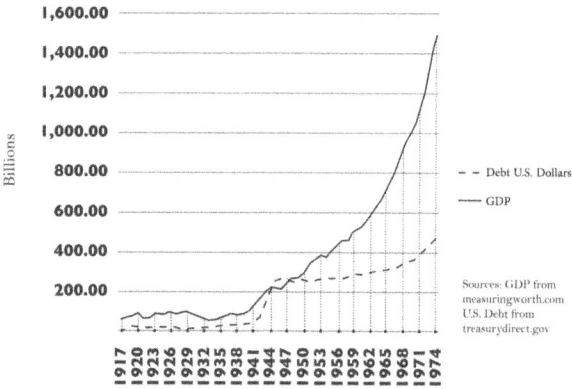

Figure 18 Debt as % of GDP reduced by economic growth

This is the general approach taken by mainstream economists when they explain that the debt crisis is not a serious matter. To them, economic growth will help us grow out of the present crisis. The problem with this approach is that economic growth does not occur in isolation: it depends on natural resources in general, and on cheap energy in particular. In fact, there is a direct link between the use of energy and economic growth in the world.

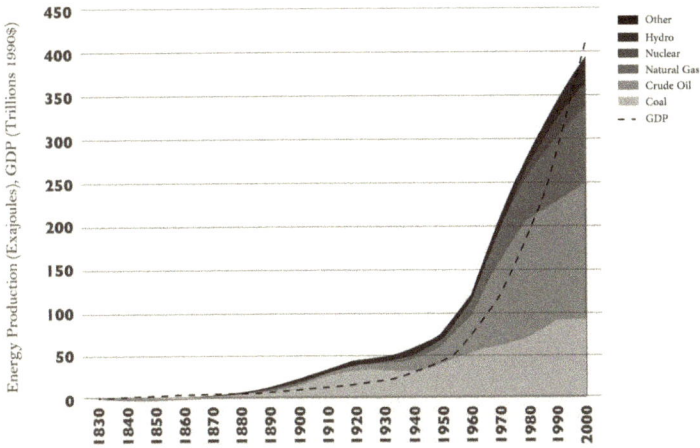

Figure 19 Link between the use of energy and economic growth in the world. [26]

As can be seen in the graph above, economic growth accelerated when human beings discovered fossil fuels—coal and oil. That is, the rate of economic growth is directly dependent on the amount of energy we use. Given the rate of growth of the debt, current depletion of oil fields and the increasing cost of exploiting newly discovered fields, it is extremely unlikely that we can reach the type of economic growth that enabled the United States to keep its huge debt burden at bay.

From 1947 to 1967, the US economy grew at an average 7 percent per year. No Western democracy has come close to that type of growth in recent years. During the same period, the debt increased at an average of 1.3 percent per year. During the last ten years, the US debt has seen a growth of over 10 percent per year. If this trend continues, the US economy would require a GDP growth in excess of 10 percent per annum to be able to reduce the debt as a percentage of GDP. Such a scenario is unthinkable today, even with unlimited availability of cheap oil. A similar case can be made for other indebted nations as well. [27]

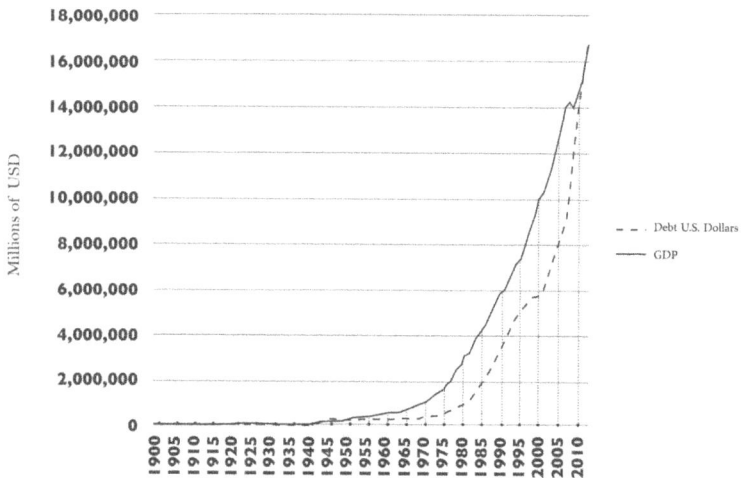

Figure 20 Debt in US dollars

But we do not have unlimited energy resources. Even though we are not in danger of running out of fossil fuels any time soon, it is indisputable that the Energy Return on Investment (ERI) is falling rapidly. [28] This means that we need more and more energy to extract a barrel of oil, which in turn means that it will become more expensive to extract that energy. The new discoveries of oil and gas are either in the form of oil shale or tar sand, which are difficult to extract due to the nature of the deposits, or are located in places where the location itself makes it both difficult and expensive to extract, such as in the desert or in the Arctic. Most of the oil shale in the world, for example, is found in the driest parts of the United States, and here are some of the main economic, technological, and environmental challenges of oil-shale extraction:

- environmental challenges, such as ground water and soil pollution
- high energy usage to extract oil shale from the ground
- lack of appropriate technology to extract
- large amounts of water needed for extraction in one of the driest parts of the world

As we can see, while there may be plenty of oil resources left in the ground, the new resources are not as easy or cheap to extract, nor are they environmentally friendly. Moreover, while energy in itself is important for economic growth, it is not enough. To secure growth we need access to cheap energy. Consequently, if we do not witness a major environmentally friendly scientific breakthrough in the near future, the growth in nonrenewable energy consumption will likely reduce rather than increase, and eventually it will be reversed. Humanity will then be forced to live with diminishing sources of energy. This in turn will dramatically affect economic growth.

Given the constraints of the current economy, which is so heavily dependent on cheap, nonrenewable energy for its expansion and growth, it is unreasonable to think that we have sufficient cheap energy available for the United States to grow itself out of the debt crisis. The same argument holds true for other Western nations.

If we cannot grow ourselves out of debt, what other options do we have? Continuing to repay the banks at the expense of the real economy is not a viable option. Diverting available funds away from productive investments, like the present austerity programs tend to do, is also a dead end. In either case, the economy will shrink to the point where the ability to repay the debt will be next to impossible.

Another option is to inflate the currencies by creating inflation. This cannot be done by one country in isolation; it would have to take place globally. In the Eurozone, monetary policy is determined by the European Central Bank, so no individual country has the means to inflate the euro. Since the only country with enough influence over the European Central Bank is Germany, which has little interest in debasing the euro, this is unlikely to take place.

For those countries that are not in control of their own currencies, inflation is not an option. The majority of loans are made in hard currencies, such as US dollars or euros, so if the local currency is devalued, it will become harder for the countries to repay their foreign loans.

The only country that could inflate its currency without worrying about external debts is the United States, since all external debt is nominated in US dollars. If the dollar began to lose its value and inflation spread in the United States, the debt burden of the US Government would be reduced. However, if the US Government decided to take that route, a series of unwanted events would be set in motion. First, countries holding US dollars would get concerned, since the value of their holdings would be reduced. They would do everything in their power to get out of the currency while it still held its value. Secondly, they would stop accepting US dollars as payment for exports, and the time for the

US dollar as the world's reserve currency would most probably end. This would put an end to the United States' biggest competitive advantage. The US would have to be in a very desperate state before its economic and political leaders would allow this to happen. At some point something would have to give, and a worldwide hyperinflation could set in. This would affect most of the world's currencies; worldwide debt would effectively be cancelled, and all bank savings would be wiped out. Such a situation would be devastating to the economy and to people, especially the middle class and the poor.

Another possibility is that debtor nations declare bankruptcy and stop payments on their debts. As we have seen, it is possible for the European Union to bail out some countries, such as Greece and Portugal, but if defaults were to spread to larger countries, such as Spain or Italy, there would not be enough existing capital to bail them out. The result would be catastrophic for the banking sector and indeed the entire world economy. Banks would fail, creating a ripple effect that could bring down the entire banking sector.

If the banking system collapses, the entire edifice of the market economy will come tumbling down. Although it does not produce anything in itself, the financial system enables all commercial transactions, including imports and exports, to function. Given the dependency of most countries on the global economy, a stop or severe reduction in international trade would have catastrophic consequences on the lives of people all over the world. Indeed, our dependence on trade is so high that without it millions of people in both the northern and southern hemispheres would face many other forms of personal and financial difficulties, such as joblessness, homelessness, and even starvation.

If a country cannot pay back its debt through austerity, then it cannot grow out of the debt. There will not be enough money to bail out such an economy. Yet we cannot allow such countries to default. What is the alternative? Basically we have two choices. One is to write off the public debt. This view is supported by economist Michael Hudson, who writes:

> This situation confronts society with a choice: either to write down debts to a level that can be paid (or indeed, to write them off with a Clean Slate), or to permit creditors to foreclose, concentrating property in their own hands (including whatever assets are in the public domain to be privatized) and imposing a combination of financial and fiscal austerity on the population. This scenario will produce a shrinking debt-ridden and

tax-ridden economy. The latter is the path that the Western nations are pursuing today.[29]

Economist Erik Reinert echoes this view. In a recent interview he states, "If we 'save' the banks at the expense of the real economy, we will dig ourselves deeper into the crisis. Let the banks go bankrupt!"[30]

Another path is to reverse the trend of extraordinary low taxes for the rich and reintroduce tax levels similar to the ones after the Great Depression. Unfortunately, this would not raise enough funds for governments to pay back their debts. If a high wealth tax, as opposed to an income tax, was levied on fortunes over USD 500,000, however, then the situation would change dramatically.

The French economist Thomas Piketty has researched national assets, and he found that in most developed countries today, government assets are around 100% of national income, while the debts are also around 100% of national income, making the net value of public assets zero. Private wealth in the same countries, however, amounts to four or six times the national income.[31]

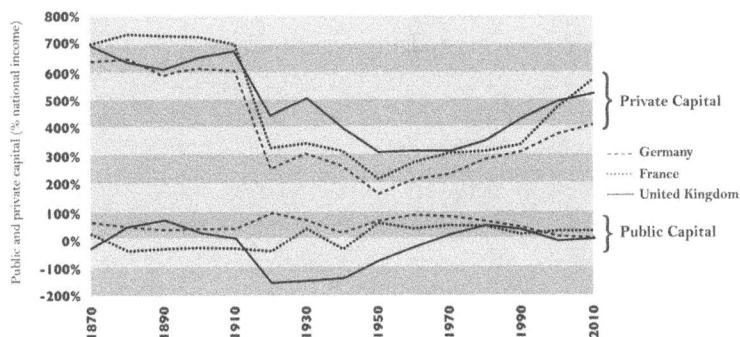

Figure 21 Private and public capital in Europe[32]

Instead of trying to sell off public property to repay the public debt, a more rational approach would be to tax the population, a legitimate right of any government. There is plenty of private wealth to pay off all the national debt and still leave many times the national income in private hands. Moreover, doing this would not reduce the wealth of the country. The question is, how much of the country's wealth should be in private hands, and how much should be in public hands? Right now most wealth is in private hands and very little wealth is in public hands.

To solve this imbalance, one could place one time the national income in public hands and four to five times the national income in private hands.

The problem with implementing such a scheme is the mobility of financial assets in the present world. If, for example, the government of Greece tried to implement this type of policy, we would see a massive capital flight out of the country. It is also likely that many wealthy Greeks already keep their money abroad, out of the reach of the government. The same is probably true of all small nations.

The only country that could fairly easily implement this type of policy would be the United States, since it has the clout to go after the assets of US citizens anywhere in the world. By introducing a wealth tax, the whole of its government debt could be removed very quickly. No country in Europe could by itself institute such a policy. However, if the EU makes it mandatory for all countries to introduce such a tax, and makes it applicable for its citizens regardless of where the money is kept, then the policy could easily be successful.

In the same way, the unfunded obligation of the United States in terms of Social Security and Medicare can actually be resolved quite easily if there is a will to do so. Presently, all income over $117,000 is exempt from Social Security tax. If this cap were lifted, then in a very short time, Social Security would be properly funded. The United States also has one of the most expensive and inefficient healthcare systems in the world. By reforming it along the lines of the much more efficient and cost-effective healthcare system in Canada, Medicare expenses, though very high, could easily be managed. There is evidence that Obamacare is already reducing the rate of increase in medical costs. The losers would be the wealthy healthcare industry, and the entire nation would be the beneficiary.

Unfortunately, without a 180-degree turn in the political winds, none of these solutions are implementable. However, if we look at the alternatives, this strategy would probably be the least painful, since the consequences of not doing it would either be to starve the real economy of needed resources or let countries go into uncontrolled default.

Resolving the public debt in this way does not address the enormous level of private debt that exists. One individual cannot tax other individuals, so the option of taxation is only open to governments. However, if implemented, it would be one step closer to resolving the crisis. We will return to these suggestions in the Solutions part of the book. But first, in order to understand the serious nature of this problem, we need to achieve a deeper understanding of the financial system and its functions.

Economic Growth and the Financial System

The economic growth that has taken place in the past 150 years is, in a word, enormous. In the UK alone, the economy grew 41.565 times (GBP 41 billion to GBP 1,330 billion in 2005 pounds) between 1830 and 2008, while the population grew less than four times (16.5 to 61 million), resulting in a tenfold increase in goods and services per person.

In recent years, economic growth in countries such as India and China has increased the availability of food and other goods, as well as reduced poverty. The increased productivity and growth has also reduced world hunger. In 1970, 37% of people globally were hungry, while 16% were hungry in 2009. Of all the developing nations, China, India, and Bangladesh have experienced the greatest reduction in poverty and hunger. In Bangladesh alone, the number of poor people has been reduced by sixteen million in a decade.[33] On the other hand, poverty in Africa has been stagnant, but as there are fewer people involved, the global poverty statistics still look relatively positive.

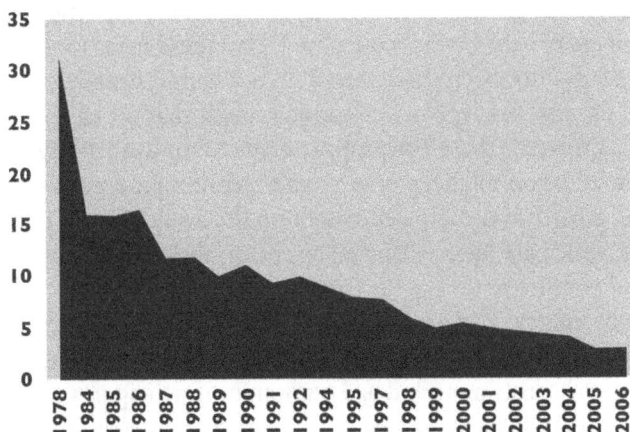

Figure 22 Poverty reduction in China[34]

In Asia the growth rate of 2.5 percent per annum has led to a doubling of GDP in the last twenty-nine years. A growth rate of 8 percent per annum (an average exceeded by China between 2000 and 2010) would lead to a doubling of GDP within ten years.

Economic growth is associated with increasingly complex systems of cooperation between individuals. These days we are dependent on literally millions of other people spread over the whole world for our supply of common items. In order to allow such massive amounts of people to cooperate in increasingly complex ways, a highly sophisticated coordinating system is required.

In today's world, the coordinating link for facilitating economic growth is the financial system, which is used by every country and every economy on the planet. The financial system is essentially a system of trust that enables people to voluntarily provide goods and services to others with the confidence that they will be compensated for it.

While the financial system helps to create wealth, it is important to remember that in itself it creates nothing. The real source of increased wealth in the world is due to increased labor productivity, or how much work each person can produce within a given period of time. This, in turn, depends on two things. One is technology and the second is energy. With the help of technology, one human being can manage a machine doing the work of one hundred human beings, but the energy to run the machine comes from coal, oil, gas, or electricity. As we saw in the previous graph, economic growth over the past 170 years is proportional to the amount of energy society has consumed. Had these new, nonrenewable energy sources not been discovered, no economic system could have provided us with the type of economic growth that we have achieved. Economic growth is therefore proportionate to the availability of cheap energy. In addition to cheap energy and technological advancements, economic growth is heavily dependent on the availability of cheap raw materials, which are often extracted by cheap labor in less economically developed countries.

While economic growth has taken place in capitalist countries, we should also not forget that socialist countries in the former Eastern Bloc during the early postwar period had economic growth figures even higher than those in capitalist countries. [35] In recent years, no country has been able to match the growth of the Chinese economy—even though it has many elements of a market economy, it is essentially state controlled.

When the Financial System Took Over, the Tail Started Wagging the Dog

As we noted earlier, while the financial system helps to promote economic growth by enabling complex patterns of cooperation, it is not by itself responsible for economic growth. Growth is produced through a combination of technological innovation, energy, and the availability of raw materials. The financial system has a very important facilitating role, but that is all. As long as the financial system is controlling the real, productive economy, it is useful, but once the financial sector grows too big and speculation dominates the economy, the real economy becomes unstable.

In the past thirty years, the financial sector has grown to such an extent that its role has outgrown its main purpose: to finance the real economy. Since the rapid growth of the finance sector in recent years, this part of the economy has taken on a role and rationale all its own—it has attracted more and more money away from the real economy. In the 1980s, 90 percent of all investments went into companies that produced real goods and services. Today, an estimated 95 percent of all investments are speculative, and only 5 percent goes to productive investments in the real economy. [36] The shadow of the speculative economy looms large in today's market economy.

Speculation redistributes wealth, and more often than not it redistributes wealth from the poor to the rich. Speculation in food products through futures contracts, for example, can create speculative bubbles aimed at increasing the profit of the speculators. And since food is essential for survival, poor people are forced to pay the resulting higher prices in order to purchase basic staples. Indian Economist Jayati Gosh calls this situation a "killing field:"

> And it's a killing field indeed, because grain, or any other basic food commodity that gets turned into a speculative bubble, means a global price spike, which causes the world's poorest to starve. In 2007-08, the number of people suffering from malnutrition globally rose from 800 million to one billion. This was the direct result of financial speculation in food. [37]

What is the difference between investment and speculation? When we invest we put money into companies or processes that will create more wealth, such as agriculture, research, manufacturing, etc. In short, when we invest we create wealth. When we speculate, however, we do not create new wealth; we simply redistribute it. Buying a share in the stock market with the expectation that the price will go up does nothing to increase the value produced by the company we have invested in. The same goes for buying commodities, metals, or any of the numerous derivative instruments that have literally taken over the world economy.

In the last thirty years, enormous profits have been recorded in the industrialized world, far higher than the actual GDP growth of many countries. But where did these profits come from? They were mostly made up of capital gains on existing wealth. In other words, prices on land and other assets increased and were considered a profit, even though no new wealth was created. American economist Michael Hudson describes this as the process of transforming industrial capitalism into finance capitalism. "The finance, insurance and real estate (FIRE) sector," he writes, "has emerged to create 'balance sheet wealth,' not by tangible investment and employment, but financially in the form of debt leveraging and rent-extraction."[38] In the current economy, according to Hudson, more and more people put up real wealth (such as land and buildings) as security for loans, and keep on extending these loans until they cannot be paid back. In the end, when the debts can no longer be serviced, the rich take over vast amounts of real wealth by confiscating the securities that were put up in the form of property.

While confiscation of assets by foreclosing on mortgages might be one of the ways that the financial system extracts wealth from the real economy, it is not the only one, nor the most common. Since the financial sector does not create real wealth, any reported profit is actually a transfer payment from the productive sector—from agriculture, industry, shipping, construction, etc. This is achieved by creating balance-sheet wealth, which later is converted into cash assets or other tangible investments. Admittedly, cash is also a financial asset, but it is comparatively more stable than share prices, options, bonds, and derivative instruments.

A company might buy shares in the stock market, for example, and once the price of stocks goes up, the smart investor sells and transfers the money into cash or physical wealth such as real estate and metals. While it may not be obvious at first glance, any profits made in the stock market must be a transfer payment from somebody else, since buying and selling stock does not create any new wealth.

This type of transaction requires risks, and the speculator may lose or gain. Banks and stockbroking firms take commissions for financial transaction, regardless of whether the customer gains or loses on the trade. The more transactions, the more commissions they receive. These transactions are net transfers from the real economy to the financial economy. Minimal at first, these transactions have steadily grown until they now make up a large portion of the economy. In 2012, 40% of United States' corporate profits came from the financial sector. In other words, the financial sector diverted an astonishing 40% of the profits of corporations to itself in the form of interest, bank charges, and similar fees. [39]

To make money by extending one's ownership of existing wealth rather than to create new wealth is commonly known as rent-seeking, something traditionally looked down upon by economists. The online magazine *Investopedia* describes the term as, "When a company, organization or individual uses their resources to obtain an economic gain from others without reciprocating any benefits back to society through wealth creation."[40] While this phenomenon has existed throughout human history, in recent times it has taken on staggering proportions. In the past, rent-seeking was accompanied by land rent and interest made on loans, but for the first time in history, the proportions of rent extracted by the financial system are so great that it is threatening to suffocate the real economy under a mountain of debt.

The key to understanding this new trend lies in realizing the enormous size of the financial sector. At the beginning of the financial crisis in 2008, the accumulated capitalization of the world's stock markets was over 60 trillion US dollars, equal to the GDP of the entire world. For the derivative market—a financial security that derives its value from an underlying asset —the amounts are even more astonishing. While the estimates of the value of this trade ranges between 600 trillion and 1.5 quadrillion dollars (yes, that's right, quadrillion), one of the world's leading experts on derivatives, Paul Willmott, who holds a doctorate in applied mathematics from Harvard University, recently set the value to 1.2 quadrillion dollars.[41] That is, twenty times the world's total GDP. This enormous wealth poses a great threat to the world's financial system. As well-known investor Warren Buffet, one of richest men in the world, has said, "Derivatives are the financial weapons of mass destruction, carrying dangers that, while now latent, are potentially lethal."[42]

Instead of simply being a tool for the productive sector to enable it to function properly, the financial sector has grown so big that it greatly outstrips the productive sector. Like a parasite, it is draining the real economy of the resources needed to reinvest in productive ventures. In spite of the enormous influence and importance of the financial system, the system in itself does not play any major role in present economic theory. It is simply considered the oil used to grease the machinery of the real economy. Many economists claim that this is the reason why they failed to predict the economic crisis. The main player of the crisis—the speculative market—did not even exist in their economic models. Incredible but true.

While rent-seeking and the effect of compound interest was clearly understood in ancient times, dating back as early as the Babylonians, neither classical, neo-classical, Keynesian, nor neo-Keynesian economic theory has considered this practice important enough to make it a part of their models. Marx, however, did analyze this sector of the economy and recognized it as a potential problem, but he believed that industrial capitalism would tame financial capitalism and put it under its control. Unfortunately, Marx was wrong.

The nature of bank lending has also changed. Presently, 80% of all debt is backed by mortgage-related securities. [43] In other words, money is lent out to increase the cost of land, which is just a sub-division of nature that nobody can claim to have made. If a loan is given to make a factory or a road or a cargo ship, we are increasing the wealth of the world, and the extra income generated by these assets can repay the interest. But a piece of land does not in itself produce anything. When we buy an existing house it does not add any new wealth to the world. The only way to generate the extra income to repay the interest is by asset inflation, where the value of land is artificially increased due to the easy credit provided. This is advertised as helping ordinary people to become rich, but in reality it only tricks people into taking on increasingly bigger loans that they will have to spend the rest of their lives paying off. Increasing land prices therefore is not a sign of prosperity. The only real beneficiaries are the banks, because as housing prices increase as a percentage of annual income, people are forced to take out ever-larger loans to buy a house, and spend a longer time repaying them. This results in the interest earnings of banks going up.

Local banks, which used to be the guardians of people's money and their future, no longer exist in isolation as they often did in the past. All banks and financial institutions today lend to and borrow from one another. Herein lies their strength but also their weakness. Since consortiums of investors and banks have come together to underwrite government debt throughout the world, ripple effects could hit the entire banking system even if only one large government were to default. [44]

Debt and Compound Interest

In 1772, Anglican minister Richard Price graphically explained the magic of compound interest:

> Money bearing compound interest increases at first slowly. But, the rate of increase being continually accelerated, as to mock all the powers of the imagination. One penny, put out at our Savior's birth at five percent compound interest, would, before this time, have increased to a greater sum than would be obtained in a 150 millions of Earths, all solid gold. But if put out to simple interest, it would, in the same time, have amounted to no more than seven shillings four and-a-half pence. [45]

And therein lies the problem. The current banking system is based on compound interest, and the rate is fixed regardless of the performance of the economy. As we can see, interest payments are only transfer payments from the productive part of the economy. Unless the real economy grows faster than the interest on debt, more and more of the real assets will be owned by the holders of that debt, since the debtors will have to sell off assets to satisfy the creditors. This is the course of action governments like Greece and numerous private individuals have been forced into.

Another aspect of high-debt service ratios is that the money that should have gone into consumption or investments end up being paid in interest charges. This has a deflationary effect on the economy, making austerity programs very ineffective. By cutting costs to pay the debtors the whole economy goes into a tailspin. According to economist Michael Hudson, "The internal contradiction here is that squeezing out more revenue to pay bondholders shrinks the economy, and hence its ability to pay taxes and debt service. The crisis deepens as national budgets and bank balance sheets fall further into deficit."[46]

The policy of paying the debtors at all costs was the basis for the IMF's Structural Adjustment Programs in developing nations. This helps save, of course, the financial system from losses, but only at the cost of draining national economies in the developing world.

One contributing reason for the situation is the indiscriminate nature of lending practices. If money is loaned to finance productive ventures, such as factories, it is possible for the added value of products to keep up with or exceed the interest charged. The biggest source of lending these days, however, is asset acquisitions, such as buying houses, lands, and stocks. None of these investments create new wealth, so the only way to find money to repay the loans with interest is through asset inflation, which results in the value of the original assets going up. The more loans given to real estate and other asset acquisitions, the more prices will increase. Hence, the very financing of asset purchases is the main reason prices are going up in the first place. When prices later collapse and buyers are unable to pay the loans, the banks foreclose and confiscate the property.

Debt servicing, interest payments, and capital gains are often either tax-free or have concessionary rates much lower than normal income and normal profits. This gives investors an incentive to borrow money for asset acquisition rather than for productive investments.

Gains from interest and capital gains used to be called "unearned profits." This term is rarely used anymore, but in the past thirty years there has been a major shift from industrial power to financial power. The real power brokers are now the money managers on Wall Street and in London. The unproductive financial sector is diverting ever-larger portions of the planet's wealth into its own treasure chests of profit. Curiously, this phenomenon, this shadow economy, seems to have gone unnoticed by the bulk of the world's academics. "It is as if the real world's power grab by the financial oligarchy does not properly belong in scientific analysis. Failure of academic models to acknowledge it produces an ideology that falsifies the way the world really works."[47]

Collapse of the Financial System

As we saw earlier in this chapter, the debt burden of most industrialized countries and the private sector is so large that drastic measures will have to be taken to resolve it. Unlike in the aftermath of WWII, growing ourselves out of the debt is not possible today; the energy resources needed for such an expansion are simply not present. Bailouts can also only be of limited assistance, since they shift the debt burden from one party to another and thus do not address the whole of the problem. The bottom line is that if the debt grows faster than real wealth is being created, the creditors will end up owning larger and larger portions of the wealth in the world. If not, it may trigger defaults, creating severe strains or even a collapse of the banking system.

Since the rest of economy depends on the banking system—from the individual salary account to the import and export of goods and the financing of expansion and new projects—a system collapse would lead to a halt of all economic activity. All imports and exports would stop. Countries without sufficient energy sources (the majority of countries in the world) will see their factories shut down and cars will remain off the roads. Heating in cold climates will be difficult and massive suffering will follow. Just consider the effect of the "polar vortex" that hit the United States in early 2014, which caused temperatures to drop below -15°C. At those temperatures, large amounts of energy for heating are necessary to keep people alive, but even at much warmer temperatures heating is still necessary. In short, the economic and social consequences of a collapse of the financial system cannot be overstated.

During a financial collapse, the effectiveness of central governments will likely deteriorate quite rapidly. A power vacuum will take place, which can easily be exploited by fundamentalists, political terrorists, populist hate groups, and other fanatic organizations and individuals. Such populist radicalizations are presently taking place in Greece, Holland, Finland, and France, where nationalist and neo-Nazi-type organizations are receiving growing support. With the breakdown of international trade, regional cooperation may seize to exist, and war and armed conflicts may arise all over the world. Some transnational corporations may retain their power, and we may witness the rise of corporate dictatorships. As trade is reduced, people in industrialized countries may face hunger and famine. If oil supplies do not reach the industrialized and oil-dependent West, whole societies may become dysfunctional. Food production may also suffer, being heavily dependent on mechanized farming. With chaos spreading, the powers that have nuclear weapons might use them in a desperate attempt to cling to power and influence.

A financial collapse, as outlined above, may remind us of fatalistic, end-of-the-world movies and conspiracy theories, but considering the present developments in the global economy, these scenarios are entirely plausible. Our dismantling of the real economy in order to pay off debts created by the financial economy is leading us closer and closer to a state of collapse. Economist and *New York Times* columnist Paul Krugman has clearly understood the magnitude of our predicament: "I'm tempted to say that the crisis is like nothing we've ever seen before. But it might be more accurate to say that it's like everything we've seen before, all at once."[48] Here Krugman is only speaking about our economic problems. If we add the inequality crisis, the environmental crisis, and the resource crisis to the equation, we are, as the saying goes, stuck in a pickle of global proportions.

As we have seen in this chapter, the debt crisis has reached unsustainable levels in most of the Western world, but how did we amass so much debt in the first place? Economist Ravi Batra argues in his latest book, *End Unemployment Now,* [49] that it was a direct result of rising inequality. As workers produce goods more and more efficiently but do not receive a proportionate increase in salaries, an imbalance occurs in the economy where the increased production goes to profits for the superrich rather than into the pockets of ordinary people. Since regular people no longer have enough money to buy the goods that are produced, Batra argues, the increase of both private and governmental debt is inevitable if economic collapse is to be avoided.

Chapter Two

The Inequality Crisis:
Poverty in the Land of Plenty

*You need some inequality to grow... but extreme inequality is not
only useless but can be harmful to growth because it reduces mobility and can lead to political capture of our democratic institutions.*

—Thomas Piketty

SINCE THE 1970S, A small segment of the population has become
increasingly rich, while common people have gotten poorer.
According to a recent report by Credit Suisse, the bottom half
of the world's population owns less than the richest eighty-five people
in the world. [1] Furthermore, in the past year 210 new individuals have
become billionaires, joining a select group of 1,426 men and women
with a combined net worth of $5.4 trillion. [2]

All human beings deserve to have a decent living standard, but when
resources are poorly allocated, the few take an ever-increasing share of
the world's wealth. Even more worrying, there is little correlation between
wealth and contribution to humanity. It is important that there are incentives
in place that reward hard work, ingenuity, creativity, and innovation. This
is what the capitalist system is supposed to do. In reality, the most unproductive persons benefit the most. Unearned income from speculation and
debt is highly rewarded, even if these activities do nothing to create wealth.

Those who really work and contribute can hardly afford a decent
life, while unproductive people are disproportionally rewarded. With
the present economic crisis, inequality has risen and unemployment in

many European countries has soared. People who worked their whole lives cannot afford to live on their pensions. Unemployment has reached levels where two-thirds of the population in some countries are out of work. Seven out of ten people now live in countries where inequality has increased. The social cost of this is hard to measure, but it includes widespread poverty and despair. The Red Cross recently issued a report on the "humanitarian crisis in Europe," detailing how inequality also increases the risk of social unrest. [3].

Although the financial crisis is often to blame for these consequences, many European countries have experienced increasing levels of inequality in times of economic growth too, which debunks the myth that growth is a necessary condition for a more equal society. Portugal and the UK for instance, ranked among the most unequal countries in which to live, according to a study conducted by the Organization for Economic Cooperation and Development (OECD). [4] Development studies teach us that inequality is in fact one of the leading causes of continued poverty, since it diminishes a country's overall productivity.

The unequal distribution of resources has contributed to increasing the gap between the rich and poor on the continent. As reported by Oxfam, the combined wealth of Europe's ten richest people is more than the total amount used on austerity measures in the two years following the financial crisis in 2008. [5] But from a global perspective this is just the tip of the iceberg. According to the Credit Suisse report cited above, 10 percent of the global population now holds 86 percent of the world's assets, while the poorest 70 percent (more than 3 billion adults) hold just 3 percent. The United States, with 5 percent of the world's population, uses 40 percent of the world's resources. This is due to a net transfer of resources from one region to another, from the poor countries to the rich countries. Even an average worker in Sweden or UK is, from this global perspective, an exploiter and part of depriving others of their due.

Inequality on the Rise

From 1974 to 2004, the richest 1% increased their share of the return on wealth in the United States from 38% to 58%. [6] In 2010, the richest 1% accounted for 93% of all income growth, and out of this, 37% went to the richest 0.1%. This means that out of 150 million households, one-third of all income growth went to just 15,000, an exclusive group with an average annual income of $23.8 million. [7]

As we can see from the graph below, the richer the families, the more they have gained in relative income in the past decades.

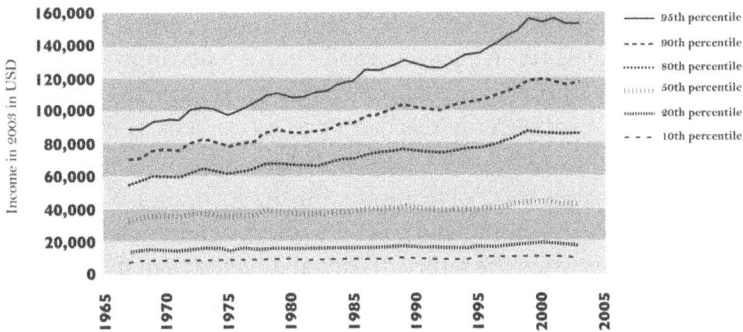

Figure 23 Income inequality on the rise

Billionaires have never been richer than today. The Mexican businessman, Carlos Slim, who has built his wealth from merging smaller businesses into monopolies, could actually pay the annual wages for 440,000 Mexicans with income derived from his own wealth. [8] Inequality is not rising only in the United States, but in the entire world. Whether in the United Kingdom, Denmark, France, or the Netherlands, inequality is on the rise. [9] While absolute poverty has gone down in China, inequality is rising in both rural and urban areas.

The rising inequality is intimately linked to the debt crisis, and the link is not difficult to grasp. Simply put, as long as income is fairly evenly distributed, there won't be very rich people to lend money or people who desperately need to borrow money. When income distribution is skewed, those who have a little money borrow from those who have a lot.

The Inevitable Rise of Inequality in Capitalist Societies

In early 2014, a little-known French economist, Thomas Piketty, burst on the world stage with the English translation of a book he had published in French the year before, *Capital in the Twenty-First Century*. [10] By April 24 it had reached the top of the *New York Times* bestseller list for nonfiction. By July 6, it had dropped to the number four spot, but for any book on economics to reach the number one spot and stay on the list for so many months is quite unprecedented.

The basic tenet of the book, based on statistical research made by the author and his team of researchers, is that when the return of capital has historically been higher than the rate of growth, a gradual concentration of wealth and income is inevitable. For much of recorded history, the return on capital has been between 4 and 5 percent per annum, while the world economy in previous centuries rarely grew more than 1 percent and in the past century only reached 1.5 to 3.5 percent. Global growth is expected to slow to below 1.5 percent before 2100.

Piketty describes this correlation with the formula $r > g$, where r stands for return on capital and g is the growth of national income. By logical necessity, when the return of capital is bigger than the growth of the economy, the income from capital will gradually take over a larger and larger percentage of the national income.

Since capital is very unevenly spread, the income from capital is also distributed very unevenly and mainly benefits the already rich. Consequently, Piketty concludes that inequality in both wealth and income in a capitalist society is bound to increase, unless something externally prevents it.

As we saw previously, the rich owns an enormous portion of the current wealth in the world. According to Piketty's figures, the bottom half of the population in the United States owns just 5% of the total wealth, whereas the top 10% owns 71%. The wealthiest 1% owns one-third of all wealth.

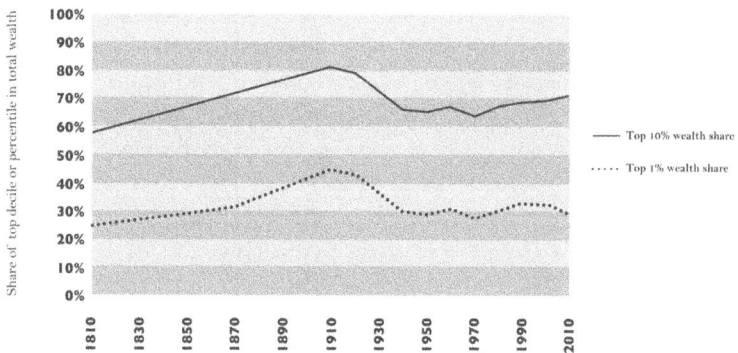

Figure 24 Wealth inequality in the US, 1810-2010[11]

As we can see, inequality rose steadily in the nineteenth century. The dip in the twentieth century Piketty explains by the onset of the First and Second

World Wars, and the Great Depression, which tended to wipe out large fortunes. Since the 1970s, the upward trend has resumed and will soon reach the same concentrations observed at the beginning of the twentieth century.

It is interesting to compare this trend with a country like Sweden, which started out with higher inequality than the US, but after the two world wars has kept inequality under much better control. But even in Sweden inequality has been rising again since the 1970s.

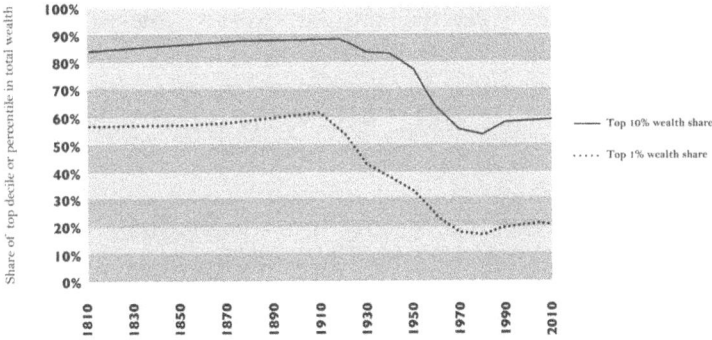

Figure 25 Wealth inequality in Sweden, 1810-2010[12]

Apart from wealth inequality, there is also an increasing income inequality. While in the 1970s the highest 10% of income earners received around 33% of income in the United States, today they receive 48%. The trend is not as dramatic in Europe, but income inequality is increasing there as well, even in Scandinavia, where historically the gap between rich and poor has been small.

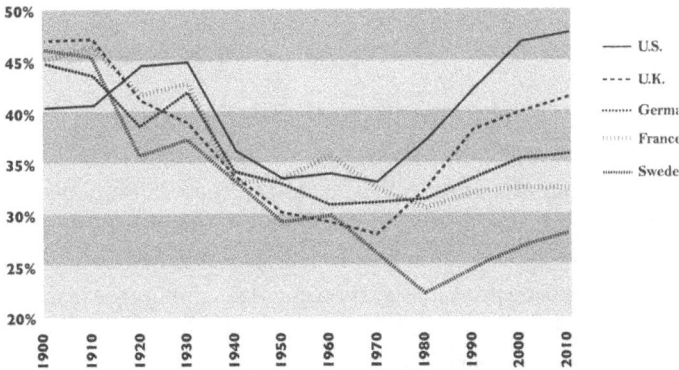

Figure 26 The top decile income share: Europe and the US[13]

In the early twentieth century, the reason for income inequality was mainly due to returns on wealth, while the differences in income from work was not so high. This has changed since the 1970s, when we have seen the rise of the super salaries of managers and chief executives.

While in 1910, 20% of all income went to the richest 1%, only 6% of total wages went to this group. This shows that the rich mainly made their money from capital. By 2010, the richest 1% received only 9% of total income, while it received 7% of total salaries. In the United States, by 2010 the richest 1% received 20% of the total income, as well as 11% of the total wage bill.

Piketty predicts that unless strong measures are taken, inequality will continue to grow until it reaches proportions that will undermine the entire social order.

Root Causes of Rising Income Inequality

Piketty has shown that return on investment is higher than the growth of the economy and that top management salaries have increased enormously compared to worker salaries, but this does not explain why this is happening. The answer, however, is very simple. If the wealth of the rich grows faster than the economy, the average citizens are getting a smaller and smaller share of the pie.

This can be explained by two facts. First, a smaller percentage of company income goes to pay worker salaries, and more goes to pay owner profits and the often absurdly high salaries and bonuses for top management. Secondly, no government actions, such as progressive taxation, have been implemented to mitigate this trend. Rather, governments have increasingly reduced taxes on the rich, giving the rich a double bonus and the ordinary people a double whammy.

The Productivity Wage Gap[14]

When the economy is more efficient, and workers can produce more per hour than before, salaries traditionally goes up. This not only helps workers but is necessary for the economy as a whole. An employee is also a consumer, and with increasing productivity more goods are put on the market. If people's salaries are kept stagnant, and the increase in productivity only goes to the owners of the businesses as profits, who is going to buy the goods? Hence, paying workers less is bad for both the workers and the economy.

Up to the 1970s, wages in Western countries more or less kept up with inflation. As we can see from the graph below, this changed in the 1970s.

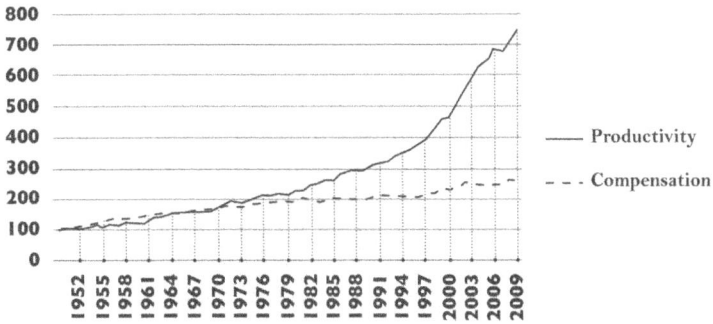

Figure 27 Productivity wage gap in the U.S.[15]

In some European countries the situation was similar. See the following example from Italy.

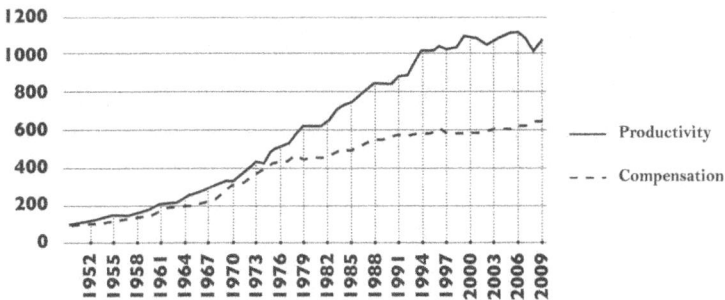

Figure 28 Productivity wage gap in Italy[16]

From a macroeconomic standpoint, there is another problem. When productivity goes up, more goods are produced. Someone has to buy these goods, and the richest 1 percent of the population will not buy them all. The workers, rather, are the main consumers of goods. But if their income does not increase, they will not have enough purchasing power to buy those goods. And to compensate for their reduced purchasing power, people borrow more money and go further into debt.

Regressive Taxation

Since the middle of the twentieth century, taxation in most industrialized nations became gradually more regressive. When taxation is progressive, the higher your salary, the higher your taxes. When taxation is regressive, the rich pay a smaller portion of the total tax burden.

The following is a chart of the highest tax bracket in the United States. Two things are notable. First, the highest tax rate for the past twenty years has been the second lowest since the First World War. The notable exception is the run-up to the Great Depression, which ended in financial disaster.

Secondly, the period with the greatest economic growth in history, the years after the Second World War, historically also had the highest income taxes.

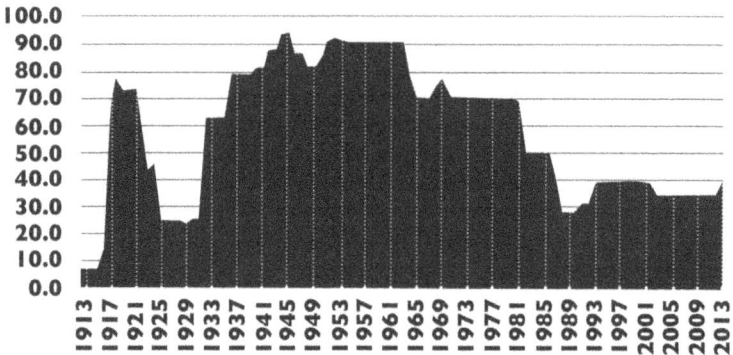

Source: Tax Policy Center

Figure 29 Highest tax bracket in the US

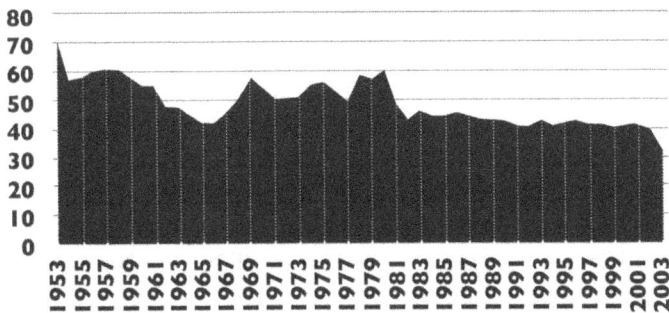

Source: Tax Policy Center

Figure 30 Corporate capital-gains tax in the US

Capital-gains tax for individuals are even lower. By 2003, the rate of capital-gains tax was only 19%. As opposed to income tax, which is higher at higher income brackets, capital-gains tax is a flat rate regardless of the amount of income earned. This is the main reason why Warren Buffet—at the time of this writing, the fourth-wealthiest individual in the world— complained in 2011 that he was paying a lower rate of tax than his secretary. "My friends and I have been coddled long enough by a billionaire-friendly Congress. It's time for our government to get serious about shared sacrifice," he wrote in a much-publicized article in the *New York Times*. [17] In another *New York Times* article a year later, he advocated for a minimum tax on the wealthy. He claimed that no investor will turn down an investment opportunity because he has to pay higher taxes, so there is no need to incentivize them with low tax rates. In Buffet's own words:

> So let's forget about the rich and ultra-rich going on strike and stuffing their ample funds under their mattresses if — gasp — capital gains rates and ordinary income rates are increased. The ultrarich, including me, will forever pursue investment opportunities. And, wow, do we have plenty to invest. The Forbes 400, the wealthiest individuals in America, hit a new group record for wealth this year: $1.7 trillion. That's more than five times

the $300 billion total in 1992. In recent years, my gang has been leaving the middle class in the dust. [18]

The biggest asset class by value is real estate, for which the government collects very little in taxes due to the tax rules that almost entirely eliminate taxes on this class of assets. This is how it works: Almost nobody buys real estate in cash; they borrow the money from the bank. The rental income goes to paying the interest, so the investment is basically free. Not only is it free but also tax free, since the interest payments are tax deductible. In other words, the government is deprived of those potential taxes. In addition, the rules of depreciation allow the investor to write off part of the value of the building every year. This is also reported as a loss, which means that the accumulated losses on the building end up higher than the gains. This loss can then be used to offset other income and further reduce taxes.

The real purpose of buying real estate is to sell when prices are high in order to profit on capital gains. As we have seen, the taxes on capital gains are much lower than on normal income. But that is not the end of it. Most countries have rules in place allowing a person to invest the money earned in new assets within a specified number of years without paying any capital-gains tax.

Such practices enable Warren Buffet to only pay 17 percent in income tax while his secretary has to pay over 30 percent. Regressive taxation policies have done much to transfer wealth from the poor and the government to subsidize the rich and thus increase inequality.

Effect of Inequality on the Economy

When wages do not keep up with increases in productivity, ordinary people do not have the purchasing capacity to buy the goods on the market. If simultaneously the government, which is the biggest consumer of all, has falling revenues due to tax cuts for the rich, the demand on goods and services falls further.

The combination of reduced purchasing capacity and lowered government spending has an immediate impact on the demand for goods and services. Factories are not able to sell their inventory and people are laid off. This further reduces demand. Under such circumstances, the rich people who have benefitted from tax breaks and low salaries for workers have no interest in investing in the real economy. Would you build a new factory if the one you already have cannot sell its products? Hence, vast amounts of money are kept out of the real economy, and the natural flow of money and goods comes to a halt. This illustrates one of the paradoxes of capitalism. While the capitalist system tends to increase inequality, the same inequality, if taken too far, will destroy the very same system.

Short of increasing salaries and raising taxes, there is only one way to avoid a deep recession, and that is debt. By relaxing loan requirements for ordinary people and encouraging them to live on credit, the economy can move again. If governments start to borrow ever-increasing amounts of money to make up for the loss in tax revenue, then the aggregate demand of the economy can forestall a recession. This is what has been going on in the world since the 1970s. Both governments and individuals have amassed enormous amounts of debt to offset the effects of stagnant salaries and lowered taxes for the rich.

The inequality, however, brought on by stagnant wages and regressive taxation, came with a price: either a deep recession or a build-up of debt. Governments chose to go the way of increasing debt. There is therefore a clear connection between the inequality crisis and the debt crisis. The debt crisis was a direct result of the inequality crisis.

In the United States, President Ronald Reagan was the first to implement big tax cuts for the rich. The theory, which was based on the supply-side economics and monetarism of the Chicago School of Economics headed by Milton Friedman, stipulated that if the rich were given more free money they would invest it in the economy, which would increase production and stimulate more growth. Monetarism is explicitly against government stimulus spending and believes that governments should mainly spend money to get out of a recession. The irony is that while Reagan proclaimed himself to follow monetarist policies, his policies provided the biggest peace-time stimulus package in the history of mankind, tripling the national debt in six years!

From the very start, Reagan's government policies were clear—provide tax cuts for the rich to increase their wealth, and protect the economy from collapse by having the government borrow and spend money. This is neither monetarism nor supply-side economics, however, nor is it Keynesian economics, but rather a set of economic policies leading to increased inequality and massive government debts.

The Debt Burden Creating More Inequality

While poverty and inequality leads to an increased debt burden, debt in itself increases inequality. The two feed on each other, aggravating the situation in each turn of the cycle. Let us try to understand how this works.

It is impossible to borrow resources from the future to use in the present. Therefore, all resources that are used are those available to us at the present moment, whether these are infrastructure projects, military spending, or social security. When an individual or nation borrows money to acquire resources, the money is borrowed from someone or somewhere. When banks loan money today, however, they "create" fictitious money while still receiving interest from the lender on the money they "created." This fictitious lending system has become popular with banks, since they make much more profit than if they loaned real money.

As the debt burden of the world increases, the interest keeps rising. In 2013, public and private debt in the United States alone amounted to roughly sixty-one trillion dollars, with interest payments of three trillion annually. [19] This amounts to a staggering 19% of GDP! In other words, 19% of the entire economic output of the United States was redirected as transfer payments to the financial sector. This is money that will not come back to the real economy, except in the forms of new loans that again will increase the transfer payments. In this way a large portion of the economic output is transferred into the hands of a small group of investors in the financial institutions. This huge percentage of resources that is channeled into unearned profits for a small group of rich people is a significant contributor to the rising inequality. Whereas capitalists in the past might have exploited the workers, they did at least contribute to the creation of new wealth. The new, modern type of financial capitalism grabs a huge portion of the economic surplus and gives nothing in return. This practice exploits manufacturers, small business owners, and workers alike. As we saw in the previous chapter, governments have increasingly been printing and borrowing money to stave off a collapse of the economy, but Batra claims that the only people to benefit from the huge budget deficits are the rich.

If there is a wage gap, then more goods are produced than what can be bought. In this case profits may actually fall. According to economist Ravi Batra, "if consumer [or government] borrowing [...] absorb the unsold goods, business revenue rises by the amount of that borrowing, and with wage cost staying constant or falling, the entire debt goes into raising profits. Any kind of borrowing raises profits by the same amount, provided the nation is not in a serious recession." [20]

"The point is," Batra continues, "that the monopoly capitalists always benefit hugely from the so-called monetary and fiscal policies. These are not policies but actually WMEs, or weapons of mass exploitation, because they create the false impression that the government is doing something for those laid off." [21]

The Broader Issue of Inequality

The problem with inequality goes beyond the issues of individual hardship or macroeconomic imbalances. Recent studies show that inequality has great implications for all aspects of social life.

In their book *The Spirit Level: Why Equality is Better for Everyone*, [22] Richard Wilkinson and Kate Pickett argue that equality is important in many ways. A society with high inequality has high levels of crime, drug abuse, teenage pregnancies, homicides, mental illness, and so on. The really interesting thing is that it is not the absolute level of wealth that matters, but the differences among the people inside a given country. Japan and the UK have similar levels of income per capita, but Japan, a much more egalitarian society, has far less crime and other social problems than the UK, a country with high levels of inequality.

Learning from History

Historically, Europe and the United States became high-income areas due to a combination of rising salaries and reduced capital costs. This combination forced innovation and labor productivity and at the same time produced workers that had the purchasing capacity to drive the economy. The key to welfare, according to Erik Reinert, lies in "the interaction between increasing wages which makes new technology profitable, and higher demand." [23]

Since 1989, this trend has stopped in Europe. Salaries have been stagnant, which have reduced the incentive to introduce new technology. At the same time, workers have lost the purchasing power to buy the goods available on the market. While China's wages are much lower and technology is less advanced, the rapidly growing nation is catching up fast. Both salaries and technology are increasing faster than in the West. While the West is stagnating, China and a few other Asian countries are moving ahead rapidly. If this trend continues, the West may find itself falling behind the Asian nations.

There are thus two types of inequality: income and wealth. While the first is troublesome, the second is even more problematic. Wealth can be inherited and passed on from generation to generation, and thus grow to gigantic proportions. Wealth inequality will therefore always be much higher than income inequality. Given this fact, it may take centuries to see meaningful changes in the concentration of wealth, even with a punitively high or progressive income tax, especially given the sacrosanct nature of property rights in our economy and culture.

Given the close interaction between the financial crisis and rising economic inequality, we cannot solve one without the other. To solve the financial crisis, we also have to fix the inequality crisis—and vice versa.

In a market economy, as opposed to a feudal or subsistence economy, people need to have enough purchasing capacity to enable the economy to optimally function. When there are extreme levels of profits, high corporate pay scales, and regressive taxations, the amount of hoarded money increases substantially, and since this wealth is not part of the real economy, the long-term viability of the market itself is challenged.

Capitalism has, in a sense, a self-destructive gene in its DNA. Through normal market forces, capitalism concentrates more and more money in a few hands until the basis of the market collapses. Hence, in order for capitalism to work, regulations and transfer payments from the government are needed to counteract the monopolistic tendencies of capitalism, and thus to ensure the viability of the market. When governments fail to fulfill these functions properly, inequality increases and society faces a crisis.

In addition, to enable poor nations to grow out of poverty, the net drainage of resources from poor to rich areas has to end. In short, a more equitable world would be a more prosperous and peaceful world.

As critical as the issue of inequality is for the economy, humanity is facing even more dangerous threats, namely the depletion of natural resources and the destruction of our environment. In the next two sections, we will discuss these crises.

Chapter Three

The Resource Crisis:
Depleting Nature's Bank Account

Until we recognize that our environmental problems, from climate change to deforestation to species loss, are driven by unsustainable habits, we will not be able to solve the ecological crises that threaten to wash over civilization.

—Erik Assadourian

W HILE DEBT, FINANCE, AND similar economic issues are human-made problems that can be managed with solution-oriented policies, natural resources have external limits placed on us by nature. Indeed, many of the resources we have been taking for granted—such as oil, fish, and fresh water—are becoming scarce, at least in proportion to the rate of their exploitation. Neither classical, neoclassical, Keynesian, nor Marxist economic theory take these vitally important facts into consideration. The cost of natural resources has in theory been considered equal to the cost of extracting them, and these resources are generally not considered to have any intrinsic value of their own. Since the dawn of the industrial revolution, the "unlimited existence" of our natural resources has been taken for granted, or if scarce, it has been assumed the market will find a ready alternative to replace them.

Modern economics does not even acknowledge the necessity of raw material and energy, but wraps these factors into "capital," with the assumption that any type of capital can always be converted into materials and energy. The commonly used Cob-Douglas production function,, implies that production = labor x capital x total-factor productivity. Mathematically, this entails that all capital inputs can be used interchangeably and can be substituted, which in theory means that production could function without raw material and energy—as long as we have money! Hence general economic theory assumes that nature exists outside of production— and is of less importance to the economy. A representation of this formula could look like the following figure: [1]

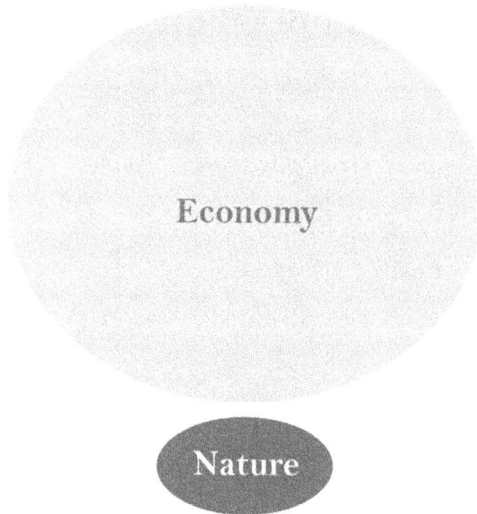

Figure 31 Economy over nature

The entire financial system is thus nothing but a mental abstraction and cannot replace or be a substitute for the real economy, real natural resources, or real sources of energy. Without natural resources, no economic activity and no life can be sustained.

In recent years there have been attempts by modern economists to incorporate nature into economics by calculating the cost of nature as externalities, etc. Such thinking would produce the following graph:

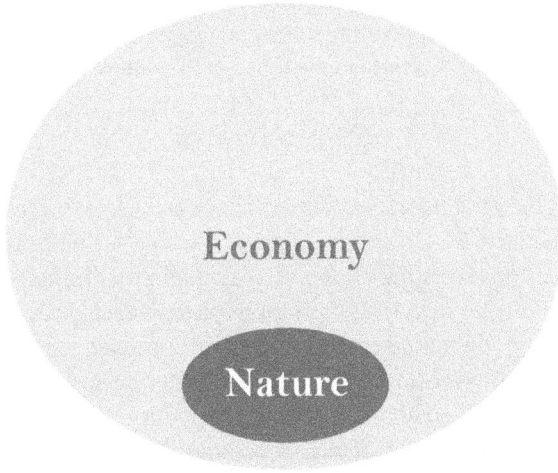

Figure 32 Nature as part of economy

This formula, however, is also not representative of the real interaction between nature and the economy. In reality, the economy is an outgrowth of nature; a small, integral part of the global eco-sphere. A representation of a more eco-centered economy would thus look as follows:

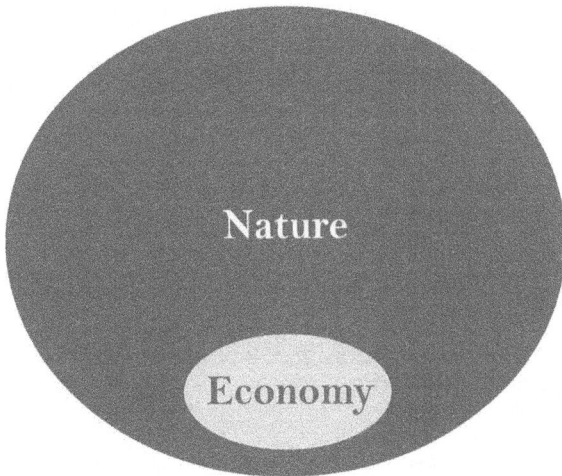

Figure 33 Economy as part of nature

In the following section, we will look at nature and natural resources, their importance for our economic life and wellbeing, and the limitations they may impose on human economic development.

Scarcity

The world is heading for an "ecological credit crunch" far worse than the current financial crisis. We humans are over-using the natural resources of the planet. *The Living Planet Report*[2] calculates that humans are using 30% more resources than the Earth can replenish each year. This results in deforestation, degraded soils, polluted air and water, as well as dramatic declines in the numbers of fish and other species. According to the report's authors, led by the conservation group, WWF International, formerly the World Wildlife Fund, we are running up an ecological debt of four to $4.5 trillion each year—double the estimated losses of the world's financial institutions—as a result of the credit crisis. The report also calculated the economic value of services provided by ecosystems destroyed annually, such as diminished rainfall for crops or reduced flood protection. The report concludes that by the year 2030, we will need two planets to sustain our consumption. Unfortunately, we have only one. "The recent downturn in the global economy is a stark reminder of the consequences of living beyond our means," says James Leape, WWF International's director general. "But the possibility of financial recession pales in comparison to the looming ecological credit crunch."[3]

In an article in *Scientific American* titled "Forget Peak Oil, We're at Peak Everything,"[4] published in March 2013, the journal claims that apart from oil, we are running out of forests for paper production; the demand for water is 40% higher than sustainable levels; and fish levels in the seas are dropping dramatically due to overfishing.

Minerals are also starting to be in short supply. In his book, *The Race for What's Left: The Global Scramble for the World's Last Resources*,[5] Michael T. Klare concludes that global shortages are forcing us to look for resources in more and more difficult places, and at an increased cost. Shortages of oil and minerals, such as silver, zinc, antimony, indium, hafnium, terbium, platinum, gallium, and many other rare but exceedingly important resources, forces us to search under the sea, in the Arctic regions, and in other hostile places. While doing so, the cost of extraction increases, and we are running into diminishing returns by having to spend more and more resources to get the same amount of oil, gas, and minerals as before. At the same time, we are damaging the ecosystem, which provides us with a complex array of services needed to sustain life. Therefore, while we are desperately trying to delay the time when these resources finally will run out, we are damaging the very foundation of our existence. We will return to this in our section on the Environmental Crisis.

Energy

Life depends on energy, and life on earth exists solely due to the energy we receive daily from the sun, about 1.5 W/m2 at the top of the atmosphere. [6] Of this staggering amount, about a quarter reaches the earth's surface. Part of this energy is absorbed by plants, which, through the process of photosynthesis, convert it into sugar and other organic matter, thus creating the base of life. Animals and fungi eat living or dead plant matter, receiving their required energy indirectly from the sun.

Without the heat of the sun there would be no wind, ocean currents, or waves. Up until recently, human energy requirements have been satisfied through the utilization of food, firewood, charcoal, wind, and water. [7] We consumed food provided by nature. Wind moved sailing ships; boiling water ran steam engines and wind powered windmills to grind wheat or to drive mechanical workshops; firewood heated our homes and allowed us to cook food; and charcoal provided a more concentrated heat source for the forging of iron and other metals.

The process of extracting energy indirectly from the sun has been going on since the beginning of life itself. All life basically consumes the amount of energy that the sun provides at any given moment, such as wind and water or harvested food or firewood. Throughout geological and human history, living beings have adjusted to the available supply of solar energy and lived and thrived within those limits.

At the dawn of the industrial revolution about two hundred years ago, when we started to mine coal on a massive scale, our relationship to nature changed dramatically. Suddenly we seemed to have an endless supply of "free energy" sources to serve our growing needs. This new development altered the course of human civilization. The industrial revolution and our economic advances have often been attributed to the increase in labor productivity, but labor productivity is in fact a product of three distinct components. The first was human cooperation, when people work together to achieve goals by specializing in various fields—also known as Adam Smith's concept of the specialization of human labor. Secondly, human ingenuity was needed to come up with inventions allowing one person to do the work previously done be several people. Finally, we needed cheap energy. Even though the industrial revolution enabled one person to operate a large machine producing the equivalent of many people's work, the machine itself required lots of energy. Without cheap energy resources, it would have been impossible to reach the levels of automation and labor productivity we have witnessed during the industrial revolution and beyond. Cheap energy was first derived from coal and later from oil, making both the underlying drivers of the industrial and agricultural revolutions. Without these resources, we would never have been able to attain the standard of living we have in the Western world today.

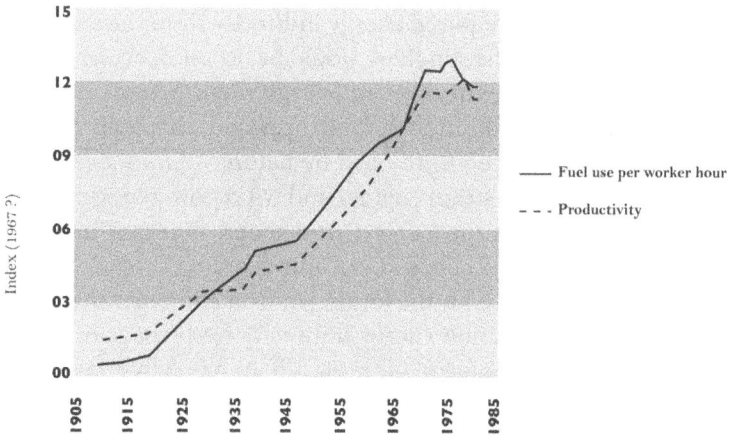

Figure 34 Correlation between labor
productivity and the use of energy per worker

As can be seen from the graph above, there is a strong correlation between labor productivity and the energy use per worker. In fact, the energy an average worker in the United States has at his or her disposal today would be equivalent to having sixty to eighty slaves performing the same labor. There is also a close connection between energy use and economic growth.

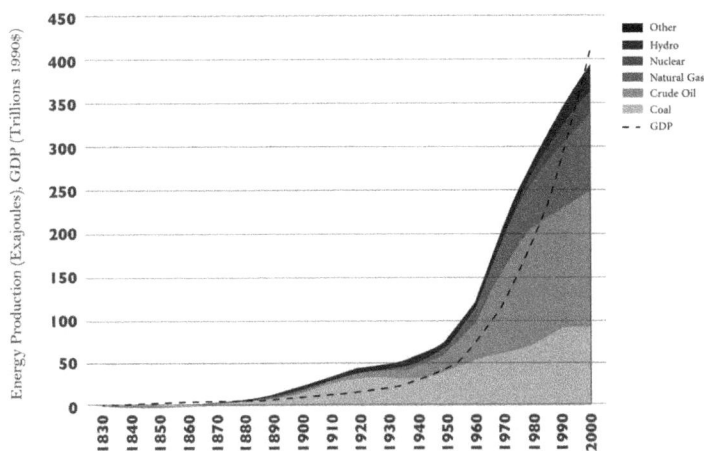

Figure 35 Correlation between energy use and economic growth

Although it is a common logical error to confuse correlation with causation, in this case it is easy to show that without an abundance of cheap energy, neither the labor productivity nor the economic growth achieved in the last century could have been possible.

By now the link between economic growth and energy use has been made abundantly clear. Financial crises may come and go, but as long as we have an abundance of cheap energy and other natural resources, the economy is bound to bounce back sooner or later. There may be a painful period of adjustment, but the economy will eventually grow again.

What would happen, however, if a major economic crisis coincides with an energy crisis? Even worse, what if the present economic crisis is triggered by the first signs of an energy crisis, where we are no longer able to increase the amount of cheap energy we use every year? The simple answer is that it would be impossible to resolve the economic crisis unless the underlying energy crisis is handled simultaneously, which is an unlikely scenario. Let us therefore look at the availability of our major energy sources to determine if there is evidence of a looming energy crisis.

Energy Squeeze

There is a distinct difference between oil, natural gas, and coal—the predominant energy sources driving our current economy—and the renewable sources of firewood, water, and wind that our forebears depended on. While these renewables directly utilize the energy released by the sun, sources such as oil, gas, and coal utilize energy accumulated and stored in the earth over a period of millions of years. Hence, we could compare oil and the other hydrocarbons to the "fat" the earth has stored up for reserve energy. This storage of energy is what we humans have been dipping into over the past two hundred years. Its easy availability made us believe it could fuel unlimited growth and prosperity. But it does not require an advanced degree in mathematics to understand that if we consume energy that has taken millions of years to produce in a matter of decades, once that energy is exhausted it will take millions of years for the earth to recreate it. According to British Petroleum, total oil reserves reached 1700 billion barrels at the end of 2014, sufficient to fuel 52.5 years of global production. In other words, there will come a time in the near future when the oil, coal, and gas reserves will run out. Barring the discovery of a thus-far unknown energy source, we will again be required to limit our consumption to the direct input of solar energy.

In academic, scientific, and political circles, there is currently a fierce on-going discussion about whether we are actually running out of the conventional hydrocarbons—oil, gas, and coal. Basically, we can divide the debate into three groups depending on their points of view.

Peak Oil advocates claim we are facing a future where oil production peaks and from which we will start a downward slope of extracting less and less oil.

Unlimited Oil advocates claim we will never run out of oil, since we will discover more efficient ways to extract hard-to-get oil that was previously unavailable.

Ecological Disaster advocates agree we will not run out of oil anytime soon, but they consider this an undesirable predicament, since the environmental consequences of the extraction and burning of fossil fuels will be environmentally disastrous.

These three groups represent the main views among a wide spectrum of experts, and naturally there are experts whose views lie somewhere in between these extremes. Let us look at the arguments of each and determine if we can find some common ground to help us decide what the actual reality is.

Peak Oil Advocates

The original theory of peak oil was proposed by M. King Hubbert in 1956. Mr. Hubbert accurately predicted that United States' oil production would peak between 1961 and 1975, and then decline. Globally, oil production peaked in 2005 with seventy-four thousand barrels of oil per day (74 mbd).

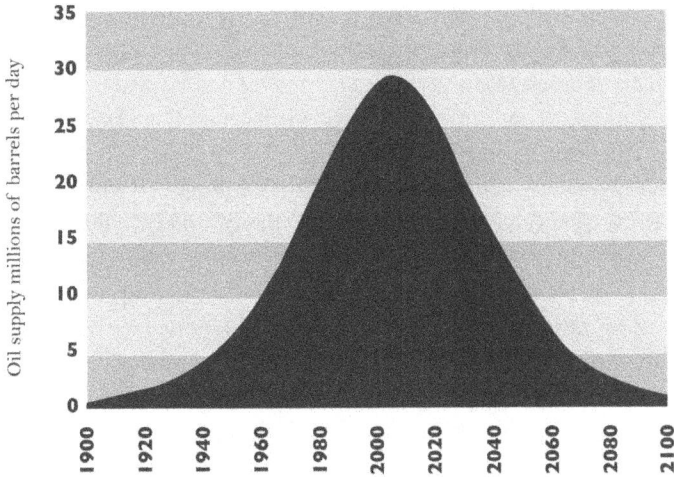

Figure 36: Hubbert's Curve
Global oil production in giga-barrels per year

At the time, the peak-oil theory seemed to have been confirmed, spelling an end to economic growth and prosperity. According to Hubbert, major oil fields were being depleted faster than new reserves were being discovered, and those that were discovered were often in inhospitable places where extraction could only be done at great cost.

In his book *The Race for What's Left*, Michael Klare writes:

> …the era of readily accessible oil and gas has come to an end: from now on, vital energy supplies will have to be drawn from remote and forbidding locations, at a cost far exceeding anything experienced in the past. The world is entering an era of pervasive, unprecedented resource scarcity. [8]

Klare gives several examples of the difficulties in exploiting the new fields recently discovered. Commenting on the vast new discoveries in Russia and Brazil, he writes:

> In Russia, for example, a major effort is now under way to develop oil and gas deposits off the east coast of Sakhalin, a large island in the Sea of Okhotsk in the North Pacific. Sakhalin Island is below the Arctic Circle, and so is spared the extreme temperatures of more northerly locations. Nevertheless, it is not an easy place to operate in. Temperatures in the winter often reach 40 degrees below zero, and the island lies in an area prone to typhoons. What's more, Sakhalin's offshore oil and gas platforms are often exposed to massive ice floes pushed toward the island by powerful currents in the Sea of Okhotsk. To withstand these floes, as well as the earthquakes that often rattle the area, the platforms have to be specially reinforced. And because an ice sheet surrounds much of Sakhalin in the winter, supply ships and oil tankers can reach the oil-production zone only during certain times of the year. The island's vulnerability to severe weather was made especially evident in December 2011, when the Kolskaya oil rig capsized and sank in a fierce storm while being towed into a Sakhalin harbor, resulting in the death of most of the sixty-seven crewmen aboard.

Equally daunting challenges are facing the developers of Brazil's new offshore oil discoveries, including the giant Tupi field in the deep waters of the South Atlantic. Known as "pre-salt" deposits because they lie buried beneath a thick layer of salt, Tupi and neighboring offshore fields are thought to hold as much as 100 billion barrels of oil, making them the largest untapped reservoir to be exploited since wells in the North Sea were brought online in the 1970s. But extracting oil from the pre-salt area will not be easy or inexpensive. The offshore deposits lie beneath 1.5 miles of water and another 2.5 miles of compressed salt, sand, and rock. New drilling technologies will have to be developed to operate at these ocean depths and to penetrate the salt dome below. The subsalt reserves are also believed to contain high concentrations of natural gas, and the separation and handling of this gas will pose additional challenges. Successful development of Tupi and other pre-salt fields will require hundreds of billions of dollars and many years of effort. [9]

Norway is also finding it challenging to exploit its new oil fields. In a recent interview in the Norwegian paper, *Nordland*, the former Oil and Energy Minister, Eivind Reiten, recommends that the country should not proceed to develop the new oil fields discovered in Lofoten off the coast of northern Norway. His argument is not based on environmental considerations, but rather on cost considerations.[10]

Some peak oil advocates, such as Kjell Aleklett, Professor of Physics at the University of Uppsala in Sweden, and retired petroleum geologist, Colin Campbell, founder and honorary chairman of the Association for the Study of Peak Oil and Gas (APSO), believe that in contrast to Hubbert's peak, we will reach what could be called an oscillating or bumpy plateau, where energy production will reach a peak, fall back somewhat, reach another peak, and continue like this until the inevitable decline. [11] Other scientists, such as Charles A. S. Hall and David J. Murphy, share this view. [12] According to them, the recent spike in shale-oil production is just a short-term peak that puts off the inevitable outcome for a few years or maybe a few decades. Campbell's predictions as of December 2013 project that a decline in total energy production will take place after 2020. In APSO's Peak Oil Review it is predicted that oil output will climb to ten thousand barrels in 2015, [13] up from eight thousand barrels at the end of December 2013. However, the Review expects that by 2017, the production will peak again since all the "sweet spots," those areas that give the most oil for the least amount of work, would rapidly become depleted.

Shale Oil and the Unlimited Oil Advocates

The decline did not continue as expected, however. The higher costs of oil have made alternative and more difficult sources of oil profitable, and as technology tackled these difficult sources, such as tar sand and shale oil, production increased. According to the U.S. Energy Information Administration, [14] in 2014 the United States total oil production was bigger than its oil imports for the first time since 1995.

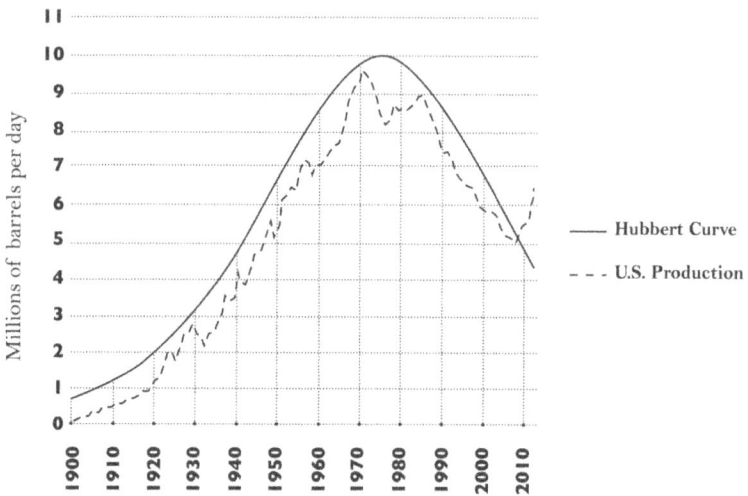

Source: U.S. Energy Information Administration

Figure 37 U.S. Crude oil production versus Hubbert's Curve

Global oil production is also rising. After a setback for a few years after 2005, new heights were reached in 2011 and 2012. This gave rise to a new group of advocates who claimed that we have so much hydrocarbons in the form of oil, gas, and similar deposits that we will never run out. Most of these resources were previously unavailable, but new technology has put them within our reach.

"'When will the world's supply of oil be exhausted?" asked MIT economist Morris Adelman, perhaps the most important exponent of this view. "The best one-word answer: never. Effectively, energy supplies are infinite."[15]

Faced with the evidence, even peak-oil advocates these days admit we have enormous amounts of hydrocarbons trapped inside the earth. While proven conventional reserves stood at 1.317 trillion barrels as of January 1, 2007, according to the IEA, the world reserves of shale oil as per a 2010 estimate stood at 5 trillion barrels. Even though just a small part of these reserves are technically recoverable, their presence changes the game dramatically.

The US is fracking so much natural gas today that the price is less than a third of the prices in Europe and Asia—a big cost advantage for

American industry. As companies switch to cheap natural gas, a recent Citigroup report argued that the US petroleum boom could add as much as 3.3% to America's GDP in the next seven years, and the International Energy Agency has predicted that the United States may soon become all but self-sufficient in energy.

Shale Oil and Oil Shale

Despite the similarities in names, there is a big difference between shale oil and oil shale. Shale oil is oil trapped in tight rock formations and released by fracking. In recent years, there has been considerable success in exploiting these types of reserves in Montana, North Dakota, Colorado, and Wyoming.

Oil shale, on the other hand, is not oil but a rock containing kerogen, a type of fossilized algae. If heated to 650 degrees Fahrenheit (343 degrees Celsius), kerogen can be converted to oil and natural gas. Though the reserves are vast, little progress has been made in extracting kerogen. The amount of energy required to heat it and turn it into oil is one of the main problems. Shell is the latest of a line of companies that have abandoned their research into oil shale after spending millions of dollars in investments.

Energy Returned on Investment

Why then, in spite of ample evidence of vast deposits of hydrocarbons, do the peak-oil advocates believe that a decline in energy, with its sure impact on the economy, is inevitable? Their arguments focus on economic feasibility and Energy Returned on Investment (EROI).

EROI, sometimes also called EROEI (Energy Returned on Energy Invested), measures how much energy is needed to extract energy from a particular energy source. It is defined as:

If it takes one barrel of oil to produce one barrel of oil, we would have an EROI of 1:1. In this case there would be no incentive to extract the oil at all, since we would end up with the same amount of oil we had when we started.

This concept is important when we consider oil reserves, since their EROI varies significantly. A comprehensive summary of the EROI of various fuels was done in 2008 by Charles Hall and a group of students. In the table below, EJ/yr stands for exajoule per year, which equals one quintillion joules (10^{18} joules) per year, or roughly 278 billion kilowatt hours. The third column from the left shows the energy return on investment.

If a source has a high EROI, it means that it requires little energy to extract it. If it has a low EROI, it means a large amount of energy is needed. If the EJ/year is small, it means that the energy source is insignificant to the total energy needs of the world.

Resource	Year	Magnitude (EJ/ yr)	EROI (X:1)
Fossil fuels			
Oil and gas	1930	5	>100
Oil and gas	1970	28	30
Oil and gas	2005	9	11 to 18
Discoveries	1970		8
Production USA	1970	10	20
World oil production	1999	200	35
Imported oil to the USA	1990	20	35
Imported oil to the USA	2005	27	18
Imported oil to the USA	2007	28	12
Natural gas	2005	30	10
Coal (mine-mouth)	1950	n/a	80
Coal (mine-mouth)	2000	5	80
Bitumen from tar sands	n/a	1	2 to 4
Shale oil	n/a	0	5
Other nonrenewable			
Nuclear	n/a	9	5 to 15
Renewables			
Hydropower	n/a	9	>100
Wind turbines	n/a	5	18
Geothermal	n/a	<1	n/a
Wave energy	n/a	<<1	n/a
Solar collectors			

Flat plate	n/a	<1	1.9
Concentrating collector	n/a	o	1.6
Photovoltaic	n/a	<1	6.8
Passive solar	n/a	n/a	n/a
Biomass			
Ethanol (sugarcane)	n/a	o	0.8 to 10
Corn-based ethanol	n/a	<1	0.8 to 1.6
Biodiesel	n/a	<1	1.3

In the table above,[16] we first notice that the current energy source with the highest EROI is hydroelectric power. The problem with this source is its limited supply. Globally, it supplies only nine hexajoules/year, and the possibility to increase this is limited, mostly due to the lack of suitable rivers.

Secondly, we can see that the EROI for conventional oil has been dropping over the years. In the 1930s, the EROI was around 100:1, which means that with one barrel of oil one could extract 100 barrels. By 2005, this had dropped to 12-18:1, which means that from one barrel of oil we only can extract twelve to eighteen barrels.

Thirdly, if we compare this with alternative fuels, such as corn-based ethanol, tar sands, or shale oil, we get EROI values between 0.8 and 1.6 for ethanol, and between two and five for tar sands and shale oil. This means equal reserves of conventional oil, tar sands, and shale oil do not give the same net benefit to society. The lower the EROI, the greater the energy needed to extract it. This can be calculated with the formula: . At a ratio of 1:1, there is no net gain of energy. At a ratio of 2:1, we need to extract two barrels of oil to get a net gain of one barrel. In the best-case scenario of corn-based ethanol, with a ratio of 1.6:1, we need to produce 2.7 units of ethanol to get a net gain of one unit.

This, the peak oil advocates claim, creates a net energy cliff. At high EROIs, the amount of energy required to extract a unit of energy is negligible. When the EROI changes from 50:1 to 49:1, it makes almost no difference in the amount of energy output. When we have low EROI numbers, however, small changes can be critical. A lowering of EROI from 2:1 to 1:1 means that instead of getting twice the energy we put in, we get no new energy at all from the operation.

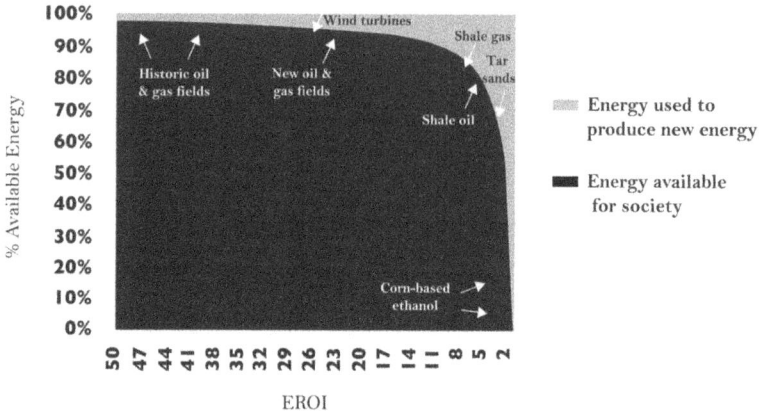

Figure 38 The net energy cliff

The argument the indefinite-oil-supply advocates use to counter EROI calculations is that it is not necessary to use the same type of energy source to extract new energy. Other critics of the peak-oil theory point out that even if shale oil and tar sands have low EROI, it is not necessary to use oil as energy to extract oil. In fact, to extract shale oil mostly shale gas is used as an energy source. But there is a big problem: shale gas has only a slightly better EROI than shale oil.

Ecological Disaster Advocates

This third group of opinion makers agree that oil and other petrochemicals are basically unlimited. In opposition to the unlimited-oil advocates, however, who view this as a positive, this group considers it a disaster. We already have problems with global warming from burning too much fossil fuel, they argue, and if oil becomes scarce, it will force humanity to turn to renewable energy sources. The fact that oil reserves seem to be unlimited is a great danger, since it will encourage us to use greater and greater quantities of it and thus cause more and more pollution. Also, the process of fracking pollutes ground water and can have severe, long-term environmental consequences. We will elaborate on this in the next chapter on the ecological crisis.

Peak Oil or Unlimited Oil Supplies

In its World Energy Outlook for 2012, the International Energy Agency declared we are using more oil than we are discovering:

> More than 70% of the increase in proven reserves since 2000 has come from revisions to reserves in discovered fields, known as reserves growth, with the rest coming from discoveries. Discoveries have picked up in the last few years with increased exploration, driven by higher oil prices, but they still lag behind production by a large margin. In 2011, twelve billion barrels were discovered, equal to 40% of the oil produced during the year. [17]

The agency still concludes, however, that improvements in technology will help us extract oil more efficiently and improve our ability to find more oil, at least up to 2035. The agency asks: "Does this mean that resources will simply not be big enough to support a continuing rise in output, such as that we projected in the New and Current Policies Scenarios and that a rapid decline is imminent? The simple answer is: no." [18]

For the United States, they predict that production of oil, boosted by the shale-oil revolution, will rise to 11 mb/d in 2020, and thereafter gradually decline. The agency does not seem to consider shale oil as a major game changer, as some other analysts claim. The 2013 report is even more explicit. In the executive summary, it sums up its position: "Light tight oil [another name for shale oil and related oil sources] shakes the next ten years, but leaves the longer term unstirred." [19]

The IEA further estimates that at 2013 consumption levels we have proven oil reserves for fifty-four years, and 178 years if we consider all remaining recoverable resources. [20] The agency also predicts that prices of energy will continue to rise in real terms, reflecting the increasing cost of production.

Instead of getting more optimistic, however, the IEA has in the past ten years reduced its predictions of future energy consumption. In 2004, the World Energy Outlook predicted that by 2030 world oil consumption would be 121 mb/d. At the time, Kjell Alkelett and other researchers at the University of Uppsala challenged this prediction, contending that it is impossible to achieve. In its 2013 outlook, the IEA revised this figure to around 100 mb/d.

Assessment of the Energy Situation

Some critics consider the views of the IEA to be too optimistic, alleging that the agency tries to deliberately downplay the risk of peak oil. [21] On the other hand, nobody has ever accused it of being pro peak oil. Let us therefore assume that the estimates of the IEA reflect the best-case scenario of energy production in the years to come and analyze what the consequences would be if these assumptions are correct.

If we look at the big picture, there is not that much difference between the IEA estimate of recoverable reserves and that of the peak-oil proponents. They mainly differ in regards to the time frame. While peak-oil proponents believe that we will run out of oil in the next few years, the IEA believes we are safe at least until 2035. After that even the IEA is unsure. But both agree on one point: the era of cheap oil is over. In her remarks during the launching of the World Energy Outlook 2013, the Executive Director of the IEA, Maria van der Hoeven, proclaimed:

> For billions more, any true sense of energy security is under-mined by high energy prices. It is now more than five years after the onset of the global financial crisis, yet the recovery remains fragile; for many consumers and businesses, energy prices remain stubbornly high. Alarmingly, oil prices have averaged over $110/barrel since 2011. Such a sustained period of high oil prices is without parallel. [22]

The IEA is also pessimistic about the environment and estimates that the targets for CO_2 emissions will not be met. The Earth, the agency claims, is on course to become 3.6 degrees warmer than it was at the start of the industrial revolution, around 1760.

In summary, here are the prospects for energy production in the near future:

- Energy will become more expensive. For energy to drive economic development, it has to be cheap. In the near future, global society will have to spend more of its resources on fulfilling its energy needs.
- When more energy is required to produce energy, more greenhouse gases and pollution will be produced.

- Most new fuel sources depend heavily on water for its extraction. As we will discuss shortly, water is also getting scarce.
- To obtain natural gas and oil, there will be increased ground-water pollution through fracking, by injecting water and up to six hundred chemicals into the ground.
- Even if we are in no danger of running out of energy anytime soon, the implications are serious. Let us analyse the consequences a bit further.

Expensive Energy

The importance of oil to the economy cannot be underestimated. Historically, oil has been a cheap resource, and its ready availability has fueled the economy for the past one hundred years or more. Water is also an important resource—in part, because it is cheap and easily available. If water were scarce and expensive, life would not flourish as readily here on earth. In recent history, economic downturns have been associated with high energy prices. If, in the near future, we are stuck with relatively high prices, raising the cost of production, which appears practically unavoidable, economic growth will be greatly curtailed.

The amount of resources we spend on energy seriously impacts the amount of discretionary spending available for other social goods and services. When oil purchases as a percentage of GDP went up in the past, the economy was thrown into a recession, even though it never passed 8 percent. In future times of reduced EROI on oil production, it is not unlikely that the cost of oil will rise to between 10 and 20% of GDP, an unprecedented situation. Indeed, if decision-makers take into account past statistics or case studies, they will have to admit to the disastrous effects this will have on the economy and people's livelihoods.

As we mentioned in the first chapter, it will be impossible to grow out of the debt crisis. With high energy prices, the necessary economic growth cannot take place, and we will be forced to deal with the debt in painful ways—through default, write offs, or inflation. This will force us to undergo a massive restructuring of the entire economic system.

Until cheap alternative energy sources are found, economic growth will be limited. With limited economic growth, unemployment will continue to be high and may rise even further in most developed countries. We may enter the Big Recession we never really recovered from.

Modern food production, which is highly energy intensive, will also be affected. Food prices will increase, and vitally important food items will be unaffordable to vulnerable groups. The trend of slightly reduced poverty and starvation over the past decades may not only be reversed, but rather increase significantly.

When economic problems are on the rise, there is often a corresponding rise in fascist and extremist parties and opinions; as mentioned earlier, this is already taking place all over Europe, in poor and affluent countries alike.

The Direct Environmental Impact of the Energy Crisis

Presently, global temperatures have risen an average of 0.8 degrees since the beginning of the industrial revolution. We already see the impact of global warming through dramatically altered weather patterns: severe storms, increased heat and drought mixed with spells of intense cold or severe rainstorms and flood.

It is difficult to predict what an increase of three degrees will have on the planet, but judging from current trends the outcome will be very serious and in many places catastrophic. According to the IEA, based on increased CO_2 emissions due to increased energy consumption, this is indeed what we can expect.

In regions where light oil and shale gas are extracted, the local environmental impact can be severe. Fracking involves the injection of water mixed with sand and chemicals under high pressure, which causes tiny fractures in the rock through which oil and gas can migrate to the well. Not only oil but also contaminated water seeps through these cracks. According to a recent report by Environment America, fracking "produces enormous amounts of toxic waste water — often containing cancer-causing and even radioactive material." [23] The report estimates that 360,000 acres of land have been directly damaged as a result of fracking since 2005. Drinking water has been contaminated in many US states, including Pennsylvania and New Mexico, and in New Mexico alone, groundwater was contaminated on more than four hundred occasions. [24]

The energy crisis is real and it is not going away anytime soon. We are optimists, however. There are energy sources with vast potentials around, and with the right effort it is likely that humanity eventually will find ways of using them sustainably. As long as short-sighted attempts to maximize private profits guide our policies, however, we are unlikely to resolve the problem anytime soon.

The Effect of the Climate Crisis on Global Water Reserves

Energy and minerals are not the only resources facing depletion. The most vital component in our life, short of the air we breathe, is water, and there are alarming signs that we are running out of this precious liquid. Water scarcity is already looming, and the increasing demand for this "blue gold" in growing biofuels and extracting shale oil and gas will lead to even more competition over water. Priorities will have to be made whether to use water for energy production or for irrigation, for example. This could put further restrictions on the exploration of unconventional oil and gas reserves, and the growing of biofuels. Food and drinking water is a fundamental necessity of life—oil exploration is not.

Most of the world's water, a total of 97%, in fact, is salty. Of the remaining 3%, over two-thirds is trapped in glaciers and polar ice caps. Fresh water is found mostly as groundwater; only a fraction is available on the surface, 87% of which is found in lakes, 11% in swamps, and 2% in rivers.

It requires two to three thousand liters of water to produce enough food to feed a person for one day. Compare this to the amount of drinking water a person requires, a mere two to four liters. With the world's population approaching seven billion people, the daily requirement of fresh water is thus reaching unprecedented proportions.

While fresh water is a renewable resource, global groundwater sources are steadily becoming scarcer. The largest depletions are in Asia and North America, although nobody really knows what the long-term effect on the ecosystem will be.

In 2012, the National Intelligence Council, Director of National Intelligence, Central Intelligence Agency (CIA), Defense Intelligence Agency (DIA) and the Federal Bureau of Investigation (FBI) jointly prepared the 2012 US Intelligence Community Threat Assessment on Global Water Security. The report concluded:

> Between now and 2040, fresh water availability will not keep up with demand, absent more effective management of water resources. Water problems will hinder the ability of key countries to produce food and generate energy, posing a risk to global food markets and hobbling economic growth. As a result of demographic and economic development pressures, North Africa, the

Middle East, and South Asia will face major challenges coping
with water problems. [25]

Furthermore, the Organization for Economic Cooperation and
Development projects said that about 47% of the world's population will
be living in areas with severe water stress by the year 2030. Water scarcity
was also put on top of the agenda in a recent UN report, urging the UN
Security Council to take immediate action.

Water scarcity is not only about the lack of water (quantity), or the
lack of access to safe water (quality), but also about the "economic scarcity" of water. Water may exist in the ground, but it is time-consuming
and expensive to extract it. Hence, as the demand for water increases,
combined with limited supplies, the cost and effort to maintain and
facilitate access to water will increase. This will require more power and
resources from other sectors and thus multiply the problems.

In many countries, groundwater levels are declining, including China,
India, and the United States. Many rivers are being diverted from their
natural flow to satisfy the ever-increasing demand for water. As journalist Fred Pearce realized when he started to study the water issue, the
situation is worse than most people realize:

> Israel is draining the river Jordan into pipes before it reaches the
> country that bears its name. There is drought on the Ganges,
> because India had sucked up the holy river's entire dry-season
> flow. The great Oxus, the Nile of Central Asia, is diverted into
> the desert, leaving the Aral Sea to dry out. Half a century of
> pumping on the High Plains of the USA has removed water
> that will take two thousand years of rain to replace. In India,
> farmers whose fathers lifted water from wells with a bucket now
> sink boreholes more than a kilometer into the rocks — and still
> they find no water. [26]

Many NGOs warn that the wars of the future are as likely to be fought over
water as they are over oil today. According to author Steven Solomon,
author of *Water: The Epic Struggle for Wealth, Power, and Civilization*:

> An explosive new political fault line is erupting across the global
> landscape between the water Haves and water Have Nots....
> Simply, water is surpassing oil itself as the world's scarcest critical

resource. Just as oil conflicts were central to the 20th century history, the struggle over freshwater is set to shape a new turning point in the world order and the destiny of civilization. [27]

We are already witnessing examples of this predicament in Sub-Saharan Africa, North Africa, and West Asia, where water scarcity is a continuing driving factor in political instability, environmental degradation, and armed conflict. Although no armed conflict has yet resulted over water shortages, time and time again control over the management of natural resources are at the root of inequalities and disputes. Some hot spots include problems over water between Israelis and Palestinians, between Egypt and the other countries sharing the Nile, and between Iran and Afghanistan attempting to share the Hirmand River.

In some places, the rising cost of water has already led to riots. One of the most well-known was the Cochabamba protests in Bolivia in the year 2000. To improve the availability of water, and on the insistence of the World Bank, Bolivia privatized the supply of water and gave the contract to Aqua del Tunari, a joint venture between the multinational Bechtel and Suez Lyonaise.

To ensure the legality of the contract, the government enacted Law 2029, which not only legalized the monopoly on water given to Aqua del Tunari, but expanded its water rights beyond the original contract. The law gave Aqua del Tunari rights to all water in the country. This meant that the company could go to community water projects they had nothing to do with and install meters and collect money for the water the community used. By law, the company could even charge people for the use of rainwater collected from their own rooftops.

When the company increased the water rates by 30 percent, raising the monthly cost to $20 per user, riots broke out. Many clients earned only $100 per month—$20 was more than they spent on food

As a response to the spreading riots, the government declared a state of emergency. After much violence the government was forced to relent and the contract was cancelled. Water prices returned to pre-2000 levels, and the officials of Aqua del Tunari had to flee the country. Since the water infrastructure was never upgraded, Bolivia still suffers from water shortages.

Privatization of water remains a hot issue. In her book *Blue Covenant: The Global Water Crisis and the Coming Battle for the Right to Water*, Maude Barlow describes recent water-privatization policies around the world that until now has been mostly under the direct control of government authorities. [28] Privatization was first implemented in some Western countries and then spread to developing countries through World Bank loans and projects. Corporations like GE, Dow Chemical, and Proctor & Gamble are now getting into the ownership, control, and recycling of water. Liberalizing and privatizing water services is a long-standing goal of the European Commission, but it is fiercely opposed by the public and many member states. Gabriella Zanzanaini of the organization Food and Water Europe says the ongoing push to privatize "really demonstrates how the Commission has lost touch with reality. Their ideological arguments are not based on substantiated facts and ignore the democratic will of the people." [29]

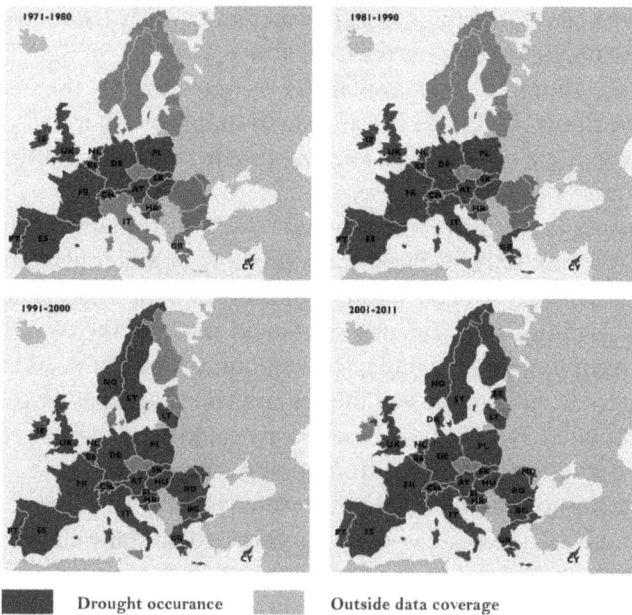

| ■ | Drought occurance | ▨ | Outside data coverage |

Source: (http://www.eea.europa.eu/legal/copyright). Copyright holder: European Topic Centre on Inland, Coastal and Marine waters (ICM)."

Figure 39 Observed drought episodes in Europe. [30]

Water is a vital resource for our survival, and the shortages we are facing will most likely make the access and control of water, along with the struggle to control oil, one of the foremost battlegrounds in the years to come.

In his essay "Lumberjacks in Eden,"[31] Peter Hall, the fund manager of the Hunter Hall Group, points to the dangers and impossibility of unrestricted growth:

> If we maintain our current trajectory of population and economic growth, by the end of our lifetime (and yours), the human footprint will be about two and a half times as heavy as it is today. Food production will need to be twice as high as today to support the expected 50% increase in population, as well as desired increases in standard of living.

But as we have argued above, we neither have the energy nor the water to support such a rate of growth. Almost all resources on the planet are being strained. Something will have to give.

In 1972 a book funded by the Volkswagen Foundation and commissioned by the Club of Rome published the results of a computer simulation of unrestricted economic and population growth with limited resources. The book, *The Limits to Growth*,[32] pictured a bleak future for humanity. It envisioned dwindling resources, a collapse in industrial output, increasing death rates, and dwindling populations.

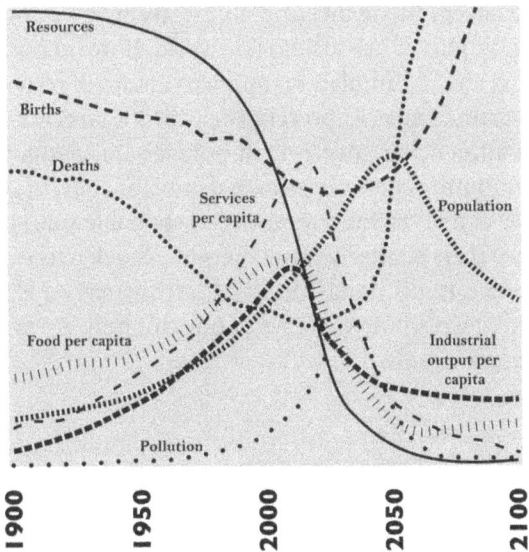

Figure 40 Limits to growth

In 2004 an attempt was made to see to what extent the predictions of the original report had come true. The new document was titled "Limits to Growth: The Thirty Year Update,"[33] and concluded:

> While the past 30 years has shown some progress, including new technologies, new institutions, and a new awareness of environmental problems, the authors are far more pessimistic than they were in 1972. Humanity has squandered the opportunity to correct our current course over the last 30 years, they conclude, and much must change if the world is to avoid the serious consequences of overshoot in the 21st century.

The 2009 article in *Scientific American*, "Revisiting the Limits of Growth After Peak Oil," [34] and other recent publications have confirmed that the computer model is on track, and that if we do not alter our course dramatically, the global system could collapse somewhere in the middle of this century.

Whatever the accuracy of the specific predictions of the report, the general trend is clear: we are using up resources faster than they are being regenerated, and we are soon going to face a situation where Mother Nature will impose severe restraints on our ability to grow our economy. If we learn to accept the reality and adjust, we may be able to make a smooth transition to a more sustainable world. If we do not, but instead keep exploiting and accumulating until we run out of resources, we are facing a very grim future. At present the world is largely controlled by corporations influencing government policies and designing a global agenda of maximum economic growth. Unfortunately, these corporate leaders' vision is neither long term nor sustainable but is focused on how to increase their quarterly profit margins. Much to the detriment of humanity's future, important issues, such as the survival of humankind and what kind of world we will leave to our children, are far from these corporate leaders' minds.

Chapter Four

The Environmental Crisis: No Nature, No Economy

In Nature, all debts are paid and no one is 'too big to fail.'

—H. T. Odum

O F ALL THE CRISES facing the world today, the one with the potential for having the most profound impact on human life is the environmental crisis. The global financial crisis that began in 2008 was a human, not a natural, catastrophe. By employing the most appropriate human interventions, we can certainly resolve such a crisis. The same goes for the inequality crisis. Through economic reform and restructuring, as well as technological innovation, production and wealth can increase and be redistributed, and poor, destitute areas can become affluent within a short time. History witnessed how rapidly the European and Japanese economies rebounded after WWII. So yes, an economy in crisis can, if proper means are applied, be restored rather quickly, but it is not so easy when faced with an environmental crisis. Especially not if we run out of certain irreplaceable natural resources.

We are currently experiencing a very grave resource crisis, an ecological "credit crunch" caused by our overuse of the world's natural elements. This is a far more serious problem for the future of humanity than the current financial crisis. Yet most people in industrialized countries are oblivious to the fact we are living beyond our means. Most are unaware, for example, that Britain, Norway, the Netherlands,

Austria, and twenty-three other countries are importing more than half the water they consume—in the form of goods such as cotton, rice, wheat, and so on.

"We are using 50% more resources than the Earth can provide, and unless we change course that number will grow very fast— by 2030, even two planets will not be enough," writes Jim Leape, Director General of WWF International in his organization's 2012 *Living Planet Report*.[1] The report concludes that if the average citizen on planet Earth lived like a citizen of the USA, four planets would be required to produce enough resources. Since the average citizen of China, with nearly one-sixth of the earth's population, will shortly consume as much as an American citizen, according to Chinese planners, we may soon run out of many resources, especially fresh water, which is already scarce in many parts of the world. That is, unless we make dramatic changes in the way we produce, use, and reuse goods that nature "freely" provides.

Shortages of oil and other energy resources will have an enormous impact on our lives. However, the nonrenewable resources we may run out of in the near future, such as hydrocarbons from crude oil and the rare minerals used in the high-tech industry, are resources nature itself is not very dependent on. Certainly, a lack of these resources may significantly alter civilization as we know it and reduce the number of people the world can support, but the very functioning of the earth as a living, breathing ecosystem will not be affected. With time, we will invent new and more effective renewable sources of energy and find other ways to develop sophisticated technology to support our energy needs.

Furthermore, there are aspects of the environmental crisis far more worrying than our dependency on nonrenewable sources of energy, such as oil and coal. If our dependency on nature's services from air, water, soil, and forests are threatened on a global scale, or if global warming reaches catastrophic levels, there will be no technological, economic, or political solution to counter these effects. We cannot simply reinvent what nature has provided for us for hundreds of thousands of years. Together with the plants and the animals, we are ecological creatures, and in order to understand the magnitude of this looming crisis, we need to have a better understanding of our partnership with nature. Most importantly, we need to understand the relationship between the economy and the ecology of the biosphere.

Destroying the Hand that Feeds Us

Human beings, like all other creatures, are completely dependent on the gifts provided to us by nature. A report issued in 1997 by a team of biologists and economists put the "business services" provided by the global ecosystem through free pollination of crops, the recycling of nutrients by the oceans, etc. to $33 trillion, twice the global GDP at that time. [2] It is not clear exactly what the commonly used definition of "business services" is, but regardless of what services were included in the report, it certainly did not include the total value of services provided to us by nature, which also includes how its beauty positively affects our health and wellbeing. What is the value of a family picnic in the grass under the trees? What is the value of fresh water in a creek to the fish and frogs, and to the human beings who relax by its banks? What is the real value nature provides us when we grow a vegetable crop in the backyard?

The many ways nature contributes to our life and wellbeing is, to say the least, priceless. We do not have any other means to bind solar energy with carbon dioxide and water to produce organic compounds. We are totally dependent on nature to accomplish this vitally important undertaking. Since we cannot replicate the enormous economic and aesthetic contributions made by nature, it is invaluable to us. It is not possible to put an accurate price tag on either its partial or total value.

The great power source that fuels the works of nature is the sun. Without this source of energy, the Earth would be incapable of sustaining life. The scale of our own attempts to harvest solar energy through solar cells and passive solar houses is miniscule compared to the amount of solar energy harnessed by nature through photosynthesis, water cycles, etc. Indeed, it is almost negligible in comparison. This said, if we can learn to more efficiently harness the energy provided by the sun, including the use of wind, wave, and geothermal energy, we can continue to sustain life long into the foreseeable future on this green planet of ours. Hence the value of the sun's energy and its many complex functions in nature is beyond comparison, beyond any finite value in pounds or in dollars.

At the end of the day, all we human beings can do is to find various ways to utilize the services nature already provide us. This observation is quite different from the labor theory of value emphasized by both Karl Marx and Adam Smith, which stipulates that all economic value derives from human labor. Far from it—it is nature that provides the underlying and lasting value for the wealth utilized by human society.

All the technological inventions, capital investments, production hours, and infrastructure involved in creating a product is but a small part of the total capital we are using. The total capital provided by nature in the form of land, raw materials, water, sun, air, and space is by far the largest of all forms of capital, but unfortunately in the current market economy natural capital is seen as free, or largely undervalued, and is thus used up at an alarming rate.

To remedy this predicament, scientists have made various attempts to put a price tag on nature's services. In 2011, The Department for Environment, Food and Rural Affairs in the UK announced the findings of a national ecosystem assessment, a project involving five hundred experts who had established "the true value of nature ... for the very first time." The report further stated that this exercise was "theoretically challenging to complete, and considered by some not to be a theoretically sound endeavor." Some of the services provided by the UK's ecosystems, it pointed out, "may in fact be infinite in value." [3]

Even the work attributed to human beings and accounted for in the world's GDP is indirectly made possible by nature. Human beings cannot exist without nature, but nature can easily exist without human beings. Given the enormous contribution nature provides, the current degradation of the natural systems that provide us with free services is a serious threat to our very survival. If nature is destroyed on a large scale, or reduces its provisions of beneficial natural services, it will have drastic and immediate effects on our life. In the worst-case scenario, humanity's very survival may be threatened.

In 2005, the United Nations Environmental Project, (UNEP), published the *Millennium Ecosystem Assessment.*[4] The report, authored by 1,360 scientists from ninety-five countries, concluded that two-thirds of the natural machinery providing free services to humanity has been damaged by human activities. The report states that "human activity is putting such a strain on the natural functions of Earth that the ability of the planet's ecosystems to sustain future generations can no longer be taken for granted."

Economists, however, have taken nature for granted virtually since the beginning of the profession. Economists do not generally calculate the value of the free services provided by nature. Regardless of how large the contribution is, nature's capital will not show up as a minus in the accounting books. For the sake of illustration, let us say that the real value created by nature in the form of a forest is one hundred, and the value contributed by the cutting of the forest and using the trees is ten. If we included the value created by the forest, cutting the forest would be a losing proposition. We would lose one hundred to gain ten, a net loss of ninety. If we ignore the contribution by the forest provided by nature, however, then we would gain ten by cutting it down and lose nothing. In other words, due to our flawed accounting methods, we have drawn the erroneous conclusion that it will add more value to cut down the forest. Indeed, we have concluded that nature's main value is its monetary value.

Naturally, the one hundred contributed by nature will not accrue to an individual company, whereas the ten gained from cutting down the forest will. Hence, from the view of the company, cutting down the forest is better, even if the world loses. This is exactly the way the market economy has conducted its business so far—by completely disregarding the value of nature.

Only when we learn to calculate the real value of nature's contributions, and start to take this value into account in our planning, can we hope to save our habitat from destruction. Insights such as these are already gaining traction among some business leaders and economists. At the World Forum on Natural Capital business and sustainability leaders come together to do just that—to discuss "how the value of natural assets like clean air, clean water, forests and other natural assets is factored into business decision-making and countries' systems of national accounting." [5] Moreover, ecological economists such as Herman Daly and Paul Hawken see economics as a subsystem of the ecosystem, and they emphasize the need to preserve natural capital.

Environmental columnist for the *Guardian*, George Monbiot, writes, "Rarely will the money to be made by protecting nature match the money to be made by destroying it. Nature offers low rates of return by comparison to other investments."[6] His point? We should protect nature regardless of whether or not it makes financial sense in the short run. Because in order to survive and thrive, we not only depend on nature as a source of energy and food, we also need nature for recreation and inspiration. And these latter provisions, as anyone who has enjoyed a hike in the wilderness, or gone for a swim in a pristine lake knows, are priceless.

The Six Most Serious Environmental Threats Facing Our Planet

The most serious threat facing our planet today is not global warming, water shortages, or pollution—these are simply the symptoms of an unsustainable economic system and culture. The main threat, and thus the main cause, is the materialistic lifestyle that the people of the "modernized" countries have become accustomed to in the last decades and continue to take for granted. Our overconsumption of material goods, and the following depletion and destruction of natural resources, has a direct cause-and-effect relationship to the state of the world we live in.

Seen from the perspective of those living in the poor part of the world, the lifestyle of the privileged nations, and the economic and political decisions it promotes, can be experienced as a direct threat to survival. In the words of Indian environmental activist, Vandana Shiva:

> Greed and appropriation of other people's share of the planet's precious resources are at the root of conflicts, and the root of terrorism. A way of life for the 20 percent of the earth's people who use 80 percent of the planet's resources will dispossess 80 percent of its people of their just share of resources and eventually destroy the planet. We cannot survive as a species if greed is privileged and protected and the economics of the greedy set the rules for how we live and die.[7]

The environmental problems facing our planet have the potential to drive us further apart, even destroy us, but they also have the potential to bring us closer together. In fact, if we do not come together as one planetary nation to solve these imminent problems, we may no longer have a planet to call our home much longer. Here are some of the most pressing environmental problems we need to solve in the immediate future:

1) Habitat Destruction
The destruction of Earth's natural habitats has at times been severe and at other times catastrophic. As mentioned above, two-thirds of the world's ecosystem is being harmed by human activity, and the destruction is being carried out at an ever-increasing rate. According to the *Guardian*, "The wetlands, forests, savannahs, estuaries, coastal fisheries and other habitats that recycle air, water and nutrients for all living creatures are being irretrievably damaged. In effect, one species is now a hazard to the other 10 million or so on the planet, and to itself."[8]

That hazardous species is us. In addition to destroying the natural cycles that sustain life, we also actively introduce pollutants into water, air, and earth, killing microorganisms and poisoning the planet. In nature, waste functions as food for other organisms, which means that there is no waste without having an ecological function. Everything is recycled. However, with modern inventions, human beings have introduced artificial and toxic particles that nature is unable to utilize or break down. Radioactive waste, industrial waste products, and many chemicals used every day belong to this group.

In his book *The Future*, Al Gore explains that "the rapid growth of human civilization—in the number of people, the power of technology, and the size of the global economy—is colliding with approaching limits to the supply of key natural resources on which billions of lives depend, including topsoil and freshwater." Topsoil and freshwater are singled out here because of their importance in meeting our most basic needs. However, as Gore also points out, limits on virtually all of the natural resources that we use are becoming apparent.

According to Greenpeace, a recent major study indicates that if global temperatures increase 1.8-2° Celsius (3.2-3.6°F), a million species would be threatened with extinction over the next fifty years. Rapid CO_2-emissions reductions on a global scale can remedy this situation, but currently there is not enough political will to enact the changes needed to stop this massive species holocaust. If temperatures rise even higher, even more species will be lost.

2) Climate Crisis

Of all the negative effects caused by the collision of industry with the Earth, "the single most important and threatening of this collision is the climate crisis."[9] An overwhelming majority of scientists believe that the climate crisis is being caused by the build-up of CO_2 and other greenhouse gases in the earth's atmosphere, the main contributor to which is the burning of fossil fuels, such as oil and coal.

However, the increase in the earth's temperature is but the tip of the iceberg when it comes to climate change, for this phenomenon causes a series of knock-on effects that are potentially devastating. These include disruptions from numerous weather and weather-related phenomena. Southern Scandinavia, where the authors are from, has experienced less snow cover and more rain and floods and even droughts in the past twenty to thirty years as a direct effect of climate change. In many other parts of the world, weather-related destruction due to rising sea levels, storms, droughts, and typhoons is beginning to impact people, plants and animals, and these natural disasters are only expected to intensify.

Barely three months before the super-cyclone Haiyan ravaged parts of the Philippines in the fall of 2013, and gained notoriety as the strongest storm to hit land ever recorded, an article in the Geophysical Research Letter reported that the temperature in the Pacific Ocean has increased steadily since 1990. This area needs to be watched carefully, the report concluded, as devastating cyclones are likely to be formed here.[10]

And the list goes on. Other serious threats due to climate change include rising sea levels, which are already impacting many island nations due to melting polar ice; acidification of the oceans due to increased carbon-dioxide absorption; oxygen depletion in the oceans that could have devastating effects on ocean life; and increased droughts in some areas and increased flooding in others that could severely affect the global food supply. As temperatures increase, the greater will be the threat to the environment and to the future of humanity.

3) Loss of Biodiversity

One of the most serious aspects of the environmental crisis is the loss of biodiversity. Losing a species is a loss of life and ecological balance, as well as a loss of food, medicine, and scientific information that can potentially be useful in the future.

If current trends continue, the polar bear—a symbol not only of global habitat loss but of climate change and global pollution trends— will likely be gone by the end of the century. Global warming and the resulting melting ice sheets threatens the feeding habits of polar bears, and dioxin pollution, caused by plastic waste in the oceans, threaten its mating habits.

If a country loses its food harvests due to natural disasters, it may cause famine and death. But as long as the knowledge of how to grow food is maintained, food harvests will eventually be restored. However, if the know-how is lost, it can take generations before that knowledge is rediscovered. Similarly, in the natural world, information is stored in an animal or a plant's genetic code. This information has taken millions of years to develop, and once it is irretrievably lost by the loss of a species, we cannot recreate it. Therefore, it is in our ethical, ecological, and economic interest to preserve cultural and biological diversity.

All life has existential value. The life of a bird or a goat is as important to them as our own lives are to us. We therefore have an ethical and ecological responsibility to preserve as many natural life forms as possible for the sake of their right to exist. This fundamental right is grossly overlooked in today's economy, where utility value vastly trumps existential value. One way to support the existential value of other living beings is to eat as low on the food chain as possible. As popular American food writer Michael Pollan suggests, we should eat 1) whole foods, 2) mostly plants, and 3) not too much. From an ethical, health, and ecological point of view, this is sound advice—plants are good for health. Eating plants causes less animal suffering, and growing plant food has less of an environmental impact, since it uses less water, less energy, etc.

Another more fundamental and political way to guarantee the existential value of nature is to follow Ecuador's example, which has included in its Constitution the chapter "Rights for Nature." Rather than treating nature as property under the law, Rights for Nature articles acknowledge that nature in all its life forms has the right "to exist, persist, maintain and regenerate its vital cycles." The Ecuadorian people have legal authority to enforce these rights on behalf of ecosystems, and the ecosystem can be named as defendant in court cases. [11]

In addition, all life forms have utility value. The extinction of a species is thus a great injustice against nature and against humanity. The utility value of bees, for example, as pollinators of crops, is unquestionable. It is estimated they add 420 billion pounds to the UK economy alone. But bees all over the Western world are currently threatened by pesticides, neonicotinoids, various pests, and also by a lack of biodiversity—fewer varieties of flowers to feed on make them more susceptible to disease. Therefore, in view of both the existential and utility value of bees, it is in the interest of human society to preserve their lives by banning neonicotinoids, as well as by preserving and even increasing the biodiversity the bees depend on to stay healthy and multiply.

Even exotic plants and animals seemingly of no real value and existing in such small populations that they cannot possibly contribute anything substantial to the global system, or to human progress, are in fact repositories of information that might be crucial should the environment change. Containing unique gene pools, these exotic species might suddenly become essential for life under different ecological conditions. We may not fully understand a certain genome's utility value at present, or what utilitarian potentials exist in certain species, but every time a species is lost, it potentially impacts our future and the ecological balance of life on the planet. Consequently, it is in the interest of all nations to follow Ecuador's example to include "the rights of nature" in their respective constitutions.

4) Waste

In the award-winning film *Trashed*, actor Jeremy Irons documents how we are slowly but surely trashing our planet with non-biodegradable plastic garbage, thereby jeopardizing the health of plants, animals, and humans. Irons, a smoker, knows full well that waste from cigarette butts contains millions of toxins that are especially deadly to marine life. According to the film's website, 4.5 trillion filters from smoked cigarettes make their way into the environment every year. Still, like most us, he continues to practice his environmentally unfriendly habits.

We are trashing the planet in small and big ways. According to the film, when you buy a plastic toothbrush and throw it away, it may end up in the stomach of a large fish a few years later. Yes, even the oceans have now become our planet's garbage dumps. Researchers from the University of California, San Diego produced a study that revealed that more than 9 percent of the fish in a certain area of the Pacific Ocean contained plastic waste in their stomachs. The study estimated that up to 24,000 tons of plastic waste per year was ingested by fish in that area alone.[12]

To save our planet from drowning in garbage, industrial innovators are learning from nature how to produce and reuse material waste. In nature, biological waste or nutrients decompose into the natural environment, into the soil and water, without causing any pollution, providing food for bacteria and microbiological life. Later these organisms become food for plants, animals, and humans. Similarly, we can design industrial, commercial, and waste systems according to these natural design mechanisms. Technical nutrients, the inorganic or synthetic materials manufactured by humans—such as plastics and metals—can thus be used many times over without any loss in quality, staying in a continuous cycle.

To save the planet from drowning in waste, we must bypass the garbage dump, whether on land or in the ocean. There are basically two ways to prevent trashing the planet: 1) make things that biodegrade just like in nature—you use it, you throw it in the compost; and 2) reuse all non-biodegradable materials as part of the industrial production cycle—your electronic gadget becomes outdated, you turn it in to the upcycling plant to make parts for new gadgets. In either scenario, nothing is wasted and no trash is created. This is our best hope for saving us from suffocating in our own waste.

5) Water

Fresh water is in short supply. Global reserves of drinkable water are only a fraction of 1 percent. One in five humans does not have access to safe drinking water, due in part to polluted rivers. Strife has already broken out in some stressed regions. In others, there is conflict due to privatization of drinking water.

Indian scientist and activist Vanadana Shiva highlights the complexities involved in the global water crisis. "The water crisis," she writes, "is an ecological crisis with commercial causes but no market solutions. Market solutions destroy the earth and aggravate inequality. The solution to an ecological crisis is ecological, and the solution for injustice is democracy. Ending the water crisis requires rejuvenating ecological democracy." [13]

Scarcity and the growing demand for water means big business for global corporations. The two largest in the water industry are the French companies Vivendi Environment and Suez Lyonnaise des Eaux, whose business operations extend to 120 countries. One of the main solutions to the water crisis is to ban the corporate privatization of water and to make it a key industry guaranteed to people by their local governments. Water is part of the global commons—it belongs to us all. In addition, more efforts need to go into water preservation, such as building rainwater catchment systems on houses and cleaning up polluted rivers and lakes.

6) Food

The way we grow and distribute food is, perhaps more than any other human endeavor, a symbol of our unsustainable planet. Food researcher and author Frances Moore Lappe has maintained for many years that we do not lack food on this planet: we have a distribution problem and a concentration-of-junk-food problem. Millions of people in the southern hemisphere are hungry and malnourished due to lack of food, and millions of people in the northern hemisphere are getting sick and obese from eating too much of the wrong kinds of foods.

We are turning food crops into biofuels to fill up our SUVs; we are giving corporations like Monsanto near absolute control of the global seed market; we import food we could grow at home from thousands of miles away; soy beans are imported from poor countries that lack protein to fatten pigs and cattle in rich countries with too much protein; and pesticides and artificial fertilizers are poisoning fields, crops, water, animals, and humans at an unprecedented rate.

The "green revolution" initiated in the 1970s by researchers, philanthropists, and governments sought to end world hunger by increasing food-crop yields worldwide. Their productivity logic went something like this: modernize agricultural techniques, make high-yield crops pervasive, and food prices will drop and poor people will be fed. This largely failed paradigm still dominates worldwide, yet a billion people go hungry despite increases in food production.

The production, distribution, and consumption of food today betray symptoms of an unsustainable economy with a lack of ecological outlook. Food production needs to become more localized; food consumption, especially in rich countries, needs to be much more plant-based—since this increases efficiency, health, and sustainability; corporations should be banned from monopolizing seed production; and organic methods of farming need to be increased and supported with research and subsidies.

Conclusion

We are in the process of gradually destroying our planet's delicately balanced ecological systems. We are compromising an extremely effective and sophisticated web that converts solar energy into life-giving energy and an atmosphere that supports an abundance of life. If we upset this delicate balance much more, the consequences are potentially catastrophic. What we do know is this: it is time to change course; it is time to become better stewards of the only planet we have—the only home we know. It is time to start creating a more sustainable, ecological, and resilient economy.

Part II:
Capitalism: An Historical Perspective

I N PART ONE WE discussed the present crisis, but not how we got there. In order to understand the state of this deeply interconnected global problem, we need to rewind. Nothing comes from nothing. Every situation we encounter can generally be explained by analyzing the events leading up to it. The present crisis is no exception. In the next chapter we will look at the history of economic thought. Economic theories have, to a large extent, guided the policies shaping the world we live in and have thus led up to the current finance, inequality, environment, and resource crises. We will assess the foundation of these theories and how effective they have been in creating a just and sustainable world.

Since much of the history of modern economics started in Europe, we will take a closer look at its history, starting with the Mercantile Era and leading up to the formation of the European Union. We will learn that the EU was formalized as an international experiment in free-market economy based on neoclassical economic ideas. Our conclusion is that this experiment has economically benefited some countries enormously while directly causing both the destruction and slow development of others.

Finally, we broaden our scope and look outside Europe to analyze the factors causing some countries to become rich and others to remain poor. This historical process, which has led to an unequal economic playing field—generally involved various forms of economic exploitation. Rich countries drained resources from poor countries to benefit their own industrialization and growth while simultaneously preventing those poor countries from industrializing. Through various free-trade agreements, this economic double standard is alive and well even today. Hence, we seriously question the viability of these agreements and the economic system that promotes them.

Chapter Five

From Mercantilism to Green Capitalism: Economic History with a Twist

Environmentalism does not bring into question the underlying notion of the present society that man must dominate nature; rather, it seeks to facilitate that domination by developing techniques for diminishing the hazards caused by domination. In contrast, ecology or social ecology refers to an approach that rests on 'the ecological principles of unity in diversity, spontaneity and the non-hierarchical nature of ecological communities.' This approach attempts to overcome the splits between society and nature, mind and body, thought and reality that mark Western images of the world.

—Murray Bookchin

The Era of Mercantilism

MERCANTILISM, WHICH LASTED FROM the late fifteenth to the late eighteenth centuries, followed the feudal era when mighty armies of kings and queens ruled over farmers, clerics, artisans, and peasants. During this time, trade and military action became closely linked. After centuries of internal conflict, Europe had become adept in warfare and was often able to dominate far-larger enemies through superior technology, better strategy, and sheer ruthlessness. In some places, such as the Americas, Europe won great victories by biological warfare. The native population did not have any resistance to the infections brought by the Europeans; hence relatively simple diseases like the common cold often killed thousands of native peoples within a short time.

Mercantilism can be described as a system where the state gets directly involved in controlling the foreign trade of a country as a means to secure its military and security interests. Since gold reserves were necessary to conduct war, it was considered of special importance to maintain a positive trade balance, so that gold accumulated in the country's coffers.

The term "mercantilism" was first introduced by critics of the system such as Adam Smith, and the term was not in use during the time the system was practiced. During its time, mercantilism was also not seen as a coherent economic theory. Writers about the system varied in sophistication from one another and the thoughts that came to be known as mercantilism evolved over a long period of time. With few exceptions, there was no mercantilist writer who covered the whole working of the economy; instead, authors usually wrote about selected aspects of it. The practices that are now considered mercantilist were hence not a result of the ideas of any one theoretical writer, but grew out of centuries of experiments and practical realities.

High tariffs, especially on manufactured goods, soon became a common, if not universal, feature of mercantilist economic policy. This protectionist policy prevented colonies in Asia and later in Africa and South America from developing their own industries and becoming exporters of finished goods. Other policies included creating networks of overseas colonies while forbidding the same colonies to trade with other nations. Mercantile nations also monopolized international trade by building ports where they stored various staples, banning gold exportation, forbidding trade that involved using foreign ships, promoting certain manufacturing practices with government subsidies, limiting wages in foreign countries, maximizing the use of domestic resources, and refining raw materials from the colonies in domestic factories.

Another feature of the mercantilist era was that gold was money. Gold, and to a certain extent silver, made international trade possible. When trade was uneven, gold payments were used to balance the accounts.

In the latter part of the mercantilist era there was a shift from accumulating gold to building up an industrial base. While gold in itself did not produce anything, a strong industry would create wealth for the country. Likewise, the emphasis gradually shifted from the capacity to conduct wars to creating general prosperity.

Mercantilist writers emphasized the circulation of money and in theory rejected the hoarding of wealth. In reality, however, the nations practicing mercantilism hoarded massive amounts of wealth and this rapidly increased the gap between the rich and poor countries. Today, neo-mercantilist theoreticians recommend using selective high tariffs for new industries or to promote the mutual growth of countries through national industrial specialization, which would, they argue, bring poor countries out of poverty through industrialization. Currently, advocacy of mercantilist or protectionist methods for maintaining high wages in advanced economies is also popular among workers in those economies.

The author who best summed up the theories of mercantilism was probably the Austrian scholar Philipp Wilhelm von Hornick in his 1684 work, *Austria over All, If She Only Will*.[1] In the document he presented a nine-point program for growing the national economy:

- That every little bit of a country's soil be utilized for agriculture, mining, or manufacturing.
- That all raw materials found in a country be used in domestic manufacture, since finished goods have a higher value than raw materials.
- That a large working population be encouraged.
- That all export of gold and silver be prohibited and all domestic money be kept in circulation.
- That all imports of foreign goods be discouraged as much as possible.
- That where certain imports are indispensable, they should be obtained in exchange for other domestic goods instead of gold and silver.
- That as much as possible, imports be confined to raw materials that can be finished [in the home country].
- That opportunities be constantly sought for selling a country's surplus manufactures to foreigners for gold and silver.
- That no importation be allowed if such goods are sufficiently and suitably supplied at home.

During the mercantile era, policies such as these were used to strengthen and concentrate wealth in the European economies. In the European colonies, however, these mercantile policies of industrialization, efficiency, growth, and protectionism were not allowed.

Walpole and the Rise of British Industrialization

Robert Walpole was the main architect behind the British mercantile system. While Britain was taking on the world as a colonial power, it was Robert Walpole, Britain's first prime minister, a position he held for twenty-one years (1721-1742), who effectively built up Britain as a strong industrial nation.

Walpole was a deft politician and financial manager. His political skills were fictionalized in Jonathan Swift's novel *Gulliver's Travels* in the form of the character Flimnap, the prime minister of the Lilliput empire. As the real-life prime minister of Britain, Walpole launched a policy that dramatically changed Britain's economy.

The British government prior to Walpole had, in true mercantile style, captured raw materials from the colonies through a policy requiring that all trade with Britain be conducted in British ships. While mercantile imperialism and the plundering of colonies of raw materials had been a great source of government revenue for a long time, Walpole introduced a new policy: the promotion of domestic manufacturing industries. As Walpole stated in an address to Parliament: "It is evident that nothing so much contributes to promote the public wellbeing as the exportation of manufactured goods and the importation of foreign raw materials."
[2] This policy, more than any other, contributed to the growth of industrialization and the wealth of Britain for many years.

English mercantile businesses would import silk from India, for example, and spin the silk in English factories. In 1718, Thomas Lombe obtained a patent for a silk-weaving engine. With his brother John Lombe he built a silk mill in Derby. Soon angry silk industry merchants from Italy claimed the Lombe brothers had stolen their invention and sent a woman to kill the two brothers. John Lombe died in 1772 and many argued that he had been poisoned. By the 1730s the brothers had employed over three hundred workers in a large factory in Derby. This inspired others to imitate their success, and silk factories were established in Manchester, London, Norwich, Macclesfield, Chesterfield, and Stockport.

However, British manufacturing was not efficient enough to compete on the world market. Indian cloth was cheaper and better quality than the cloth produced in England. Even the introduction of machines to mechanize the industry, such as the Hargreaves's spinning frame (1764), Arkwright's spinning frame (1769), and Crompton's mule (1779), did not make British textiles competitive on the world stage. If it had not been for extreme protectionist measures, the industrial revolution would have been stopped in its tracks. To protect the infant industry, duties on textiles were gradually raised, until by 1813 they reached 85%. [3] If Britain had not protected its markets, it would never have become industrialized.

Such industrial expansion was made possible by a combination of British technical ingenuity, mercantile policies, and colonialism. While Britain tried to maintain its position as an exporter of manufactured goods and importer of raw materials, it was not able to impose its will on everyone. Most European countries followed in Britain's footsteps and built up their own industries by fiercely protecting them. They followed their own mercantilist agendas. In addition, these countries also used other economic measures, such as government subsidies for research and development, the nationalization of banks and key-industries, and government-funded railroad projects.

In its colonies, Britain had much greater success. With the exception of America, most colonies were kept as exporters of raw materials and markets for manufactured goods produced in Britain. All industries were effectively banned in the colonies.

America, on the other hand, broke loose from British rule and with great determination started to build up its industries behind a wall of protectionism. It was the young, ambitious Alexander Hamilton who became the intellectual leader of the movement arguing for the development of industries and the use of government subsidies to achieve that end. President Abraham Lincoln also supported these policies, and under his presidency he charted a course that eventually would make the United States one of the nineteenth century's most protectionist countries and fastest-growing economies.

Adam Smith, Ricardo, and the Rise of Free Trade

In 1776, one of the most influential books ever written on economic matters was published—Adam Smith's *An Inquiry into the Nature and Causes of the Wealth of Nations*. Adam Smith broke with the mercantilist tradition, forcefully arguing that free trade was always beneficial to all parties involved. He opposed protectionism in all forms and believed that it favored special-interest groups and not the nation as a whole. For that reason he believed that the American colonies would be better off importing industrialized goods from England, rather than protecting and developing their own industries. He felt that tariffs and other protectionist measures were justified in only two situations: when it was in the national security interest of the country and to balance protectionist measures taken by other nations.[4]

Smith's theories were ahead of their time, and it would take another eighty-four years before Britain engaged in large-scale free trade on the global stage. By that time Smith's ideas of free trade had been adapted and refined by British political economist David Ricardo (1772 —1823), whose influence on classical economics was at least equal to that of Adam Smith. A member of Parliament and a businessman, he amassed a considerable personal fortune. His most significant contribution to economics was the theory of comparative advantage, presented in his 1817 book, *Principles of Political Economy and Taxation*. Before Ricardo, people thought that foreign trade only made sense if one country could produce something cheaper than another country. Ricardo stood this common-sense argument on its head and proved with brilliant logic that two countries could trade even if one country could produce everything cheaper than its trading partner. Both countries would benefit, Ricardo argued, if each one concentrated on what it did best, even if this "best" was not as good as its trading partner. This theory, with its undeniable logic, provided a strong argument for those in favor of free trade.

Regardless of the beauty of the logic used in arguing for free trade, it is unlikely that protectionism would have ended in Britain based on these arguments. After all, protectionism was what had built up British industry into its leading position and nobody would willingly have given it up, no matter how rational the arguments. What really changed were the economic realities that suddenly made free trade advantageous for Britain. Free trade, to paraphrase Victor Hugo, was an idea whose time had come.

During years of protectionism, the British industry had grown so strong and efficient that it now could produce goods cheaper and more efficiently than its competitors. When Britain's industry was less efficient than its competitors, it needed protectionism, but after becoming more efficient than its competitors, it did not. Until it reached this dominant stage, the country followed a double standard that has become common economic policy among Western nations: practice and campaign for free trade when it suits your interests and practice mercantilism when protectionism is better suited for national or corporate bank accounts.

In Britain this dual policy was implemented when cotton manufac-turers agitated for a ban on exports of spinning machines that might help foreign competitors. In contrast, the abolition of the Corn Laws enabled the importation of cheap grains—that is, raw materials from poorer countries. Cheaper grain was beneficial to manufacturers, since it would enable their workers to buy cheaper foods and this would keep wages low and increase profits. This double standard is still in vogue today, as evidenced by the enormous subsidies that are poured into agriculture in both the United States and Europe, the one area where developing countries might have a competitive advantage against the industrialized nations.

Ricardo's Error

According to Ricardo's theory of comparative advantage, everyone benefits from free trade. If history has proven this to be wrong, then where is the flaw in Ricardo's theory?

In his book *Bad Samaritans*, Harvard economist Ha-Joon Chang dedicates a whole chapter to this issue.[5] The chapter, which is called "My Six-Year Old Son Should Get a Job," compares a developing country to a young child and says that even though in the short term it would be better for such a country to specialize in what it has a relative advantage in, such as growing rice, in the long run it would prevent it from acquiring the skills needed to do more advanced things. He considers it the same as sending a six-year-old child out to work instead of to school. In the short run the child might be able to make more money shining shoes, but if he spends his time shining shoes, he will never get the chance to learn the advanced skills that would enable him to get a better job, such as an engineer or a doctor.

"Ricardo's theory," Ha-Joon Chang writes, "is absolutely right—within its narrow confines. His theory correctly says that, accepting their cur-rent levels of technology as given, it is better for countries to specialize in things that they are relatively better at."[6] But—and this is the crucial part—levels of technology can be developed and are not fixed. The best way to develop technology is to protect it while it is not yet competitive, just as you would subsidize a small child until he or she has become an educated adult ready for employment. "Such protection is costly," writes Chang, "because the country is giving up the chance to import better and cheaper products. However, it is a price that has to be paid if it wants to develop advanced industries."[7] Ha-Joon Chang concludes by writing, "Ricardo's theory is, thus seen, for those who accept the status quo, but not for those who want to change it."[8]

Economist Erik S. Reinert is even less kind to classical economist David Ricardo than Ha-Joon Chang. He believes that Ricardo's theory of comparative advantage simply made colonialism morally acceptable. Ricardo's theory was advantageous for rich countries, in other words, but disadvantageous for the poor, since it forced some countries to only produce raw materials and thus to be exploited and remain poor. It was for this reason the eighteenth-century German economist Johann Heinrich Gottlob von Justi argued, that colonies would rebel—in order to create their own industries. But that rarely happened. Unlike the USA, which rebelled and liberated itself from Britain in 1776, most poor countries, even if they are politically independent, have yet to free themselves from the oppression of economic colonialism.

The Invisible Hand

While Adam Smith is known for his views on free trade, his most famous and most quoted idea is that of the invisible hand. The idea behind the invisible hand is that if every individual works for his or her own benefit, without any intention to support the larger community in which he or she lives, the result will be no different than if the person would have consciously worked for the benefit of others.

It is not from the benevolence of the butcher, the brewer, or the baker that we expect our dinner, but from their regard for their own interest. We address ourselves not to their humanity but to their self-love, and never talk to them of our own necessities but of their advantages.[9]

This simple and fairly obvious idea was developed by later authors as a wholesale support for greed and selfishness. It is questionable if Smith would have agreed with this. Smith was foremost a moral philosopher. In his first major work, *The Theory of Moral Sentiments*,[10] he tried to prove that human beings are fundamentally good and generally act according to the dictates of conscience, what Smith calls "the man in the breast," even if it goes against the person's own interest.

Furthermore, Smith often took the side of the consumer over the producer, the worker over the factory owner. He was very suspicious of traders and manufacturers and claimed that their interests were directly opposite to those of society as a whole. These sides of Adam Smith are rarely brought forward, but they are clear to anyone who reads the original works. As for the famed invisible hand itself, Smith says surprisingly little about it. In fact, it is mentioned only once in *Wealth of Nations*, and once in *Theory of Moral Sentiments*.

Reading *Theory of Moral Sentiment*, one can only marvel at the idealistic simplicity of his ideas:

> The rich only select from the heap what is most precious and agreeable. They consume little more than the poor, and in spite of their natural selfishness and rapacity, though they mean only their own conveniency, though the sole end which they propose from the labours of all the thousands whom they employ, be the gratification of their own vain and insatiable desires, they divide with the poor the produce of all their improvements. They are led by an invisible hand to make nearly the same distribution of the necessities of life, which would have been made, had the earth been divided into equal portions among all its inhabitants, and thus without including it, without knowing it, advance the interest of the society, and afford means to the multiplication of the species. [11]

In *Wealth of Nations*, Smith has this to say about the invisible hand:

> By preferring the support of domestic to that of foreign industry, he intends only his own security; and by directing that industry in such a manner as its produce may be of the greatest value, he intends only his own gain, and he is in this, as in many other cases, led by an invisible hand to promote an end which was no part of his intention. [12]

In 1,700 pages of writing, Smith mentions the invisible hand only twice. He never develops the idea into a consistent theory. He left us only these brief observations. Compared to the little Smith actually wrote about the invisible hand, its importance in modern economic theory has been truly staggering. It is mentioned in almost every textbook of economics, and in all references to Adam Smith and his ideas. Adam Smith's comments have been proffered as proof that the market, through the invisible hand of some equally invisible power, will automatically bring harmony and equality to society. The influence of this idea in modern economic theory has been enormous and the consequences for real-life economics quite unsettling.

One of the problems, according to Reinert, is that the free-market idealists do not see any difference between the "real economy" and the "financial economy." Ideally, the financial economy represents the capital that drives the real economy, while the real economy consists of a chaotic complex of production, sales, and innovation of numerous goods and services. [13] Today's theories about globalization assume that all the various economic activities in the real economy result in economic harmony, more wealth that can be shared and utilized by everyone as long as the right economic conditions (free trade) and financial and government institutions are in place. But economic reality is not that simple. In order to create more economic equality, there is a need to control and to redistribute the real economy with the help of government regulations and by controlling the size and power of corporations and the wealth of the rich. Here are the simple facts: both free trade, especially between countries of unequal levels of wealth and industrialization, and economic self-interest create inequality and often economic chaos.

In the 1840s there was a technological revolution based on the steam engine and the use of coal. In the 1990s there was a technological revolution based around the popularity of computers and the Internet. Both eras inspired an almost-religious faith in the rise of the stock market, and as long as people believed it worked, it did. But when reality set in, it became clear that the cause of real wealth is not speculation but the inventions that create real productivity and trade. It was the steel industry, the steam engine, and the coal industry in England in the 1840s, and the computer-technology revolution in the USA in the 1990s, that created the wealth, not the speculation these developments inspired, in the stock market. The stock-market frenzy in England led to the crash of 1844, while the dollar frenzy on Wall Street and the artificial rise in dot-com stock-market values led to the stock-market crash in 2001. Similarly, the Asian economic crisis of 1997 occurred when too much of the investments in Asia, which resulted in the so-called Asian Economic Miracle, had been invested in capital rather than in economic productivity. This caused the Asian economies to amass enormous levels of foreign debt, which they were unable to repay, hence the collapse and the need for a forty-billion-dollar IMF bailout. When the market runs ahead of the economics of the real world, which it inevitably ends up doing, we eventually suffer the consequences: the economy comes crashing down.

In each period, the myth of the invisible hand was at the forefront of economics and the end result was the same: theoretical stock-market speculations that eventually led to stock-market crashes. That is, the economic crashes of the 1840s and the Asian crisis of the 1990s, as well as the dot-com crisis of 2001 and the financial crisis of 2008, were all caused by the commercial (or speculative) economy's disconnect from the real economy. Despite what Adam Smith and the other classical and neoclassical economists claim, when left on its own the market does not regulate the economy. Without institutional structures, governments, and laws, the economy will—due to the forces of self-interest and the myth of the invisible hand—become chaotic and self-destructive. Economic self-interest creates economic inequality, a divide between rich and poor, and the dogma of the invisible hand leads to economic chaos. That is, the two theoretical foundations that underpin capitalism have not stood the test of time. As seen throughout history, unregulated capitalism has not delivered on its promise—plenty for all. Well, it has delivered plenty, but not for everyone and often only for the few.

Karl Marx and the Birth of Socialism

Karl Marx (1818-1883) came from a well-to-do middle-class family in Germany. After his studies he wrote for radical newspapers in Cologne and subsequently moved to Paris in 1843 where he met Frederick Engels, who was to become his lifelong friend and collaborator.

His first major publication, which was coauthored by Engels, was *The Communist Manifesto*, published in 1848. It was commissioned by the Communist League and laid out the league's program. It was to become one of the world's most influential political documents.

Far from seeing capitalism as a system that would benefit all people, Marx saw it as an exploitative mechanism where the interests of the working class were diametrically opposed to those of the capitalist class, who used their capital to enrich themselves through investments in factories, etc. Furthermore, Marx saw no possibility to lessen this gap through reforms. He predicted that the only way to improve the lot of the working class was through a violent revolution. This revolution would overturn the order of the day and put the ownership of what Marx called the "means of production"—the factories, mines, farms, and other operations that generated a surplus—in the hands of the proletariat.

In order to maintain control, the proletariat—in reality, the leaders of the revolution—would, after a successful revolution, institute a dictatorship. This new political structure would remain in place until the entire state gradually disappeared, leading to a worker's utopia in which all things were collectively owned.

Apart from a few transitional policies mentioned in *The Communist Manifesto*, Marx did not say anything about how the communist society would function, or how its economy would work. He also said very little about the capitalist system itself, apart from rhetorical condemnations. In short, *The Communist Manifesto* was just that: a manifesto with strong rhetoric but devoid of analysis.

As a result of his revolutionary activities, he was expelled from France and settled in England in 1849 with his family. Here he lived a life of deep poverty, trying to make a living as a journalist.

During his exile in London, Marx sat down to work on his theoretical masterpiece, *Capital: A Critique of Political Economy*. The first volume was published in 1867, while Marx was still alive, and the second and third volumes were published after Marx's death by Engels.

Capital was everything that *The Communist Manifesto* was not. It was a highly sophisticated analysis of capitalism and totally devoid of the rhetoric that characterized *The Communist Manifesto*. Marx liberally quoted Adam Smith, Ricardo, and other classical economic sources, and thus illustrated that he had a good understanding of production and how it translates into profits—the effect of trade; the workings of money creation and credit; and the boom and bust cycles of modern economies.

In addition to the economic analysis, *Volume I* of *Capital* paints a graphic and touching portrait of the deprivation and suffering of the working class in Britain in the middle of the nineteenth century, with numerous examples of those injustices.

Although Marx in many ways broke with the norm, he also accepted many of the orthodoxies of classical economics, such as the labor theory of value, which he borrowed, although in a revised form, from Adam Smith. This prompted Nicolas Kaldor (1908-1986) to write that "the Marxian theory is really only a simplified version of Ricardo, clothed in a different garb." [14]

The influence of Marx's ideas was monumental. Even though few Marxists would read, and yet fewer actually understand, the heavy volumes of *Capital* that laid the foundation for Marx's thinking, Marxism became the driving force in labor unions and socialist political parties at the beginning of the twentieth century.

The communists followed a three-pronged strategy:

- They had a formidable economic theory that, although difficult to digest, was equally hard for classical economists to refute. Indeed, it gave a good description of the prevailing capitalist mode of production.
- They had a theory of history that claimed that the rise of communism was inevitable, and that a successful revolution and the fall of capitalism were destined by history. This gave communism almost a religious undertone of faith.
- They had a superb organizing structure that penetrated factories and working-class neighborhoods. Communist leaders stood side by side with the workers, supported them in strikes, and helped them to press demands from the factory owners.

Many of the gains of socialist and social democratic movements in Britain, Scandinavia, France, and other places in Europe were due to the influence of Marx and the movements he inspired. Marx was also the inspiration behind the Bolshevik revolution in Russia in 1917, which led to the formation of the Soviet Union and about ten years of a relatively positive development. But the revolution became isolated, and degenerated into Stalinist oppression and a bureaucratic dictatorship. More significantly, Marx's revolutionary ideas also inspired a softer revolution in Western Europe where workers fought for better pay and better working conditions through strikes and political agitation. It was indeed the Marxian impetus for revolutionary struggle against the excesses of capitalism that inspired this global movement of labor unions, leftist parties, and feminist groups. Collectively, it was this pragmatic movement, rather than the markets of the classical and neoclassical economists, or the abstract theories of communism, that would create more economic equality and more wealth for everyone. It was this movement's struggles, from the 1920s onward, that would serve as a counterweight against the market forces of capitalism and eventually create the mixed economies that Europeans today have become accustomed to.

More popularly known as the "welfare state," the economic system that emerged is a mixture of capitalism and socialism, a mixture of state-owned and privately owned enterprises. The welfare system or the mixed economy of Scandinavia has been hailed by *The Economist* as the economy of the future, the Next Supermodel. "The main lesson to learn from the Nordics," *The Economist* writes, "is not ideological but practical. The state is popular not because it is big but because it works. A Swede pays tax more willingly than a Californian because he gets decent schools and free healthcare. The Nordics have pushed far-reaching reforms past unions and business lobbies. The proof is there." [15] The Nordic countries achieved these results by assembling the best of both worlds, the best of capitalism and socialism.

While Marx analyzed capitalism and inspired social movements, he contributed little when it came to proposing a new economic order. Apart from general statements that the means of production should be collectivized, he offered almost no ideas on creating a socialist society or how its economy should run. This may come as a surprise to most people, and to quite a few Marxists as well, but in the almost-three-thousand pages of *Capital*, there are no concrete proposals for a socialist economy. If we contrast this with the enormous care Marx put into analyzing capitalism, the contrast is stark. The closest we come to Marx pointing toward a vision of a socialist society in *Capital* is this quote from *Volume 1*: "Let us finally imagine, for a change, an association of free men, working with the means of production held in common, and expending their many different forms of labor-power in full self-awareness as one single labor force." [16]

Marx goes on to explain that free men in a communist society would produce goods with a difference: the profits made would be "social instead of individual." Such ideas, however, are not enough to form the basis of a socialist economy or to use as a guideline for a socialist society. Whether Marx had ideas of how a socialist society would work or not is not known, but if he did, he never passed them on to the world. This might possibly be the root of the failures of communist regimes such as the Soviet Union. These countries had to invent the economy as they went along, since Marx did not provide any practical guidance. Marx's primary contribution to economics was his analysis of capitalism and the inspiration he provided to socialist groups. As a contributor to a new vision of how a socialist economy should work, he had a very limited role.

Considering Marx's insightful analysis of capitalism, it may seem surprising that his ideas have had so little impact in classical and neo-classical economic theory. Unable to refute Marx's analysis, it seems that classical economists decided to ignore it. Interesting as Marx's ideas are, apart from the inspiration they gave to social and labor movements, they were less influential in informing economic policy in capitalist countries. We will therefore leave Marx and his ideas and continue our survey of economic thought where we left off.

A Brief Critique of Self-Regulating Markets: List, Keynes, Schumpeter, and Polanyi

During the second half of the nineteenth century, influenced by Adam Smith and Ricardo, the arguments for self-regulating markets dominated economic discourse. The wind had changed and there was a belief that markets, if left to themselves, would efficiently utilize resources, ensure full employment at living wages, maximize the economic gains of society, and ensure that no company would reap unfair profits. In short, an economy free from government interference would regulate itself and perform much better than if the government tried to control it. However, there were still some dissenting voices, and we will discuss them in the following section.

George Friedrich List

George Friedrich List (1789-1846) was a German economist who emigrated to the United States in 1925. He was influenced by the works of Alexander Hamilton, the mastermind of United States policies to nurture its fledging industries behind a wall of tariff protection and subsidies.

In his opinion, the talk of free trade by industrialized countries who had built their industrial base behind a barrier of tariffs was hypocrisy. In his *The National System of Political Economy*, he writes:

> Any nation which by means of protective duties and restrictions on navigation has raised her manufacturing power and her navigation to such a degree of development that no other nation can sustain free competition with her, can do nothing wiser than to throw away these ladders of her greatness, to preach to other nations the benefits of free trade, and to declare in penitent tones that she has hitherto wandered in the paths of error, and has now for the first time succeeded in discovering the truth. [17]

List was not opposed to free trade. From historical evidence he understood that free trade can be good in some instances and bad in others. His recipe for trade was to first protect industries until they are competitive, and then gradually open them up to trade by creating trading blocs with neighboring countries before finally allowing unrestricted international trade. This is, to a large extent, the economic policy followed by Japan, Korea, China, and other successful newly industrialized nations.

John Maynard Keynes

By the onset of the Great Depression in 1929, it became clear that so called self-regulating markets were unstable and tended to destroy themselves. Before and after the onset of the depression, voices started to be raised against the wisdom of allowing markets to regulate themselves. One of these was John Maynard Keynes (1883-1946), who during the 1920s and 1930s published several papers and books on the need for the active participation of the government in regulating the economy.[18]

Keynes argued that during a recession the government should boost the economy by borrowing and spending, and that these activities would be balanced by budget surpluses when the economy was booming. He also criticized the idea that unemployment will automatically be removed by free markets. Keynes argued that if the money saved is more than the money invested unemployment will rise. These ideas went against the neoclassical economic thoughts prevailing at the time.

Germany was one of the first countries to adapt Keynesian economic policies. Those policies succeeded in turning around Germany and gave rise to Hitler and the Second World War.

In 1936, Keynes published his most important work, *The General Theory of Employment, Interest and Money*. Keynes believed that classical economic theory was a specific case that only held up in specific circumstances, whereas his theory was a general one that would hold up under all conditions. In classical economics, supply governs demand as summoned up in Say's Law.[19] According to Keynes, the situation is the reverse: demand governs supply. If there is nobody ready to buy, nobody will produce. Consequently, the book advocates active government action to stimulate demand when the economy has a downturn.

While mostly ignored at first, Keynes's theories gradually gained dominance and were almost universally adopted from the end of the Second World War up to the 1970s, when the wind changed back towards free unregulated markets.

Joseph Schumpeter

A strong critic of Keynes was the contemporary Austrian economist Joseph Schumpeter (1883-1950). Schumpeter was not only critical of Keynes, but of Adam Smith and David Ricardo as well. He felt that economists were suffering from the "Ricardian Vice," making abstract economic models without any empirical foundation. He maintained that these theories, even if interesting and beautifully framed, had little relevance to the world we live in. Schumpeter claimed that this gave rise to the false idea that correct policy decisions can arise from simple abstract models. According to Schumpeter, you cannot oversimplify economic realities. If you do, what you come up with will be meaningless, with no connection to the real world. "[T]he general reader," he writes, "will have to make up his mind, whether he wants simple answers to his questions or useful ones — in this as in other economic matters he cannot have both."[20]

Schumpeter followed the historical school of economics and believed that innovation and creative destruction of outmoded ways and technologies were the driving forces of economic growth, not capital per se. These can never be captured in simple economic formulae, and so in order to take policy decisions we need to pragmatically look at the world as it really is and learn from history. Following abstract economic reasoning will only lead us astray, he argued.

According to Schumpeter, for development the economy depended on the entrepreneur and new ideas and technology. Without these, any amount of capital and other resources would be useless. He thus echoed the ideas of Johann Beckmann (1739-1811), who considered production, technology, and knowledge as the basis for wealth creation.

While in mainstream economics the ideas of Schumpeter and Beckmann have almost totally disappeared at the expense of more abstract theories, it is interesting to see that they still live on at Harvard Business School and other major business schools throughout the world. Real businessmen have little use for abstract theories. They are concerned with making money.

Karl Polanyi

In 1944, eight years after Keynes published *The General Theory of Employment, Interest and Money*, a much harsher critique of free-market theory was published by Karl Polanyi (1866-1964). Polanyi, a Hungarian economist, had emigrated to London, where he wrote his major work, *The Great Transformation*. [21] According to him, the great transformation was the transformation from previous societies—where the market was only a small part of society and the mechanism of the markets were under social control—into a new world where the market controlled society.

Polanyi was critical of Adam Smith and the idea of the market being the central focus of human society in general and the economy in particular. "In spite of the chorus of academic incantations so persistent in the nineteenth century," he writes, "gain and profit made on exchange never before played an important part in human economy. Though the institution of the market was fairly common since the later Stone Age, its role was no more than incidental to economic life." [22]

Polanyi argued, in effect, that the economics of laissez-faire was not a natural aspect of human life but was "abstract' and "planned," while social and economic protectionism was a natural reaction to the inequality and social dislocation created by the very same market. He acknowledged that the capitalist market had brought "unheard of material wealth," but this narrow focus was also the market's inherent problem or contradiction.

The transition to a free-market economy was not, according to Polanyi, spontaneous but a deliberate act imposed with much effort by governments that needed to be kept in place by government coercion. In fact, there was nothing natural with free markets at all since they go against the very fabric of society. His central thesis is that self-regulating markets do not work but rather are destructive and dangerous. "Our thesis," he writes, "is that the idea of a self-adjusting market implies a stark utopia. Such an institution could not exist for any length of time without annihilating the human and natural substance of society; it would have physically destroyed man and transformed his surroundings into a wilderness." [23]

The reason for this is that the market turns nature, people, and money into commodities to be traded as if they were goods in a market. The problem is: they are not commodities.

> [L]abour, land and money are essential elements of industry; they also must be organized in markets; in fact, these markets form an absolute vital part of the economic system. But labor, land and money are obviously not commodities; the postulate that anything bought and sold must have been produced for

sale is emphatically untrue in regard to them. In other words, according to the empirical definition of a commodity they are not commodities. Labor is only another name for a human activity which goes with life itself, which in its turn is not produced for sale but for entirely different reasons, nor can that activity be detached from the rest of life, be stored or mobilized; land is only another name for nature, which is not produced by man; actual money, finally, is merely a token of purchasing power which, as a rule, is not produced at all, but comes into being through the mechanism of banking or state finance. None of them is produced for sale. The commodity description of labor, land and money is entirely fictitious. [24]

It is impossible, Polanyi maintains, to treat labor as a commodity without affecting the human beings that constitute this very commodity. While disposing of the labor power contained in human beings, it would also dispose of the physical, psychological, and moral sides as well. As a result human beings would be removed from protective cultural institutions and would "die as the effect of acute social dislocation through vice, perversion, crime, and starvation."[25]

The effect on nature would be equally grave. Polanyi predicted that treating nature as a commodity would "reduce it to its elements, neighborhoods and landscapes defiled, rivers polluted, military safety jeopardized, the power to produce food and raw materials destroyed."[26] Finally, treating money as a commodity would "periodically liquidate business enterprises, for shortage and surfeits of money would prove as disastrous to business as floods and droughts in primitive society."[27]

These predictions, made in 1944, have come true with a vengeance. Polanyi sums up his conclusion thus: "[N]o society could stand the effects of such a system of rude fictions even for the shortest stretch of time unless its human and natural substance as well as its business organization was protected against the ravages of this satanic mill." [28]

As a reaction to social dislocation, society takes steps to protect itself from the ravages of the market. In effect, once the free market attempts to separate itself from the fabric of society, social protectionism is society's natural response. In the last minute it will always pull back from the brink and reinstitute social controls on the markets before it meets its destruction. These lessons of history are periodically forgotten, and experiments in free trade are reintroduced until the next crash.

Largely ignored and forgotten by mainstream economics, Polanyi's ideas are gradually being accepted by the economic profession. In the preface to the 2001 edition of Polyani's book, Nobel Laureate Joseph Stiglitz recognizes that "[e]conomic science and economic history have come to recognize the validity of Polanyi's key contentions."[29] Economic policy at present, however, is almost in every instance quite contrary to Polanyi's ideas, a topic we will treat in more detail further on.

Two Distinct Schools of Economic Thought

According to Norwegian economist Erik S. Reinert, the history of economic thought can be divided into two distinct schools. One is the classical economic school with roots in Smith and Ricardo, and the other is the "Other Canon," the experience-based tradition of the economics of Alexander Hamilton, Friedrich List, the German Historical School, and Joseph Schumpeter. While the Other Canon has almost died out and is hardly discussed in universities these days, it was, according to Reinert, the policies and tool set of the Other Canon that largely built the industrialized world.

Economic Policies from the Second World War to the 1970s

The evolution of the welfare state and the mixed economies of Europe were strongly influenced by the economists mentioned in the previous sections, and in particular by John Maynard Keynes, who was instrumental in the Bretton Woods meetings in the 1940s and 50s. These international meetings between the USA and many European nations led to the formation of the International Monetary Fund (IMF) and the World Bank, which remain powerful forces in world trade and development, but which have been heavily criticized for mostly furthering the interests of the rich northern economies over those in the South.

During the period from the end of the Second World War until the 1970s, governments were generally active in the economy and it was understood that regulations and government interventions were needed to ensure that the purchasing capacity of the people was sufficient to drive the economy. In general, productivity increases in industry led to higher wages; there were high taxes on the rich and transfer payments were made to the poor and middle class; and internationally, poor and war-ravaged countries in Europe were assisted to rebuild their industrial base through the Marshall Plan. Exchange rates between countries were fixed, capital controls common, and selective tariffs in place in most countries.

European capitalism during the post-war period has been molded around a plethora of systems and ideas: class struggle, capitalist innovation and accumulation, as well as governmental policies of taxation and subsidies according to the Keynesian school of thought. This enabled European countries to allow capitalists to create profit, labor to earn higher wages, and governments to collect taxes, distribute subsidies to farmers and industries, and to create a welfare state of mostly free education and healthcare services.

This period laid the foundation for the relative prosperity in Europe and the United States. It also saw the rise of Japan's economy and, from the early 1960s, the Asian Dragon economies of Taiwan, South Korea, Hong Kong, and Singapore.

The Chicago and Austrian Schools of Economics and the Fall of Keynes
    While Keynesian economics was the dominant economic theory from the Second World War to the early 1970s, a formidable challenge emerged from Milton Friedman and the Chicago School of Economics.

The Chicago School of Economics has its roots in the conservative influence of Frank Knight (1885-1972). While he agreed that free markets could be inefficient, he considered governments even more inefficient and hence supported free markets and minimum government intervention.

One of the most prominent faculty members of the Chicago School was Nobel Prize Laureate Ronald Coase (1910-2013). In "The Problem of Social Cost (1960),"[30] he argued that if there were no transaction costs, people would bargain with each other to produce the same results they would have gotten had a court of law decided the case. Essentially, he argued that if we prevent a manufacturer from harming its neighbors with noise and pollution through fines or a court injunction, one could equally say that the neighbors are harming the manufacturer by preventing him from doing his business. Therefore, it is not a question of one harming the other, but of conflicting interests where both parties have the same right. He suggests that the judgment should consider the most efficient solution, one which results in the greatest economic output. In the case of a manufacturer polluting a river, the question would be whether the commercial value of the goods produced is higher than the commercial value of the fish that were killed by the pollution. Coase's solution would be to have the manufacturer pay the community for the lost fish. If the extra profits from polluting the river are higher than the cost of paying compensation for the fish killed, the company should keep on polluting and simply pay the community. The community, according to his argument, has not lost anything and the company has made a profit. This of course brings up the problem of putting a monetary value on a polluted river, and the extremely complex ecological damage that can be caused by it, an important problem that Coase does not address.

In recent years, the most influential economist to have come out of the Chicago School of Economics, and arguably the most influential economist of the post-Second World War era, was Milton Friedman, who almost singlehandedly refuted the mainstream Keynesian economic theories.

While Milton Friedman admired Maynard Keynes and considered him a great economist with a fascinating theory, he had doubts of its validity. In an interview conducted on January 10, 2000, he commented:

> Let me emphasize [that] I think Keynes was a great econo-mist. I think his particular theory in The General Theory of Employment, Interest, and Money is a fascinating theory. It's a right kind of a theory. It's one which says a lot by using only a little. So it's a theory that has great potentiality. And you know, in all of science, progress comes through people proposing hypotheses which are subject to test and rejected and replaced by better hypotheses. And Keynes's theory, in my opinion, was one of those very productive hypotheses—a very ingenious one, a very intelligent one. It just turned out to be incompatible with the facts when it was put to the test. [31]

Milton Friedman thus disagreed with Keynes, not because he found flaws in the theory but because, according to him, the theory did not correspond to the facts of the real world. Indeed, Friedman and the Chicago School of Economics were of the firm opinion that economic theories should be predictive, and that a theory is good if it can be used to predict future events. If it does not, then it is bad, regardless of the logic and beauty of its arguments.

There are several differences between the ideas of Keynes and Friedman:

Keynes believed that aggregate demand controlled the economy, while Friedman returned to the ideas of classical economics, which believed that supply was the important factor and that supply created its own demand (Say's Law).

Both Friedman and Keynes believed that governments should be active in correcting markets, but their opinion on how to do so varied. Keynes believed in fiscal policies—that is, during times of depression governments should spend more money, and during good times they should save money. Friedman believed in monetary policy, i.e., controlling the amount of money that is in circulation. Beyond this, the government should let the market manage itself.

While Keynes believed that the government should control interest rates as a means of stimulating or slowing the economy, Friedman believed that interest rates should be determined by the loanable funds markets.

While Keynes saw the Great Depression as a failure of the capitalist system, Friedman saw it as a failure of the Federal Reserve Bank to boost liquidity during the downturn by increasing the money supply. Basically, apart from the control of the money flow, Friedman and the Chicago School of Economics believe in free markets, free trade, and minimum involvement of government. In *Capitalism and Freedom,* for example, Milton Friedman advocates the elimination of:

- taxes on corporations
- the graduated income tax
- free public education
- social security
- government regulation of the purity of food and drugs
- the licensing and qualifying of doctors and dentists
- the post-office monopoly
- government relief from natural disasters
- minimum-wage laws
- ceilings on interest rates charged by usurious lenders
- laws prohibiting heroin sales, and nearly every other form of government intervention that goes beyond the enforcement of property rights and contract laws and the provision of national defence

An economic school advocating even more liberalization is the Austrian School of Economics. Not only does this school support free trade, it also believes that the government should not get involved in monetary policy and should even let the money supply be handled by the market. In addition, the Austrian School believes that money should be backed by a definite value in terms of a commodity, such as gold. The Chicago School, in contrast, believes in government-issued money as the basis of monetary policy.

While the Austrian School of Economics traces its roots to the followers of St. Thomas of Aquinas in the fifteenth century, the modern era of the Austrian School of Economics can be considered to have started with Ludwig von Mises (1881-1973), who promoted praxeology, a type of deductive study of human behavior based on certain axioms. Mises believed that the subjective choices of individuals underlie all economic activity. As opposed to the Chicago School of Economics, von Mises did not believe that statistics and scientific testing were useful or necessary in economics; he thought you could arrive at absolute knowledge through logical deduction and established truths.

Other important personalities of the Austrian School were Friedrich Hayek, Karl Menger, and Israel Kirzner. Of the contemporary followers of the Austrian School, Robert P. Murphy is the most well known.

The rivalry between the Chicago and Austrian schools is fierce. While the Chicago School argues that the Austrian School is unscientific and detached from reality due to its disinterest in statistical proofs, the Austrian School accuses the Chicago School of accepting any assumption, regardless of how unrealistic or silly, provided they can find a statistical correlation to use it in predictions. The Austrian School seems interested in explaining the data at hand with a coherent theory, while the Chicago School argues that a theory need not be elegant or conclusive as long as it can be used in predictions.

The Austrian School critiques the Chicago School's belief in the efficient-market hypothesis. In an article describing the difference between the Austrian and Chicago schools of economics, Robert Murphy argues that the hypothesis not only fails to explain market bubbles, but in its strongest form the hypothesis denies that bubbles such as the housing bubble theoretically take place at all.[32] He also pokes fun at Ronald Coase's paper "The Problem of Social Cost" (quoted above).

The Rise of Reaganomics

When Ronald Reagan became president in 1981, he turned to the Chicago School of Economics and Milton Friedman for support and guidance to implement his economic programs. Milton Friedman sat on Reagan's Economic Advisory Board during the eight years of the Reagan administration, and he was also awarded the Presidential Medal of Freedom.

The main thrust of Reagan's economic policies was ostensibly to boost the supply of goods and reduce the size of the government. He drastically reduced taxes on the rich and cut spending programs on social welfare. These policies, which made the rich richer and the poor poorer, were supposed to stimulate the economy in line with Milton Friedman's ideas.

The concept of small government was never realized, however. Rather, the government grew bigger than ever. The difference was only in where the money was spent. Instead of spending it on social services for the poor, Reagan's government spent it on military hardware, thereby significantly boosting aggregate demand. In eight years, Reagan's "small government" more than quadrupled the US debt, from seven hundred billion to three trillion.

It is therefore extremely hard to say whether the supply-side policies had any impact on the economy. Whatever the tax breaks might have achieved was likely dwarfed by the enormous stimulus packet that Reagan implemented.

With the emphasis of the Chicago School of Economics' idea that economic theories should be able to predict future events, and that, in the words of Milton Friedman, "One of the greatest mistakes is to judge policies and programs on their intentions rather than their results,"[33] it is rather ironic to note that the result of Reagan's policies have been far from those expected. While the economy received a temporary boost, the long-term cost was an enormous rise in public debt. As a result of similar policies in many other countries, the world now faces a debt overhang that threatens to destroy the whole financial system. Furthermore, the expectation that putting more money in the pockets of the rich would increase aggregate supply was never fulfilled. The increased money for rich speculators, combined with aggressive borrowing by the government and the middle class, only fueled asset and financial bubbles without adding any real economic growth.

The 1970s to the Present Day: A Return to Unregulated Markets

In the middle of the 1970s, a distinct change took place in economic thought. The distinctly Keynesian character of economics following the

Second World War diminished in importance while the world returned to classical supply-side economics, informed by neoclassical economists influenced by the Chicago School of Economics and the works of Milton Freedman, Margaret Thatcher, and Ronald Reagan. The influence of Keynes subsided fast while free trade and unregulated markets gained new momentum. Instead of helping the consumer through increased wages and improved purchasing power, the new emphasis was on help-ing producers increase their profits in order to save more money, and, according to the theory, invest more.

In the United States, Britain, and many other countries, in line with supply-side economic ideas, marginal tax rates on the rich were reduced from 80 to 90% down to 30%. Taxes on capital gains were lowered; thus higher taxes had to be paid by those doing an honest job. But if you made money from financial speculation, your tax rates were lowered.

Salaries did not keep up with productivity gain, and in many coun-tries, including the United States, the poor and middle classes started to struggle and had to work longer hours and borrow more money in order to keep the same standard of living. The rich and the superrich, on the other hand, were doing very well and executive pay reached unprecedented levels. As noted in the chapter on the inequality crisis, the gap between the rich and poor grew steadily. Between 1974 and 2004, the richest 1% in the United States increased their share of the national income from 38% to 58%.[34]

The support of the already wealthy was theoretically meant to free up more capital for the rich to invest in the economy and thereby create new jobs and generate more economic activity. That is indeed the theory behind supply-side economics. However, this did not happen. Most of the freed-up capital went into speculation and fueled financial and housing bubbles, laying the foundation for the crises we discussed in detail in the first section of this book. As detailed in Chapter Two, this also created a debt crisis, since governments and individuals had to borrow heavily to maintain the aggregate demand that kept the economy running.

A simultaneous move to deregulate the economy and allow greater flexibility for bankers and financiers to create new and sophisticated financial instruments, such as the 1.4-quadrillion-dollar derivatives market, increased financial instability.

While the financial sector expanded, income from this sector was growing as well. By 2012 the profits from the financial sector accounted for 40% of US corporate profits.[35] There are problems with these profits, however. The financial sector does not create any real wealth. When the financial sector is reporting higher profits, these profits are in reality transferred from the real economy. In other words, the larger the financial profits, the more blood is drained from the real economy to be swallowed up by financial investors. Michael Hudson, Distinguished Research Professor of Economics at the University of Missouri, Kansas, considers this a "free lunch" extracted from the economy and wrongly labeled as earnings on a par with wages and profits. [36]

Hudson considers the whole free market a myth, that due to the financial strength of a handful of players, no real market, in the way it is defined by neoclassical economics, truly exists.

The euphemism "free market" means central planning by banks and high finance — by Wall Street, the City of London, Frankfurt, the Paris Bourse, and centers further east. This shifts the allocation of capital and policy planning out of the hands of government and into those of the banking sector. [37]

Erik S. Reinert also sees parallels between the free market and central planning. In his book *Why Rich Countries Become Rich and Why Poor Countries Stay Poor*, he observes, "the close kinship between communist planning and neo-liberalism makes it easy for economists to move from one political extreme to the other, from being Ricardians on the left to being Ricardians on the right." [38]

Internationally, the 1970s and beyond ushered in the era of free trade and the free movement of capital. In 1995, GATT, the General Agreement on Tariffs and Trade, was upgraded to the World Trade Organization (WTO), which was given unprecedented powers to regulate world trade. After several rounds of negotiations, tariffs were reduced on most industrial goods, restrictions that all member states were forced to abide by.

Simultaneously, the International Monetary Fund (IMF) through its Structural Adjustment Programs (SAP) forced free-market reforms on all recipients of aid, and the World Bank made such reform a condition for its loans.

This set of reforms pushed upon the world are often called the Washington Consensus. The term was first coined by the economist John Williamson in 1989 to describe ten prescriptions for economic reform for developing countries in crisis, including trade liberalization, removal of customs, tariffs and trade protection, deregulation of financial markets, encouragement of direct foreign investment, privatization of state enterprises, and removal of government subsidies. Later on, the term was broadened and now often signifies a neoliberal agenda of free-market fundamentalism.

The trend towards free trade has been gradual, and the strength of the free-trade forces has slowly but surely increased. Free trade has become the economic gospel of our times. Beneficial for countries whose industries are already mature and strong, free trade can be disastrous for those whose industries are in their infancy. All rich nations today adhere to free trade in most industrial products. But as we have noted earlier, these countries did not become strong economies by engaging in free trade. They became industrially strong through mercantilist protection. Now it is in their interest to impose free trade on everyone else, thereby weakening the industrial capacity of developing countries and ensuring their own industrial supremacy.

As economists Erik S. Reinert and Ha-Joon Chang have emphasized in their writings, countries that became rich and industrialized during this period, such as the "miracle nations" of South Asia—Japan, Korea, Taiwan, and China—became so by not following the policies of the Washington Consensus. All of these countries had a strong state involvement in the economy, and they had severe restrictions on imports, capital movement, and foreign investments.

With the latest round of WTO talks and regional free-trade agreements, the options of protecting infant industries and following in the footsteps of other industrialized nations have been closed by the developed nations. Rich countries have kicked away the ladder of poor countries by forcing free-trade policies on them before they are ready to compete. This, in effect, was what Britain did to the American colonies by not allowing them to develop industries, and this is what the US and the EU are doing to African, Asian, and South American countries today by allowing free trade when poor countries export raw materials but not when they want to export ready-made goods.

As an economic historian, Erik S. Reinert maintains that today's global market is neocolonialism under the guise of free trade. "Africa," he writes, "is being divided into a complex network of areas with different trade agreements—the so-called spaghetti bowl—in which the EU and the USA try to increase their fields of interest." [39] He describes how the treaties being signed today are similar to those signed during colonial times over 150 years ago. One recent example is how Egypt has been pressured into buying strongly subsidized apples from the EU. This allows the EU to outcompete apple growers in Lebanon, who traditionally have delivered apples to Egypt, thus destroying the local apple trade. Another example of this economic double standard is seen in the very foundation of the EU itself. When the EU was called the European Economic Community (EEC), it was sold to the European electorate as a market that would give, according to the best capitalist principles of Adam Smith, an increasing rate of return. That is, the market within the EU would, they claimed, increase wealth for everyone. When the same politicians needed a theory for trade with Africa, they chose another model more fitting for neocolonial circumstances, namely the theories of David Ricardo, where increasing returns are assumed not to exist. The vested interests of powerful European politicians, who in return represent the even more powerful vested interests of corporations, make their choices based on what makes the most profit for them according to the circumstances, not on what is right or wrong.

As opposed to physical science, where there is general agreement between scientists as to what theories are correct, there is no such agreement in economics. This is probably due to the lack of an effective feedback mechanism to test the validity of economic theories in the real world.

This has led to a situation where we have many different schools of economics that are recognized within the profession, yet which have diametrically opposite views on almost everything. What makes an economist famous is the clarity and cleverness of his ideas and thoughts, regardless of whether their colleagues agree with them or not. For example, Milton Friedman was a great admirer of Keynes, even though he considered his theories completely wrong and was instrumental in overturning the Keynesian orientation of government policies.

With so many different views, it is almost always possible to find an authority or a theory to support every conceivable policy. Any businessman or politician, who for whatever reason, likes to pursue certain economic policies, can almost certainly find an economic theory to support it.

There is growing inequality within the European Union as well. Reports from the EU commission show a steady upward trend in inequality since 2000. The countries with the most income inequality, such as Italy, Spain, Portugal, and Lithuania, are also those countries with the least industrialization, the lowest wages, highest unemployment, and thus the highest private debts. This combination of low wages and high private debt was, at least in part, the cause of the European financial crisis. Income inequality has further increased with the entry of new member states such as Romania and Croatia, both countries with a high level of poverty and unemployment. As land in these countries is bought by wealthy farmers in the UK, Denmark, and the Netherlands, the local farm economy will likely crumble and thus increase unemployment and inequality. There is also a growing trend within the EU itself to see some of its less developed member countries as sources of cheap raw materials. This trend toward more inequality can be seen wherever there is "free trade" between countries of unequal development and income levels. This kind of trade favors the already powerful and rich. Indeed, the whole of EU is based on the idea of the free movement of goods, services, capital, and people, so if free trade benefits those with the most advanced level of industrialization, it is no surprise that the more developed countries inside the EU will benefit at the expense of the less industrialized ones. We will return to a detailed analysis of the EU in the next chapter.

The Environmental Crisis and the Rise of Green Capitalism

While the financial and inequality crises can be seen as a direct consequence of economic policies backed by neoclassical economics, the problems with resource shortages and environmental degradation are more appropriately linked to the industrial revolution and economic expansion in the past two hundred years. The strain on resources and the degradation of the environment have been going on throughout the mercantile, classical, Keynesian, and neoclassical eras, and there are few or no aspects of traditional economic theory that address this problem.

As we noted earlier, the resource and environmental crises are the most serious threats facing humanity today, and hence a renewed interest in the problem has emerged through various green parties that have gained influence in many countries. While there are technical challenges in solving the environmental crisis, these challenges can be overcome with the right political will. The main problem is that the policies needed to implement changes are generally contradictory to short-term profit motives, and thus classical or neoclassical economic thought largely ignores environmental problems.

Economic historian Karl Polanyi was perhaps the first to warn us of this issue. In 1944, he asserted in his milestone book *The Great Transformation* that society needs to control the market economy and not, as today, allow the market to control society. He also warned of the ecological consequences of unbridled markets. Even though Polanyi's ideas have been largely ignored by mainstream economists, his message that economics is inseparable from the way we live has come to the forefront of today's green movement.

The first modern economist who specifically talked about this topic, which now is at the heart of green political thinking, was the British economist E. F. Schumacher. What Adam Smith did for classical economics and Marx for socialism, Schumacher did for green capitalism: he laid the foundation for further ideological thinking. In his path-breaking work published in 1973, *Small is Beautiful: A Study of Economics as if People Mattered*, he presented a thorough critique of material capitalism's main shortcomings and suggested a way to live on our planet of finite resources without going beyond the inherent boundaries of ecology. He suggested we develop a sustainable lifestyle and economy nearly twenty years before the word sustainability was made fashionable by the 1987 Brundtland Commission at the United Nations.

Schumacher's book introduces the term "natural capital," which brings Polanyi's message into the arena of the environment. If we create an economy that abstracts itself from nature, they both argued, we will inevitably destroy this invaluable resource. The many serious environmental problems facing us today have brought home the huge costs of the market economy's faulty abstractions. We have interfered with many of the life-supporting systems of this planet, and if this trend continues, the capacity of our planet to support future generations can no longer be taken for granted. Without a sustainable environment, there can be no sustainable economy.

Green economists since Schumacher's time have made a compelling argument that we need to account for natural capital. "Today we understand natural capital," writes green economist Paul Hawken, "as the sum total of renewable and nonrenewable resources, including the ecological systems and services that support life. It is different from conventionally defined capital in that natural capital cannot be produced by human activity." [40] Most importantly, natural capital, such as fossil fuels, fish, and animals, cannot be replaced by human activity. Once they are lost, they are lost forever.

The green movement contends that the problem with the capitalist system is that it is not rooted in an ecological understanding of how the world works. The source of the word "economics" comes from the Greek *oikos*, which means "earth household." Understood in an ecological context, economics is about taking care of the earth as if it were our own household, our home. But neither socialist nor capitalist theorists have seen economics that way. Neither theory realized that those earlier cultures who disregarded the limits of nature, who saw nature as a limitless and free resource, such as the people on Easter Island, are now gone. Both socialism and capitalism, in all their variants, have contributed to the ecological-resource and economic-systems crisis we are now in.

Schumacher did, however, understand this predicament. He pointed out that our ethical and philosophical worldviews have great political and economic consequences. He suggested two main reasons for our economic and environmental problems: 1) basing an economy on the individual's desire for wealth, and 2) separating economics from ecology. Schumacher was one of the first to provide these revelatory insights into an economic system he aptly described as "the institutionalization of individualism and non-responsibility." [41]

Directly or indirectly inspired by Schumacher's *Small is Beautiful* worldview, American businessman-turned-environmental-activist Paul Hawken wrote the book *Natural Capitalism*; physicist and third-world farm activist Vandana Shiva developed a new vision for rural economies in India; architect William McDonough and chemist Michael Braungart created revolutionary cradle-to-cradle industrial-design innovations by copying the way nature works; European green movements inspired and founded political parties influencing governments all over the EU; and third-world bottom-line economics became a new standard by showing corporations that profit, people, and planet need to be part of economic planning and accounting.

Vandana Shiva argues that what the proponents of free markets see as proof of underdevelopment can actually be signs of a good and balanced life:

> I come from the Himalayas and even today we have villagers in the high mountains who have zero cash income, but they are not poor for that. They have good woolens…that can keep you warm even in the snows, beautiful homes, lovely structures that protect you from climates,… nutritious foods, clean water, to me those are the indicators of whether you have the good life or you don't. Now without a dollar a day you can have the good life

if your ecosystems have not been spoiled, your rivers flow, your forests are intact, your agriculture has not been destroyed, your knowledge has not been eroded, your rights have not been taken away, and your culture gives you the means and mechanism to organize life in a way that gives dignity to all. [42]

Green Parties have, in the past three decades, sprouted up in most of the countries of Europe and in other industrialized nations. The first Green Party to achieve national prominence was the German Green Party, famous for their opposition to nuclear power. Founded in 1980, the party has been in coalition governments at the state level for some years. In 2001, it reached an agreement with the government to end reliance on nuclear power in Germany and agreed to remain in the coalition and to support the government of Chancellor Gerhard Schröder in the 2001 Afghan War. The support for the war, however, put them at odds with many Greens worldwide. The Swedish Green Party has had up to twenty-five members in government, while the European Green Party is represented in the EU parliament and is supported by thirty-four Green parties from all over Europe. There are also green parties in the United States, Brazil, Australia, New Zealand, and Lebanon.

The support for green values and sustainable economics has become so ubiquitous in our society that world politicians and corporations such as Wal-Mart, Shell, and Exxon have subscribed to sustainable green and third-bottom-line practices, in which not only profit but also community and environmental goals are described in their business's mission statements. But as green activist Paul Hawken lamented in his book *Blessed Unrest*, even with three million grass-roots organizations struggling to make the world more equal and green, and corporations and politicians promoting green values, the actual sustainable green changes we have made are but "drops in a bucket." The world is more polluted, more unequal, and more unsustainable than ever.

There are two main reasons for this dire predicament. First, while there are many green parties and people with interest in the environment, none of these parties have become a leading force in any major country. But even if that were to happen, it is unlikely that much would change due to the simple reason that it seems impossible to reform capitalism and make it truly "green." The driving force behind the capitalist system is the profit incentive of individuals and companies. And, as we have seen throughout modern economic history, the profit motive, or the so-called "bottom line" of capitalism, has always been antithetical to environmental interests. But what are the reasons for that?

Human beings have many motivations; the desire for wealth and profit is just one of them. Regardless of the observations of Adam Smith, very few people consistently try to maximize financial gain at the expense of everything else. Everyone is not always motivated by greed and selfishness.

The capitalist system is rigged in such a way that the people with the most money have the power. Those who fit the stereotype of the rational profit-maximizer, those who put their financial interests above everything else, are the ones who eventually achieve the most power in a market-capitalist economy. It is in their favor to put short-term financial interests above environmental interests. Consequently, in free-market capitalism the political will for ecologically sound industrial policies is rather weak. Trying to make capitalism greener and sustainable is therefore not a practical strategy. As both Polanyi and Schumacher have pointed out, capitalism is by its very nature not green, sustainable, or cooperative.

Green politicians urge us to build upon the best of the market economy, but as we have noted above, capitalist reform strategies from Keynes to neoliberalism, from the welfare system to the greens, have one thing in common: they are attempts at circumventing, denying, or glossing over the systemic shortcomings of growth-capitalism's basic principles. As history has shown, this only gives the multinational corporations more time to continue with their green-washed propaganda. Similarly, taxing corporations only makes them work even harder to find tax loopholes or tax havens to hide their profits.

While most politicians today support the cause of stopping global warming, very little is being done about it. Capitalism is a colossal system imbedded in its own self-fulfilling mission to increase profit at any cost. Unless it fundamentally alters its main premise, meaningful ecological reform is not possible. As Schumacher wrote, "the idea of unlimited economic growth, more and more until everybody is saturated with wealth, needs to be seriously questioned on at least two accounts: the availability of basic resources and, alternatively or additionally, the capacity of the environment to cope with the degree of interference implied." [43]

Since the publication of Schumacher's green classic in 1973, the world has not become any more sustainable or greener. In spite of the popularity of everything green, corporations are ahead of the game. They find new loopholes to pollute and to pay less tax in order to maximize profit. Green Capitalism is a contradiction in terms, and it is therefore unlikely that its vision can develop a truly sustainable economy or save us from the environmental crisis we described earlier in the book.

Conclusion

In this chapter, we have traced the history of economic thought from the days of Mercantilism to Green Capitalism, to show how economic thoughts and theories have shaped the world and created the present multidimensional crisis.

While neoclassical economic theories and free markets have been strongly criticized in this chapter, it does not seem that any current economic theory by itself holds the solution to the complex problems confronting us today. A return to the economics represented by the Other Canon could certainly help poor nations, but this economic school does not specifically address the debt crisis. The resource crisis is also not addressed by any of the above economic theories. Green capitalism is praiseworthy, and to some extent it addresses both resource problems and environmental degradation. Unfortunately, it is a contradiction in terms. At best it is an attempt to reduce the impact of environmental degradation within the constraints of the free market system.

As long as free markets, or rather banks and the financial system, decide the allocation of resources, it is hard to conceive of a sustainable economy where environmental concerns are properly addressed. Even though there are many lessons to be drawn from a review of economic history, it shows us no clear and easy path forward. In the last section of this book we will lay out a more comprehensive path by addressing some of the main limitations of both the free market and the green capitalist system. For now, we will turn our eyes to Europe and the European Union, to take a closer look at what this powerful economy holds for the future.

Chapter Six

The European Union: The Future of the World or the End of an Era?

I N OCTOBER 2011, THE German prime minister, Angela Merkel, warned that peace in Europe could be endangered if an agreement was not reached on how to manage the crisis that had engulfed the euro and the whole of the EU economy. Speaking to the German parliament she said, "No one should think that a further half century of peace and prosperity is assured. It isn't. And that's why I say if the euro fails, Europe will fail, and that mustn't happen." [1] A grave warning from the head of Europe's most prosperous economy, and in view of Europe's violent and poverty-stricken past, a warning millions of Europeans can easily relate to.

A Continent of War and Strife

During the past one thousand years, Europe was engulfed in almost constant war with only short periods of relative peace. This led the Russian anarchist Peter Kropotkin to write that "war is the natural condition of Europe." [2] As technological advancements improved weapon technology, the destruction and loss of life increased exponentially. So did the amount of collateral damage, the deaths among the general population not taking part in the war. While one soldier a thousand years ago could kill one person at a time with a sword, a bomber pilot in the Second World War could kill hundreds of people with one bomb, mostly civilians.

After the Second World War, it became clear that continued large-scale warfare could permanently destroy the whole of Europe, or set it back hundreds of years. The point of fighting wars is, after all, to gain an advantage. If total destruction results, there are only losers. It thus became clear that a drastic change of direction had to take place if Europe were to survive as a continent. Europe needed lasting peace. But how could this be achieved?

After the First World War, at the Paris Conference of 1919, an attempt had been made to emasculate Germany—who was seen by the victors as the main reason for the war—to make sure it could no longer be in a position to threaten its neighbors. In the Treaty of Versailles, blame for the war was squarely put on Germany for "the aggression of Germany and her allies."[3] Severe reparations were demanded, far beyond the capacity of Germany to pay. The aim was to weaken Germany to the point that the nation would never be able to pose a threat again. Comparable treaties were made with Austria, Bulgaria, Hungary, and Turkey, and the Hungarian Empire was broken up into many pieces.

The Paris Conference virtually acted as a world government, creating new countries and bankrupting its enemies. The purpose of the new demarcations was to create ethnically homogenous countries. The conference also set up the League of Nations, which was a precursor to the creation of the United Nations after the Second World War.

While most politicians seemed to agree on this course of action, there were also critics. One of the most outspoken critical voices of the punitive reparations Germany was forced to pay was Maynard Keynes. Keynes felt that high reparations would punish innocent German citizens and reduce Germany's ability to import goods from other countries, thereby damaging the entire European economy. In his book *The Economic Consequences of the Peace*, Keynes writes:

> The policy of reducing Germany to servitude for a generation, of degrading the lives of millions of human beings, and of depriving a whole nation of happiness should be abhorrent and detestable, even if it were possible, even if it enriched ourselves, even if it did not sow the decay of the whole civilized life of Europe… [N]ations are not authorized, by religion or by natural morals, to visit on the children of their enemies the misdoings of parents or of rulers. [4]

Keynes made the prediction that the unfair peace treaty would lead to a new war more terrible than the previous, and his prediction came true with a vengeance. German hyperinflation, the collapse of the Weimar Republic, and the subsequent rise of Hitler and the Nazi party were, in many ways, a direct consequence of the terms set by the Treaty of Versailles.

Peace, Power, and Prosperity through Economic Integration: The Marshall Plan, Bretton Woods, and GATT

After the Second World War, the initial reaction of the victors only served to repeat the mistakes of the Paris Conference. Henry Morgenathau, Jr., Secretary of the US Treasury from 1934 to 1945, came up with a plan to ensure that Germany would never be able to attack its neighbors again. The plan, which was implemented after the allied victory in 1945, aimed at destroying all industry in Germany and turning the country into an agricultural nation. All industrial equipment was to be destroyed and all mines flooded with water. [5]

It soon became clear these policies were causing economic hardships for Germany. Former US President Herbert Hoover was sent to investigate, and his report on March 18, 1947 concluded, "There is the illusion that the New Germany left after annexation can be reduced to a 'pastoral state.' It cannot be done unless we exterminate or move 25,000,000 out of it." In other words, an agricultural Germany without industry could never feed its people. The lesson? If you destroy the synergy between industrial and agricultural development, then agricultural production will also fall.

This became the turning point in the effort to achieve peace in Europe. Instead of trying to muscle peace through impoverishment, the new thinking was that harmony between nations could best be achieved through economic integration, by making every nation more prosperous. If people trade with each other and are economically dependent on each other, it was thought, the motivation to go to war would no longer be there.

This change in political direction was accompanied by several policy initiatives. The first was the Marshall Plan, which aimed to help European nations to industrialize and build up their economies. Similar assistance was given to Japan after the end of the Second World War.

Another part of the strategy was to set up rules for the world economy and international economic institutions to oversee trade and economic cooperation. This work had already started before the end of World War Two, at Mount Washington Hotel, Bretton Woods, New Hampshire, where representatives from all forty-four allied nations gathered from July 1 to July 22, 1944. The aim of the conference was to avoid the mistakes of the 1930s, when each country followed the policy of "beggar thy neighbor." By protecting their markets, devaluing their currency to promote exports and reducing imports, trade stopped and each country became worse off. There was a widespread belief, spearheaded by Cordell Hull, the US Secretary of State from 1933 to 1944, that both world wars were the result of trade warfare. If international trade was fair, he believed, it would promote peace and stability. Keynesian economic ideas of state intervention in the economy still prevailed, and it was thought that coordinated action between countries was preferable to the actions of individual states.

The aim of the conference was not only to promote peace. The United States firmly believed that free trade and the lowering of tariffs would be in its interest. After all, the United States was the world's most advanced industrial nation; few countries could compete with its dominance. The outcome of the conference reflected two different objectives: achieving a lasting peace, and promoting the economic interests of the industrialized nations. Initially, the first objective might have been more important in driving reform, but as peace in Europe became a reality, the second objective started to dominate policies. We will return to this topic further on.

The conference delegates agreed on a set of general rules for the global economy, and two international organizations were set up: the International Monetary Fund and the International Bank for Reconstruction and Development (IRBD), which later became part of the World Bank Group. The provisions agreed upon included the following:

- Fixed exchange rates. All currencies were fixed to the US dollar, which in turn was fixed to gold at a rate of $35/oz.
- Members could only adjust their exchange rates within 10 percent of the original rate.
- The IMF was to help member countries with temporary current account deficits (trade deficits), by lending money to be repaid within eighteen months to five years.
- Voting rights in the IMF was not on a per-state basis, but was based on the quota of contributions members gave to the IMF, akin to shareholders in a corporation. Since the US contributed the most,

it also had the strongest voting power and the most influence.

- The IBRD (now the most important part of the Word Bank) was capitalized with $10 billion and was expected to lend funds and underwrite private loans to help in post war reconstruction.

In 1947, three years after Bretton Woods, another institution to promote world trade was put in place, the General Agreement on Tariffs and Trade (GATT), which aimed at lowering tariffs and duties in international trade. As opposed to the Bretton Woods conference, which had as its primary objective securing peace, the focus of GATT was to promote free trade. In line with the economic theories discussed earlier, the justification was that free trade will benefit all members. History would prove over time, however, that the more industrialized a nation was, the more the nation would benefit from free trade.

The initial reductions in tariffs were modest, but subsequent iterations of the agreement increased their scope and included more and more products, cutting the previously agreed-upon tariffs further. By 1995, GATT was replaced by the World Trade Organization (WTO), which considerably increased the scope and powers of the institution. Presently, tariffs on most industrial goods have been removed, while tariffs on most agricultural products remain. This means that in the areas where industrial countries have an advantage, free trade is the norm. In areas where undeveloped countries could have an advantage, heavy government subsidies and tariffs are the norm. Intellectual property rights are also enforced by the WTO, which again benefits developed countries and is a disadvantage to the less industrialized countries, those who are most in need of development.

Global Dominance and Global Disparity

Have these institutions brought prosperity and peace to the world, as was promised during their creation? The record is mixed. The volume of trade in the world has increased dramatically. While levels of absolute poverty have been reduced, inequality has increased. And while Western Europe has experienced peace and relative prosperity, international tensions have not been greatly reduced. There were prolonged wars in Kosovo, Bosnia, Herzegovina, Iraq, Syria, and Afghanistan, wars and famines in Africa, a refugee crisis in Europe, an increase in terrorism, and continued conflicts in the Middle East, but no world war has erupted in the past seventy years.

One emerging trend is that with the introduction of global financial institutions, the power to regulate world trade has been heavily centralized, mostly to the benefit of the advanced industrialized nations. "Much of what happens in the global economy is determined by the rich countries," writes Cambridge economist Ha-Joon Chang. [6] And much of what the rich countries do to the global economy, especially to the poor countries, is determined by the policies of the IMF, the World Bank, and the WTO. This heavyweight economic trinity is often responsible for implementing policies that in theory are supposed to help poor countries achieve economic growth, but which too often, due to their lending and development practices, lead to the rich countries getting richer and the poor countries getting poorer.

After the so-called Third World debt crisis of 1982, the IMF and the World Bank began to exert a much stronger political and economic influence on the countries in the Global South. In the words of Indian novelist and anti-globalization activist Arundhati Roy, these powerful institutions went "beyond the jurisdiction of sovereign governments, international instruments of trade and finance" to institute multilateral laws and agreements that "puts colonialism to shame." Economist Ha-Joon Chang terms such institutions Bad Samaritans—institutions who claim to help but instead control and extract wealth.

According to Ha-Joon Chang and Erik S. Reinert, once the free market controls the economies of the Third World they become enmeshed in an elaborate, carefully calibrated system of economic inequality. Western countries flood the markets of poorer nations with subsidized agricultural goods and other products with which local producers cannot compete. Countries that are thus plundered by these sophisticated colonizing schemes are steeped in debt to the powers who designed them. The newly colonized free-trade nations in the Third World are today repaying the rich nations at the rate of about $382 billion a year. The rich get richer and the poor get poorer—not accidentally, but by economic and political design.

A graphic depiction of these developments is illustrated by the combined wealth of the world's billionaires in 2004 (587 individuals and family units). According to *Forbes* magazine, their wealth amounts to $1.9 trillion—more than the gross domestic product of the world's 135 poorest countries combined. This stark contrast in wealth between people and nations often has tragic human consequences. Since 1997, the Indian National Crime Bureau estimates that forty-six farmers have committed suicide every day due to economic hardships, often imposed by heavy debt burdens from loans to pay for fertilizers, hybrid seeds, and pesticides produced by multinational corporations. In the words of Vandana Shiva:

In 1998, the World Bank's structural adjustment policies forced India to open up its seed sector to global corporations like Cargill, Monsanto, and Syngenta. The global corporations changed the input economy overnight. Farm saved seeds were replaced by corporate seeds which needed fertilizers and pesticides and could not be saved. As seed saving is prevented by patents as well as by the engineering of seeds with non-re-newable traits, seed has to be bought for every planting season by poor peasants. A free resource available on farms became a commodity which farmers were forced to buy every year. This increases poverty and leads to indebtedness. As debts increase and become unpayable, farmers are compelled to sell kidneys or even commit suicide. [7]

With the free trade policies advanced in the wake of the Bretton Woods conference, a new phase began in global development that created unprecedented economic prosperity but also economic inequality, poverty, and environmental destruction. In the vision of Western capitalism, the world, both conceptually and literally, was soon divided into under-developed, developing and developed nations. This economic divide and worldview reflected, in large part, the dominance of US policies in world trade and the economic inequality built into the US capitalist economy. The more regulated European economy has, in contrast, created a less unequal capitalist economy on its prosperous continent. But is free trade, even when regulated as per the European model, the optimum economy for local populations, international trading partners, and environments? We do not think so. Let us thus take a closer look at how the European dream of an economic union started and how it has affected the world.

The Formation of the European Union

After World War II ended in 1945, Europe was left divided, and in 1946 the European Union of Federalists formed to campaign for a United States of Europe. In September of that same year, Churchill called for a United States of Europe spearheaded by France and Germany to increase the chances of long-term peace. The dream of a federalist Europe, how-ever, remained elusive, as few Europeans were willing to give up their national identities and join a federation.

With Winston Churchill's call for a United States of Europe gaining support among politicians throughout the continent, the Council of Europe was established in 1949 as the first pan-European organization. In the following year, French Foreign Minister Robert Schuman proposed a community to integrate the coal and steel industries of Europe—to control the two elements necessary to make weapons of mass destruction. In other words, the initial impetus driving the call for a united Europe was, in part, a desire for peace in the name of international cooperation—a seemingly benign political dream.

It is doubtful, however, that it is only the creation of the EU that has maintained peace in Europe over the past five decades. The divisions of Western and Eastern Europe, the military influence of NATO and the US, as well as the "static balance" of peace during the prolonged Cold War, have had more impact on maintaining peace than European integration. In the words of Harvard professor and bestselling author Niall Ferguson, "the creation of the European Union was not about war and peace, otherwise there would have been a European Defense Community, and that was vetoed by the French National Assembly in 1954." [8]

A Union of Coal and Steel

Business interests may have had a lot more to do with the formation of the EU than peacemaking. In 1951, France, Italy, and the Benelux countries (Belgium, Netherlands, and Luxembourg), together with West Germany, signed the Paris Treaty, creating the European Coal and Steel Community. This took over the role of the International Authority for the Ruhr area and lifted some restrictions on German industrial productivity. The first institutions, such as the High Authority (today called the European Commission) and the Common Assembly (today called the European Parliament) were soon formed, and the first presidents of those institutions were Jean Monnet and Paul-Henri Spaak respectively.

After failed attempts at creating defense and political communities, leaders met at the Messina Conference and established the Spaak Committee, which produced the Spaak report. The report was accepted at the Venice Conference in 1956, where it was decided to organize an Intergovernmental Conference focusing on economic unity, leading to the Treaties of Rome, which was signed in 1957. Soon thereafter, the European Economic Community (EEC) was formed.

The era of "peaceful cooperation" that followed united Europe for years in a common sentiment of cultural and political unity. In addition to this peaceful union, the economy was relatively good. Interest rates were low throughout the 1960s, 1970s, and 1980s, labor unions were strong, the salaries of workers rose rapidly, and people's living standard increased year by year. Up until 1980, as productivity increased, there was a corresponding increase in real wages. Hence the living standard progressively increased. [9] After 1985, however, with the introduction of more liberalism and free trade, the growing postwar economy began to unravel, and lower wages, debt, inequality, and unemployment increased. It was in the wake of this increasingly unstable economic climate that the EU was formed.

EU and the Four Freedoms

The European Union (EU) was formally created in 1993 as a result of the Maastricht Treaty.[10] The EU is an economic and political union of twenty-eight member states operating through a system of supranational institutions and intergovernmentally negotiated decisions by the member states. Institutions of the EU include the European Commission, the Council of the European Union, the European Council, the Court of Justice of the European Union, the European Central Bank, the Court of Auditors, and the European Parliament. The European Parliament is elected every five years by EU citizens in Brussels, EUs "capital city." This parliamentary city is also home to thousands of bureaucrats lobbying politicians to enact their economic dreams and policies. The largest multinational companies have upward of two hundred lobbyists representing them.

The latest major amendment to the constitution of the EU, the Treaty of Lisbon, took place in 2009. The EU has developed a single economic market through a standardized system of laws that apply to all member states. Within the Schengen Area (which includes twenty-two EU and four non-EU states) passport controls have been abolished. Due to the growing refugee crisis in Europe, however, passports are now required at some borders within the Union. In theory, however, EU policies aim to ensure the free movement of people, goods, services, and capital; enact legislation in justice and home affairs; and maintain common policies on trade, agriculture, fisheries, and regional development.

The formation of the EU was a logical extension of the EEC, in an attempt to draw European countries even closer together into one common market. It is a far-reaching concept, which for the first time in human history has united five hundred million people from twenty-seven different countries without a centralized state behind it.

The economic foundation of the EU, as established in the Maastricht Treaty, is the Four Freedoms. These are not the same four freedoms envisioned by Franklin Roosevelt—freedom of speech; freedom of worship; freedom from want; and freedom from fear. While Roosevelt's freedoms concerned the rights of the individual, the EU freedoms were the commercial freedoms of an open market: the free movement of goods, services, persons, and capital.

With the four freedoms, most tools that individual governments traditionally have had to influence their economies were removed, and the whole of Europe turned into a large experiment in free-market capitalism. While the original vision might partly have been to preserve peace in Europe, the foundation of the EU has more to do with a certain economic worldview than that of promoting peace—the worldview of neoliberalism, a deregulated economy of unlimited competition. The four freedoms of the EU were designed to forward a neoliberal economy in all its member countries, coupled with democratic but centralized government regulations from the European Parliament in Brussels and monetary regulations from the European Central Bank.

As expressed earlier, so-called free-market capitalism has economically benefitted the developed nations and the largest corporations most. At the same time, it has often reduced the ability of less developed countries and communities to catch up and develop their industries. This leads to uneven development, where rich countries and regions prosper and poorer areas often fall behind, a situation that has become a reality in present-day EU. Indeed, free markets do not automatically bring about freedom from want, the fourth of Roosevelt's freedoms. Yet this is the gospel propagated by free-market economists and politicians.

Another favorite myth of free-market neoliberalists is that open free markets are always better for business and for people. Here are a few reasons why this is not always so:

—Free markets favor large companies; those with the most money and power will generally outcompete smaller companies. Hence, free trade reduces freedom of choice for smaller companies and people in general—they are forced to compete within an economic environment fixed by the larger companies.

—Free markets do not favor investments in smaller businesses, such as farms and specialized industry in poor areas because they are not competitive. For the growth and sustainability of a poor area, however, investing in smaller, local businesses, even if they make a loss for several years, is, in the long run, good for society and the economy.

—Free markets do not allow less developed areas to protect themselves against competition from larger companies from other countries.

—Free markets often create an economic "race toward the bottom." Examples in Europe are an increase in zero-hour companies such as UK's Sport Direct, where employees do not have fixed salaries, don't know how many hours they can work, and have no health benefits.

—Free movement of labor between rich and poor areas can be greatly profitable for corporations but can also create a shadow economy of low wages, illegal employees, brain drain, and increased economic and human stresses within the social welfare system,

—Free markets do not recognize that certain state-owned companies, such as in the alternative energy, health, and oil sectors, can be better for the stability of the local economy and for the environment.

With these factors in mind, we will now take a closer look at the EUs Four Freedoms—Free Movement of Goods, Free Movement of Capital, Free Movement of People, and Free Movement of Services.

Free Movement of Goods

Article 30 of the Maastricht Treaty prohibits EU member states from imposing custom duties and any other charges having the same effect as custom duties on any goods moving between countries. In addition, article 110 prohibits member countries from imposing any other type of taxes on imported goods that are different from the taxation of domestic goods. Article 34 prohibits nontariff restrictions on imports such as import quotas. Finally, any rule that directly or indirectly discriminates against imported products to the favor of domestic products by making it more cumbersome, costly, or time consuming to market the imported product is prohibited under Union Law.

This freedom makes it difficult for a country to protect or subsidize local industry until it becomes competitive, the method all industrialized countries used in the past to develop their local industries. After the introduction of the free movement of goods, Greece and Portugal were forced to compete on equal terms with technological and industrial powerhouses such as Germany and France.

Member states may restrict the free movement of goods only under certain special circumstances, such as when there are risks associated with public health, the environment, or for consumer protection.

Free Movement of Capital

Capital of any quantity can be moved between member countries within the EU at the same cost as transfers within a single country. In addition, any EU citizen or corporation is allowed to buy any type of property in any part of the Union. It is interesting to note that this "freedom" has suddenly been suspended for Cyprus, even though Cyprus is a member of the Euro Zone. In order to prevent capital flight following the crash of the banking sector, movement of capital out of the country has now been severely restricted.

Hence, the European economy is not a completely free market. Indeed no market, in spite of the economic rhetoric by neoliberal economists, has ever been free—it is always regulated by government policies. While the US economy is considered one of the world's most deregulated economies, the European mixed economy of soft deregulation and state control is considered a less aggressive form of capitalism. Nevertheless, due to increased deregulation through the four-freedom agenda and a rise in speculative wealth and corporate power, the European economy resembles the US economy more and more every year.

Free Movement of People

Within the EU, anyone can move to a different country and work, settle, and retire there; your professional qualifications in one country will be recognized in any of the other member countries. Due to language and cultural barriers, the actual mobility of people has been fairly limited. Even from depressed areas in Greece and Portugal, there has not been a mass exodus to Germany, Denmark, or other more prosperous countries in search of jobs. There has, however, been an increased flow of people into Scandinavia and other countries, mostly single men and women from Eastern European countries such as Romania and Poland, who send part of their wages back to support their families. This economic migration from less developed EU countries to richer countries, coupled with an increase in legal and illegal immigration from Middle Eastern, Asian, and African countries, has created a backlash of protests from primarily right-wing extremist groups, thus fueling strong anti-EU sentiments. These protests, however, are often ignoring the underlying economic issue: that free trade between unequal economies creates a migratory flow from poor to rich areas, and when that migration crosses barriers of country, culture, and language, then complications arise, including increased crime, black-market economies, economic dependency, and as the breaking up of families. The moral of the story is this: when economic conditions are good, people don't want to move away from their native culture and their family and friends to seek greener economic pastures; they only do so when the going gets tough, when the local economy is unproductive.

Free Movement of Services

The free movement of services is established in Articles 56 and 57 of the Maastricht Treaty. Services are defined as anything provided for remuneration that does not fall under goods, capital, or persons. In other words, a cleaning-service company in Denmark can, under this law, set up shop in any of the EU countries and compete on the same level as a local company. APCOA Parking AG is Europe's largest parking-service company, with more than 4500 employees. The company's Scandinavian division is AuroPark, which monitors parking lots outside shopping centers and businesses in Sweden, Denmark, and Norway. Even in areas where there is "free parking," if drivers stay past the allotted time, they have to pay hefty fines of over one hundred dollars. These corporations are not very popular since they are owned by outside interests and thus compete with and drive local companies out of business.

The Four Freedoms, the Environment, and the Local Economy

In theory, we have few reservations regarding free trade. Given optimum conditions, which we will discuss later in the book, free trade as set forth in the EU's Four Freedoms can have great cultural and economic benefits. But free trade can also be detrimental to the local areas within an economic union when local interests are not protected. Hence a market economy needs regulations to protect the interests of local economies, the environment, and local cultures, because free trade is a misnomer—trade of any kind is always regulated, either by the state or by the corporate powers. Free trade is never really free.

Take the case of fishing. The fishing industry has a long tradition in Europe and is deeply tied to the local culture, economy, and environment, especially in Norway, where the support of fishermen and farmers helped to ensure a NO vote in the EU referendums of 1972 and 1994. The argument put forward against EU membership was that it would not be wise to allow fishing boats from other countries to compete with local fishermen— they feared it would wipe out the industry. Today the Norwegian fishing industry is as healthy as ever, with exports to over 150 countries exceeding three thousand tons per year. In contrast, Great Britain also joined the EU and that country's fishing industry has not fared so well. Spain has Europe's biggest fleet and the largest quotas with most of its fishing done in British and Irish waters, while Britain has lost nearly half of its jobs in fishing since the 1970s. The EU has also not done a very good job at protecting its ecosystem in the sea—75 percent of EU fish stocks are overfished and near extinction. [11] To prevent overfishing and preserve the ecosystem, Norway has negotiated fishing agreements. A study conducted by The Poseidon Aquatic Resource Management consultancy and Pew Environment Group found that EU subsidies had been linked to overfishing. They analyzed data from the EU›s Financial Instrument for Fisheries Guidance (FIFG), which paid almost £4 billion in fishing subsidies between 2000 and 2006. The worst offenders were Spain, Portugal, and France, who used subsidy payments to increase fleet capacity in Europe, thus exacerbating the problem of overfishing of depleted stocks such as cod and blue fin tuna. [12]

There are increasing complaints from small farmers about how the bureaucracy in Brussels prevents them from continuing with local, more environmental- and community-friendly farming methods. A beef farmer in Norway complained to the newspaper *Nationen* that EU regulations prevented him from slaughtering his herd at home, which, according to him, would be much less stressful for his cows and thus better for the consumer. Bulgarian goat farmer Petyo Ivanov from the village of Razhevo produces cheese but says he is not selling it due to all the "administration and documentation." The overwhelming bureaucracy makes him question the purpose and sustainability of small farming within the EU, since the regulations favor large industrialized farming operations over small local farms.

Dessislava Dimitrova, an organizer with the Slow Food Movement in the Balkans, believes all Bulgarian small farms face the obstacles Ivanov described:

> As a result of the formal operations of EU regulations, the small producers, the family farms, have actually been deprived of the opportunity to produce and sell their products, and we, the consumers, have been deprived of our right to choose whether to buy industrially produced foods offered by international chains or opt for healthy foods that we really like.[13]

EU foreign-trade policies, which are generally in line with WTO policies, also affect local economies outside its borders, such as in Africa. These policies represent a resource war, which has intensified even more after the European finance crisis. "The countries in the North," according to Ugandan economist Yash Tandon, "are trying to export their economic crisis to the South through trade." This kind of trade is leading to a state of deindustrialization in Africa. It forces the countries in the South to export cheap raw materials to the EU and the US to safeguard higher profits for Western corporations.[14]

There are often big gaps between the rhetoric of free-trade policy makers and what takes place in the real world. Free trade often does not deliver what it promises, not even within the EU and the rest of the Western world. It has promised growth, but growth has actually slowed down in the past two and a half decades after trade liberalization policies have been aggressively enacted worldwide. Secondly, the war on resources and local economies that the Africans complain about is also taking place within the EU itself, as seen in the rapid depletion of fish stocks and in the rapid decline of small farms and agro-industries in rural areas.

The Euro Zone

While the four freedoms created the foundation for a free market and removed many of the tools national governments used to control the economic development of their countries, there still remained one obstacle to a fully open market. That was the exchange rates used to protect local industry and promote economic growth. If a country started to become less productive than its neighbors, the balance of trade would become negative and its exchange rate would fall. This would help local producers, encourage exports, and discourage imports.

But from the perspective of international business, national currencies increase transaction costs, make import and export burdensome, and introduce uncertainties in financial calculations. Flexible exchange rates also went against the interests of the most productive countries, such as Germany, who prior to the euro saw its currency appreciate, which in turn partially offset the advantage it had from increased productivity. When the currency appreciated, it became more expensive for other nations to buy German goods, and so it lowered exports.

In order to remove this one final obstacle to an open market, the EU introduced the euro as its common currency on the first of January, 1999. At that time it was only an accounting currency. Bank notes were issued three years later in 2002. The euro is currently used by 334 million Europeans.

Initially, the move was welcomed by several scholars, such as the British historian Niall Ferguson. The main problem, he thought, would be a monetary union without a common fiscal policy; that is, without a central government that controls expenses. Right after the euro came into existence in 1999, Ferguson warned in an article published in *Foreign Affairs* in 2000 that "a monetary union without a fiscal union would fall apart after about ten years because of the divergence between the member states."[15] Today, Ferguson says, he is running around Europe trying to remind politicians that it was a banking crisis similar to the one Europe is now experiencing that caused the Great Depression in the summer of 1931.

Historically, monetary unions have not been successful. In his book *The End of the Euro*, Belgian business editor Johan van Overtveldt writes that a monetary union between different countries has been attempted but failed in Europe before. The two main monetary union failures were the Latin Monetary Union (LMU), formed in 1866 between France, Belgium, Italy, and Switzerland, and the Scandinavian Monetary Union (SMU) formed in 1872 between Sweden, Denmark, and Norway, who joined in 1875. The LMU never established a common monetary standard and this eventually led to its downfall in 1927, but it had essentially already failed during World War 1. Despite the fact that the Scandinavian countries were largely integrated politically, culturally, and monetarily, their independent political systems created monetary policies that proved to be incompatible with the union. By 1924, each member country no longer accepted coins from the other countries as legal tender, and by 1930 the SMU officially disintegrated when all three countries abandoned the gold standard. [16]

There are many advantages to having a common currency, such as ease of monetary exchange and reduction of transaction costs, but historically no monetary union has ever succeeded without a common fiscal policy. That is, without a common central authority controlling the purse strings. So far only a national government has been able to provide the functional structure needed for a common currency. This fundamental fact was ignored when the euro was introduced. Short of forcing the countries of Europe into a much closer fiscal union, which would be tantamount to creating a federal republic of Europe, there is little hope that the euro can survive. As this is extremely unlikely, the future of the euro is highly uncertain.

In the meantime, the clear winner is Germany, who has benefitted immensely from the euro. The great losers are Greece, Spain, Portugal, and other countries with smaller economies and a weak industrial base. Those who opted out of the euro, such as the UK and Sweden, have probably benefitted, since imports and exports to the rest of Europe have been simplified, and they have been able to control their own monetary policy.

Uneasy Progress: Increased Inequality and Mobility

The EUs social charter, as envisioned by Jacques Delors, one of the original architects behind the EU, is based on a fundamental vision of basic economic and social security for all Europeans. According to the *New Internationalist*, however, "This social vision was also tied to the notion of a 'free' single market encompassing all of Europe. Compatibility between the market and society was simply assumed — a fatal error not just for the EU but in the entire approach of mainstream social democracy." [17] Indeed, free trade is no guarantee for social security or prosperity, not to speak of economic democracy and environmental sustainability.

While the creation of a common European market has brought the continent closer together and has made war less likely, the free market has had different effects on different parts of the Union. At the inception of the EU, large transfer payments were made to assist the poorer nations, such as Greece and Portugal, to develop infrastructure, health, and education, and to support agriculture. However, since these funds were not primarily used to modernize the industrial sector and make the countries competitive, the long-term effect of a common market made the poorer nations less competitive and more dependent on aid.

The initial boom created by transfer payments from the rest of the EU was followed by another capital infusion from cheap loans after the formation of the common currency. These were both short-lived stimuli, and the resources were not used to increase labor productivity but to create infrastructure and support consumption. In Spain, the economic growth was due to more people entering the market place, rather than labor becoming more efficient. The loans given to Spain resulted in a property boom with real estate prices going up, but not in industrial growth. "To be sure," writes Bill Dawidow in *Atlantic Monthly*, "the economies of southern Europe would have struggled even without being yoked to the euro. But I think it's reasonable to blame the euro for turning those problems into a catastrophe." The euro, he argues, enticed these countries to borrow money at very low interest rates. "Real estate bubbles," he continues, "were just one of the consequences. Cheap money enabled countries to run up big debts, pay high wages to government employees, and create false prosperity that encouraged consumers to spend and borrow."[18]

Now that transfer payments have been reduced and borrowed money is due for repayment, the real effect of EU's free-market system can finally be evaluated. Free trade between unequal economic partners, such as between Mexico and the United States, or between Germany and Portugal, divides the economy into high- and low-income zones where industries in lower-income countries cannot compete with those in the industrially advanced nations. After the North American Free Trade Agreement (NAFTA) was signed between the United States, Canada, and Mexico, creating the largest free-trade economy in the world, the Mexican economy started deteriorating quickly. Economist Erik Reinert terms this three-stage process "de-industrialization, de-agriculturalization and de-population." As a result, the Mexican farm economy was devastated. Local staples like maize and beans had to compete against the much cheaper imports from the North. Soon millions of illegal immigrants from rural areas migrated to the US to seek work; in many local areas only people over sixty still remain.

A less dramatic but similar development is happening within the EU itself. Parts of the EU are becoming a miniature developing world, with similar problems as developing countries in Asia and Africa. In these areas, the industry and technology sectors cannot compete internationally or within the EU, and so they are forced into mainly promoting agriculture, services, and tourism. Since no country in history, apart from some island tax havens, have been able to prosper without a strong industry, the future for these countries is grim.

With free trade and the mobility of capital and labor, people move from one area to another in search of work. This movement of people is advantageous to corporations, since it brings a steady flow of labor, and, in the short run, to the mobile laborers and their families. But this free flow across national borders also creates problems for countries, local communities, and individual families. Even though Norway is not a full member of the EU, a large percentage of the nurses and waitresses working in Norway are from Sweden, while a large percentage of carpenters and painters are Polish men, who are forced to stay away from their families for months at a time. Such labor mobility across national borders contributes to an increased black economy, a lowering of wages, and a reduction in skilled labor in the mobile laborer's home country. In addition, it adds stress to the families concerned.

Another complex side effect of European free trade has been the "brain drain" phenomenon—the outflow of highly qualified workers from key industrial areas is increasingly becoming a challenge for many countries of the Eurozone. Poor career prospects, constraints on freedom, low wages, unemployment, bad living and working conditions, social insecurity, and political instability are just some of the factors that play into young professionals' decisions to leave their home countries and seek more profitable environments elsewhere.

The direct negative consequences of brain drain includes the loss of intellectual potential and the indirect loss of economic investment, diminished tax revenues, and staff shortages in economically disadvantaged areas. While the brain drain exodus is economically beneficial for the richer regions, the poorer regions experience a loss of human capital in the form of a reduced skilled labor force, which is vital to the development of society. In the case of skilled labor, researcher and author Gazi Mahabubul Alam recognizes this emigration as "essentially providing personal benefits for individuals rather than public benefits." [19]

Recipient countries with positive economic growth patterns, such as Germany and countries outside the Eurozone, benefit from the brain drain through decreased labor shortages, enhanced average labor skills, and decreased wage pressure in the national labor market.

In the case of Europe, three major directions of brain drain are apparent:

- From developing countries to the EU
- Inter-European (East-West) flows
- From Europe to the US, and, more recently, to developing countries

When the financial crisis struck in 2008, the knowledge economy was one of the greatest victims. In its aftermath, a major common concern is the inequality of European wages. Some say "equal pay for equal work" in the Eurozone might be a remedy, but this is more often not the case.

Inequality is not only growing between countries but between people inside the same countries. Since economic liberalization has been widely accepted within Europe, taxation policies and government rules have become increasingly regressive, favoring the rich. People who work pay higher taxes than those who live on what used to be called unearned income, such as capital gains and interest from investments. Social safety nets are being dismantled. As some politicians argue, we no longer can afford to pay for many aspects of the social security system, while the rich are getting richer, taking an increasingly larger piece of the economic pie.

Historically, the European economy, and especially the Nordic economic model, reduced economic disparity by letting the trade unions and employers negotiate wages. If they did not come to an agreement, the unions would go on strike, and if they still did not agree, the state would mediate a solution agreeable to both parties. According to Norwegian historian Edvard Mogstad, "This system gradually improved the wages of the workers and worked quite well for decades until the 1980s, when European capital and industry got an upper hand by following a Thatcher/ Reagan-style neo-liberal agenda." [20] This point of view is supported by the Organization for Economic Cooperation and Development (OECD), which states that "inequality in Europe has risen quite substantially since the mid-1980s. While the EU enlargement process has contributed to this, it is not the only explanation since inequality has also increased within a 'core' of 8 European countries." [21] Although the increasing wealth disparity in Europe is troubling, it is inevitable given the economic policies pursued by the EU and its member states.

How to Unite the Many Nations of Europe?

The unity of a nation or the international unity among many nations, such as within the EU, is generally built around certain sentiments, whether religious, linguistic, or cultural. The vast continent of the Soviet Union was united based on an anti-exploitation sentiment among the peasantry against the rich. This sentiment fueled the Bolshevik Revolution and established a strong communist state. At the end of the Cold War, however, when the proletariat's dream of justice and equality had become an oppressive regime, Marx and Lenin's socialist ideals were no longer able to unify the nation. Consequently, the Soviet Union broke up into many nations united around linguistic, religious, ethnic, and geographical sentiments. Is it too farfetched to consider that something similar could happen in Europe?

Countries with less socioeconomic disparity have traditionally shown rapid economic growth. Examples of this are the Scandinavian countries. Norway, for example, is one of the most equitable nations in the world, but in the current economic climate, economic inequality is increasing even in Norway, and even more so in the rest of Europe. Instead of a lessening in income disparity and widespread economic development, countries and people are getting increasingly polarized between the haves and have-nots. Dreams of social cohesion and peace are not enough to maintain economic and social stability in Europe. In order to maintain peace, relative prosperity has to be widespread among the countries of the Union.

There are also problems on the political front. As the Union has increased in size from its original six member countries to twenty-eight, the distance between the political decision-makers in Brussels and the people on the streets of Sweden, Portugal, Ireland, Romania, and Italy has increased. As the economic crisis has intensified, there is a growing perception among people in the various member nations that the European Parliament is less responsive to people's interests and is instead increasingly beholden to the interests of corporate lobbyists. In the words of antipoverty campaigner John Hilary:

> Having spent much of the past 15 years fighting for fairer policies within the European Union, I now have a profound distrust of its institutions. Bitter experience has taught me just how great is the democratic deficit at the heart of the European program. The

EU's supreme policymaking forum, the Council of Ministers, meets in camera without any form of external oversight. The powerful but unelected European Commission closely follows the steer given to it by the tens of thousands of corporate lobbyists who operate within the Brussels bubble. The European Parliament (EP) remains a toothless wonder, even after the recent Lisbon Treaty reforms. [22]

The EU struggles with deeper and more complex problems than mere historical tensions and incompatibilities between market and social forces. These fundamental problems are systemic and inherent in the original political architecture of the EU and the market economy it serves.

Increased Mistrust

In the 1980s, the disintegration of the countries behind the Iron Curtain was thought of as unthinkable. Yet by the early 1990s, the unthinkable became inevitable. The eastern European leap from the unthinkable to the inevitable makes this watershed historical moment an important backdrop in our attempt to contemplate the future history of Europe.

Indeed, the disintegration of the European Union was unthinkable just a few years ago, but now that the UK has decided to leave the union, this has, according to many experts, become a real possibility. The European economic crisis has demonstrated that the risk of a disintegrated EU is not just a rhetorical device employed by nervous politicians to enforce austerity measures. The problems currently facing the EU are real, and they are not solely economic. Europe's political system is also facing opposition by the people whose futures it was created to protect. Statistics show that political engagement and public trust in the EU has never been lower.

Fears that the Eurozone might enter into a new recession are real. This raises a number of fundamental questions about the future of both the EU and the euro. Economists, politicians, and common people alike are asking themselves: Just how strong is the economic and political foundation the Eurozone is built upon?

Elector participation in the Eurozone is at its lowest point in history, prompting many to question the motives of the political decision-makers and how democratic and sound their decision-making processes are. The financial crisis has sharply reduced the life expectancy of governments and inspired new populist parties opposed to the EU. The public mood has become a quiet chorus of pessimism and anger.

The latest Future of Europe survey funded by the European Commission and published in April of 2012 showed that most people agree that the EU is a decent place to live, but the lack of confidence in the economic performance of the Union and its capacity to play a major role in global politics is increasing. More than six out of ten Europeans are now convinced that the lives of those who are children today will be more difficult than the lives of people of their own generation.

Even more alarming, almost 90 percent of Europeans see a big gap between what the public wants and what their governments do. Only a third of Europeans feel that their vote counts in the EU and only 18 percent of Italians and 15 percent of Greeks feel that their vote counts even in their own countries. [23]

What will happen to the EU if impoverished states such as Portugal, Italy, Spain, and Greece quit the euro, cut their losses, and chart a new economic path with different economic policies? As the Soviet experience demonstrated, not only the lack of reform but more importantly a series of misguided reforms from the center itself can also lead to disintegration of an economic union or a country. In times of crisis, politicians are in search of a silver bullet to solve all problems. But when the problems are more systemic than the superficial solutions contained in the proposed bail-out reforms, these sudden measures can easily become the cause of further problems.

It is not only possible that the EU will disintegrate from the periphery, as it already has started to do, but it could even disintegrate from within the center itself. Yes, some economists have even predicted that Germany, the heart of the union itself, could, because of its close ties to the euro, be a substantial cause of an eventual collapse.

The euro has become a symbol of the crisis Europe is facing. As economist Paul Krugman has pointed out, a common currency requires a strong common political and cultural system, and unlike the United States, Krugman maintains, Europe lacks the most important ingredients for a common currency. "America has a currency union that works," he writes, "and we know why it works: because it coincides with a nation—a nation with a big government, a common language, and a shared culture. Europe has none of those things." [24]

Will the European Union, with powerful countries such as Germany and France at the helm, weather its current economic storms and maintain its current formation, or will this dynamic and diverse continent break up into more decentralized economic regions? Will we see the development of a Nordic Economic Union? Will the British Isles regroup into a localized economic zone? Or will Europe's old national sentiments flare up and the union splinter into many nations, each fending for its own? What we do know is that the current union is not working as it was theoretically intended, because its castle walls have been built on the unstable foundation of neoliberalism and capitalist free trade. Indeed, not all European citizens have been applauding the EU and its existence.

Why Norway Refused to Join the EU

In 1972, the streets of Norway were filled with protests against the EU when by referendum a majority of Norwegian voters rejected EU membership. The same situation repeated itself in 1994. Throughout the years, opposition against the EU has been dominated by political groups from the center-left, and especially by farmers, fishermen, and workers on the coasts and in the north. These early protests against the EU reflected, with almost farsighted precision, many of the same topics discussed today in countries like Portugal, Greece, and Ireland: lack of democracy, lack of economic justice, lack of freedom and independence, and lack of concerns for the environment.

According to the Norwegian movement against the EU (Nei til EU), which has been active for the past four decades, the main reasons for remaining an independent nation are as follows:

- Democracy: The authority of new areas is transferred from the nation states to the EU. The citizens of the EU are rarely aware of what is happening behind closed doors in Brussels. Consequently, only around 45 percent of the people of the EU participate in elections. As an independent nation, Norway has a better participatory democracy.
- Solidarity: As a strong force in the World Trade Organization (WTO), the EU is pressuring poor countries into allowing multinational companies to set up shop. The EU also enters into unfair trade agreements with former colonies and has reduced its aid to poor countries in Africa. The EU pressures poor countries to accept liberalization and privatization of the economy.

- Environment: The EU is not effectively helping to solve the world's environmental problems, such as global warming. The EU's economic policies lead to centralization and large-scale production, resulting in overconsumption of resources, increased transport, and pollution. The EU has proven to be ineffective in solving global environmental issues and too big and cumbersome to solve local issues.

- Freedom: Since the signing of the Lisbon Treaty, many of the EU's foreign-policy decisions are made during elite political dinners in Brussels, and these decisions increasingly favor rich countries. Before membership, Sweden used to vote for the interests of the south in the UN, but as an EU member, Sweden rarely does so. As an outsider, Norway can remain an independent voice in the world.[25]

Two themes have been fundamental to Norwegians against membership in the EU since the Treatise of Rome was signed in 1957: 1) the perception that democratic values at the national as well as the local level are best retained outside the EU, and 2) skepticism towards the market liberalism embedded in the EU constitution. As we have noted, these concerns have become increasingly prevalent in new member countries, especially those at the periphery of power in Brussels, and in those countries suffering the most from the European crisis, such as Portugal and Spain.

According to the No to EU movement in Norway, the EU has largely designed a society "where local and national communities are replaced by companies and banks as the fundamental building blocks." This popular movement has been supported by the majority of Norwegians over the years and has been very critical of the fundamentals in the EU's economic program, namely the four economic freedoms mentioned above. These neoliberal policies, it is argued, restrict local authorities and states from the right "to limit the market freedoms if it is necessary in order to achieve important social purposes." In other words, this movement has, from its very inception in the early 1970s, pointed directly to the heart of EUs weak links as an economic and social Union, namely its tendency to centralize and monopolize both economic and political power.

According to the No to EU movement, "The Norwegian Parliament, like Westminster, is far from the individual voter: Brussels, however, is much farther away and too detached from democratic control. If we want politics based on solidarity values, and if we wish to take the people with us on that endeavor, we must begin at the level where democratic power is real. This is a thesis of equal significance to both Britain and Norway."[26] Indeed, similar concerns are echoed amongst EU skeptics all over Europe today, from Ireland to Portugal.

EU Trade Policies

While the EU has maintained a common market, it has also pushed other countries to adapt free-trade policies and not to impose tariffs on exports from the EU. If countries would impose tariffs on EU exports, it would make those goods more costly and less competitive. Therefore, the EU has argued, it is in the best interest of the Union to always insist on free trade.

However, these policies are not totally consistent, but are rather an expression of political expediency. In areas where the EU has a comparative advantage, they push for free trade. In areas where the EU cannot compete, it imposes severe import restrictions on other countries. In particular, agricultural products are heavily restricted. Some examples:

For key agricultural exports like sugar, rice, and dairy products, the EU maintained tariffs of 350–900%.

The European Union pays tomato farmers a minimum price that is higher than the world price while the processors are also subsidized. As a result EU tomatoes "dumped" into West Africa now make up 80 percent of the local supply and have nearly destroyed the domestic industry.

Due to the skewed policy of stopping imports of products developing countries could compete in, developing-country exports have not increased significantly over the past forty years, with the exception of East Asia and Central America. South America, Central and Eastern Europe, and Africa's share in total world exports was actually lower in 2002 than in 1960.[27]

In other words, free trade conducted by the EU or the US in poor countries with the help of the World Bank and the World Trade Organization is often applied selectively and only when it benefits the powerful industrial nations.

A few years ago, the EU reformed its Common Agricultural Policy (CAP) to discourage overproduction by big farms and instead encourage "preservation of traditional rural landscapes, and bird and wildlife conservation". This policy sounds nice on paper, but in the real world, the four freedoms underlying the EU charter will make capital-strong farmers from foreign countries compete with local cheese makers on small milk farms in Romania. Hence, free trade in the form of the free movement of people, capital, and goods now inundates the Romanian countryside—from England, Denmark, and Germany they come to start megafarms to raise crops for export.

In Transylvania, Romania, cheese farmer Ion Duculesu operates a small dairy farm that is unlikely to meet EU health and safety standards. He tells BBC reporter Mark Mardell that he will eventually have to buy machinery in order to compete with foreign companies, but he wants to carry on milking by hand as he has always done. "They'll fine us," he says, "and we'll go out of business, so I will be out of a job. But I've always worked with animals since I was a child so I will still raise them." In this way, the local economy's interests are often pitted against more powerful economic interests from abroad. [28]

Would it not be better if Brussels could help Ion Duculesu and other small Romanian farmers expand and modernize their own production while maintaining their jobs and traditions? But that is not Brussels' job. Instead, Brussels's policies in the name of market freedom let farmers from England, Denmark and Germany invade the Romanian country-side, thus ensuring that the future of Romania's agricultural economy will be an uneven and unfair playing field.

Conclusion

Both the EU and, in a broader context, the financial institutions that have shaped economic policy during the latter part of the twentieth century and into the twenty-first, were based on the idea that prosperity for all will promote peace and stability. If there were no trade wars or unjust treatments of countries, there would be no need or incentive to engage in war. The best way to achieve this, it was thought, was by the introduction of free trade and open markets. These markets were thought of as being self-regulating, or possibly requiring some limited government intervention, and were in the end going to give economic prosperity to all.

In this way, the free markets that were supposed to achieve this reality were built into the very foundation of the EU, making all of Europe a common free market. Internationally, a similar free-trade agenda was established through the WTO, the World Bank, the IMF, and various bilateral trade agreements.

The premise that widespread prosperity will lead to peace is, at least in theory, probably undeniable. The weak link in this argument is whether free and open markets actually lead to prosperity for all, or rather to a concentration of wealth, making some areas rich and other areas poor.

As outlined earlier, there is increasing evidence that free markets benefit those who are already rich and lead to increasing economic disparities, the very condition that free markets were supposed to remove. Given the fundamental free-market rules that formed the basis of the European Union, the current polarization of wealth and the financial crisis was inevitable. The assumption that the capitalist market, the environment, and people's interests are compatible lies at the heart of the EU experiment and also embodies the Union's inherent limitations and possible failure. If these conclusions are correct, then the continued economic integration of Europe will not lead to peace and prosperity but to inequality, increased environmental degradation, fragmentation, protest, and perhaps even war.

New economic policies are needed to empower each region and country to develop its industrial and technological potential, and to sustainably utilize and maintain local resources in order to compete on equal terms in an open market. We cannot put economic toddlers in a boxing ring with heavyweight corporate champions and expect fair trade and fair wages to be the result.

One of the main reasons we have spent considerable time in this book analyzing the EU is that the European economy is often hailed as the best in the world and worthy of emulation. However, the EU economy does not hold all of the answers to the world's economic and environmental problems. Since the very foundation of the EU is built on free markets, and these free markets are creating conditions that often have gone counter to the prosperity and unity of Europe, a new union based on different ideals and policies will sooner or later have to emerge. Economies are complex and simple solutions often go wrong. The idea that free markets will solve all economic and social problems is as false as saying that centralized planning will solve all our problems. We need to accept the inherent complexities of human and economic interaction, and carefully build new systems and institutions that are not based on dogmatic theories but on a careful study of society, the environment and the consequences of our past and present economic policies. As we study and learn from history, we will become more humble, and we will be better able to rebuild an economy that is not the conqueror of people and the environment but rather the servant of people and the environment. We will return to these new economic ideas in the final chapters of this book.

Part III:
Capitalism: Its Myths and False
Promises

Chapter Seven

Free Markets and Fictitious Commodities

When the institutions of money rule the world, it is perhaps inevitable that the interests of money will take precedence over the interests of people. What we are experiencing might best be described as a case of money colonizing life. To accept this absurd distortion of human institutions and purpose should be considered nothing less than an act of collective, suicidal insanity.

— David Korten

FREE MARKETS ARE NEVER really free. All economic markets follow certain rules that define the market, and such rules are given by and enforced by society. As economist Ha-Joon Chang puts it, "A market looks free only because we so unconditionally accept its underlying restrictions that we fail to see them."[1]

Since it is pointless to critique something that does not exist, for the purpose of this chapter we will adapt the common usage of the phrase "free market" as a system where:

- the market allocates resources and government interference is kept to a minimum;
- where prices are set by competition and speculation, whether it is done by small players or large monopolistic companies;
- where trade is free with a minimum of customs tariffs or other trade restrictions;

- and where intellectual property is protected and enforced.

Today, the free-market economy is more or less taken for granted as the only form of economy suited for a modern society. And yet there is much evidence pointing toward the fact that a free market is less than a perfect economy and often leads to wastage of resources, increased inequality, poverty in the developing world, and destruction of the world's environment.

While there is much criticism that can be directed towards free markets, and this book has already brought up quite a lot, in this chapter we will focus on three specific critiques of free markets. The first critique is based on the works of Karl Polanyi, who provided one of the most comprehensive critiques of free markets ever written. His main work, the highly influential *The Great Transformation*,[2] was published in 1944.

The second critique, which is actually an extension of the critique made by Polanyi, is that free markets set themselves above both society and nature. Markets are unable to calculate the value of things not sold and bartered, and hence the most valuable things we have, such as the capacity of nature to produce food from sunshine, water, and carbon dioxide, go unaccounted for.

The third critique is based on historical records of development and is in part inspired by the works of economists Erik S. Reinert and Ha-Joon Chang.

Karl Polanyi and Fictitious Commodities

Karl Polanyi defines a commodity as a product produced for sale in a market. The problem, according to Polanyi, is that free markets by necessity have to include labor, land, and money which are not commodities and do not naturally behave like commodities in a market. In the foreword to the 2001 edition of the book [3], Nobel Prize winning economist Joseph Stieglitz writes:

> Labor is simply the activity of human beings, land is subdivided nature, and the supply of money and credit in modern societies is necessarily shaped by governmental policies. Modern economics starts by pretending that these fictitious commodities will behave in the same way as real commodities, but Polanyi insists that this sleight of hand has fatal consequences. It means

that economic theorizing is based on a lie, and this lie places human society at risk. [4]

Polanyi argues that the self-regulating market is a totally new concept and a reversal of previous trends of development:

> True, no society can exist without a system that ensures order in the production and distribution of goods. But that does not imply the existence of separate economic institutions; historically, the economic order has been a function of the social order. Neither under tribal, feudal, or mercantile conditions was there a separate economic system in society. Nineteenth-century society, in which economic activity was isolated and imputed to a distinctive economic motive, is a dramatic departure. [5]

In past societies, the economic system was absorbed in the prevailing social system and was and formed and shaped by it. Markets in commodities have always existed, but they were regulated according to the norms of society. What has changed is that the relationship has been turned on its head: markets are now regulating society.

A self-regulating market that includes land and labor requires that human beings and nature itself are turned into commodities, and this leads to the destruction of both society and the natural environment. In the words of Karl Polanyi:

> [L]abor, land and money are essential elements of industry; they also must be organized in markets; in fact, these markets form an absolute vital part of the economic system. But labor, land and money are obviously not commodities; the postulate that anything bought and sold must have been produced for sale is emphatically untrue in regard to them. In other words, according to the empirical definition of a commodity they are not commodities. Labor is only another name for a human activity which goes with life itself, which in its turn is not produced for sale but for entirely different reasons, nor can that activity be detached from the rest of life, be stored or mobilized; land is only another name for nature, which is not produced by man; actual money, finally, is merely a token of purchasing power which, as a rule, is not produced at all, but comes into being

through the mechanism of banking or state finance. None of
them is produced for sale. The commodity description of labor,
land and money is entirely fictitious.[6]

If a market is to appropriate the role of organizing society, then the vital
aspects of society must be under its sway: human labor, nature and her
resources, productive capital and money. Like other commodities, these
had to be subjected to supply and demand. Economic liberalism was
thus the primary organizing force during the nineteenth century. Its
goal was to turn the ideology of self-regulating markets into a reality by
enforcing free trade and laissez-faire. The market required the creation of
three institutions: the poor had to be freed from ties to community and
geography and organized into a labor market; nature, the resources and
land, had to change hands and be used according to international free
trade; and money had to be regulated by the market, not controlled by
the government, and the gold standard was seen as the only guarantee
that an international market system could be trusted.

Free trade implied that industrial England would sacrifice its agricultural communities and import grains grown more cheaply elsewhere.
The labor market, regulated by hunger, would adjust its price according to the reduced price of grain, and this (in theory) would allow the
manufacturer to produce goods more cheaply, as he must, in order to
keep up with the deflation that the gold standard would create — if
money was controlled by the market then demand implied deflation,
and the government could not simply print more money as long as the
gold standard was in place. In the countryside, gold was rarely used for
commerce because it was not available, but taxes had to be paid in metal.
People sacrificed everything of value to the tax collector, eventually
paying with pots and pans.

It is impossible to treat labor as a commodity without affecting the
human beings that are the bearers of this commodity. While disposing
of their labor power, their physical, psychological and moral sides get
disposed of as well. As a result human beings are removed from protective cultural institutions and "die as the effect of acute social dislocation
through vice, perversion, crime, and starvation."[7] The identity of a person
is distorted and replaced by an alienated automaton. Smith and Owen
foresaw this and, after the market system was in place, there arose an
endless stream of humanistic writers who detailed the destruction of
the humanity of the workers, Marx being the most influential.

The effect on nature would be equally grave. Polanyi predicted that treating nature as a commodity would "reduce it to its elements, neighborhoods and landscapes defiled, rivers polluted, military safety jeopardized, the power to produce food and raw materials destroyed."[8] Land is not simply an economic commodity; it is nature herself. Focusing on its economic value and deny its existential value has a disastrous effect on human psychology: it creates an economic outlook that sees things abstractly, according to monetary value. Markets delete the realness of land in its valuation, and in doing so, the relationship that land has in a healthy society is lost. On the one hand, rural life and culture was gradually destroyed. The social ties that had developed over hundreds or even thousands of years, which held society together without the need for regulation, were dissolved so that land could be fluid and move according to the control of a market system. The ground upon which society was founded was thus fractured and sometimes removed altogether. The productive role of land and nature in providing services upon which the economy itself depended was threatened. The knowledge of how to live with the land, how to produce food in a harmonious way, was also lost and ecological destruction became inevitable.

Finally, treating money as a commodity caused society to "periodically liquidate business enterprises, for shortage and surfeits of money would prove as disastrous to business as floods and droughts in primitive society."[9] Money is not simply another commodity, for if it is in limited supply then trade becomes impossible and society becomes parsimonious. Marx saw it as an abstract representation of human labor. Regardless of the philosophical completeness of this definition, the monetarization of society was, in reality, the market regulation of the productive capacity of industrial society. That is to say, it made economic productivity into a commodity to be organized in the market.

These predictions, made in 1949, have come true with a vengeance. Polanyi sums up his conclusion thus: "[N]o society could stand the effects of such a system of rude fictions even for the shortest stretch of time unless its human and natural substance as well as its business organization was protected against the ravages of this satanic mill."[10]

We can further sum up Polanyi's critique of free markets as follows: It is a logical fallacy to expand the concept of commodities to be regulated by the market to include human beings, money, and nature itself, none of which are actual commodities. The consequences of treating people and nature as commodities are catastrophic and destructive to both. Treating money as commodities creates financial crisis and destroys businesses. Markets are simply the way human beings trade commodities. Both human beings and nature exist separately from markets, but markets cannot exist outside of nature and human beings.

Distorting Reality

Markets are human constructs, and the rules that control them are also made by people. Markets are organized ways for humans to cooperate and interact in ways they agree upon. There is nothing fundamental in this mutual agreement, and it can take various forms. Thus markets are subject to decisions made by human beings. Furthermore, human beings are part of nature and are subjected to the laws of nature. This is the humanistic and ecological way to view the economy.

The modern market, however, has disrupted this holistic role of the economy. In market capitalism, economic forces are expected to dominate and decide the fate of both human beings and nature. Blind adherence to market ideology leads to these kinds of distortions. But nature is far too complex to be governed by a few simplistic market rules of human interaction, and any attempt to do so will, as we have seen, lead to disastrous results. Individual profit motive is not a sufficient criterion to provide for the long-term progress and survival of humanity and life itself. What is required is a system that provides for maximum utilization and rational distribution of resources, in a way where both humanity and the entire ecosystem thrives, not only in the short term but for generations to come. Markets are distinctly unsuitable to achieve such a balance between economy and ecology.

Moral and Humanitarian Considerations

In human society, ethical, moral, and humanitarian considerations are always relevant to scientific and economic progress. Economics, therefore, cannot simply be a study of what is, but rather a vision of what we want the future to be. It cannot be seen separately from ethical and moral issues, and needs to tackle issues such as welfare and inequality.

To pretend that economics is neutral and does not involve political and moral decisions is to deceive ourselves.

The Forgotten Contributions of Nature

As we noted earlier, most classical economists considered value to be produced exclusively by human labor—the work done by nature did not add any value to a product. If a person thus carries water up a hill and fills a cistern, this action, according to classical economic theory, creates value, whereas if nature does the same thing by evaporating sea water and depositing it in the cistern in the form of rain, then no value is added.

The moment Mother Nature does not provide something for us, such as heat, we need to use human labor to create a heat source. If it is cold in the winter, we need to have a stove and to find fuel to warm our houses. If this has a value, why does direct sunlight not have a value too, even if we do not pay for it?

According to neoclassical economists, the prices determined by the market also account for the value of the services provided by nature. But in reality that is not the case. The studies cited earlier concluded that the value of nature's services in production is many times the global GDP. This, in effect, proves that the value of nature is not adequately reflected in market prices. One might contend that resources such as sunlight are virtually limitless — their use does not diminish the supply. However, the studies did not include such "unlimited" natural resources, because firstly, their inclusion would have made the study an illogical critique of the market, and secondly, the value of sunlight is immeasurable since life cannot exist without it. The studies did include, however, those of nature's services that are being destroyed due to their exploitation. The financial worth of nature's contribution to the economy is literally immeasurable, but unfortunately the earth's natural environment is being depleted at an alarming rate. The environmental crisis is a direct result of how grossly underrepresented nature is in the market economy. Without photosynthesis, plants could not grow and there would be no food. Human beings may plant the seeds, but the food is directly produced by nature without human intervention. We cannot replicate this even if we wanted to. Since we depend upon food for our survival, nature's contribution is fundamental and irreplaceable; it is impossible to place a value on it.

If we are to have a sustainable future on this planet, nature's contributions have to be included in economic science. So far, the market's short-term profit motives have enabled us to destroy far more natural wealth than we are producing. The clear-cutting of Amazon rain forest to provide grazing land for cattle is an example of such folly. Unless we calculate the economic value of a rainforest and compare it to the value of cattle, we cannot make an informed decision whether the project is really in our best interest or not. Some economists have started to make such calculations. And what kind of economic value are we talking about? According to an article in *Time* magazine, "research cited in the TEEB, [The Economics of Ecosystems and Diversity] report, an annual investment of $45 billion to biodiversity conservation worldwide could safeguard about $5 trillion in ecosystem services — a benefit-to-cost ratio of 100 to 1." [11] Hence, it is clearly more economically and ecologically rational to safeguard the biodiversity of the rainforest than to let short-term cattle-industry profits graze it into annihilation.

Markets can also not account for the intrinsic value of plants or animals. A flower has value and a purpose, even if human beings do not directly profit from its existence. Markets can trade in commodities that are owned, but not with the processes of nature (regardless if they are vital or trivial), because natural processes are part of nature, they are not made by humans and cannot be owned; they are grown and must be experienced through being. This concept, which is far beyond the present scope of economics, requires a completely new approach to economic theory. [12]

Free Markets: The Historical Record

The best way to test an economic model is to devise policies based on its principles and then test the effects of these policies. We will thus take a closer look at what free-market economists advise poor countries to do to become wealthy, and then see what happens to countries that follow their advice. We will then compare these results to what wealthy countries actually did to achieve their wealth status.

The open-market policies summed up in the Washington Consensus are:

- Remove all restrictions to trade by removing import duties and import quotas.
- Let the local currency be freely convertible to other currencies, and allow it to find its own value.
- Remove subsidies to local industries.
- Remove all subsidies on essential commodities so that local prices will be equal to internationally traded prices.

- Allow the free flow of capital, including foreign investments and the free repatriation of profits from such investments.
- Deregulate financial institutions so that interest rates can be determined by the market.
- Abolish regulations that restrict the free entry of new firms along with any measure that restricts competition.
- Privatize all state enterprises.
- Secure intellectual property rights.

The aim of most of these policies is to try to create the "perfect market," which allegedly will benefit all participants.[13]

Since these policies have been implemented in many countries, it is easy to determine the effect they have had. The results show that the effects vary greatly depending on the competiveness of the local industry.

Countries like Germany, Sweden, and the United States, who opened up their markets in the late 1970s, have clearly benefitted from free trade. However, states that had poorly developed industries, or industries of average efficiency, did very poorly.

Historical Evidence

Let us take a look at Mongolia. According to the research of Norwegian economist Eric S. Reinert, Mongolia had developed a large industrial base during the twentieth century.[14] It may not have been competitive on the international stage, but it provided employment and produced goods efficiently enough for the local market. After the collapse of the communist bloc, Mongolia was approached by the World Bank with a promise that economic prosperity would automatically follow if the country opened up its borders and specialized in areas where it had comparative advantage.

It turned out that Mongolia's comparative advantage was in cattle, but the amount of land available for grazing was limited. It was an area of diminishing return, since it was impossible to expand the activity without reducing its efficiency. Soon the industrial sector, which had slowly been building up over the past fifty years, was completely destroyed. Between 1991 and 1995 most of Mongolia's industry was effectively annihilated. The country's industries had effectively disappeared, beginning with the most advanced. Even the production of goods where imports had not supplanted local production was down drastically. The production of bread was down 71 percent, and the production of books and newspapers 79 percent. In other words, Mongolians ate and read less than before. In a few short years, real wages were almost halved and unemployment was rampant. The country's imports exceeded the value of exports by a factor of two, and the real interest rate, corrected for inflation, was 35 percent.[15] As the displaced workers struggled to survive, they were forced into cattle herding. The land had already more cattle than it could support and in the year 2000 between two and three million animals died due to lack of adequate grazing lands.

Other countries have faced similar fates. When Russia, at the recommendation of the IMF and the United States, adopted the "shock therapy" of suddenly opening up its borders to international trade, the economy collapsed. The GDP shrank by 40% between 1991 and 1998, and half the industrial jobs were lost. Poverty, until then relatively unknown, reached unprecedented levels. Hyperinflation set in and state industries were sold off to party cronies.

This has not been the case only with former communist states: most countries who have opened up their markets have had similar experiences. In Peru, the implementation of market reform wiped out the industrial sector. As in the case of Mongolia, the opening of their markets destroyed local industries, leaving the country solely dependent on the export of raw materials and agricultural goods. These are activities of diminishing returns that put pressure on the wages of a country. As a result, the average person's income was reduced by half.

The countries that are often quoted as the prime examples of the success of free markets, the "Asian tiger" economies, such as Japan, South Korea, Taiwan, and of late, China, are actually examples of the opposite. All these countries protected their local markets, allowed free export but restricted imports, and imposed severe restrictions on the movement of capital and foreign investments. None of them followed the policies recommended by neoclassical economics. Why would these economies, which did not follow the model of free markets, be used as examples of successful use of that model? Perhaps because success stories were needed to justify the continued use of those policies, and since there were none from the countries that implemented the reforms the model insisted on, some sleight of hand was needed to show that the successful emerging markets had followed the advice of the Washington Consensus, when in fact they had not!

Going back to the beginning of the industrial revolution, what type of policies did the early industrialized countries follow? Let us start with Great Britain, where the industrial revolution started.

In the middle of the eighteenth century, the main exporters of textiles were India, China, and Europe, with China making up 33 percent and India and Europe 23 percent each.[16] At this time, Indian cloth was cheaper and better quality than the cloth produced in England. Even with the introduction of machines to mechanize the industry, such as Hargreaves' spinning frame (1764), Arkwright's spinning frame (1769), and Crompton's mule (1779), British textiles were not competitive on the world stage. If it had not been for extreme protectionist measures, the industrial revolution would have been stopped in its tracks. To protect the infant industry, duties on textiles were gradually raised until by 1813 they had reached 85 percent![17]

Britain was a prime example of infant-industry protection. It became an industrialized nation not by following but by violating the modern doctrines of free trade promoted by neoclassical economics. According to the free-trade theory, Britain should not have bothered to develop a domestic textile industry, since they were able to get Indian cotton for 50–60 percent below local prices. Had they followed this course, Britain would probably have remained a poor developing nation.

Other industrialized countries have followed closely in Britain's footsteps. Since the time of the first secretary of the US treasury, Alexander Hamilton, in 1790, the United States pursued a course of industrialization by protecting its budding industries with high tariffs. Hamilton understood that a country without industry is doomed to be poor and backward and thus set out to protect the infant industries until they were strong enough to stand on their own feet. This policy of protectionism lasted until well past the Second World War, when the United States was the world's largest economy and had the biggest industrial base.

In all its colonies, except the United States, Britain succeeded in preventing industrialization by forcing them to become exporters of raw materials and importers of British industrial output. As a result, the United States became the world's biggest economy and the most powerful nation, whereas the other colonies remained underdeveloped and are still far behind the industrial nations.

Most European countries followed in the footsteps of the United States. They realized quickly that a country needed an industrial base to become powerful. Germany, Sweden, Norway, Holland, France, and others imposed high tariffs on imports and effectively subsidized their infant industries until long after the Second World War. There were exceptions, such as Spain and Portugal. Relying on gold from their colonies in South America, they ignored the path to industrialization and instead protected their agriculture. As a result, they fell behind the other European nations and became relatively poor from a European standpoint.

The conclusion seems to be that the countries that followed the policies now promoted by neoclassical economics, whether in the past or at present, all ended up impoverished, whereas those who did the exact opposite flourished.

The lesson from history is clear: free trade is beneficial to industrially advanced countries, but for a country to reach that level of industrialization, it needs to protect its industries. In other words, free trade does not benefit everyone, but only those that are already ahead.

The Other Canon

In his book *How Rich Countries Got Rich… ….. and Why Poor Countries Stay Poor*, Eric Reinert explores different types of economic thought and concludes that the prevailing theories that rest on the work of Adam Smith, Ricardo, and other classical economists stand in contrast to what he calls the "Other Canon," a lineage of economic theory "that provided the guidelines for economic policy when today's presently wealthy nations made their historical transitions from poverty to wealth; for example, England's progression from 1485 to the post-Second World War Marshall Plan."[18]

Reinert claims that there are basically two types of economic theories. The first, from which the neoclassical school of economics is derived, takes metaphors from physics and builds up simple theoretical models that they apply to real-life economics— often, as we have seen, with very poor results. The other approach is experience based and often draws parallels with nature and the human body. It cannot be captured in simple economic formulae. One of the early proponents of this type of economics was Joseph Alois Schumpteter, who stated that "the general reader will have to make up his mind, whether he wants simple answers to his questions or useful ones — in this as in other economic matters he cannot have both."[19]

Reinert concludes that current neoclassical economics has chosen simplicity in favor of relevancy. It is detached from the real world and recommends policies based on its theoretical assumptions rather than what historically has proven to work. Victor Norman, an international trade theorist, claims that "One of the nice things about economics as a science is that it is just a way of thinking, factual knowledge does not exist."[20]

In the Other Canon tradition, knowledge on the macrolevel is achieved exclusively through detailed factual knowledge of what happens at the microlevel. In fact, this type of understanding requires the economist to move constantly between these levels, taking the elevator, so to speak, between the high and low levels of abstraction. Relevance is at the core, and form is only considered as it reflects relevant facts. Other Canon economics has a large toolbox and all tools that may reflect relevant reality are allowed. In today's standard economics, the focus is on mathematics and precision more than on the object of analysis itself, the economy. As has been observed by others, the toolbox and the incentive system of the profession combine to make most economists prefer to be accurately wrong than approximately right.[21]

Reinert agrees with our conclusions that the methods used by present-day industrialized countries to become rich is diametrically opposed to the advice they offer developing countries. He maintains that the poor developing countries are actually prevented from using the methods European countries used to get rich. Reinert explains: "History reveals how rich countries got rich by methods that by now have generally been outlawed by the 'conditionalities' of the Washington Consensus." [22]

Not surprisingly, the methods used by European countries to become rich were based on the Other Canon, not on neoclassical economics or the Washington Consensus. Historically, poor countries got rich by emulation. In other words, instead of selling raw materials to the industrialized nations and importing finished goods from them, they tried to imitate the industrialization process of those rich countries. In doing so, they fiercely protected their local markets. They banned importation of foreign goods or imposed punitive tariffs on them. This policy of trade protection and developing local industry was accepted policy up until the 1970s, when the wind changed towards neoclassical policies. Prior to that time, there was no free movement of labor, capital, goods, or services.

These two opposing views of economics were, after 1970, competing for dominance. The vision of the Other Canon was represented by Swedish economist Gunnar Myrdal. While Paul Samuelson and other economists of the neoclassical school set out to "prove" mathematically that free trade would lead to equal salaries all over the world, Myrdal was of the opinion that "free trade would increase already existing differences in incomes between rich and poor countries." [23] Reinert elaborates:

> The economic policies of the Washington Consensus — the basis for the economic policies imposed by the World Bank and the International Monetary Fund — are exclusively built on the type of theory which is represented by Paul Samuelson. The developments of the 1990s are in sharp conflict with Samuelson's ideas, but confirm Myrdal's assertion: rich nations as a group seem to converge into a cluster of wealthy countries, while the poor seem to converge towards poverty, with the gap between them rising. Paul Samuelson's theory seems to be able to explain what goes on inside the group of rich nations, while Gunnar Myral's theory seems to be able to explain the development of relative wealth between the group of rich nations and the group of poor nations. Samuelson's theory is not harmful to nations which have already established a comparative advantage in increasing returns. It is, however, extremely harmful to those nations that have not passed the mandatory passage point of a conscious industrialization policy. [24]

What the neoclassical theory lost, which was present in the Other Canon, was the importance of innovation, economic synergies, and the fact that different types of economic activities have various qualitative differences. With the free-market economy, the emphasis shifted from producing things to distributing things. Free trade became the bringer of prosperity rather than innovation and the proper utilization of human and natural resources, which had been the emphasis in the past.

According to the Other Canon, free trade is a double-edged sword. As early as the 1840s, Friedrich List opined that underdeveloped economies needed to protect their own industries through high customs tariffs in order to become competitive. After these economies gained partial success in industrialization, they should start to open up to the neighboring countries in regional trading blocs before finally opening their borders to free trade. If they opened up their economies too early to international competition, he argued, their budding industries would be destroyed. In recent history, this has proven the case for many developing countries that have been forced to take the path of globalization under pressure from the IMF and WTO.

Intellectual Property Rights

The policies inspired by the Washington Consensus are consistent in their attempts to create a perfect market where market forces alone determine the price of everything. However, there is one major policy that does the opposite, and that is the insistence on protection for Intellectual Property Rights (IPR).

Perfect competition removes opportunities for large profits, and squeezes the profit margins of businesses. Under those conditions it is impossible to innovate and to establish new factories and businesses. To solve this problem, there are two ways to create a temporary monopoly or protection that will allow new ideas to grow and new factories to become profitable before they are wiped out by competition.

The first is tariff protection, which allow the geographical spread of industry, and the second is patents, which allow new ideas to be protected for a period of time until everyone can use them. Both are tools to interfere with markets and create imperfect competition, and extraordinary profits that are not possible under perfect competition. According to Reinert:

> Today's economic policy and the Washington institutions vigorously defend only one of these institutions — the patents that create ever-increasing income flows to very few and very rich countries — while the very same Washington institutions vehemently prohibit the tools that allow the geographical spread of imperfect competition in the form of new industries to other countries. Protecting imperfect competition in the rich countries is accepted, but not in the poor.[25]

In essence, it is clear from past and recent history that free-market policies do not have the predicted results for poor countries. The policy of free trade does not benefit all countries equally. It is to the advantage of the developed countries, but goes against the long-term interest of countries that have yet to develop a strong industrial base.

Furthermore, all exports and economic activity are not equal. Exporting agricultural goods is not equivalent to exporting industrial goods. The former is a market that approximates perfect competition and gives diminishing returns, while innovation and industrial production is a market of imperfect competition and increasing returns. No company or country willingly encourages perfect competition, regardless of what neoclassical economic theory states; rather they go to great lengths to avoid it. Patent law is a way to prevent perfect competition and emulation, and to force poor countries to remain in the business of being producers of raw materials or exporters of unskilled labor.

Indeed, no industrialized nation has ever followed the policies of the Washington Consensus. They do their best to create imperfect competition or no competition for their own products. They compete through innovation, for which they take out patents to prevent others from emulating them. At the same time they insist that poor developing countries should follow a path of free trade, which reduces them to being exporters of raw materials and cheap labor, which is a market with close to perfect competition, diminishing returns, and constantly lowered salaries. In the few instances where the industrial countries are at a disadvantage compared to the developing countries, such as in food production, they have no qualms about breaking their own rules and often resort to massive subsidies.

Chapter Eight

Neoclassical Economics:
A Grand Theory on Shaky Grounds

Ultimately, every successful treatment for a medical problem begins with an accurate diagnosis. The sooner we face up to the fact that our financial system is suffering the equivalent of a neurological disorder, the sooner the real healing can begin.

—Mark Roeder

I N THE PREVIOUS CHAPTER we looked at so-called "free markets." In this chapter we will look at neoclassical economics (NCE), which is a theory of how the free market operates. NCE is not the only such theory. The Austrian school of economics has a different view on how free markets work. NCE is the most widely accepted theoretical framework to explain the operations of markets, however, and 90 percent of the world's economists subscribe to NCE. The remaining 10 percent are considered heterodox, a term that applies to everyone from New Keynesians and Marxists to followers of the Austrian School of Economics. Due to the prominence of NCE and its influence in guiding policy decisions in many countries, we have chosen to give special attention to this theory. Much of what will be discussed is of a technical nature, and some parts require a basic understanding of mathematics.

Why Economists Failed to See the Recession

During the recent economic crisis, there was much discussion about why economists failed to predict the onslaught of such a catastrophic downturn. One of the arguments put forward is that debt, the root of the Great Recession, does not form a part of economic theories of how markets work. Modern economic theory takes into account only the producer and the consumer and the flow of resources between the two. It totally ignores banks and debt, [1] considering these to be unimportant, merely "oil" to lubricate the working of the real economy. Debts these days, however, are very large compared to the size of the economy. Government debt alone, as we saw in the first chapter of this book, corresponds to the output of the entire economy for one whole year. While this is very high, private debt is even higher.

Furthermore, income from the financial sector used to be around 2 percent of GDP, but by 2010 it had reach 9 percent.[2] In spite of this, economic theory totally ignored this problem. The economic profession failed to see the recession because their models did not take debt, the root cause of the recession, into account.

However serious this omission may be, it is only the tip of the iceberg. In this chapter we will look at the foundation of neoclassical economic theory and demonstrate that assumptions of perfect markets are frequently applied in situations where no such assumptions can be made, and that there are serious problems with the underlying mathematical models that NCE relies on.

Faulty Assumptions: A Critical Review of the Assumptions of Perfect Markets

The world is too complex to analyze in its entirety, so whenever we try to understand the world we create models that simplify things enough for us to be able to grasp and analyze them. There is nothing wrong with this approach; indeed it is the only possible way for us to analyze the real world. In a sense, all the assumptions we make in a theory are unrealistic, in the sense that they are simplifications, but these simplifications can be considered justified if they help us come to a better understanding of the real world and how it functions.

For example, while calculating the velocity of a ball rolling down a slope, a physics student will probably ignore the friction of the ball against the slope. Technically speaking, this is incorrect, but it turns out that the friction is so minute compared to the force of gravity that puts the ball in motion that even if we ignore friction in our calculations, we get almost exactly the same result that we would have gotten if we had taken friction into account.

NEOCLASSICAL ECONOMICS 189

However, if we would have placed a rough piece of wood on the same slope, the friction of the rough piece of wood would have been significant. If we did not take it into account our calculations might be substantially off. For example, if we calculate that the wood will reach the end of the slope after one second, and the piece of wood can't even move at all due to the friction, then naturally the underlying assumption of no friction is wrong and will totally distort the result.

NCE, like any other model, also makes assumptions that simplify the issues it studies. One of the fundamental concepts of NCE is the assumption of the perfect market, which neoclassical economists usually believe to be a good approximation in most markets in the world.

While NCE also has models for monopolistic and oligopolistic markets, neoclassical economists believe that perfect markets are more efficient and preferable to other market types. Furthermore, most of them believe that the assumption of the perfect market applies to many cases in the real world with sufficient accuracy to help us get a better understanding of what is taking place in the world.

While there might be situations where the perfect market is a good approximation of the real world, in most cases it is probably not. Unfortunately, economists tend to apply the assumption of the perfect market even in cases where it is obviously unjustifiable.

Most economists would agree that it is important for assumptions to be realistic. The notable exception was Milton Friedman, who was put on record as stating that the validity of assumptions is irrelevant as long as the theory had predictive power. This extreme view makes little logical sense. If the assumptions are wrong, then any predictive power is due to luck or to unknown factors that might change. If these unknown factors do change, the predictions of the theory will fail the next time it is tested. In other words, even if the theory works once, it may never work again. After researching the actual behavior of free markets, the famed mathematician Benoit Mandelbrot came up with a definitive answer: Friedman's theory, Mandelbrot claimed, has no predictive power.[3]

Before we look at instances where NCE has inappropriately applied the concept of the perfect market with predictable results, let us first review what constitutes a perfect market.

A perfect market is defined as a market where:

- Every actor is consistently acting in a manner to maximize profits.
- No participant is big enough to influence prices on his or her own.

- There are no barriers to entry and exit.
- Everybody has perfect information available to them.
- There is equal access to the factors of production.
- There are no externalities.

A perfect market is, according to NCE, supposedly self-regulating, so no government interference would be necessary. Indeed, since perfect markets are supposed to be very efficient, any government interference would distort the market and make it less efficient.

Maximizing Utility and Profit

The first assumption is one that concerns the very nature of human beings. Everybody, whether a person or a business, is supposed to consistently, at all times, act in a manner that would tend to maximize the gains of that particular individual. Companies are supposed to maximize profits and individuals are supposed to maximize utility. We will return to the concept of utility in the mathematical section. For now we will just mention that utility represents the satisfaction experienced by the consumer of a good or service.

The assumption of the "rational profit/utility maximizer" has been taken for granted as an article of faith by all classical economists since the time of Adam Smith. Not only is it an article of faith that this is how people really act in the world, this tendency of selfishness is something that should be encouraged rather than restrained, since it is the driving force in the economy.

The refutation of this point is simple. First of all, we know by personal experience that everyone is not a "rational utility maximizer." People often choose to do things that go against their chances to maximize personal gain, and they do so for a variety of reasons, such as the willingness to sacrifice for an ideal, a country, or a religion; or simply due to selflessness. People sometimes prefer a lower-paid job to be able to spend more time with their kids, or to reduce stress.

When the Europeans colonized African lands and forced people to work hard in exchange for meager salaries, it was necessary to create a situation of dependency. Traditional institutions had to be destroyed, culture and history reduced to ashes, farms and natural sources of food demolished—in short, the mutually supporting society that existed had to be ruined and replaced by a disjointed collection of poor individuals who would serve as a willing labor market. According to Karl Polanyi, "[T]he white man's initial contribution to the black man's world mainly consisted in introducing him to the uses of the scourge of hunger. ... the smashing up of social structures in order to extract the element of labor from them." What colonizers did rapidly in Africa and India, capitalists did more slowly in Europe and America through what Polanyi called the "Ricardian construct of the labor market: a flow of human lives the supply of which was regulated by the amount of food put at their disposal." To create a situation where people worked as utility maximizers, Polanyi wrote that "it was necessary to liquidate organic society, which refused to permit the individual to starve."[4]

Of late there have been psychological studies backing up the intuitive certainty that people usually do not act as rational utility maximizers. Quoting a study by Henrich, J. et al., Hall and Klitgaard write that "Heinrich and their colleagues, after examining the results of behavioral experiments in fifteen societies ranging from hunter-gatherers in Tanzania and Paraguay to nomadic herders in Mongolia concluded, "[T]he canonical [NCE] model is not supported in any society studied." In experimental settings and under real world conditions, humans consistently make decisions that favor enforcing social norms over ones that lead to their own material gains.[5]

It is also interesting that while greed is considered bad in almost all cultures, in economics it has been turned into a virtue. In discussing Adam Smith's invisible hand, Duncan K. Foley writes:

The moral fallacy of Smith's position is that it urges us to accept direct and concrete evil in order that indirect and abstract good may come of it. The logical fallacy is that neither Smith nor any of his successors have been able to demonstrate rigorously and robustly how private selfishness turns into public altruism. The psychological failing of Smith's rationalization is that it requires a strategy of wholesale denial of the real consequences of capitalist development, particularly the systematic imposition of costs on those least able to bear them, and the implacable reproduction of inequalities that divide people from one another in society.[6]

John Maynard Keynes sums it up more succinctly. He said that capitalism is "the astonishing belief that the nastiest motives of the nastiest men somehow or other work for the best results in the best of all possible worlds."[7]

The view of human beings as seen through the moral lenses of the major religions or philosophers cannot be reconciled with Homo Economicus. Indeed, Adam Smith himself contradicts this view. In *The Theory of Moral Sentiments* he goes to great lengths to demonstrate that human beings are intrinsically good and tend to act according to the dictates of their conscience, even if this goes against their own interests. He spends the entire book arguing that human beings are bound by conscience, or the inner "impartial spectator," to act in a moral way. Smith considers the very thought of taking advantage of other people to promote one's own self-interest to go against the nature of human beings. He writes: [F]or one man to deprive another unjustly of anything, or unjustly to promote his own advantage by the loss or disadvantage of another, is more contrary to nature than death, than poverty, than pain, than all the misfortunes which can affect him, either in his body, or in his external circumstances."[8]

As the inconsistency between people's actual behavior and the ideal of the rational profit maximizer became obvious, rather than giving up the notion, the economics profession tried to expand the idea of utility to correspond with reality. In 1992 the economist Gary Becker received the Nobel Prize in economics "for having extended the domain of microeconomic analysis to a wide range of human behavior and interaction, including nonmarket behavior." Becker's definition of utility was expanded to include things like spending time with children, preferring a good working environment to a high salary, and even to include altruistic behavior. While this expanded definition of utility is more in line with actual human behavior, it makes predictions on what human beings will do in a certain situation much more difficult. If people consistently maximized utility by getting richer, then their actions would be predictable. But if a selfless person maximizes utility by giving away his or her wealth, or by not taking advantage of his market position so as not to hurt his competitors, then the concept of utility becomes so vague as to be almost useless for economic predictions.

In 2002, the psychologist Daniel Kahneman was awarded the Nobel Memorial Prize in Economic Sciences for his work on decision-making. Through numerous studies under controlled situations he was able to show that people often take economic decisions that are not in their best interest by relying on what he refers to as "System 1," a method of thinking that "operates automatically and quickly, with little or no effort and no sense of voluntary control."[9] As Kahneman demonstrates, although this thinking is necessary in our daily life as a way of coping with day-to-day problems, when used as a tool to guide us in taking economic decisions, we consistently make "irrational" choices that would not be expected from a "rational utility maximizer." From the evidence, it seems that most of the time people are not acting as utility maximizers, and when they do, there is no guarantee that they necessarily will act rationally.

It is undoubtedly true that people sometimes put their economic interests first, but to say that all people at all times put their economic interest first and act rationally on that interest has no foundation in reality.

No Participants Big Enough to Influence Prices on Their Own

The next assumption of perfect markets is that all players are so small that nobody can, on their own or in cooperation with other players, set or influence prices. Contrary to the assumption, economic concentration is endemic in the capitalist system, and the fact that a few huge corporations dominate the market is the rule rather than the exception. According to Hall and Klitgaard:

> In most of the developed world monopolized or concentrated industry is neither rare nor an anomaly. This is true despite the textbook model of businesses favored by mainstream economists: competitive industries of many powerless firms operating in impersonal markets that allocate resources with maximum efficiency. Rather, economic concentration is an explicit strategy on the part of firms themselves to control their economic environments and protect their opportunities to achieve profits in the long run. [10]

Technology companies like Microsoft, Netflix, Intel, Facebook, Amazon, Apple, and PayPal have such a powerful market presence that they are monopolies in their areas of the economy. Other technology companies are what one can best describe as oligopolies, part of a handful of companies that dominate the market. Almost all PCs, for example, are made by a handful of companies. This holds true for other consumer goods as well, such as TVs and DVD players. These markets are as far from perfect as one can imagine. In the energy sector, a few companies dominate the world market, such as ExxonMobil, BP, Shell, Statoil, and a few others. Likewise, in mining the world is also dominated by a handful of companies. The same goes for the retail market, where chains like Ikea, Wal-Mart, Seven Eleven, Starbucks, and others are the dominating corporate giants.

In a developed capitalist economy, concentration of wealth is the norm not the exception, and concentration of wealth allows individual players to influence markets. However, it is not only that they influence prices— they also use economic power to influence the market in non-economic ways. IBM is subsidized; so are big industrial farms. NATO and GATT provide big corporations access to cheap resources and labor that are not available to local companies. Fruit companies own major portions of foreign countries. The United Fruit Company used to own over 60 percent of Guatemala and paid no taxes there. When the country's democratic leader, Jacobo Arbenz, was elected, his popular land-reform policies were opposed by the United Fruit Company, since they would have reduced the landholdings of the company. The company then successfully lobbied the CIA to overthrow the new president. Arbenz was replaced by a military junta that scrapped the land reforms and returned things to the status quo.

Capitalism cannot function without a system of state support. It never has. Even if it could potentially survive, why would big corporations that have the power to manipulate special advantages for themselves choose to lose profits by not taking advantage of their political clout?

Wal-Mart and Ikea actively remove local competitors. Wal-Mart's model is to create a superstore at a strategic hub between many towns or small cities and then undersell the local trades (food markets, tire stores, toy stores, clothing shops, furniture stores, etc.). Thereafter they may put smaller Wal-Mart stores in small cities. Once the local job market and industry is ruined, they can employ part-time labor to operate their stores. Not only can they influence the selling price; they also dictate purchasing price and make exclusive deals with suppliers.

Large bread companies require that supermarkets receive deliveries once or even twice a day. The retailers are required to sell so much cheap bread that they must push it on their customers. Once a product has become a standard consumption item, sellers (such as Coca Cola, Pepsi, etc.) can enforce preferential treatment by retailers. Large technology firms, defense contractors, and computer companies get access to university departments, NASA, and defense contracts, which allows them to have access to publically funded research and even get paid for their involvement.

Big companies often use every manipulative, devious, unfair, unjust, political, or destructive means available to insure the slightest advantage. They have ousted governments, displaced populations, written constitutions, violently attacked strikers, and despoiled the earth simply to get a price advantage. It is not only the selling price that they influence but also the price of raw materials and labor.

No Barriers to Entry and Exit

Another condition for perfect markets to function is that there are no barriers to exit and entry. That is to say, anyone can enter a market on the same conditions as existing players. In a perfect market, new participants will enter the market if profitability goes up, suppressing profits till they reach an equilibrium, and inefficient participants will leave the market if they cannot produce at a profit.

Apart from any regulatory governmental framework that may prevent certain players to enter the market, there is one huge obstacle that always exists as a barrier to entry and exit: fixed capital.

Only in industries where there is no fixed capital can we even theoretically talk about eliminating barriers for entry and exit. As soon as we need to invest in machinery, software, expertise, etc., in order to enter a market, we automatically have a barrier to entry. In order to produce aluminum or drill for oil, we need billions of dollars in investments. The general population cannot afford this. Consequently, there are only a few huge companies that are engaged in activities like oil, natural gas, power stations, nuclear energy, mining, aluminum production, microprocessors, the building of cars and airplanes, etc. According to Hall and Klitgaard:

The only way to ensure a perfectly competitive equilibrium, however, is to ignore the problem of fixed cost. In fact the initial assumption of the economists of no barriers to entry precludes the analysis of the cost of long-lived fixed productive assets. But industrialists operated in the real world where large-scale industry required substantial investment in fixed capital. If, at the same time, the cost of producing one more unit of output (what economists call marginal cost) is low, real-world producers face a dilemma.[11]

If there truly were no barriers to entry and exit, it would mean that a Bushman from the Kalahari Desert could set up a nuclear power plant as easily as a big European corporation. This is naturally not the case.

The problem of fixed costs not only poses a problem to entering a market, but to exiting it as well. Let us assume that a company has fixed assets that run into billions of dollars. If, due to excess competition, the price falls below the production cost, the company has one of two options: either it produces and sells below cost—possibly with the view of either reducing costs later on or hoping that the prices will pick up—or it closes down production. Closing down production and writing off billions of dollars of assets is often not an option at all, so the company is forced to stay in business even though it is losing money. Many of today's airlines, such as SAS, British Airways, Asiana, Kingfisher, and Kenya Airways, as well as several American airlines, are in this position.

Patents are an institutionalized barrier to entry. Patent legislation is becoming an increasingly important tool for Western economies to stay ahead of the competition and ensure that they maintain their affluence even as more and more of the manufacturing is done in China and in other low-cost countries.

In the past it was industrial production that made a country rich. Today, the rights to produce something have been divorced from the actual production in such a way that someone who owns this right can make more money than the people who are doing the actual production. A patent owner can prevent anyone else from producing whatever he or she has a patent on, or can license out the patent to production firms at a fee.

Patents and intellectual property rights stand as impassable barriers to entry as long as the patent is in force. Far from being something to promote world trade and free markets, it is actually one of the greatest hindrances to free markets. In areas where the barrier to entry is not that big, artificial barriers of entry are erected purposely to protect the profits of a few businesses or industries.

In a broader sense, all companies strive to prevent competitors from entering the market. Every company wants to maximize profits, and the easiest way to do that is to restrict competition. Therefore, all successful companies try to create artificial barriers to entry for their competitors if no natural barriers exist. This is as true for the small drug store on the corner as it is for multinational corporations. Obviously, multinational corporations are far more successful in this regard than small private businesses.

In conclusion, the assumption of no barriers to entry and exit is a not only a myth; it is an assumption that contradicts the assumption of rational profit maximizing business because the activity of any rational profit maximizer would, knowingly or unknowingly, create barriers to entry, and hence barriers invariably become the norm.

Perfect Information Available to Everybody

While perfect information is the stated condition for a perfect market, the unstated condition is that everyone also has the same ability to understand and act on this information. If this were true, stock markets, future markets, currency markets, and all other means of speculation that is a hallmark of the free-market system would cease to exist. If everybody knew the same information and had the same intelligence to act on that information, nobody could be more successful in trading than anyone else, except through random events and luck.

But the condition of perfect information has even bigger problems. If everybody had equal access to information and equal intelligence to utilize this information in the most productive way possible, then education, intelligence, and training would be meaningless. A barber in India would have an equal chance to develop software as Bill Gates. Economists believe that this assumption is reasonably valid, provided there is perfect information within an industry or among consumers.

In reality, this is not the case. Within industries, information is one of the most valuable assets in the world, because information is what makes it possible to convert other material resources into useful commodities. Information and knowledge are not equally spread, and those who possess it often try to hide it to maintain an advantage over those who don't. When it is impossible to keep the information secret, patents and other restrictions on intellectual property are used to make sure that even the information that is freely available cannot legally be used except by a few.

As for the consumers, their situation is even worse. Politicians and businesses, advertisers and media sources, do everything to keep consumers from being able to make rationally informed decisions. In fact the market system itself deletes the information that consumers would need if they were to even attempt to make a rational choice.[12] Media sources incorporate ideologically manipulative content in order to seemingly produce a better product to present to their consumers (the advertisers).

Voters are taught to see the political world as a personality contest, and they know painfully little about the economic ramifications of what happens behind parliamentary walls. And lastly, businesses advertise products to create artificial desires and brand loyalty, to silence concerns about health risks and associate themselves with popular sentiments or famous people—in other words, to specifically undermine people's rationality so that they will buy things that are useless or harmful.

Even in the hypothetical case that all information is available to all, for example through the Internet, the sheer volume of it would make it impossible for each person to fully digest it. Therefore, even in these circumstances people will specialize in different areas and gain more knowledge than others in their areas of specialization. This is one of the driving forces of modern society: specialization. We all specialize in various areas and thus through cooperation achieve more than if all of us tried to do and know everything.

Our ability to absorb and understand the implications of what we see is different from others' ability to do this. In a fundamental sense, the idea of perfect information being equally available to all parties goes against nature itself. The assumption of perfect information also disregards physical distance. A person who is present where something is happening will naturally have a better knowledge about it than someone who is on the other side of the globe. Hence, the condition that everyone will have all information available to him or her goes against common sense, science, and personal experience, and can never be fulfilled.

Equal Access to Factors of Production

It goes without saying that everyone cannot have equal access to factors of production. How is it possible for Vietnam or North Korea to have access to the same factors of production as the United States? How can nomadic people in the Sahel Region of Africa have access to the same factors of production as industrial captains in Tokyo?

The proposition that all people have equal access to the factors of production is so ridiculous that it would be absurd to spend any further time disproving it. Is it ever a reasonable assumption at all? Almost never, at least not in situations where anyone would actually take the time to use NCE: situations where all the players are insignificant and no one is trying very hard to get ahead, i.e., in marginally noncompetitive markets. Such markets were common at the time of Smith, when it was considered foul play to undercut your fellow sellers or tradesmen or to make special deals. In rural towns or in well-knit communities, where markets are embedded in an environment of cooperation, such ideals still exist—but the other assumptions of NCE do not apply in such situations because the human influence is too significant for people to display economically rational behaviors.

No Externalities

Externalities in economics are costs or benefits borne by a third party that didn't chose to bear that cost. For example, if an industry pollutes a river, and a community down the river has to cover the cost of the cleanup, then this is an externality for the company causing the pollution. In other words, someone else is bearing the cost and the company pockets the extra profit or increased market share by lowering the cost of its products.

The conditions of a perfect market demand that there are no externalities, but in reality externalities make up a large part of the economy. The true cost of oil, if we include the military operations to protect the oil fields, the environmental impact of pollution, and the effect of greenhouse gases produced when burning the oil, would be many times higher than it is at present.[13]

The same holds true for nuclear energy. Recent studies have shown that the cost of dismantling old nuclear stations is far higher than anyone had previously thought. For example, it is estimated that it will cost more than $900 million to dismantle the Three Mile Island Unit 2 nuclear power plant, which was the site of the worst nuclear disaster in US history.[14] The recent disaster in Fukushima and the subsequent leaks into the ocean have not been factored into the cost of the electricity. Finally, the cost of processing and storing the final waste has also become much higher than originally anticipated. Including these costs in the price of electricity generated by nuclear power plants would make nuclear energy much more expensive.

NCE recognizes that externalities exist, but believes that they can and should be dealt with by the market, rather than by government regulations. On the theoretical level it assumes that externalities are internalized into costs and therefore are technically not externalities. On the practical level, it supports policies that find a way to internalize the externality, generally by extending property rights—for example, by inventing carbon credits so that the company now owns negative pollution, which is consumed as a cost in carbon-emitting activities.

One externality that NCE does not account for is the free work provided by nature. As we mentioned earlier, nature provides free services to us on a scale that dwarfs the global economic output. Since nature's total contribution is greater than all business activities on earth, it is a stretch to consider its contribution unimportant. We are in fact absolutely dependent on nature for our daily survival, even if we do not consider natural resources as adding economic value. Neither do we take note when our economic activities destroy the "free" resources that nature provides us.

Whatever NCE may assume, there exists an overwhelming amount of actual externalities in the real world that are not internalized or dealt with by the market. A self-regulating market creates externalities, and far from eliminating the needs for government intervention, makes such intervention necessary to avoid total destruction of the planet. It cuts no ice to simply talk about externalities—when the trees are gone and the oceans have no fish left, when the topsoil is destroyed and there is no water to drink, then the externalities will be internalized in the economy en-masse as the wheels of production grind to a halt due to a lack of ecosystem service.

Drawing Conclusions on False Premises

While the assumptions of the perfect market may be a good approximation in certain narrow cases, no such assumption can be made regarding the economy as a whole, and definitely not in many key areas, such as financial markets. We will look at some of the consequences of falsely assuming a perfect market in places where it is clearly inappropriate.

General Equilibrium Theory

In 1874, Leon Walras introduced the General Equilibrium Theory in his book *Elements of Pure Economics*. [15] The theory states that a general equilibrium in all markets can be obtained simultaneously if the assumption of perfect competitive markets holds. If these assumptions do not hold—in particular, if the assumption regarding return to scale is violated—then neoclassical economists have not been able to demonstrate that a simultaneous equilibrium is possible.

It can be clearly shown that many, if not most, of today's markets are not perfect markets, whether they be markets in energy products such as oil and gas (due to the small number of big firms), financial markets (due to imperfect information), agricultural products (due to farm subsidies), etc.

Financial Markets

Financial markets are a perfect example of a situation where perfect markets do not exist. First of all, the near-perfect information available to all required by the theory does not exist. Indeed, if everyone had the same information and the same ability to act on it, there would not be any financial markets, since nobody would be able to make any money from them.

Financial markets transfer wealth, but by themselves they do not create any wealth. Therefore, the smarter or luckier party gains on the less informed or unlucky party. It is like a big gambling floor. If everyone knew what the price of stocks would be tomorrow, nobody could make money at someone else's expense.

The assumption that nobody is big enough to influence prices is also false when it comes to financial markets. Remember when George Soros, as chief architect of a group of speculators, successfully broke the British pound on September 16, 1992? This is a typical example of speculators acquiring enough resources to manipulate prices in the face of determined resistance from central banks and regulators.

Energy Markets

The energy markets, as well as the markets of many raw materials, such as aluminum, are controlled by a limited number of large companies that can influence supply and prices. This was demonstrated at the end of 2014, when oil prices dropped to half their value in a few months.

Factor Prize Equalization

For example, the conclusions of modern trade theory that free trade will benefit everybody and lead to factor-prize equalization is a direct consequence of the assumptions of a perfect market. [16] The prediction is that under these conditions the cost of production, prices, and salaries would end up being the same all over the world. Naturally, if there is perfect information, perfect competition, no increased returns on scale, equal access to factors of production, no barriers to exit and entry, etc., then everyone and everything would be equal everywhere. If everything were equal everywhere, then prices, production costs, and so on, would also be equal. Why would these be exempted?

The obvious truth is that things are not equal the world over. Differences do exist and they cannot be theorized away. Since the assumptions are wrong, the conclusions are equally wrong.

What would happen, however, if these assumptions actually were true? According to Nobel Laureate in Economics James Buchanan, it would lead to the cessation of all trade: "[In a model] which embodies constant returns to scale of production over all ranges of output, all of which are private, this economy would be without trade. In such a setting, each person becomes a complete microcosm of the whole society." [17]

So if the assumptions of NCE theory are correct, then all economic activity would stop. But since the assumptions of NCE theory are not correct, the theory itself is obviously meaningless, and any policies based on this theory are bound to fail.

Free Markets and Government Intervention

As we mentioned above, NCE states that in a perfect market there is no need for government intervention, and if the government does intervene unnecessarily then it will be harmful.

Evidence from the real world, however, strongly suggests that the idea of self-regulating markets without government intervention is a myth. There are no successful economies in the world where the state did not play a major role in promoting economic growth. Active state involvement in the economy is indispensable for any economy to function well. Edward Herman, Professor Emeritus in Finance of the Wharton School of the University of Pennsylvania, writes:

> In the actual history of capitalism, however, public ownership has played a substantial role, and state intervention in other forms such as subsidization, protection from competition, the underwriting of risk, and the carving out of foreign markets by imperialist wars, has been of enormous importance and integral to the rise of the great capitalist states… The essential principle

operating in defining the relation of private capital to the state has been opportunism: that is, the state has been mobilized as needed for a vast number of services, funded by the general taxpayer but benefiting important business interests.[18]

In the United States, the government subsidy of big business generally goes through the Pentagon system, where lucrative contracts are given to the defense industry, serving as a means for the government to pump massive amounts of capital into the economy.

Many weapons that are produced are hardly ever used. But the arms race is on and newer and newer versions of weaponry are developed, with the help of a constant stream of state subsidies. The US's military power is overwhelming. Its budget is 50 percent of the total defense spending of all the other countries combined. Besides any legitimate security needs, it functions as a machine to subsidize the rich corporations.

Subsidizing business through the Pentagon system is much easier to justify than any other type of subsidy. Nobody would agree to lower their living standards to subsidize IBM to make a new computer chip. However, if people are told that there is an imminent threat of communists invading the country, or that terrorists will attack, then any expenditure can easily be justified.

Other countries have other ways of intervening in the economy. In Scandinavian countries it is done through the social spending programs, and in Holland through the Ministry of Economic Affairs, which coordinates business cartels. But all governments of industrialized nations intervene in their respective economies in order to ensure that they keep running.

The idea of the liberal market and laissez-faire originated after Malthus's *Dissertations on Populations*. The great philosophers were looking for laws that applied to society; they were looking for human laws—moral, psychic, and spiritual concepts upon which the edifice of society could be constructed. Townsend and Malthus introduced the idea that the laws of nature, of wolves and sheep, also govern human beings. In nature there was no need for government: hunger and the scarcity of food kept everything in good order. In Ricardo's eyes, this removed the need for government's role in the economic sphere and established the basis for laissez-faire economics. The laws of economics were the laws of nature, and so labor had to find its price in the market. Burke and Bentham thought that pity for the poor interfered with the functioning of society, and since the natural law of hunger and scarcity was sufficient to impel them to work, government regulations and political sanctions were superfluous.

Laissez-faire means to let the laws of the market govern society, and to not let the government impose any such human laws. For these thinkers, to hand society over to the control of a market was not an idea based on any previous theory or observable evidence. Their ideas were partly based on the interests of an emerging business class, and from the combination of the ideological conception of the poor as animalistic, and a confusion among social administrators over how to utilize this emerging class of paupers in a profitable way.

Robert Owen was the first and perhaps the only one to clearly foresee the degraded plight that awaited the laboring class and the ensuing deterioration of culture and community. But Ricardo's vision was enforced in the English countryside and on the factory floor. The exploitation of the poor was ruthless and their sufferings went unnoticed. Rural life was dismantled and the cultural tradition of countless generations was suddenly erased. In the words of Karl Polanyi:

> The road to the free market was opened and kept open by an enormous increase in continuous, centrally organized and controlled interventionism…. Just as, contrary to expectation, the invention of labor-saving machinery had not diminished but actually increased the uses of human labor, the introduction of free markets, far from doing away with the need for control, regulation, and intervention, enormously increased their range. Administrators had to be constantly on the watch to ensure the free working of the system. Thus even those who wished most ardently to free the state from all unnecessary duties, and whose whole philosophy demanded the restriction of state activities, could not help but entrust the self-same state with the new powers, organs, and instruments required for the establishment of laissez-faire. [19]

For most, the irony of the situation went unnoticed: the state was forced to enforce a doctrine of noninterference. The sufferings inflicted on the poor, combined with food shortages and unemployment, led to revolts. The market was not working and the poor were paying the price. After the Peterloo Massacre, the Six Acts of 1819 and the Libel Act made unapproved meetings illegal and allowed for government censoring of newspapers through taxes. Training in the use of arms was criminalized and soon afterward the Habeas Corpus Act was suspended. This was to limit the rights of people to prevent what was a human reaction to an inhuman situation. "Insofar as individual liberty was destroyed, it was destroyed by and in pursuance of Acts of Parliament."[20]

But it was enforced selectively. Labor, according to the principles of laissez-faire and self-regulation of the market, should have been allowed to set their price and sell their labor according to what manufacturers were able to pay (indeed businessmen had this right to sell their commodities at their chosen price), but such activities would have interfered with the cost of labor being regulated by grain prices and the pangs of hunger—in these cases the government would protect the functioning of the all-important market, with violence if necessary. But when industry artificially depressed wages below market value, below that which people needed to feed their families, leading to workers striking and prompting the police to break up the strikes, the government would call in temporary workers to keep industry running.

Laissez-faire is largely a mythical concept that the business community has seen as a useful device to be selectively applied—to complain about government spending on human services or to rationalize privatization, but of course not to remove subsidies, tax breaks, government spending on contracts, etc., that benefit the same community of business owners.

Since the Second World War, the governments of successful industrialized countries have been intensely involved in the economy, be they made up of social democrats or conservatives. "The economic doctrines preached by the rulers are instruments of power, intended for others, so that they can be more efficiently robbed and exploited."[21] That is to say, just as the early industrial successes (England, USA) had flourished by not following the recommendations of the self-regulating market, modern success stories are nations that largely abandoned the dictates of NCE.

A study done by twenty-four economists concluded that the economic miracle of postwar Japan was not a miracle, but was due to the Ministry of International Trade and Industry (MITI) following a policy of disregarding prevailing economic theory and giving the "predominant role in the formation of industry policy" to the state. The industry in each sector of the economy works closely with a corresponding section of the MITI. Relying on tariffs, subsidies, financial controls, etc., MITI flatly rejected the standard NCE prescription. Japan's economy is "rather similar to the organization of the industrial bureaucracy in socialist countries."[22] Some of the economists suggested that Japan's statements in support of economic doctrine were intended to befool its rivals into following them.

China, although remarkably repressive, is another example of a mixed economy that has experienced rapid economic development while disavowing standard neoclassical practices. "One phenomenal success has been 'township and village enterprises', for the most part factories owned by rural farmers," which "now account for close to 20 percent of China's GNP, employing more than 100 million people," financial correspondent David Francis writes, quoting a World Bank spokesman who predicts that they "will most assuredly be the single most dynamic form of enterprise on the Chinese scene." [23]

Postwar Germany is also a telling case. The country allowed for strong government involvement in business and a large welfare state to ensure that the system worked for the people in the form of re-education, life-long welfare, and comparatively high wages and benefits. *The Economist* observed that "bank-owned industries unbothered by shareholders, secure from predators and heedless of profit" did very well. Germany is like a bee that theoretically should not be able to fly, but "the German economy's riposte to this ancient caricature is to fly."[24]

According to a World Bank study in *Journal of Economic Development and Cultural Change*, other rapidly developing counties such as Taiwan, South Korea, Hong Kong, Singapore, and Thailand have similar stories: import substitution by local production, government control of vital economic intuitions, restricted trade and industrial policy, high tariffs, and long-term goals rather than quick rewards. Import substitution (producing at home rather than importing) and export growth was a key to their development, along with government intervention in industry. Government policymakers are "insulated…from interest group pressures," and make policies focused on "sustainability, poverty reduction, and decreasing income inequality." [25] Other reforms include tying wages to productivity growth, public-sector savings, public and private risk sharing loans, government-backed repayment guarantees, councils to transmit information between institutions, and government interference in the financial markets.

The above countries' success was in strict violation of the suggestions of NCE. Every country that has achieved recent economic growth is called an economic miracle, but it achieved that growth without following NCE policy. Hence it is not a miracle, but rather an example of government administrators examining reality and thinking logically rather than misapplying free-market ideas that have no historical success record whatsoever. Brazil, by comparison, was keeping pace with the Asian NIC's until it took a loan from the World Bank (due to the debt crisis) and was forced to follow mainstream economic policy, which led to social and economic disaster. In fact, every country where the US and Europe had significant influence is struggling with poverty, which has only been exacerbated by the World Bank's NCE policy.

As we have seen in the recent financial crisis, when the financial sector messes up to such an extent that a collapse is imminent, governments line up to solve the problem. Their aim is to privatize profits and socialize losses. In other words, when the rich banks and other financiers start to lose money due to their incessant gambles for higher profit, the citizens bail them out. Taxpayers and poor people are forced to squeeze their consumption to offset their losses.

Economics as Pseudo Science

The early economists called their subject "political economy." The term itself indicated that it was related to politics and the government policies. It had no pretentions of being scientific in the same way as physics or mathematics.

While early economists, starting with Ricardo, made thought experiments based on simplified assumptions, such as his arguments for the effects of various types of taxes on the economy and his famous principle of comparative advantage, he did not present any statistics to demonstrate whether his reasoning actually had any correlation with the real world. This trend has continued since then. While mathematics have become more advanced, the lack of a link between theory and real economic data has continued to be the norm even today. In spite of this, contemporary economists like to view economics as a science, and they liberally employ many of the mathematical tools used in physics.

The first serious attempt to make economics mathematical was made by Alfred Marshall, who up until then had pursued a career in mathematical physics. In 1865 Marshall abandoned his career in physics and after a passing glance at philosophy and ethics went into economics, which he saw as a way to combine his ethical and mathematical interests, with the intention of making it into a mathematically precise science. He became the most influential economist of his generation. Other influential economists of this time were French mathematician and economist Antoine Cournot, scientist-economists William Jevons and Böhm-Bawerk, mathematical economist Léon Walras, Vilfredo Pareto, a civil engineer who studied physical equilibrium principles while earning his doctorate in engineering, and Irving Fisher, whose doctoral thesis was written under the great American physicist Willard Gibbs and which drew extensive and specific parallels between mechanics and economics.

The founders of what would become neoclassical economics were educated in the world of physics and wanted to describe the social world using the same analytical tools that were successful in describing the physical world. According to Mirowski, et al., they borrowed from physics and thermodynamics and remade economics in the image of mid-nineteenth-century vector mechanics: utility became a vector field corresponding to energy. "The progenitors of neoclassical economic theory boldly copied the reigning physical theories in the 1870s...they copied their models term for term and symbol for symbol, and said so."[26] Walras, for example, stated the economic need to be scientific in this way: there is "no need to take into account the morality or immorality."[27]

During the initial period of making economics mathematical (1870s–1920s) the vast majority of economists were not able to grasp what was happening. In the words of economist Schumpeter:

> Mathematical theory is more than a translation of non-mathematical theory into the language of symbols, but its results can, in general, be translated into non-mathematical language. This is the reason why the non-mathematical majority of economists never realized the full extent of their obligations to the mathematically trained minority: the typical theorist never realized, for instance, that he did not fully understand Marshall.[28]

New methods of proof arose; problems became increasingly definite and abstract. Those who were most mathematically inclined changed the discourse of economics, focusing on issues to which they could apply their mathematical training, but their conclusions were translated into traditional language so that they could be understood by the general audience of economists, and so the older breed of economists were not aware of the significance of this shift in the ideology of economics.

"In appropriating the formalisms of mid-nineteenth-century energy physics and adapting them to the language of utility and prices, the progenitors and their epigones adopted a certain worldview..."[29] that would determine what was economic orthodoxy and what was heterodox, a worldview that would filter out the logic of the softer social sciences, labeling it as "unscientific," and limit economic discourse to a narrow, quantifiable domain within the vast spectrum of social science.

Economists, mathematically modeling the effects, were stuck in an endless variety of incompatible ways, while the causal factors remained beyond the purview of their mathematical models. Here was hidden the Cartesian blunder of assuming that higher truths are inferior to lower truths because the latter are measurable. Here also was Malthus' naturalism, the rationalization that human beings' behavior is mechanistic, dressed in the garb of scientism. With his General Theory, Keynes made an effort to halt the process of mathematical abstraction and lead economics towards a logical rigor that respected the inescapable value of higher truths—that society was human. This might have led to a social science of economics that let go of the market ideology and its mathematicians. But this never materialized.

From the mid-1930s to the 1960s there was an increasing push for rigor in economics. The Econometric Society was founded in 1930 to promote "rigorous thinking similar to that which has come to dominate in the natural sciences."[30] Rigorous thinking implied mathematical precision using abstract axioms "This period, from the 1930s to the 1960s, was exactly when economics became a predominantly mathematical discipline.... the requirement that theories be mathematically rigorous meant that economists had to deal with increasingly abstract models."[31]

Samuelson from MIT was a dominant figure during this period who shaped, in many ways, the outlook of economists. "For Samuelson, being scientific meant deriving operationally meaningful theorems...the main source of such propositions lay in optimization because equilibrium typically involved maximizing or minimizing something."[32] Kenneth Arrow, another American economist, produced a proof that the equations for equilibrium had a solution (1954), but he could not show uniqueness, nor was he concerned if the quantities (e.g., utility) were well defined. He also showed that markets, in general, do not produce an ethically acceptable allocation of resources. Although this was not considered a relevant question in the search for models, it led Arrow and Samuelsson to agree that markets cannot be relied on to solve social problems and that the government had to have a role in the economy.

The question then arises: How far did these attempts to making economics into a science go? We can look at this from two viewpoints. First, to investigate if the mathematical techniques that were used were theoretically applicable to economics, and second, to see if the techniques really had predictive power.

To answer the first question, we will limit ourselves to investigating three issues. The first is the economists' concept of utility, which lies at the heart of NCE; the second is the nature of randomness; and the third is the distribution of random events.

Utility

The fundamental basis of NCE is the concept of "utility." People are said to inherently optimize utility, to consistently do things to maximize utility for themselves. But what is this utility and how is it measured? Buying a new car provides some utility, and having a good education is also a form of utility. But in economics the concept of utility is different from such goods and services; it is considered the psychic evaluation by an individual of these goods and services.

It is easy to measure goods and services, but how can this psychic evaluation of these goods and services be measured in numbers? In his book *More Heat than Light*, Philip Mirowsky sets out to prove that the mathematics behind economics does not work, and his critique centers on the vague nature of utility.[33]

Leon Walras, who attempted to make a direct analogy between physics and economics, asked the opinion of the famous French mathematician Laurent Schwartz regarding utility. His purpose was to bolster his points using the mathematics of physics in economics, but Laurent did not agree that utility was something that could be measured mathematically. "How can one accept that satisfaction is capable of being measured? Never will a mathematician agree to that."[34] Still Walras maintained that marginal utility, even if it were not measureable, could be treated as if it were measurable.

Walras began a correspondence with another great French mathematician, Jules Henri Poincaré, to clarify the validity of this trick. Pointcaré also had clear criticism of Walras's use of mathematics and said that satisfactions can be ordered but not measured. [35]

To say that utility can be ordered but not measured would mean that if I prefer to have a safe neighborhood rather than a luxury car, it would be impossible to calculate how many luxury cars equals a safe neighborhood. This means that none of the simplest mathematical tools can be applied to the concept of utility. In short, any mathematical treatment of the concept of utility would be so rudimentary that it would have little value at all.

In spite of the criticism from the mathematicians he contacted, Walras went ahead and treated utility as a measurable entity, which is at the heart of his main work, the General Equilibrium Theory.[36] But utility is not measurable, and hence creating complex mathematical formulas based on this theory is at best impractical and at worst rather nonsensical.

Randomness

Natural science tries to understand the world as it is. It has successfully used mathematics to describe the world and its natural laws, and thus often predicts the outcome of different circumstances. We know how to build a bridge that will be able to stand the weight of the cars travelling across it, and we know how to build a rocket that can bring us to the moon and back. These are wonderful achievements, and it has made it possible for us to control and predict many aspects of the environment around us.

During the time of Newton, we assumed that physical phenomena were fixed and ordained, and that a given cause always gave the same effect. With the introduction of quantum mechanics, this is no longer true. All subatomic events in nature are random, but—and this is very significant—the randomness follows very specific patterns. While the individual event is random, the probability distribution of the events never changes. This, in science, is called the ergodic principle, and it is why the world works in a predictable manner.

If the probability distribution of physical events changed, mathematics and formulas would become meaningless, because a formula that worked at one time may not work at another time. For example, if I drop a ball from the roof, one time it may fall and another time it might float. Nothing could be determined any longer.

The same is true in any other field of science. If the randomness of events do not follow certain patterns, it is impossible to use statistics or any other mathematical tool. For this reason, most economists, such as Samuelson, Cochrane, Stiglitz, Mankiw, Friedman, and others, have taken the ergodic axiom as the foundation for the scientific method in economics. They "either implicitly or explicitly have assumed that observable economic events are generated by an ergodic stochastic [or random] process."[37]

If a process is ergodic, then a past data sample will be statistically equivalent to a future data sample, and hence the probability distribution of the past data is the same as the risk in the future. The implication is that if economics is to be (and it's assumed by modern economists that it should be) on par with the hard sciences, then the axiom of ergodicity must be accepted. Without the ergodic axiom, the proof of efficient markets falls apart; that is to say, the backbone of NCE depends on ergodicity. However, none of the hard sciences involved the interaction of human beings (that is why they are called hard sciences). When human behavior is introduced, ergodicity no longer applies.

If we made a survey of clothing habits on a given day in a given town, for example, and we found that most women wore short skirts, we could probably use those statistics to predict how many women would wear short skirts in the same town the next day. But if we used the same statistics to predict what women would wear ten years later in the same town, or in another town on another continent having a different culture, then the statistics would be useless. Human beings change interests; they have differences in culture and preferences based on time, place, and person, and so the ergodic principle does not apply when human beings enter into the picture. In the words of Paul Davidson:

> Efficient market theory, Arrow-Debreu models, Ricardian equivalence, etc., require the households, business enterprises, and politicians to possess a significant correct and accurate message of things that are going to happen in the future if they are to make efficient (optimal) decisions today." And although the conclusions reached based on these theories may be applicable to highly constrained circumstances, they are "inapplicable to the world of experience because in the real world, households do not have any significantly reliable information about the future, and neither do budgetary policy makers, nor entrepreneurs." The primary blunder is that in their effort to be a hard science they required the ergodic "assumption of people having significantly reliable knowledge about the future," which was artificially created by "accepting bad axioms as the basis for mainstream theory.[38]

To cover up this fundamental flaw in the economic theories, many economists ignore the real world and never seriously correlate their theories and equations with the cold facts of the real world.

In their famous paper "On Tests and Significance in Econometrics," Keuzenkamp and Magnus compared 668 econometrics articles and found less than a dozen that attempted to statistically test any theory whatsoever, and only in a few was any conclusion reached about the validity or invalidity of the model. "In cases where a decisive conclusion is obtained, the same volume may contain a test of the same hypothesis with the opposite result." And when a theory was rejected, it was not clear what was implied, and the conclusion often contained caveats: "not very constructive conclusion," "worth remembering," or "rejection of the theory is not necessarily implied." In the end, because the hypotheses in economics are so shaky, "a rejection does not necessarily mean a rejection of the hypothesis of interest, as auxiliary hypotheses might be false instead."[39]

The econometric profession recognizes that "if the confrontation of economic theories with observable phenomena is the objective of empirical research, then hypothesis testing is the primary tool of analysis."[40] However, the impact of testing the theory is painfully limited. They quote economist Aris Spanos, who said that "to my knowledge, no economic theory was ever abandoned because it was rejected by some empirical econometric test, nor was a clear-cut decision between competing theories made in lieu of the evidence of such a test." And other economists echo similar feelings. Even to estimate an empirical estimation of a parameter is virtually unheard of.

Distribution of Random Events

Most random events in the physical world follow the so-called normal distribution, which requires that variances among random variables are finite. The normal distributions used in economics simply cannot be applied to economic data: economic data have too many points far from the mean. Mandelbrot discovered by actually looking at financial data that the random variables had infinite variance and that it was a mistake to treat anomalies and periods of crisis separately.[41]

Mandelbrot discovered that distribution of prices is approximately scale invariant. Normally, if you look at data over a long period you get a better understanding of the trends than if you look at it over a short period. However, if the distribution is scale invariant, it does not matter if you look at the performance of the stock market for one hour or for ten years—you still will have no better chance of predicting what the market will do in the future.

Furthermore, the combination of non-Gaussian distributions with infinite variance and scale invariance imply yet another strike against the idea of rational expectations. Rational expectations require an ergodic stochastic process (see above) that depends upon rational buying and selling to stabilize the price. What all this means is that the talk of "constrained maximization of rational behavior" is meaningless drivel.

Mandelbrot et al gave a definitive answer to Freidman's statement that the realism of a theory or its axioms is irrelevant as long as they have predictive power: Friedman's theory has no predictive power. Mathematics is not so inelegant that one may use baseless axioms and manipulate poorly defined objects, and produce something useful.

As we can see, in order to make its models seem scientific, NCE has applied the wrong mathematics for the wrong reasons. Math has been introduced for the sake of using math alone, and not because its use has created greater insights into economics.

Conclusion

Can economics be said to be a science on par with physics? The answer is an emphatic no. The works of Smith, Keynes, Freidman, and others, though commendable, do not contain the insight, rigor, power of thought, and conviction of seminal works in science, and yet they are romanticized and referred to endlessly as if they were scientists. There are likely two main reasons for this: 1) the study of economics did not begin as an objective investigation, but with ideological quibbles about how to manipulate social functioning; and 2) economists insisted on copying sciences that were of a fundamentally different character, and in the effort to imitate never developed its own identity. In no other discipline are there so many schools and so much bickering, nor so much backward glancing. Newton said that he saw further because he stood on the shoulders of others, for science is a synthetic union of concepts that progressively discerns truth. Economics has not followed this pattern.

In their book *Energy and the Wealth of Nations: Understanding the Biophysical Economy*, Charles A. S. Hall and Kent A. Klitgaard write:

[M]any of the assumptions that conventional economists must make to generate their world of theoretical economics, the associated equations, and their applications, defy logic to anyone trained in the natural sciences, the scientific method, or even possessing a reasonable degree of common sense. As some support for that point of view we note that as of 2010 ten of the last eight most recent recipients of the Nobel Prize in economics were people whose work challenged, in various very fundamental ways, the basic existing neoclassical paradigm.[42]

In their conclusion, which we agree with, they contrasted economics with the physics it seeks to emulate:

So our answer to the question posed by the title of this chapter is that, no, the dominant economics at this time is not a science. … In theory there is a model of physics behind it, but the equilibrium model is just a copying of the equation form without any understanding of the actual physics … In addition, the assumptions of "rational actors" required to make this model work are inconsistent with how real humans in fact interact with each other. The generation of theory based on a market concept of perfect information and equal power of interacting buyers and sellers that has not existed since agrarian England, if indeed they ever existed, combined with failure to make and test hypotheses makes an acceptance of the basic neoclassical model an article of faith, not rationality. Unfortunately the ascendance and the power of the ideas of the advocates of market theory and self-interest have spilled over to our public and political life, destroying many economies in the less-developed world.[43]

Chapter Nine

Green Capitalism:
Why it is not as Green as They Say

Narrow interpretations of 'sustainable development' are convenient for planners of gigantic destructive policies, because it is difficult to convince people that future generations will lack the ability to take care of themselves in the aftermath of whatever we find suitable to do.

—Arne Naess

C APITALISM HAS CREATED UNPRECEDENTED wealth but also growing economic inequality; it has given Western nations easy access to consumer items people in other parts of the world can only dream of, but it has also created a world of rich and poor. Market capitalism's exploitation of energy from oil and coal, as well as raw materials such as steel, wood, and agricultural land, made the Western world industrious and materially abundant. But this wealth creation also resulted in environmental damages—pollution and destruction of land, sea, and atmosphere—most notably the potentially catastrophic effects of global warming. But why did our economic system end up destroying what it depends on for its resources to grow and survive? Why did we end up biting the hand that feeds us?

There are many complex reasons we humans destroy the environment. The main ones can be grouped into four categories: psychological, economic, political, and scientific. Human psychology, for example, forms cultures and drives human behavior, which again informs our economic, political, and scientific decisions and inventions. The way we feel and think make up who we are as individuals and groups. The psychological reason for environmental destruction is related to the fundamental human trait we call greed: our insatiable need for more. If we desire more meat, for example, we will justify our "need" by cutting down the rainforest to grow soy beans to feed our pigs, and we will imprison chickens in inhumane cages and pump them full of growth hormones to fulfill our desire for more "lean white meat." Not coincidentally, our modern economy is centered around fulfilling these personal "needs." Indeed, the very heart of modern capitalism rests on the psychology of rewarding this behavior. By gratifying the human compulsion for more, modern consumerism—the so-called shop-'til-you-drop culture—has been shaped. And this reward system, this culture, is based on capitalism's main driving force: the profit motive. Scientific inventions and political laws are thus developed to support the psychology and economy based on our insatiable need to have more material goods and money.

The complexity of our environmental problems and how they often involve a spectrum of issues can be witnessed in how we currently try to solve them. Or, more often than not, in how we try to avoid taking the trouble to solve them.

Faced with the growing realization that global warming caused by carbon emission is a real threat to the future of life on planet Earth, oil-rich Norway, our birth country, continues to attend climate conferences and to project itself as an international leader in climate politics. For years, Norway's left-green government policies have been based on international trading schemes designed to set caps on greenhouse gas emissions. The right-wing government, elected in 2013, has promised to continue these policies, which allow producers in excess of the allocated amount of emissions to "purchase so called 'carbon credits' from businesses or nations that are producing greenhouse gasses below their set emissions cap." [1] For Norway, this has meant a continued increase in carbon emissions at home while helping Bangladesh improve rural cooking stoves, allowing this developing country to reduce its carbon emissions.

In return, Norway has been able to grow its economy, support its citizen's ever-increasing consumer habits, and expand its oil industry. All the while, the country's own carbon footprint has naturally increased—a habit justified by purchasing carbon credits from Bangladesh. Norwegian journalist and author Erik Martiniussen calls this contradictory phenomenon "the climate politics that disappeared."[2] While Norway early on in the climate debate promised to reduce its production of CO2—an effort that would have required economic, political, scientific, and psychological changes on a national scale—it has instead, like so many industrialized countries and businesses, chosen a much easier route: to purchase carbon credits in poor countries. Unfortunately, within the current market economy this is too often how we "solve" our environmental problems. But why?

Sustainable Capitalism: Just Another Green, Mean Machine

While our lack of environmental awareness, and the destructive habits it has led to, has many causes, the growing trend toward a world of more and more material stuff is certainly one of the main causes of environmental destruction. In her book *Green Gone Wrong*, Heather Rogers dispels the common myth that if we just buy enough green consumer goods we can solve global warming, pollution, and rainforest clear-cutting. We cannot simply buy our way out of the very problems Western consumer culture has caused in the first place, she proclaims. The green capitalist consumerism now favored by many corporations, environmental activists, and green political parties falls way short of providing solutions to our environmental crisis. She demonstrates, with startling facts and first-person accounts from all over the world, that corporate green capitalism often increases environmental problems instead of fixing them.[3]

Large corporations, such as American-based General Mills, with seven production facilities in Europe alone, are buying up smaller organic companies like jam producer Cascadian Farms, and in the name of profit they relax many of the strict organic standards smaller growers abide by. In the US, General Mills is avoiding Genetically Modified Food (GMO) labeling of its products despite growing consumer demands. "Seeking the lowest cost, Western food processors and retailers," writes Rogers, "increasingly source from large producers in developing countries where land and labor are cheap, and environmental protections lax." In South America, multinational corporations are now growing organic sugar and other crops on clear-cut land in the Amazon rainforest. The Paraguayan organic sugar producer, AZPA, which exports most of its sugar to the US and the EU, exemplifies how the growing corporate organic agricultural business works.[4]

In the last fifteen years in the US and Europe there has been double-digit growth in the corporate organic food market. According to *Wall Street Fact Sheet*, an online business magazine, "The organic foods business is worth over $50 billion globally, and with a new trade agreement between the United States and the European Union opening up new markets, that number could double within the next few years."[5] Meanwhile, smaller organic farms and coops have a difficult time staying in business while competing against the pressure from these larger, organic agribusiness companies, often specializing in making organic food more processed, packaged, fat and sugar laced. Rogers sums up her findings with a stark warning for green capitalism's future: "If the profit motive stays in place economic growth in all its destructiveness will continue apace."[6]

The Ethics of Economics: What Do We Really and Truly Need?

If, as the saying goes, money cannot buy us happiness or a better planet, what is the true value of money? Authors Robert and Edward Skidelsky promote the idea that economics is a moral science and that what we ultimately want and need are not more material things but better health and education, more creativity, and more time to cultivate hobbies and spiritual practices. Rather than having more electronic gadgets, we need to experience the nonmaterial rewards of living in "the good society." Creating such a society—by applying the psychology of "less is more"—we would not only take care of people's basic needs, we would also be saving the environment.

But why aren't we heading in that direction? Because we live in an economic system fixated on satisfying our selfish needs through hedonist materialism. We have let capital forces driven by the advertising industry dictate our needs, our desires. Consequently, we have become a world in which a small minority owns most everything and where the majority desires to have the same as the rich minority. The philosophical pillars of capitalism rest solidly on this psychology, this "endless expansion of wants." That is why, "for all its success, it remains so unloved. It has given us wealth beyond measure, but has taken away the chief benefit of wealth: the consciousness of having enough."[7]

In other words, if we lived in a society governed by the awareness that material things cannot provide us with a good society, then everyone could indeed have enough. Then our economic, political, scientific, and psychological decisions would be more environmentally sound. We would not need to plunder the environment. Instead, we would make political and economic decisions based on the awareness that when we wrong nature, we destroy the foundation for our very own existence. [8]

The Price We Pay for Environmental Pollution

A growing number of people today are concerned about the impact the economy has on the environment. We have learned there is a price to pay when we pollute. But for hundreds of years, since its origin in the fourteenth century, the word "pollution" simply meant to make something dirty or to defile something. It was only in the late 1950s that the word took on its contemporary meaning: to contaminate the environment.

Science has concluded that pollution causes individual as well as collective problems—various cancers, as well as polluted rivers and oceans full of plastic waste. All of Earth's inhabitants—plants, animals, people, communities, businesses, governments—everyone pays a price for environmental contamination and destruction. Sometimes the price is very costly. When an animal or plant species is lost, such as when the Caspian Tiger became extinct in the 1970s, and when the last drop of oil is extracted from the bottom of the North Atlantic, these species and resources are lost forever and will not be available for future generations.

With large sums of money at stake, businesses often hide the cost of environmental destruction. On a cold day in January 2000 a dam burst in Romania. The dam contained toxic waste—one hundred thousand cubic meters of cyanide-laden water—from the Baia Mare Aural gold mine. The deadly effluent flowed downstream and into the tributaries of the Tisza, the biggest river in Hungary. Cyanide is extremely toxic. Even a small dose can be deadly to humans and animals alike. The toxic water measured a hundred times the limit for safe drinking water. Since pollution in water and air knows no national boundaries, the liquid effluent flowed to the Danube, which runs through Romania, and into Bulgaria and Serbia. The mining disaster killed at least 80 percent of the fish in the region, the water became unsafe to drink, and environmental disease was no longer just an abstract medical term—it became a personal health problem for many people. The disaster also destroyed known and unknown areas of vital natural habitat.[9] We will never know exactly how much damage the toxin caused.

To date there has been no study on the long-term effects of the cyanide spill on people, animals, plants, and waterways. As is customary in the current economy, the polluter did not pay much for the damages. While the victims and the environment in several countries are still suffering the impact, only one village near the dam received any restitution. The EU paid for some of the environmental cleanup; local governments paid for the rest. For the polluter, the Baia Mare Aural mining company, this monumental disaster had very few serious consequences.

This is very common in business today: when a company pollutes, someone else pays the bills and suffers the consequences—the community, the government—not those responsible for the destruction. But destruction of the environment is not free—there is always a price to pay, and common people, through taxes, illness, relocation and other forms of distress, often end up paying the environmental debts acquired by the corporations.[10]

Thanks to global warming and a host of other global ecological problems, this time we may not only destroy an island or a few mountainsides, we may destroy the whole planet. What is also new is that we are aware that we are destroying life, and still we seem not to care. What are the reasons for this apathy? First, as Marx predicted, human alienation has advanced to such an extent that we are often psychologically and culturally numb to the consequences of our actions. Secondly, a culture oriented towards owning and consuming will place higher value related to cost rather than according to usefulness and relatedness. A glass or a steel water bottle, for example, which is purchased and a plastic bottle received for "free" when purchasing water have nearly identical levels of usefulness, but the latter is simply thrown away, even though it can be reused many times. We have corresponding attitudes towards having experiences. A beautiful sunset is often taken for granted while an expensive trip to an amusement park is highly valued. In contrast, traditional peoples invested their personal items with much love and care because they valued their possessions as a part of their life. Thirdly, there is the notion of owning personal items vs. owning capital. If ownership is limited to that which I can productively use, then my possessions are limited, and I relate to them as productive extensions of my creative ability. Naturally, I would not desire to have more than I can effectively use. But if ownership is an abstract right to land, resources, people, and capital—all of which I have no personal relation to—then it is much easier to exploit these things to generate wealth. If I simply own something, the logic goes, then I also have the right to destroy or ruin it. [11]

What is also new in human history is that modern civilization, unlike most previous civilizations, no longer feels informed by an ethical compass about what is enough. Traditional Indian society was, to a large extent, informed by deep spiritual ethics, including yogic concepts such as *aparigraha*, living a life of material simplicity, the wisdom of knowing what constitutes enough money for thriving in the world without depriving others or destroying nature, ideas that are generally absent in informing economic decision-making in modern society. Most traditional societies had similar attitudes toward the use and accumulation of things. Unlike today, where money often has an abstract function in the economy, they lived in what philosopher and economics writer Charles Eisenstein calls a "gift economy," in which ritualized exchanges between people characterized society. [12] Eisenstein advocates a "sacred economics" in which tradition and innovation is wedded to a sustainable vision of a new economics where both people and planet can thrive. While a gift economy is too simplistic for the complexities of modern society, its underlying spirit—that material things are sacred rather than throwaways or things to hoard—can inform a new economy.

A History of Environmental Ignorance

Pollution of water and air, loss of habitat, global warming, overfishing, water scarcity, deforestation—these are only some of the many environmental problems we are experiencing today. Faced with these daunting and often global problems, many wish to turn back the clock to a simpler time when humans lived in harmony with nature. But that time may never truly have existed. "If we carefully examine both our past and present," writes popular author and social activist Riane Eisler, "[W]e see that many peoples past and present living close to nature have all too often been blindly destructive to their environment." She warns against idolizing ancient tribal cultures, since they, like us moderns, also overgrazed and deforested land to feed growing numbers of people. [13] While many tribal habits were ecologically sound and ancient peoples often lived within their means, they also lacked the capacity to destroy the environment on a global scale. But locally, their environment sometimes suffered severe blows.

Easter Island was so depleted of natural resources that most of the Rapa Nui had evacuated the area when white explorers arrived in 1772. The once thriving forests were gone, and only large, mysterious stone sculptures welcomed the newcomers to the denuded and depopulated island. Perhaps religious concerns trumped their concerns for the environment, we may never know. Similarly, large portions of New Zealand had been deforested by the Maoris before the whites arrived, and the Mediterranean basin was overcut and overgrazed thousands of years ago, the scars of the erosion still visible today. Theodore Roszak, the late ecopsychologist and staunch advocate for tribal peoples and their wisdom, pointed out that tribal societies "in their ignorance, blighted portions of their habitat sufficiently to endanger their own survival. River valleys have been devastated, forests denuded, the topsoil worn away; but the damage was limited and temporary."[14]

Ecological Wisdom, Ecological Science

Despite our ancestors' ability to destroy parts of their environment, they also acquired deep knowledge about the natural habitat they lived in, and they often protected it for future generations to behold and to draw nourishment from. They were knowledgeable in herbal medicine, and they protected the forests to make sure their medicines were available for those who came after them. Their low-impact economies were indeed often sacred. The Indians of South America had developed vast forest gardens in the Amazon more than 1500 years ago. It is estimated some of these large gardens could feed over a hundred thousand people. The topsoil in these bountiful gardens was six feet deep and the soil was mixed with charcoal, enabling the soil to hold nutrients much longer than before and thus give greater harvests without depleting the soil.

Science writer Charles C. Mann, the author of *1491: New Revelations of the Americas Before Columbus*, a book about life in the Americas before the European colonizers arrived, suggests that the Amazon is not just a vast and wild jungle but, in part, a planned garden gone wild, a true cultural and ecological wonder. Mann claims that these ancient peoples possessed deep knowledge about ecology and were practicing a form of agriculture similar to modern permaculture. Based on the science of systems ecology, the three main permaculture principles are: 1) to take care of the earth, 2) to take care of the people, and 3) to return the surplus. Permaculture is thus a new form of agriculture integrating both old and new science with the goal of creating a future for people and planet to flourish together in greater ecological harmony.[15] Rather than letting surplus wealth created by farming accumulate in the hands of a few corporations or private enterprises, such as is common in today's industrial farming, a permacultural operation merges economic and ecological interests—all surplus is recycled back into the system itself.

While the ecological wisdom exhibited by indigenous peoples is as old as humanity itself, modern ecological science has its roots in the natural science that emerged from the Greek philosophers Aristotle and Hippocrates. The word itself stems from the Greek *oikos* (house) and is, in a sense, the study of our earth household, the scientific study of the interactions between organisms and their environment. The word "economics" comes from the same root, pointing toward the important interrelationship between the two sciences.

Modern ecological science emerged at the end of the nineteenth century as the interdisciplinary study of evolution, ecosystems, and biology and their relations to the larger environment or ecosystem. An ecosystem maintains life-supporting functions for animals and humans and produces natural capital in the form of food, fuel, fiber, and medicine; hence, the need to maintain a close relation between ecology and economy. Indeed, a growing number of economic thinkers maintain that economics needs to be deeply rooted in ecological awareness. When ecological thinking—the idea that the global ecosystem includes nature as well as human society—will be used to inform economic planning and action, we will be better equipped to prevent environmental disasters such as humanity is currently experiencing.

Confusing Needs and Wants

Our needs are few but our wants are many. This sentence sums up our message—that we have to build an economy that takes care of our basic needs of housing, medical care, employment, education, and food without leading us astray into thinking that more and more sophisticated versions of these basic needs will satisfy our main need: the need for inner fulfillment, for happiness. Such an economic vision is very different from the capitalist philosophy that selfishness, our many wants, is the best driver of the economy.

There are various reasons why humans have destroyed the environment. There are economic, cultural, and political reasons. But the main cause is rooted in human nature and psychology itself, in our insatiable need for more—more money, more things, more pleasure. We humans come hardwired with two innate characteristics: the need to take care of ourselves, and the need to take care of others. We may call the first need self-interest and the other group-interest. Our modern insatiability for more things originates in the human psychology of self-interest.

We have built our economic system on the principles of selfishness and insatiability, of confusing our few basic needs with more material wants. Moreover, capitalism is based on the idea that selfishness and the desire for more are not only necessary drivers of the economy, they are also virtuous human qualities. President Ronald Reagan, with his Hollywood persona and neoliberal ideology, epitomized this mythic vision of capitalism: that the dream of wealth and the wrath of scarcity are two opposing principles that are essential to form a dynamic economy. Since the Reagan era, this vision has become an economic dogma, and, we think, one of the main reasons we are a global society in deep economic and environmental trouble. Unlike Reagan and his ideological ilk, we think human needs are basic and few and that providing these needs for all, without compromising the environment, is the new economy's main priority. Does that mean the economy in the rich countries needs to stop growing in order to save the environment?

Growth or No Growth?

Our environmental problems, now spanning the globe, have painfully taught us the limits of economic growth. The industrial and commercial growth machinery of capitalism has taught us at least three things:

Capitalist growth creates economic inequality. Over the past thirty years, as GDP growth has risen, economic inequality has also risen dramatically in the Western world, while at the same time global inequality between rich and poor countries has also increased.

Capitalist growth is often environmentally disastrous. Thanks to ever-expanding loans and credit lines, we in the Western world are able to purchase fancier cars and upgraded electronic gadgets at increasingly shorter intervals, exotic foods from faraway places, and bigger houses filled with more stuff than ever before. At the same time, the Chinese and Indian middle class is growing by tens of millions of people every year who demand cars and more consumer goods. The escalating rise in production of these goods puts a growing strain on the environment by rapidly reducing nonrenewable resources such as oil and gas while also increasing pollution and toxic waste.

Capitalist growth has manifested economic globalization, but in our estimation it has not created a good global society in the spirit of

Aristotle. It was he who first outlined some of the qualities of the good life—individual courage, moderation, generosity, wisdom, and the social and economic requirements needed for the individual to realize those qualities. We think it is environmentally wise to aspire for the good society, where human expressions such as art, music, ethics, spirituality, literature, and sports, rather than material qualities, are favored. But capitalist materialism does not consider these valid notions of progress. For the true believers in unrestricted neoliberal capitalism, the good society is a society where the most successful have the most toys, and where everyone else's dream is to one day have even more toys, even more money, than the most successful have today. In Europe, and to a lesser degree in the US, this cut-throat form of capitalism has been tempered by some government control over the market, redistribution of wealth, and environmental regulations, but these checks and balances have not been enough to stem the growing increase in environmental problems.

Economist John Maynard Keynes looked forward to a time when growth would end, a time when we were materially satisfied and had plenty of time to pursue leisure activities. Not unlike a contemporary environmentalist, he had already realized in the 1930s that capitalist progress was a "soiled creed, black with coal dust and gunpowder." In an address to students at Cambridge in the 1920s, he outlined his prophetic vision of a society one hundred years hence where "the economic problem may be solved, or at least within sight of solution." We would work no more than three hours a day and spend the rest of our time in a joyous spirit of artistic and intellectual pursuits—not just the privileged few but society as a whole.

So far, Keynes' prophecy has not been realized. The reason is simple, according to the environmentalists: we cannot grow our way into the future and expect to live in harmony with both nature and ourselves. The influential Club of Rome sponsored book *Limits to Growth*, published in 1972, has set the tone for much of the environmental writings ever since: growth is bad, reduced growth is good, going back to nature and living the good life of simplicity and sustainability is the answer to capitalist excess. From John Stuart Mill to John Maynard Keynes to contemporary ecological economist Herman Daly, the vision of steady-state economics has been strong and consistent. According to Daly, a steady-state economy, like the idea of the good society, will enable any nonphysical component of the economy to grow indefinitely, despite occasional limits to economic growth as per ecological constraints.

The basic tenets of steady-state economics are: (1) maintain the health of ecosystems and the life-support services they provide; (2) extract renewable resources like fish and timber at a rate no faster than they can be regenerated; (3) consume nonrenewable resources like fossil fuels and minerals at a rate no faster than they can be replaced by the discovery of renewable substitutes; and (4) deposit wastes in the environment at a rate no faster than they can be safely assimilated. [16]

While many, if not most, environmentalists adhere to this form of ecological economics, there are technological optimists within the sustainable-economy camps who promise ecological designs "beyond sustainability" ensuring abundance and ecological balance in perpetuity. In other words, economic growth and ecological balance is possible, argues architect William McDonough and chemist Michael Braungart in their book *The Upcycle*, if "technical nutrients" such as metals, plastics, and other materials not continuously created by the biosphere become, in an industrial ecological cycle, "resource food" for another product and yet again for another product—forever and ever. [17] Inventers of various industrial designs, they and a growing number of ecological activists and scientists now believe economic growth is possible through ecological designs by turning sewage plants and houses into alternative energy generators and industrial plants into nonpolluting facilities where waste is cycled back into productive use.

We agree, but what is missing in this optimistic green vision is an economic structure to ensure that such ecological designs do not only become a feature of a privileged few countries. As Heather Rogers suggests in *Green Gone Wrong*, in the name of profit, corporations could easily start to dominate these new industrial concepts as well, ensuring monopoly and control. Unless there is economic restructuring of the economy, green capitalism will not be able to deliver what it promises: a sustainable world for all.

Global retail giant Wal-Mart, to name one example of a corporate giant gone green, is one of the most profitable businesses in the world. It is one of the largest sellers of organic produce, but despite four billion dollars of profits each year the company is still paying their workers low wages without medical benefits. Their environmental focus has not translated into better business practices. As is common in capitalism, the bottom line, rather than a new-found progressive conscience, dictates Wal-Mart's business practices. Moreover, wherever Wal-Mart sets up shop, the aggressively competitive company inevitably drives smaller firms out of business. In our observation, this is not only green gone wrong, this is green gone mean.

Selling environmental products is therefore not enough. This practice must also be supported by economic policy changes and economic restructuring. Otherwise, the profit motive will continue to dictate environmental concerns. And that kind of sustainability is too shallow, too green washed to have any meaningful impact on the economic and environmental crisis we're in.

Economic growth or no growth thus depends on the situation. Currently, the Western world does not need to grow in the production of luxury goods, or in constructing bigger houses, or more coal-fired power plants, or in designing more weapons of mass destruction. The Western world needs to grow by providing more fuel-efficient cars, greener homes, greener industrial plants, less waste and increased recycling. The Western economy needs to grow leaner and greener companies and products, and its economy needs to decentralize, to localize.

Regarding localization of the economy, the online retail giant Amazon is a case in point. The heavily centralized yet global company employs sixty-five thousand people, most of whom earn only a fraction of what the shareholders earn. If all the operations of Amazon were decentralized, according to economist Robert Reich, the various companies it would create would employ nearly 850,000 people. This would not only ensure growth in the economy by spreading the wealth around to more wage earners and away from the wealthy one percent in the shareholder class now running the company, it would also result in fewer shipping miles and thus less impact on the environment—in sum, the economic impact would be more equitable and the carbon footprint would be drastically reduced, a win-win situation for both the economy and the environment.[18]

In recent years we have painfully learned that capitalism has created an economy mainly based on material growth. We have also learned that material resources are limited; that their utilization sometimes creates pollution, and that pollution has a cost—economic, social, personal, and environmental. We have learned that we cannot simply grow the economy without paying off these debts to nature and to humanity.

But for most of modern life, politicians and business leaders have told the public that economic growth is the single most important pursuit of society. Today we know this economic goal is the number-one cause of the environmental crisis. We have also learned this: of all the crises that humanity is faced with today, no matter how devastating they may be, the one with the potential for the most profound impact on human life is the environmental crisis.

The True Cost of Air: Upsetting the Carbon-offsets

According to Rajendra Pachauri, the chairman of the Intergovernmental Panel on Climate Change (IPCC), the financial markets are humanity's only hope in reducing global warming. He said this in late September 2013 while presenting the most air-tight case ever that humans are responsible for rapidly increasing the Earth's temperature. Pachauri proclaimed his organization's latest report provided "unequivocal" evidence that the oceans and the atmosphere had warmed since 1950. He said furthermore that scientists are now "95 percent certain" that humans are the "dominant cause" of global warming. [19]

A few years before Pachauri made that statement, the popular British rock band Coldplay made headlines by making an environmentally activist decision to "neutralize" the carbon-dioxide emissions generated from the production of its second CD. To do that, the band paid The Carbon Neutral Company (TCNC) about $50,000 to plant ten thousand mango trees near Gudibanda, India. Since then, rock bands such as the Rolling Stones and the Dave Matthews Band have followed suit, thus popularizing the act of voluntarily shrinking one's carbon footprint. This type of carbon offset is sold by private firms to individuals, corporations, and organizations to reduce the impact of their carbon pollution. The other type are mandatory offsets based on the regulations set forth by the Kyoto Protocol, which requires polluting businesses to either purchase additional CO2 credits from another company or invest in new credit offsets. The whole process is overseen by a UN body. [20]

While these attempts at curbing global warming are commendable, they are also fraught with limitations. The voluntary carbon-offset business, which is now driven by the guilt and concerns of many celebrities, including actors Brad Pitt and Jake Gyllenhaal, politician Hilary Clinton, and of course green activist and former US vice president Al Gore, is according to an increasing number of environmentalists distracting us from the real problem: how to stop producing more greenhouse gases in the first place by investing in and using more alternative energy. More importantly, by creating a more localized and greener economy that requires less transportation, uses more fuel efficient and electric cars, less oil-based fertilizers, and is less dependent on meat and dairy production—since methane from cattle, according to UN reports, is one of the greatest contributors to greenhouse gasses—we can more effectively curb the rise in global temperatures.

Environmental writer Heather Rogers's conclusion is that carbon off-sets so far have only a small impact on reducing global warming, in part because the trees planted by volunteers today will only start to reduce CO_2 in several decades. More importantly, she thinks the carbon credit system will serve Wall Street well by using "the earth's atmosphere as a casino," but not become an effective way to avert increased global temperatures.[21]

While mandatory greenhouse taxes and voluntary efforts are steps in the right direction, it would be much more effective, she argues, if we stopped producing greenhouse gasses in the first place, such as by installing solar water heaters on homes in sunny cities all over the world. This has been done in cities like Bangalore, India, and such efforts can easily be copied in other cities. In other words, we do not need Band-Aid solutions; we need real economic and environmental changes from the grassroots up.

Rethinking Green Economics: Beyond the Triple Bottom Line (TBL)

The popular sustainability phrase, "People, Planet, Profit," was coined by John Elkington in 1995, and in 1997 it was adopted as the title of the Anglo-Dutch oil company Shell's first sustainability report. As a result, the three P's of sustainability have become a well-known icon of green economics in the Netherlands, as well as in the rest of the industrialized world. Since its coinage, many private companies and even multinational corporations pride themselves in adhering to TBL tenets.

For a company incorporating TBL guidelines, it means that all business decisions ideally address the question: Are the company's business practices financially, socially, and environmentally responsible? Can the company continuously self-regulate its business practices and move beyond bottom-line profit motives and optimize its performance to enhance its contribution to the environment and the community in which it operates? Today, the three P's have become a hallmark of the green business movement and are largely promoted as a panacea to creating a more sustainable world.

The following is a short review of TBL and how the concept differs from the old business model, where financial profit is generally the sole indicator of a company's success.

"People" refers to a company or corporation's fair and beneficial business practices toward the employees, people, and community in which it conducts its business. In practical terms, a TBL business would not hire child labor, would pay fair salaries to its workers, maintain a safe labor environment and reasonable working hours, and would not otherwise exploit a community or labor force.

"Planet" refers to the natural resources utilized by a business and thus to its sustainable, green, or environmental practices. A TBL company endeavors to minimize its environmental impact, or reduce its "ecological footprint" by, among other things, carefully managing its consumption of energy and nonrenewables and reducing manufacturing waste as well as rendering waste less toxic before disposal or recycling.

"Profit" is the economic value created by a business after deducting the cost of all inputs, including natural resources, pollution costs , capital, etc. Profit within a TBL framework, therefore, differs from traditional accounting definitions of profit, which would take for granted the free services rendered by nature and not account for the company's environmental impact. Normally, profit is limited to the monetary profit made by a company or organization, but in the TBL approach, profit also refers to the positive economic and service impact a company has on people and the planet.

The TBL formula quite effectively points out the essence, as well as main defect, of capitalism: that the totality of the private business enterprise, even the totality of the goal of economic life itself, can be reduced to one word: profit. "This means," wrote economist E.F. Schumacher as early as 1973, "that an activity can be economic although it plays hell with the environment, and that a competing activity, if at some cost it protects and conserves the environment, will be uneconomic." In other words, according to capitalist economics' rather irrational economic philosophy of selfish needs creating altruistic results, money is the highest of all values, and profit is the driver of progress, indeed of civilization itself. Schumacher understood the inherent flaw in this theory and the market on which it is based, which he aptly described as "the institutionalization of individualism and non-responsibility." [22]

Building upon Schumacher, the green movement of the 1980s until today has carefully developed a new economic reform model, which some call sustainability and others call green capitalism. The value system of green reform capitalism strikes at the heart of the simplistic errors of classical as well as those of neoclassical capitalism, and it points out that the pursuit of profit takes nature for granted and avoids the negative effects business can have on people and the environment. With these defects in mind, TBL was developed to right the wrongs of business as usual. But is reforming this staggeringly flawed system enough? Is it indeed possible to reform an economic system that has brought us an increasingly divided world of rich and poor nations, that has given us a financial system run amok in speculative ventures creating mega-profits but no real jobs, while effecting nature so negatively that many scientists think we are on the brink of worldwide collapse?

The green movement surely thinks so. Green reforms can indeed tame the capitalist beast, the movement bravely claims. Since Schumacher's influential book came out in the 1970s, the greens have been busy implementing all kinds of economic, political, and activist ventures in pursuit of a market system that is benign for people and the planet while also good for the bottom line. But one of green capitalism's most ardent proponents, however, popular writer Paul Hawken, admits that progress has been small. So small, in fact, that Hawken likens its impact to mere "drops in a bucket."[23] The reason green capitalism has so far made very little impact is partly political—lack of comprehensive changes in environmental and economic policies; and partly economic—corporate capitalism still makes up the larger wheels of the predominant economic system. And as long as we have an economic system acting as a predator in relation to nature, and politicians acting as its ombudsmen and spokespeople, we can only expect superficial changes to the status quo. We cannot wait, in other words, for corporations to voluntarily change their habits; it is simply unrealistic to expect them to voluntarily change their economic practices quickly without mounting public, political pressure.

We need to implement systemic and lasting green reforms in general, and more specifically, we need to restructure the economy so that it can better serve both people and the planet. For that to take place, we need to demand political and economic changes so fundamental that we may have to accept that capitalism, even green capitalism, is unsuitable for restructuring—that we need a new economic system altogether.

Creating A Green Economy

There are many vitally important aspects of green economic theory and activism as well as ecological science, which, if combined into a cohesive set of policies, hold many if not most of the answers to a more sustainable economy. What is missing in the green and environmentalist critique of capitalism is a systemic analysis and critique of capitalism itself, its philosophical foundation and economic principles. We have attempted to do just that in this book. In the previous chapters, we analyzed capitalism from a philosophical, historical, and economic perspective in relation to the EU and the world economy, and in this chapter we looked deeper into environmentalism's and green capitalism's response to some of humanity's important ecological challenges. Despite daunting challenges, many ground-breaking ideas and initiatives are making lasting and positive changes. In fact, we probably already have enough know-how—economically, politically and scientifically—to create a sustainable economy.

Each year, the World Watch Institute publishes a report called "Vital Signs" that tracks "key trends in the environment, agriculture, energy, society, and the economy to inform and inspire the changes needed to build a sustainable world." Here are some of the trends documented in 2012, with our comments in square brackets:

1. Fossil fuel consumption subsidies fell 44 percent in 2009, to $312 billion—reflecting changes in international energy prices rather than a change in policies. [Governments are subsidizing the oil industries, the world's most profitable and polluting companies. Imagine if similar amounts of subsidies went into alternative energy production.]
2. Continuing its rapid ascent, installed global wind-power capacity increased 24 percent to 197,000 megawatts in 2010—nine times as much as a decade ago. [This is a positive trend, but what is lacking and needed is massive governmental support for the alternative energy industry.]
3. Solar-photovoltaic generating capacity grew even faster. The 16,700 megawatts that were newly installed in 2010 surpasses the total PV capacity that was in place in 2008. [This is also a positive sign but still far short of the increase needed.]
4. Global biofuel production increased by 17 percent in 2010 to reach an all-time high of 105 billion liters. Rising portions of the US corn harvest and Brazil's sugarcane production are turned into ethanol—giving rise to fears of increasing food and fuel trade-offs. [This is a disturbing trend that should be stopped—using farmland for fuel production instead of food production. This trend is driven by the higher profits made

by the farmers and the fact governments often subsidize such production.]

5. Organic farming methods were used on 37.2 million hectares worldwide in 2009. This represents a 150 percent increase since 2000, yet the organic area amounts to just 0.85 percent of global agricultural land. [In other words, organic farming is still in its infancy, and as we have documented above, corporations are beginning to control the production and distribution of organics. Not a truly green or sustainable trend at all.]

6. Per capita meat consumption in the developing world doubled to 32 kilograms over the past quarter century, but this is still far below consumption levels in the industrial world. [Meat production results in methane gas from cattle, one of the main sources behind increased levels of CO_2 in the atmosphere. Reducing meat production and producing and eating more plant food is an effective way to combat global warming.] [24]

As we can see, to create a more sustainable world, we need deep-rooted political, economic, cultural, and scientific changes, since the negative trends far outweigh the incremental positive changes currently implemented. Buying organic food, recycling plastic bottles, driving a hybrid car, and voting green is not enough to bring about the monumental changes needed to create a truly green economy. Hoping that "good capitalists" and individual lifestyle changes will save the environment is not enough.

Conclusion

Our economy is dependent on nature for its survival and continued growth. With better economic and environmental policies, which will include creating a new post-capitalist economy, it is possible to create an economy that will continue to exist and thrive, just like nature herself, in virtual perpetuity. Such a new economy will be more localized, restructured, democratic, and circular. But it will not come about unless there is political will for such change, political will that is guided by new economic principles and a deeper ecological psychology and culture than currently prevails.

Part IV:
Economic Solutions for People and Planet

Make the world work for 100% of humanity, in the shortest possible time, through spontaneous cooperation without ecological offense or disadvantage of anyone.

—Buckminster Fuller

S O FAR, WE HAVE analyzed the history of economics by journeying back to the early mercantile era and forward to the modern era of green or sustainable capitalism, and we have also analyzed the various theoretical models underlying capitalism and the free-market economy. Now it is time to leave our critical outlook behind and put on some visionary glasses to look into the future of economics.

Economist Ravi Batra attributes the ailments of the economy to the productivity wage gap; in other words, part of the gains realized from work done by individuals does not benefit those individuals but instead are channeled into profits for a small elite. This leads to increasing inequality, which unbalances the economy and brings about unemployment, debt, and exploitation on a worldwide scale. Batra's solution is to close the wage gap so individual workers benefit fully from the work they do. Put the economy back in balance and everyone prospers.

We concur with Ravi Batra that the cause of the ills facing our world is largely related to inequality. If inequality can be reduced and ordinary people become more prosperous, and if the superrich are brought down from their high perks, then most of the economic ills of society can be cured. But how to do it?

With economic power comes political power, so a society where ordinary people hold the economic power is more likely to be able to solve issues like environmental destruction and shortages of resources. Average citizens have a range of priorities that are more down-to-earth than those of economists, corporate shareholders, and bankers, including the survival of the environment and the wellbeing of their children and grandchildren. Only those whose minds are obsessed with accumulation of wealth will choose short-term profit over jobs, healthy communities, and long-term survival. Judging by the recent historical decisions taken by large corporations, bankers, and many politicians, greed has inflated their reason. We already know what it will take to solve the environmental crisis as well as the economic crisis. If average citizens were given sufficient economic power, better decisions about economic and environmental affairs would be taken, and we could finally get out of the mess we are in.

While we agree with Dr. Batra's conclusions, and we are sympathetic to his suggestions to resolve the immediate crisis, we do not think his suggestions go far enough. As long as the present power structures remain, any limited reform is likely to be reversed quickly. Therefore, while we will discuss actions that any government can take, including those presented by Dr. Batra, this book goes much further, culminating in a program for a comprehensive restructuring of the entire economic system.

The first chapter in this section, "Resolving the Immediate Crisis," outlines suggested reforms to save the financial system. The next chapter, "Making Poor Countries Rich," deals with inequality between rich and poor countries, and also addresses the inherent problems of free trade. The chapter on "Economic Democracy" goes further and suggests reforms to reduce inequalities among people and the development of local economies. "Green Solutions" suggests ways to resolve the resource and environmental crisis, and the final chapter, "A New Economic System," introduces a comprehensive new economy as an alternative to both capitalism and socialism as they are known and practiced today. We are not suggesting to entirely do away with either economic system; rather we suggest ways to restructure and thus radically improve and coordinate both in a synergistic fashion.

This progression of ideas is deliberate. In the next chapters, we start by elaborating reforms that can easily be accommodated within the present economic system; at each step, however, you will see that these reforms will not be sufficient to solve the long-term problems of humanity. Thus, step by step, we have been compelled to conclude that the only way to achieve long-term prosperity and sustainability is through a radical departure from the way our economy now works.

We invite you to join us on this explorative journey. We will lay out the arguments and the conclusions we have drawn, but ultimately it is you, the reader, who will decide if our economic and environmental vision rings true or not.

Chapter Ten

Resolving the Financial Crisis:
Short-term Reforms That Will Work

At present people and nature are in service to the economy, which itself serves the desires of the financial sector. The economy we need would demote finance to its proper role as a tool, and ensure the creation of an economy in service to well-being.

— Camilla Obreg

T HE MAIN PROBLEM WITH the financial crisis is that those most responsible for it, the large banks, such as Bear Stearns and Lehman Brothers, and large corporations, such as Ford and Walmart, are benefiting from its continuation by increasing risk and debt and by reducing real wages and benefits. The people interested in ending the crisis, people like us, do not have the power to facilitate that change. Furthermore, the next generation of economists, those potentially able to turn the economic ship around, have been taught the same economic theories that created the current crisis in the first place. In other words, we are caught in a vicious cycle where the common people do not have the political or economic power to create change, and the economists and politicians lack the vision and interest to go beyond the status quo.

New ideas and a new political momentum are desperately needed to fix the financial crisis. Here are the three most important measures we think are needed:

1) New policies to reduce debt.
2) New regulations to control the financial sector.

3) New measures to reduce inequality and restore the purchasing capacity of the average citizen.

These measures are closely related, and if successful, they will put the brakes on the financial crisis and improve the lives of ordinary people. Implementing such measures will effectively move the burden of the crisis away from the average citizen and toward the rich, those who have profited from the situation and thus have the greatest capacity to shoulder the problem. Naturally, the rich will prefer that the financial burden be placed on the common people, and so they are likely to take their money out of any country that tries to implement these policies. And they can accomplish this easily, since the free movement of capital is one of the foundations of the new world order and one of the "four freedoms" the EU is based on.

The policies suggested in this chapter will only work if they were implemented across the industrial West, as well as the rest of the world. Both Europe and the United States are powerful enough to implement these policies unilaterally, but the greatest effect would come if they were applied globally.

1) Resolving the Debt Crisis

Current Strategies for Handling the Debt

So far, the customary means of "solving" a debt crisis has been to socialize the debt—to transfer the obligation to repay the debt to the citizens. But socializing private debt has repercussions for the whole economy. In Ireland, Iceland, and Spain, bankers gave out loans on housing and other ventures, and when the property boom burst, the banks were in serious trouble. In order to bail out the depositors and the institutions that had lent money to the banks, the EU pressured its governments to bail out the banks. That is, public money was used to prevent private individuals and speculators from taking losses. Private debts were taken over by the state and transferred to the public, who had no say in the matter. Such actions go against capitalist principles, however. Had there been no crisis, profits would have gone to the investors. Normal market principles dictate that an investor can either win or lose, and if he loses, he has to accept his lot. But a system that privatizes profits and transfers the losses to the public is not capitalism per se—it is socialism for the rich and capitalism for the poor. This is the tragic irony pf today's economy.

Standard debt reduction requires that money that is otherwise used for consumption or investments be diverted into paying back the debt. By thus socializing the debt, money is removed from people's pockets and their purchasing capacity is reduced. This initiates a downward spiral where transfer payments stop, salaries are reduced, and government employees are laid off. Since people in general have less money to spend, shops and businesses have a more difficult time selling their goods. As a consequence, private employers start to lay people off, resulting in still more people filling the unemployment ranks. With reduced business activity, the government collects less tax and thus needs to cut costs even more. The number of local businesses facing bankruptcy increases and the crisis gradually gets worse and worse.

This whole approach to debt restructuring, whether in third world countries or in the EU or the USA, is aimed at saving the banks and investors. Unfortunately, this is achieved at an unacceptable cost to regular citizens and does not address the underlying causes that created the crisis in the first place.

Since the debt crisis was caused by increased inequality, it cannot be solved by adding more debt, public or private, nor by further increasing inequality through austerity measures. However, that is the economic insanity we are now facing.

We need a more practical way to solve the debt crisis. The following approach aims to resolve the debt overhang in a structured way, without saddling with a crushing debt burden those who are least able to absorb it.

A New Approach to Solving the Debt Crisis

Essentially, the lending business is a speculative activity. Loans do not directly produce new wealth. They are extended in the hope that they will be repaid with interest. Loans always carry risk: the borrower may not be able to repay the loan.

Why should the general public be responsible for the losses created by profit-hungry banks and individual speculators? It makes sense that small depositors are protected from bank failures, but it is not at all logical that the general public, who had no say in either creating the debt crisis nor the know-how to resolve it, should bear the losses created by speculative banks and greedy corporations.

Piketty has demonstrated that all net wealth in industrialized countries is owned by private individuals, since the debt and public assets cancel each other out. Private wealth is generally between four and six times the national income, while the public debt is roughly equivalent to the national income. [1] Thus by taxing private wealth with a onetime tax of twenty percent, the entire public debt could be cleared at once. Alternatively, a lower-rate wealth tax of two percent could be introduced over a number of years, which is the approach Piketty advocates.

A progressive wealth tax makes a lot of sense. It could serve to balance the budget and revive the economy by forcing the richest persons in society, those who can easily afford it, to give up a small share of their wealth in order to infuse the economy with renewed vitality. A traditional bailout, on the other hand, leads to a contraction in economic output and initiates a downward spiral, dragging the real economy deeper into recession. As we have witnessed numerous times throughout history, the resulting economic crisis wastes both human and natural resources and reduces the amount of wealth created.

When the burden of a financial collapse is placed on those who have gained from previous speculative activities, and not on the consumers, the real economy will revive and jobs and lives will be protected. By targeting the wealthiest in society, unutilized financial assets, those virtually outside the productive economy, can be used to offset the debt. A large portion of the wealth of the superrich is purely speculative assets, such as derivative products, and these assets do not add anything to the real economy. By using these assets to pay back loans, interest payments will be reduced and more of society's assets will remain in the productive economy. Aggregate demand will be maintained, since the purchasing power of people will be stabilized, which will further stimulate continued production and economic activity. The net effect will be positive and will effectively defuse the financial crisis without a contraction of the real economy. While indiscriminate cutbacks in public spending are hurtful to the economy, cutting unproductive and wasteful spending will have the opposite effect. It will act as medicine for a sluggish economy.

In many countries, governments are spending large sums on unproductive ventures that only benefit limited interest groups, ventures that do not directly contribute to the economy or the well-being of the larger population. In some cases there is also direct wastage of money, corruption, and the siphoning of funds to politicians and their cronies.

Identifying Assets and Income to be Taxed

In order to utilize the resources of the rich as a means of resolving the crisis, the first step will be to identify these financial assets in greater detail throughout the global economy. With the mobility of financial assets, it is very easy to hide income and wealth from tax authorities by moving them to offshore tax havens. The United States and the EU have in fact begun to identify and target tax havens, but there are still many loopholes through which wealth can be hidden. For such global efforts to be effective, an international system of financial transparency needs to be introduced so that all international assets can be identified and disclosed. This would require close international cooperation, but if the United States and the EU agreed to such measures, their combined financial and political power would provide a good foundation for other countries to build on.

A compulsory declaration of all assets and income—regardless of which territory they belong to, or under which form of corporate structure they are hidden—should be the first policy. All banks, land registries, and other entities that track financial and tangible assets should be required to report the owners of all their assets. This would include derivatives. The quadrillion-dollar derivatives market must also be opened up for inspection and regulation. Today derivatives are private contracts between two parties; they are not regulated in any way and are thus impossible to track. A possible way forward would be to push for legislative reform that deems derivative contracts illegal and unenforceable unless they are properly registered with and regulated by a central exchange.

Naturally such controls will have to implemented internationally. In this way, the shadowy world of secret financial transactions will be reduced and eventually eliminated.

Deciding How to Tax the Identified Assets and Income

Through Piketty's research, we have learned that all wealth is in public hands, and that 70 percent of this wealth is owned by only 10 percent of the population (the top 1 percent holds 25-35 percent while the bottom

50 percent holds only 5 percent). The simple solution to resolve the debt and inequality crisis, therefore, is to have the wealthiest foot the bill and thus ensure that the lower-income groups receive a bigger part of the pie. This can be achieved with the following measures:

- Introduction of a progressive tax on wealth.
- Reintroduction of a progressive tax on income.
- Increase marginal income rates.
- Increase taxation on return on capital, and reduce tax on work and productive economic activities.
- Differentiate between productive use of wealth, such as profits from manufacturing, and unproductive profits, such as capital gains and financial income from interest. Tax unproductive profits higher. Take steps to protect and preserve the real economy.

Progressive Wealth Tax

If private wealth in a particular country is six times the national income and the government debt is equal to the national income, this means that the private wealth is six times the government debt. A 17 percent onetime flat tax on private wealth would thus wipe out the government debt. If the richest 1 percent owns 35 percent of the wealth, the next 9 percent owns 35 percent, and the next 40 percent owns 20 percent, we could achieve the same result by placing a 28 percent wealth tax on the richest 1 percent, an 18 percent tax on the next 9 percent, 2.5 percent tax on the next 40 percent, with the lowest 50 percent not being taxed.

An alternative would be to introduce the tax gradually so that the debt is removed within 10 years. In this case the richest 1 percent could be taxed 2.8 percent of the total wealth per year, the next 9 percent richest taxed 1.8 percent, and the next 40 percent taxed 0.25 percent. Since historically the return on wealth is 5 percent per annum, and higher than that for the really rich, these annual taxes would not even reduce the wealth of the rich, but simply prevent it from growing too fast. Governments would have the income to pay off their national debts with sufficient resources left over to invest in real people and the real economy, for example, in the development of green technology.

Naturally, this is only one possible structure for introducing a wealth tax. We are presenting it to illustrate that there is an easy way to reduce the collective debt in any given nation. The optional percentages may vary from those used here, but the general formula is rational and workable.

Progressive Tax on Income

Taxes on the rich, especially in the US, have steadily decreased since the time of Ronald Reagan and Margret Thatcher, with the expectations that this would free up more capital for productive investments. This near-religious promise did not materialize as expected, however. While investments actually shrunk, what grew was the level of speculation and the vast amounts of debt accumulated by governments and individuals. By reversing the trend and returning to higher taxes on the rich, we can reduce the amount of resources wasted on speculation, reduce debt levels, and put more resources into the productive sectors of the economy.

Therefore, in addition to the introduction of a wealth tax, governments should also reintroduce a progressive income tax. In the past, the top tax rate on income was nearly 80 percent, while in most industrialized countries today it has been reduced to around 35 percent. With exemptions and lower taxes on capital gains and other income from passive holdings of wealth, the rich actually end up paying even less.

We also need to draw a distinction between different types of income. Basically, there are two types: income from work and income from return on capital. In the second category, we need to make a distinction between income that constitutes profits from productive activities, like running a factory, and income that comes from speculation and financial activities, such as capital gains and earned interest.

During the Progressive Era a century ago, it was generally accepted that rent and income from property should be taxed heavily. The idea was to make these activities unattractive so as to free society from unnecessary interest and rents. Society's costs were supposed to reflect the costs of production, not unearned rents that are simply transfer payments from a productive producer to those who produce nothing so the latter can get a free lunch.

Today, we have a completely reversed system. Real work is highly taxed, while capital gains, interests, and other unearned income have low or no taxes. This is the reason why rich people in general pay a lower percentage of tax than their employees. In order to save the economy, encourage real production, and discourage people getting rich while contributing nothing, this policy must change. As long as speculation and rent-seeking exist, they should be taxed much higher than income from real, productive work. The basic problem is simple. If someone does not work but earns from the work of others, he is a burden to society. There is no logical reason why such antisocial behavior should be rewarded with tax exemptions.

Real-estate speculators have other means to avoid taxation. They borrow money from banks to buy property and rent out buildings, and the income from the rent is used to pay the bank interest. Since bank interest is tax-deductible, they pay no tax for the rental income. In addition, they depreciate the buildings every year, and although the value of the building is going up, from an accounting perspective they are actually losing money. Since their income is eaten up by bank interest, they have no taxes to pay on the property, and with the depreciation they will report losses, which they can use to offset other income.

Finally, when they sell the property at a price much higher than what they bought it for, this income is taxed at a much lower rate than operating profits or salaries, and if they reinvest the money into another property within a certain period, they will pay no tax at all.

The following are suggestions to address these problems. If followed, these suggestions will help increase government tax revenues, reward work, and reduce the incentives to borrow huge sums for real estate and other speculative purposes:

- Reduce taxes on income within normal tax brackets, but increase marginal tax rates to 50 percent for extremely high incomes. This will put more money in the pockets of those who are sure to spend it, thus putting it back into the real economy and removing it from those who would hoard it or use it for speculation.
- Increase the marginal tax rate to up to 75 percent for realized capital gains and income from other speculative activities and finance income. The lowest rate for income from capital should be consistently higher than for the same amount earned through salaries.
- Remove corporate income tax but introduce up to 60 percent for income from dividends in companies outside the finance sector, where a 75 percent maximum tax rate will apply. This rate should be consistently lower than the rate from income from speculation and financial services, but higher than tax rates from real work.

- The following additional policies could be introduced to discourage real-estate speculation:
- Disallow fictitious tax-deductible expenses for the depreciation of buildings that are actually increasing in value. This would remove a big tax shelter for the rich.
- Interest payments on speculative purchases, such as stocks, real estate, etc., should not be considered a tax-deductible expense.

A note on the removal of corporate tax: In the final analysis, all companies are owned by an individual. Taxing corporations for profits is just a way to prevent people from hiding their income in companies, but it actually constitutes a form of unproductive, double taxation.

Corporate tax is also a way to tax companies who do not distribute dividends and keep reinvesting their profits each year. Since this practice will increase a company's assets, the owners would be forced to pay an increased wealth tax, if one is in force.

The rates given here are only meant as suggestions for a nation's tax policies. The actual rates will change from time to time according to the needs of the people, the government, and the economy.

These rules would need to be revised regularly to check for any possible loopholes. As can be seen from the above proposal, income from work is taxed the least, income from owning productive assets is taxed more, and income from speculation and financial gains are taxed the highest.

Steps to Reduce Monopoly Profits

In his book *End Unemployment Now*, Ravi Batra presents a set of policies the US Government could take, without having to resort to legislation, to combat monopoly profits by large corporations and eliminate debt and unemployment. While some of these policies are very specific to the United States, here are a few that can be applied in most parts of the world:

As we have demonstrated in this book, we do not have free, competitive markets in financial services. This sector is controlled by a small group of players that aim to increase profits at all costs. Interest on credit-card debt, to mention just one, ranges from 15 percent to 200 percent per annum, depending on the country. Given that the cost of borrowing for the banks is close to 0 percent, these are enormous spreads. Thus a simple way governments could drastically bring down these rates would be to compete in the credit-card market. They could start a bank and offer to take over credit-card debt at, say, 5 percent interest. The government could also issue its own credit cards with low interest rates. This would force the banks to follow suit. With a simple stroke, consumers would benefit, debts would decrease, and the superprofits of the rich would be reduced.

Patent rights in the pharmaceutical industry protect new products for up to thirty years. While some governments, in exchange for the patents, regulate the prices of pharmaceutical products, others, such as the government of the United States, do not. This means that prices in some countries are many times higher than in others. This is an area where free trade actually could benefit people. By allowing free trade in pharmaceutical products, prices would fall drastically in many places and end up the same as in the cheapest markets. This would benefit people and reduce the superprofits of the big pharmaceutical corporations.

In India and many other developing countries, a system existed where subcontracts were extended to people to produce textiles, pottery, ornaments, machine tools, etc., in their villages and towns. These cottage industries thrived for hundreds of years and coexisted with larger enterprises. In today's world with computer technology and better communication, this system could work even more effectively.

Increase the minimum wage. This will not depress the economy. Rather it will put more money in the hands of the people, increase demand, and actually increase employment. The amount of jobs available depends on how many goods can be sold, not on the fixed level of salaries. It does not matter how low salaries are. If nobody can afford to buy anything, no jobs will be created.

Do not permit mergers of large, profitable companies, since the new megacorporations monopolize the economy, keep prices high, and reduce industry competition. [2]

Bail Out People Rather Than Banks

While a tax on wealth would solve the government's debt problem, it would not resolve the indebtedness of private citizens. Since a private person cannot tax another private person, a different approach has to be taken.

The largest portion of the current debt is related to the real-estate market. In many cases, poor people were tricked into buying expensive houses at the height of the property bubble. They ended up owning houses with debts higher than the value of the home, and with no possibility of paying the debt back or selling the house.

In a crisis economy, when people lose their savings and their jobs, their homes are often repossessed and they become impoverished. If, on the other hand, the homeowner's debt could be readjusted to the current market value of the property, the owner would have the opportunity of either staying in the home or selling it. The banks would not be any worse off than if the owner defaulted, since a default would not increase the house's value. On the whole, the economy would be better off if such policies were introduced—people would be able to stay in their homes and have higher purchasing power than if they lost their properties.

A possible way of structuring such a bailout would be to use the state's power of eminent domain to purchase properties at market prices from the bank and then sell them back to the original mortgage holders at the current market price.[3] This will keep more people in their homes and prevent many defaults. The banks would have to write down the value of their loans, but the overall impact on the economy if such policies were enacted would be immense, since it is the people's purchasing power that drives the economy. It is people like us, people with regular jobs—not banks, speculators, or financiers—who produce and purchase most of the goods in our economy. Therefore, bailing out the people is much more beneficial to the economy than bailing out the banks.

Take Steps to Protect the Real Economy

To protect the economy, we must limit as far as possible transfer payments from the productive sector to unproductive sectors—to the finance, insurance, and real-estate markets. When funds are moved into these sectors, we starve the real economy of needed investments, job creation, and economic prosperity.

Reduce Unproductive Government Spending

No matter how much money a government raises, if it wastes it on unproductive projects the national debt will keep on rising. In deciding which spending to cut and which not to cut, it would be helpful if government accounting standards were the same as those used in corporations. All companies distinguish between expenses and the acquisition of assets, but government accounting does not. Government accounting is essentially a cash flow of how money goes in and out; it does not take into account national assets. In normal accounting, an expense is something that is gone the moment you spend it, while an asset is something that adds to the long-term value of the company. For example, salaries of workers are expenses, but the purchase of stocks or new factories are assets.

If such distinctions are made in government accounting, then we can distinguish between a subsidy to a certain industry, which can be considered a cost, and the building of necessary infrastructure, which can be considered an asset. Even during an economic downturn a government could promote economic growth by investing in infrastructure and other assets without serious financial implications. In fact, government spending on productive ventures is essential in an economic downturn to ensure a swift recovery.

The Unintended Monetary Consequences of Debt Reduction

Any measure to reduce debt has unintended monetary consequences. With the present economic system, money is essentially a debt obligation. Part of the money is supplied by governments and central banks, but approximately 90 percent is created through bank loans.

Giving out new loans increases the money supply, while paying back loans decreases it. Hence, repaying loans will reduce the total money supply, which will in turn make money scarcer and contract the economy.

The fractional reserve bank system of money creation is a very blunt instrument that makes it difficult for governments to control the money supply. Although it is beyond the scope of this book, serious thought needs to be given to the issue of monetary reform.

2) Reforming the Financial Sector

The Importance of Protecting the Financial System

The financial system is essential for our continued operation as a society; it enables us to cooperate with one another in productive ways. Without a financial system, cooperation is limited to societies on a local scale only, such as in small tribes where people know, trust, and depend on one another.With a financial system, cooperation is extended to the whole world, with many ensuing benefits. When the financial system is not functioning to the benefit of the common people, however, then it disrupts people's lives and livelihoods.

A breakdown of the financial system can indeed have disastrous consequences for society. When people can no longer trust that they will get reimbursed for the cooperation extended to others, such as the supply of goods or services, they tend to hold back on such trades. Without banks, no international trade can take place. Without money and a functioning banking system, we won't receive salaries for the work we do. The savings we have in the bank will no longer be accessible. Money can no longer be raised to finance larger projects. Our entire society is based on the relationship and trust created by the finance system, and without this, society will soon collapse and enter a state of chaos.

The current governmental preoccupation with safeguarding the world's financial system to prevent it from collapse is understandable, even commendable. The problem is the way it is being accomplished, by transferring the economic excesses of speculators, banks and corporations to ordinary citizens. It is an easy and cheap way out, but it is economically counterproductive and damaging to the public trust.

At the same time, any reform has to ensure that the financial system itself remains intact. We can reform it, alter it, and improve it, but we cannot afford to let it collapse in a disorganized fashion.

Suggested Reforms of the Financial Sector

When the financial sector grows out of proportion to the real economy, it changes from being a necessary tool to a destructive weapon, threatening the very fabric of the economy. The purpose of any reform of the financial sector must therefore be to ensure that it serves the production of real goods and services and does not end up as a gambling house for idle money. In particular, speculative activities—where an individual or institution makes money on the variation of prices of financial assets— should be banned, unless such an activity can be directly shown to contribute to a better utilization of resources. Here are a few suggestions on how to reform the financial system:

Banks

- Keep investment banks separate from commercial banks. In other words, don't mix the banking processes of taking deposits and lending money with the trading of securities and derivatives.
- Limit banks to activities that are needed to help the real economy. This is the real purpose of banks. These days, however, banks either trade in derivatives, brokerage activities, mutual funds, options, and other financial instruments, or assist clients to do the same. None of these activities help the real economy; they only create instability and asset bubbles. Therefore, all these activities should stop, except in cases where they are used to hedge risks for genuine manufacturers.
- Nationalize distressed banks. It is not at all advisable to use public means to subsidize a private enterprise.
- Let small insolvent banks go bankrupt but protect depositors.
- Small countries should not be allowed to grow their banking sector larger than what is needed to finance the local economy. We have already seen the disastrous effect a bloated banking system can have in small countries like Cyprus, Iceland, and Ireland. Countries like Switzerland and Lichtenstein do have successful banking sectors that are much larger than their economies, but they specialize in asset management where the banks do not trade or lend money but simply handle clients' assets.
- If governments are to guarantee deposits, they must make sure they have the resources to do so. In Iceland the banking sector became much bigger than the government, so it was illogical for the government to try to guarantee the deposits. This is particularly dangerous when a tiny country, like Iceland, takes deposits from abroad. It is therefore important that governments do not guarantee deposits if they do not have resources.

Derivative Instruments

A derivative is a private contract between two parties that could relate to anything at all, such as the prices of commodities, whether a bank will default on a debt, or even if it is going to rain tomorrow. Presently derivatives are not regulated in any way, even though their size of trade is far greater than any other financial product. Since derivatives are not regulated, there is no guarantee that the contracting parties can fulfill their obligations, and they can therefore destabilize the entire market. It was losses on derivatives which bankrupted AIG, the world's biggest insurance company.

The derivatives market should be regulated like any other financial activity, and any new derivative product should be explicitly approved before it can be put on the market. Here are some specific aspects of the economy that should be limited:

- Credit defaults swaps (CDS) should be regulated, just like the insurance industry, and one should not be allowed to buy CDS with assets that one does not own.[4]
- Naked short selling should be banned.[5]
- The options market should be used solely for mitigation or risk, and not for speculation.[6]
- In short, any derivative that cannot be shown to directly benefit the real economy should not be allowed.

Stock Markets

As long as corporations exist, stock markets may serve the function of enabling companies to raise capital. Naturally, someone who buys shares would also like to be able to sell them at some point, and the stock market is the place where this is done. However, apart from the initial offering that capitalizes the company, all further buying and selling adds nothing to the real economy, and it should therefore be limited. A transaction tax, which charges a higher tax the shorter time a share has been held, might be a first step forward. This discourages short-term speculation but does not hamper real, long-term investments.

Currency Markets

In 1980, 80 percent of all currency traded was for genuine business purposes, and 20 percent was used for speculative trading. These days, only 2.5 percent of currency transactions are for genuine purposes, and 97.5 percent are speculative. Currently between $1 trillion to $2 trillion are traded on the currency exchanges every day. These speculative transactions distort the real market and create economic instability.

- Allow free purchase of currencies for commercial transactions.
- Prevent foreign exchange purchases for speculation.

Future Contracts

The original purpose of future contracts is to protect a company from fluctuating commodity prices so that it can properly plan for the year's production. These days, however, future contracts are mainly used for speculative purposes, as a gamble on whether costs will go up or down. One of the important groups of future contracts is that of food staples, such as rice, sugar, wheat, etc. Since the amount of speculative money is larger than the legitimate uses of future contracts, the speculative volumes basically set prices. This can have disastrous consequences for the poor, since it can artificially push up prices of staples such as rice and wheat, even if there is no actual shortage.

- Limit future contracts to those who are actually going to buy the commodities. That is, do not allow anyone to buy a future contract and then sell it without taking possession of the goods. This will effectively stop speculation.
- Specifically, make sure that no speculation in food products takes place.

The financial sector has taken over the real economy. The servant has become the master. In pursuit of ever-increasing profits, and without actually producing anything, the financial sector has grown into a behemoth that threatens to destroy both itself and the real economy. The reforms we have suggested are a first step toward reclaiming a more balanced economic order, where the financial sector serves the real economy and promotes real growth rather than recklessly redistributing wealth into the hands of a few.

One of the main functions of the economic system is to facilitate the effective use of resources. This can only take place if money and other financial wealth is kept rolling and thereby put to effective use. The hoarding of financial wealth that is not invested in the real economy is unproductive and inefficient. It is one of the main problems with the present system, something that economic reforms need to address.

Reducing Inequality

The tendency to concentrate wealth is inherent in a market economy, and as long as we have a market economy, this fact cannot be changed. Because extreme concentration of wealth destroys the necessary conditions of a market economy, the whole system eventually self-destructs.[7]

In order to prevent this and maintain a level of equality that will create sufficient demand to allow the markets to function, outside intervention in the economy by the state and trade unions has always been required. An interesting situation thus arises: the forces that oppose free-market policies become the forces that maintain the conditions that make free markets possible.

A prime example of redistributive policies within the framework of a market economy is the Scandinavian model. Scandinavia has in the past had comparatively low inequality, a robust economy, and the highest living standard in the world. In recent years, Scandinavia has followed the trend to deregulate the economy. Not surprisingly, economic inequality is now on the rise.

Below we present some suggestions for avoiding extreme inequality within the framework of a market economy. Please note that some of these points have already been mentioned earlier in this chapter but are repeated here for the sake of completeness.

Suggested policies:

- Bail out people rather than banks.
- Ensure wages increases on a par with productivity gains.
- Reintroduce progressive taxation and welfare payments to reduce the gap between rich and poor.
- Tax unearned income at a higher rate than income from work. Interest, capital gains, and other financial income should be taxed higher than income from employment, trade, and manufacturing.
- People's incentives should be realigned with their contribution to society. Make bonuses for loss-making companies illegal. Place a much lower cap on salaries for top executives and restrict bonuses and incentives in the financial sector. Use the money saved to increase the minimum wage.
- Give incentives to cooperatives. Worker-owned-and-managed cooperatives are a sizeable part of the economy in many countries and need to be supported as a counterbalance to private corporations since they ensure higher wages and worker involvement in the economy.

- Reduce salaries before firing people. If cost cutting is necessary, the option to reduce the salaries for all workers (or reduce working hours) should always be explored before firing staff.
- Ensure low unemployment. If not enough private-sector work is available, then the government could introduce public-works projects to provide jobs, particularly public works that are constructive and beneficial, such as improving the infrastructure of roads, bridges, energy grids, etc. These new jobs result in added assets for the country, thus providing a net gain of value compared to keeping people unemployed. High unemployment rates are indeed very expensive for society.

Chapter Eleven

Making Poor Countries Rich: Economics from Free to Fair Trade

What is called 'capitalism' is basically a system of corporate mercantilism, with huge and largely unaccountable private tyrannies exercising vast control over the economy, political systems, and social and cultural life...

—Noam Chomsky

T O IMPROVE THE CONDITIONS of poor countries, including the poorest members of the industrialized world, we suggest the following five actions, all of which are closely related:

- First, the government must actively participate in the economy. No country has ever succeeded in advancing its economy without a strong state sector to support the private sector.
- Second, the country needs to develop its own industrial and technological base. Apart from a few oil countries, no nation in history ever became rich by selling raw materials from the agricultural, oil, or mining sectors.
- Third, trade policies have to be adjusted in order to provide fair trade that is mutually advantageous for developing countries. Today's so-called free-trade agreements benefit those countries already ahead, but not those who are trying to catch up.
- Fourth, patent laws must be reformulated to promote the maximum benefits for humanity rather than the entrenched privileges of a handful of corporations.

- Fifth, the unindustrialized countries are in a unique position to not make the same environmental mistakes as the polluted industrialized part of the world; thus all industrial policies should be framed with long-term sustainability in mind.

The actions proposed above are not based on a theoretical model or an ideology, but rather on historical observations. The important question is, "How did rich countries become rich, and how did poor countries stay poor?" All our suggested policies aim to emulate the process rich countries embarked upon in order to become rich, while avoiding their economic and environmental mistakes.

The policies we propose are, in many instances, the exact opposite of the advice given by the World Bank, the G20, the International Monetary Fund, and the World Trade Organization. As we have seen in earlier chapters, the suggestions and policies formulated by these organizations to the developing countries are often the opposite of the policies the rich industrialized countries applied in order to become rich themselves.[1]

Strong State Involvement

For an economy to be successful, the state needs to have a key role in investing in industrial development, protecting infant industries, regulating trade, and providing key infrastructure and services required by society. Nowadays, there is a tendency to condemn any kind of government involvement in the economy, but all successful economies have had, and continue to have, very strong government involvement in subsidizing enterprises directly or indirectly and providing direction for the economy.

In the US, this was achieved through the Pentagon's military-procurement system, and in the Scandinavian countries through state enterprises and a massive welfare state. In Japan it was accomplished through the powerful Ministry of International Trade and Industry, which was directly involved in making economic plans for the country. In South Korea, Taiwan, and Singapore, the state had a prominent role in protecting local industry, subsidizing it whenever needed, planning the economy, and even directly participating in economic ventures. All these countries are hailed as proof of the success of the free-market system, but they were in fact notable exemptions from the free-market system, which is why they succeeded. The latest economic miracle, China, openly operates as a state-run enterprise. Although private players are tolerated, the Chinese government controls every aspect of the economy; it is the owner of the banks and many of the most important industries.

Today there is a strong aversion toward state-run enterprises, but there are numerous examples of successfully run government business projects. Singapore, for example, is considered a successful model of a capitalist society. However, this Asian country's government directly invests in large sectors of the economy. Singapore Airlines is one of the world's most successful airlines—it has never posted a loss in its entire history. Fifty-seven percent if the airline is owned by Temasek, a holding company owned by the Singapore Ministry of Finance. Temasek owns controlling shares in many efficient and profitable enterprises that are termed "government-linked companies" (GLCs). In his book *Bad Samaritans*, economist Ha-Joon Chang elaborates:

> The Singapore government also runs the so-called Statutory Boards that provide certain vital goods and services. Virtually all land in the country is publicly owned and around 85 percent of housing is provided by the Housing and Development Board. The Economic Development Board develops industrial estates, incubates new firms and provides business consulting services.

Singapore's SOE [state-owned enterprises] sector is twice as big as that of Korea, when measured in terms of its contribution to national output. When measured in terms of its contribution to total national investment, it is nearly three times bigger. Korea's SOE sector is, in turn, about twice that of Argentina and five times bigger than that of the Philippines, in terms of its share in national income. Yet both Argentina and the Philippines are popularly believed to have failed because of an overextended state, while Korea and Singapore are often hailed as success stories of private-sector-driven economic development.[2]

Norway's Statoil is one of the world's largest oil companies, and the Norwegian government owns 70 percent of its drilling operations in the North Sea. In China, 40 percent of industrial output comes from state-owned enterprises. The very foundation of Taiwan's economic ideology, the "Three People's Principles" of Dr. Sun Yat-Sen, the inspiration behind Taiwan's economic miracle, state that key industries—energy, transportation, education, etc.—should be owned by the state. Many of France's largest companies, such as Renault, Alacatel, Thomson, and many others, used to be SOE until the recent wave of privatization hit France. In Finland much of the modernization of steel, forestry, mining, and chemical industries was led by SOEs.[3]

Naturally, state-owned enterprises, like any other enterprise, can also be poorly operated, but simply privatizing them is not the solution to a nation's problems. A strong state sector directing and supporting private enterprise is a fundamental aspect of successfully turning a poor country into an industrial nation. There are no historical examples of a major nation becoming economically strong by letting market forces loose while the government takes a back seat. Hence, for any country wishing to become successful, the neoliberal policy of reducing state involvement in business and letting multinational corporations take over the planning process is bound to be an economic and environmental failure.

The question is not whether an economy is planned or not—economies are never entirely free or unregulated. The question is: Who will do the planning and for whose benefit? Should the sovereign state harness market forces for the good of its citizens, or should international banks and multinational corporations do the planning for the benefit of their executives and shareholders? With these important questions in mind, we have formulated the following policies:

General Policies

- The government must take a strong lead in promoting the economy.
- The government should not take over the entire economy and micromanage the economy from above, as was the case in former communist countries.
- The government should create long-term policy objectives.
- The government should take control of key industries and utilities and use its leverage to promote the success of private businesses and cooperatives.
- The government should not be in competition with private and cooperative enterprises but should act as an enabling force to ensure that they can reach their full potential.
- The government should emulate the role governments have played in success stories such as Scandinavia, Japan, Korea, and Singapore.
- The government should develop a sustainable industrial and business framework that prioritizes organic agriculture, decentralized

economics, and alternative energy, and that utilizes local raw materials in an environment-friendly manner.

Industrial Policy

The government must support and promote the development of domestic industry, sustainability research, alternative energy, and high-tech ventures, and make a long-term strategy for the development of the nation.

Government has a pivotal place in the economy, and one of its main functions should be to create a long-term national industrial strategy. Creating a future vision for a country's development should not be left to free-market forces alone, since the main interest of a corporation is to maximize short-term shareholder wealth. Corporate interests are too limited to help formulate a nation's long-term economic strategies. No nation without long-term government involvement has ever succeeded in developing a sophisticated industrial economy. Indeed, history has taught us that government involvement is the best way for a nation to overcome poverty.

The Necessity of Industrial Development

Historically, countries that focused on the export of raw materials have always fared worse than those who produced finished goods for export. In the words of Norwegian economist Erik Reinert: "For centuries, it was understood that having an industrial sector — even if the sector was less efficient than those of the richest nations — produced higher real wages than having no industrial sector at all. So, if inefficient, the industrial sector ought to be made more efficient, rather than be closed down." [4]

In today's economy, knowledge industries, such as computer software and patenting companies, play a similar role to that of manufacturing in the past. It is difficult, however, to make the jump from being producers of raw materials to being a country of advanced knowledge industries. Besides, regardless of how much technological progress there is, the production of basic necessities, such as food and shelter, will have to be prioritized. Therefore, there is a limit to how far technology replace the rest of the economy. Its role is a bit like that of the finance sector. It can make the manufacturing and agricultural sectors more productive, but it cannot replace them. [5] Moreover, as Ha-Joon Chang and Erik Reinert point out, inefficient industries that create jobs and services is better than no industry at all. In fact, these fledgling industries represent the beginning of a new future for a poor country's march toward economic independence.

Prevailing Policies

Current economic policies focus on trade and on removing those barriers that may impede its expansion. Increased international trade is generally seen as the solution to all economic problems. If trade barriers are removed and intellectual properties protected, the economic pundits proclaim, then all other issues related to economic development—research, production, and job creation—will take care of themselves. But this is wishful thinking. The fact is, global free trade has created a world divided in two halves—one rich and one poor—and the economic gulf between them seems to have no end in sight.

Indeed, large sections of the world still suffer from extreme poverty, illiteracy, and no access to clean drinking water, prenatal services, or proper medical care; thus additional emphasis must be placed on creating programs to specifically address these issues. The latest efforts in this regard are the UN's Millennium Development Goals, which aim to eradicate extreme poverty and hunger; achieve universal primary education; promote gender equality between men and women; reduce child mortality; improve maternal health; combat diseases; ensure environmental sustainability; and develop a global partnership for development, which, while also supporting a free-trade agenda, aims to alleviate some of the direct negative effects of free trade on poor nations.

While these goals are commendable, they tend to address the problem rather than the cause. Instead of creating the economic structures developing nations need to become wealthy, they are designed as handouts, thus keeping poor countries dependent on wealthy nations. Erik Reinert calls the Millennium Development Goals "palliative economics." Combined with global policies that destroy local industry in the name of free trade, these goals create a relationship of dependency, stirring up memories of the colonial ages.

Naturally, if a country is poor and people are starving, catastrophic aid is a good and righteous choice. But rather than doling out aid and thus creating long-term dependency, a more rational approach would be to also facilitate economic development so that the poor country can grow itself out of the long-term need for foreign aid and assistance.

Develop Areas with Increasing Returns

In order to prosper, a country needs to focus on those areas of production that yield the best increasing returns. When an activity has increasing returns, the more that is produced the higher the productivity. Industrial production falls under this category. A factory becomes more efficient the more units it produces. In this way, technology and other factors are combined to increase wealth creation.

Agriculture, on the other hand, has diminishing returns—the most fertile land is utilized first. If production is to be expanded, less fertile land will have to be used. Therefore, the more production grows, the less efficient it becomes. In a typical area of increasing returns, such as industrial production, the following is generally true:[6]

- There is imperfect competition, which leads to higher wages and higher profits.
- Prices are generally stable.
- It mostly requires skilled labor.
- Salaries tend to stay high.
- Technological changes lead to higher wages.
- Increased market share can get you ahead of the learning curve.

In areas of diminishing returns, such as mining, raw-materials extraction, and agriculture, the following is generally true:

- There is perfect competition, which squeezes wages and profits.
- Prices are generally volatile.
- It requires mostly unskilled labor.
- Salaries are reversible and can fall to very low levels when market prices go down.
- Technological changes tend to lower prices for consumers.
- Increasing market share drives you against the wall of diminishing returns, where every investment made gives lower and lower returns.

For a country to be economically successful, it needs to consciously direct its efforts into developing areas of increasing return. Even if a country has vast amounts of raw materials and agricultural potential, it needs an industrial base to put a floor on how low salaries can go and to stabilize the cost of agricultural products and raw materials. Whenever possible, the country should try to process its raw materials locally and then produce products from these raw materials before exporting them to other countries. This will create increasing returns. Extreme examples of the opposite are seen when Norwegian salmon exported to be processed in China is bought back again to be eaten in Norway, or when chicken produced in the US is exported to China for packaging before being shipped back to the US to be consumed in American homes or restaurants.

One way for a poor country to move up the ladder of increasing returns is through emulation, which essentially entails copying someone else's skill sets. Japan, China, Taiwan, and South Korea did not have to invent new technology to boost their economies and move their countries into the modern era. They emulated techniques from other industrial countries until they were wealthy enough to develop their own technology. Emulation is a powerful tool to help developing countries catch up. All Western nations did the same. They freely copied inventions and techniques from their rivals to increase their own prosperity. But in emulating the West, developing nations may also make many of the same mistakes: they may develop unsustainable industries. These nations have a great opportunity but also a challenge: to not repeat the same environmental mistakes that were made in the Western world. Instead they can invest in alternative energy and sustainable technologies, as well as in sustainable agriculture and agro-industries, and thus become world leaders in those areas.

Policies

- Develop areas of increasing returns.
- Emulate the technological achievements of other countries.
- Let the government subsidize the development and adaption of these technologies.
- If the country has raw materials and agricultural production, it is essential to complement this with an industrial base, even if it is not competitive internationally.
- Base industries on locally available raw materials and resources and develop new environmental technologies.

Trade Policy

Promote fair trade rather than free trade. The level of openness of the economy has to be determined by the state of local industry and the advancement of the economy.

Free Trade is Not Free

The prevailing views expressed by WTO officials and others involved in negotiating free-trade agreements, is that free trade helps everyone. Among other things, they point to the increase in world trade, which generates more jobs globally. In reality, the benefits put forth in these agreements are uneven at best. The industrialized countries benefit greatly, while poor countries only benefit short term through additional economic activities. In the long run, however, free trade agreements undermine the prosperity of developing countries by outcompeting their industries and technologies.

Current trade theory ignores the role of learning and technological improvement in developing future industries in poor countries. As individuals, we become proficient at the things we practice and concentrate on. The same goes for companies and nations. Instead of dismantling an inefficient industry, it would be better to find ways to make it more efficient until it can compete and produce quality products. The alternative is an economy indefinitely stuck in areas of diminishing returns.

With free trade, however, the door of learning and improving is often closed forever. A budding industry in a developing country has little chance to compete with established industries in advanced nations. As we noted in previous chapters, these third-world industries are quickly wiped out when the doors are opened to foreign competition through the imposition of free trade. Free trade, therefore, becomes a tool to maintain the competitive advantage of those countries who are already ahead, and an impassable obstacle for the countries trying to catch up. Free trade, therefore, is not always a tool for economic freedom, but often a straightjacket preventing developing countries to advance their economy and technological development.

Fair Trade Policies

The concept of fair trade proposed here should not be confused with the activities of Fair Trade International and other organizations, which focus mainly on improving export conditions for agricultural commodities in third-world nations. While improving the terms of trade of agricultural products is good and commendable, it cannot substitute the need for developing domestic industries.

Free trade is advantageous for a country that is already technologically advanced. Free trade, without any barriers, between two technologically advanced nations will benefit both of them, and any trade restrictions would be counterproductive. But for less advanced nations, free trade with a more advanced nation can be disastrous and can permanently prevent any possibility for long-term technological and economic growth.

For that reason, fair-trade agreements must make allowance for a country's right to protect and develop its industry and technology.[7] Nations that are currently negotiating free-trade agreements should carefully consider their impact on their industry and ability to develop technologically before signing them. Those who have already signed free-trade agreements that are detrimental to their national interests should consider all possible options to get out of them, even the option of unilaterally repudiating them. Naturally, such repudiation should not be taken lightly, since it might have severe consequences. A large nation with strategic resources has a better chance of getting away with it than a small nation with few resources. If a trend is created, however, where countries stand up for their rights to develop their industrial and agricultural base in a more sustainable manner, the ideological climate in the world will eventually change.

Powerful industrial nations have everything to gain and nothing to lose by maintaining and extending free trade, but for poor developing countries the reality is quite different. It will be difficult to buck the trend, but we may start by increasing the awareness that the benefits of free trade largely depend on a country's economic and technological development. Once this fundamental truth is acknowledged, the rhetoric that free trade helps everyone will be discredited. The fiction that free trade is best for all nations will then lose some of its moral force. Once the true face of free trade has been uncovered, it will be easier for individual countries to fight for their economic and environmental rights.

Step-by-step Expansion of Trade [7]

In the initial stage, developing countries have to protect their budding industries with tariffs and import policies. But once a country's industry has begun to develop, it will be best to gradually extend trade to neighboring countries, creating regional trade blocks with economies at a similar level of development. By gradually increasing the area of trade, these nations' industries will eventually become more advanced and competitive, and eventually they will be able to compete on a global level.

Policies

- Free trade between industrially advanced countries is of mutual benefit and should be encouraged.
- Countries that are attempting to build up their industrial capacity will have to protect their infant industries by imposing tariffs and other import restrictions.
- Developing countries need to carefully consider the impact of free trade on their local industry before signing any agreements.
- Countries that have signed an agreement preventing them from developing their industrial base, leaving them trapped in diminishing-return activities, have to consider all available options to renegotiate these agreements.
- Once industries have been developed sufficiently enough to compete, they can gradually be exposed to trade through local trading blocks that can expand geographically over time.
- For countries with limited foreign exchange, barter trade can be very advantageous.
- Developing nations should export finished and semi-finished goods rather than raw materials.
- Raw materials should only be exported if the country has such a vast supply that it cannot productively utilize all of it domestically or process it into products for export.
- An exception to the above rule may apply to oil-rich countries with small populations. Having far more energy than they need themselves, exporting to other countries can be beneficial for all parties concerned. But even these countries would benefit from diversifying and developing a petrochemical industry, or by utilizing their oil resources and revenues to develop alternative energy sources.

Patent Rights and Innovation

Patent laws and treaties should be reworded to promote maximum development for the benefit of humanity as a whole rather than to protect minority interests in advanced countries.

Patents and Trade Restrictions

Intellectual property rights (IPR) and patents are very similar to customs duties and import restrictions. Both try to prevent free trade and open markets. But while customs duties and import restrictions protect budding industries and help them to flourish, patent rights do the opposite. They protect established industries and prevent new competitors from emerging. Ha-Joon Chang writes, "the foundation of economic development is the acquisition of more productive knowledge. The stronger international protection for IPRs is, the more difficult it is for the follower countries to acquire new knowledge."[8]

Historically, countries have done everything they could to prevent innovation and knowledge from falling into the hands of foreigners. The British banned the emigration of skilled workers as early as 1719 to prevent know-how from being exported and thus competing with British industry. Later on, Britain banned the export of the "tools and utensils" used in the textile industries. In 1785, the Tools Act banned the export of various machinery and tools. Further on, patents became the main weapon to control the distribution of technology and ideas.[9]

Initially, a patent was only legal and valid in the country of origin, and it was thus perfectly legal for Germany to steal industrial secrets from England. The smuggling of machinery across borders was common, and the machine would be dismantled to see how it worked, and then copied. In some countries, such as Britain, France, and the US, it was even possible to take out a patent on an innovation that had been stolen from abroad. In the nineteenth century, this type of copying, smuggling, and stealing of ideas was an established practice in much of the Western world. "The historical picture is clear," writes Ha-Joon Chang. "Counterfeiting was not invented in modern Asia. When they were backward themselves in terms of knowledge, all of today's rich countries blithely violated other people's patents, trademarks and copyrights."[10]

Japan, China, India, South Korea, Taiwan, and a host of other countries have, during the last century, industrialized by copying ideas and technology from the West. Copying from existing sources of knowledge is almost the only way for any person or country to get ahead in this world.

What has changed in recent years is that this window for progress is being closed. In 1994, at the end of the Uruguay round of General Agreement on Tariffs and Trade (GATT), the Agreement on Trade Related Aspects of Intellectual Property Rights (TRIPS) was added, setting down minimum standards for various forms of intellectual property (IP) that are now binding for all members of the World Trade Organization. Since then, further tightening of IP has been done incrementally, and efforts to expand its scope and lengthen the period granted for patents have increased.

For the first time, global agreements are in place where even the so-called "technologically behind" countries have to sign documents ensuring that they will not try to copy the latest technology. This is an enormous step backward, further institutionalizing the existing economic gap between rich and poor countries.

Purpose and Justifications for Patents

Patents impose restrictions on the flow of information and ideas that ideally would be left free and unhindered in a modern society. All present knowledge builds on previous knowledge that humankind has collected over millennia, and it is only by sharing existing knowledge that we can increase our understanding of the world and find innovative ways to solve our problems. Anytime restrictions are put on the free flow of ideas and information, such restrictions need to be justified.

The justification for patents and IP is that they promote innovation and help society progress. Without such protection, the argument goes, no person or company would invest time or effort into solving new problems. Hence patents are necessary for society to progress. While there are merits to these claims, they are not true in all circumstances. For example, these days, patents are sought and granted for knowledge that has existed for centuries but which has never been patented before. There have been attempts to patent neem and turmeric, for example, traditional Indian medicines that have been in use for centuries.

Much of the research in airplane technology was funded by government resources as part of defense contracts with the justification that it was for national security reasons, and yet private companies end up taking out patents and thus gaining financial benefits from this research.

270 GROWING A NEW ECONOMY

Much of the research in the world is in fact accomplished by using government funds and by educational institutions that do not take out patents. The fact that this research is not protected by patents does not diminish the amount or quality of research taking place. In fact, the individuals who actually carry out the research are rarely granted patents for their inventions. In most cases, they work for a company, a government institution, or a university, and to the extent that a patent is granted, it is most frequently given to the body that employed the researcher, who has signed an explicit waiver to any intellectual rights to their inventions during the time of their employment.

Innovation is fueled by human curiosity and the drive to discover and understand things. Given the resources, scientists will always strive to break new barriers. It is unlikely a scientist will ever proclaim, "Unless the shareholders of the company employing me will make lots of money on my inventions, I will not invent anything."

If individual companies cut down on research due to their inability to take out patents on some of their inventions, society could easily step in and provide the necessary incentives to universities and other institutions to participate in the process. By employing collaborative creativity and shared solutions, those inventions would benefit humanity on a larger scale and increase the economic and social benefits far more than if the invention had been monopolized by a single individual or company.

Furthermore, in most areas patents are not necessary to protect the financial interests of companies. It is not easy to copy new technology, and by the time competitors have caught on, the original inventor will already be ahead of the game. As long as a company keeps innovating, it will remain ahead. Only if they stop innovating can a patent make a difference between the long-term success or failure of the business. In such cases, patents will only inspire companies to become complacent, and thus the whole rationale for patents will be defeated. In the words of Ha-Joon Chang, "Most industries actually do not need patents and other IPRs to generate new knowledge — although they will be more than happy to take advantage of them, if they are offered to them. The patent lobby talks nonsense when it argues that there will be no new technological progress without patents."[11]

However, we do not favor the complete abolishment of patents. In some cases, patents are useful and maybe even necessary. What we want to convey is that there must be a balance between the individual interests of the inventor and the public interest. To paraphrase Adam Smith, we are of the opinion that the interest of the inventors should only be taken into consideration as far as it promotes the benefit of society as a whole.

In the following section, we put forward suggestions for rational policies on IP and patent rights.

Rational Patent Policies

- Patent laws and treaties should benefit society as a whole.
- When there is a conflict between the interest of the patent holder and the interest of society, the interest of society should prevail.
- The granting of patents should be done only when the invention is easy to copy and the inventor would be unable to get a reasonable return on investment should no patent be granted.
- The time limit of patents should be reduced to a maximum of ten years so developing nations can benefit from the total knowledge of humankind.
- When many different patents involving a specific product, such as a cellular phone, are granted to many different parties, it can lead to a paralysis that prevents a fully functional product to reach the market. In this case, patent pooling should be introduced, where all parties holding a patent are forced to license it to their competitors so that the total of human knowledge can be put into use in the production of specific products. If necessary, this can be enforced by the government.
- Medical patents for common ailments should either be banned or licensed by the patent holders to developing countries at reasonable costs. It is unconscionable that people should die because the knowledge needed to produce the medicine is restricted to the patent holder.
- No patents should be granted for existing traditional knowledge, such as herbal medicines, even if this knowledge was previously restricted to a limited geographical area or a certain people.
- No patents should be granted for things already existing in nature, such as human genes, nor simply on the basis of someone having understood how a natural object or organism functions or works.

Capital Movements

While the free movement of capital is often seen as a fundamental right in today's world, it encourages opportunistic speculation rather than long-term development. While long-term investments in a country can bring benefits, the movement of speculative capital in and out of local stock and bond markets can wreak havoc on countries that are not prepared. The deregulation of the financial sector was a direct cause behind the collapse of the economies in Iceland, Ireland, and Cyprus. It also wrecked the Asian economies during the Asian crisis in the late 1990s.

Even foreign direct investment (FDI), when the investment is made on a long-term basis, can have a negative impact on a country if it is accompanied by large outflows of wealth in terms of repatriation of profits, etc. If the investor merges his or her interest with the country he or she is investing in and is prepared to reinvest the profits into the country on a longer timescale, foreign direct investment can have positive consequences for the country.

Policies

- Regulate the capital flow in and out of developing countries.
- While specific rules have to be decided on in each specific instance, the main aim is to use capital for constructive development that benefits the economy and the people, and restrict speculative activities that do not add anything except instability to the economy.

The Implementation of Polices: Creating the Change

Most of the policies presented in this chapter are directly opposed to present economic trends and will not be popular with the economic powerhouses of today. In an intrinsically intertwined global economy, the consequences of pursuing these policies for an individual county, especially one in the early phases of development, can be unpredictable and possibly grave. When the financial interests of nations and large corporations are at stake, charity, morality, and decency usually take the backseat. Unfortunately, in a war between ideals and power, power always wins.

Introducing and implementing such policies must therefore be a gradual affair, keeping in mind possible reactions from the big political and economic powerbrokers. The time to change the status quo is during the time of crisis, and that time is now. As it becomes more and more clear that we no longer can continue doing "business as usual," a window of opportunity will open for comprehensive changes to take place. With the financial system on the brink of collapse, steps in line with those outlined in the previous chapter will have to be taken to prevent a disaster. In the climate that will follow these comprehensive changes, the appetite for free-market capitalism will be reduced, the power of the big financial institutions weakened, and the interest in more equitable global development increased. At such a time, we believe, the policies suggested in this chapter will have a much better chance of being implemented on a larger scale.

Chapter Twelve

Economic Democracy: Changing the Economic Ground Rules

Economic democracy is essential not only for the economic liberation of human beings, but for the well-being of all —including animals and plants.

—P. R. Sarkar

THE FINANCIAL-SECTOR REFORMS MENTIONED earlier in this book, as well as those outlined to reduce inequality between nations, can, if implemented, have a positive impact on the overall economy. But unfortunately, even these comprehensive reforms are not extensive enough to resolve other aspects of the crises and thus save us from a potential perfect storm.

Unless we have deeper structural change—what we refer to as economic-systems change—we will never be able to solve such global and systemic problems as the environmental and inequality crises. History has demonstrated that political democracy is not enough. We also need economic democracy.

In theory, democracy distributes power equally to all people, but in reality it is a small elite who generally form parties, run for office, and own newspapers and TV stations. Those with money and power control the flow of news and opinion, not the average citizen, and politicians are more often than not beholden to corporations rather than to the people they represent. In order to have a more true and just democracy, we need economic democracy; we need to fundamentally change the distribution of income and wealth; we need a power shift in economic decision-making—from the corporations and the wealthy elite to the people. Presently, the production of wealth is socialized—everyone contributes—but the financial benefit of the production is privatized. A small minority reaps the economic and political rewards from everyone else's hard work.

Since money is power, economic democracy is the only way that power can be transferred to the people in a meaningful and sustainable way—a change in the distribution of wealth and income, where the fruits of economic activity are distributed more widely across the population.

By implementing economic democracy, the inequality crisis will gradually be resolved. The gap between rich and poor will be greatly reduced through higher salaries for the working poor and the middle class and by lowering the salaries for the rich. The cure lies in not repeating the same patterns as before in a trickle-down economy, but rather to do quite the opposite—to build the economy up from the grassroots, to let the economy trickle up. Economic democracy also removes the foremost obstacle preventing us from solving the resource and environmental crisis. It does so by transferring power away from those who benefit from the crises to those who will have to bear the ultimate cost of the destruction of our habitat: people living in rural areas. We will return to specific recommendations for green solutions in the next chapter, but for now our main point is this: without economic democracy, the corporate class, the rich and powerful, will prevent any long-term solutions of economic reform from being implemented.

An additional benefit of economic democracy is that it works not only on Election Day but every day. If economic democracy becomes widespread, people can exercise their decision-making powers locally every day, rather than once every two or four years.

Policies for Economic Democracy

The main objective of economic democracy is to guarantee the minimum requirements of life to all members of society and to make efforts to improve these conditions over time. This means that progressively higher incomes and access to technology must become more widely spread throughout the global population. Presently, we see the opposite.

There is rampant economic inequality, both between geographical areas and between individuals. Some countries are extravagantly rich while others are dirt poor. Even within rich countries, some areas are wealthy and wasteful while others are malnourished and poor. In some wealthy areas, such as in metropolitan cities, you find some people living in luxury while others are barely able to eke out a living.

A society rooted in economic democracy must therefore create a wholly different environment based on policies that limit the unequal distribution of wealth between geographical areas, as well as among individuals. This is a three-step process. First, limit how much wealth an individual can accumulate. Second, transform large-scale businesses and enterprises (excluding small businesses with few employees) into worker-owned businesses. Third, increase economic development in rural areas. What we are suggesting is a decentralized economic system with elements of local planning, and a balanced economy with a sustainable combination of agriculture, manufacture, and services.

The policies suggested in previous chapters can be achieved by reforming the capitalist system. To avert a perfect storm in the economy and the environment, however, we need economic democracy; we need to change capitalism as we know it; we need comprehensive economic restructuring—beyond the boundaries of the present market system.

Limits on Wealth

The traditional way to limit income is through progressive taxation: the higher your income, the higher percentage you pay in taxes. In the United States in 1910, the highest income-tax rate was nearly 80 percent. In the years preceding the Great Depression, it dropped to just above 20 percent. The low tax rate for the rich led to greater inequality, and many have argued that it was an important factor in the 1929 stock-market crash. After the depression, the top tax rates shot up again to more than 90 percent, until they again were reduced in the 1970s. Currently the maximum tax rate is 35 percent.

While taxing the rich at a higher rate than the poor does transfer income from the rich to the less well off, a more direct approach would be to introduce a minimum and a maximum wage. The concept of a minimum wage exists in most countries in the world, even though it is often circumvented through various loopholes in the laws. But a minimum wage that is lower than a living wage, which is common in many countries, will not give people enough purchasing capacity to maintain a decent life, nor will it build a healthy economy. Similarly, a minimum wage is of little benefit to the unemployed. Thus minimum wage legislation needs to be accompanied by economic policies that ensure full employment. By implementing economic democracy through the policies recommended in this chapter, an economy ensuring low unemployment will emerge.

A maximum wage, placing a legal cap on a person's take-home salary, is a lesser-known concept. The extravagantly high salaries and bonuses paid to bankers and financiers after the financial crisis shocked the world in 2007, causing widespread scandals and spawning a movement for the introduction of a maximum wage. On November 24, 2013, Swiss citizens voted on a law to cap executive pay to twelve times the lowest salary in any company. The measure failed, but similar movements have emerged in the US and other countries.

Salaries are not the main income for the rich. Most of their wealth is passive—it comes from capital gains, dividends, stock options, etc. Warren Buffet and Bill Gates did not become billionaires because of their high salaries. To limit the income of the superrich, not only salaries but all types of income have to be taken into consideration. A maximum salary will not be enough to redistribute wealth. To achieve the desired effect, we need to set an income ceiling that includes salaries, interest, rent, capital gains, and all other sources of income.

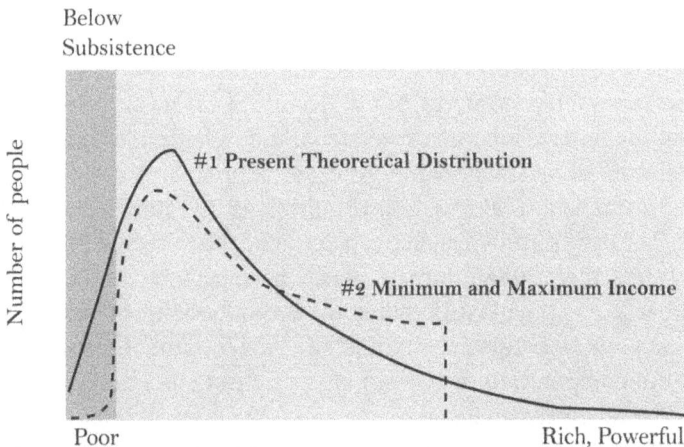

Figure 41 The effect of the introduction of maximum and minimum income on income distribution

The introduction of a minimum and maximum income would go a long way toward reducing income inequality. But income is only part of the problem. While the difference in income between the rich and the poor is huge, the difference in wealth is even greater. Due to inheritances, past-income disparities, and other reasons, wealth distribution in the world is much worse than income distribution. According to a recent Oxfam "Briefing Paper", the wealth of the eighty-five richest people in the world is now equal to the wealth of the bottom half of the global population, and the richest 1 percent owns sixty-five times more than the bottom half.[1] Limiting income would not in itself change these facts. Maybe, with centuries of limits to income, we could finally achieve some type of equality, but in the meantime the rich would still continue exercising power in the world. The control of assets, rather than actual income, is the source of real power, and in order to curb this wealth, measures to limit the extreme hoarding of wealth also need to be put in place. In short, in addition to limits on income, there must be limits on how much assets a person can own.

But what should the difference be between the maximum and minimum wage? The income gap should be narrow enough to prevent the extreme accumulation of wealth but wide enough to promote industry and give incentives for people to be inventive, smart, and hard-working. The Swiss suggestion of a difference of twelve times seems a reasonable start for most industrially developed countries, but in principle the income gap needs to be flexible, periodically adjusted in accordance with the times and the economy.

How can we determine what the ceiling on wealth should be? Two possible approaches come to mind. The limit on wealth should be such that the passive income earned from that wealth does not exceed the maximum allowable income. Another approach would be to cap the maximum wealth allowed to a multiple of the maximum yearly income. The upper limit of such a cap could be the expected lifespan of an individual, the same amount of wealth that a person could save up if he or she received the maximum income throughout his or her life and never spent any of it. This may sound like a vast amount of accumulated wealth, but compared to the wealth of the richest one 1 percent today, it would be relatively small.

Introducing restrictions on income and ownership could happen suddenly, through policy changes after a sudden crisis, or gradually, through changes in inheritance law and other reforms. Some may be of the impression that redistribution of existing wealth has taken place in communist countries, but in reality that is not the case. No communist country actually confiscated wealth from the rich and distributed it to its citizens. Instead, property was confiscated from both the rich and the poor and then turned over to the state.

On the other hand, many of the successful capitalist tiger economies in the Far East instituted widespread distributive measures after the Second World War in the form of land reform. Land was confiscated and distributed to poor peasants, and the result of these reforms resulted in the strong economies of Japan, Taiwan, South Korea, and Thailand. Such policies created a fairly well-to-do middle class with the purchasing capacity to drive the economy, educate their children, and build a foundation for increased wealth.

While the distribution of land ownership is important and has stimulated growth, the distribution of the ownership of businesses and corporations will have an even greater impact on the world's economy. (See below our alternative proposal to decentralize ownership of businesses, factories and farms.)

In a society limiting the accumulation of private wealth, the primary aim of production will be consumption rather than maximization of profits. Interestingly enough, Adam Smith, the founding father of capitalism, also believed that the interest of the consumers were more important than those of the producers. "Consumption," he wrote, "is the sole end and purpose of all production; and the interest of the producer ought to be attended to, only so far as it may be necessary for promoting that of the consumer. The maxim is so perfectly self-evident, that it would be absurd to attempt to prove it."[2]

In an economy with a maximum income, what happens if a successful entrepreneur's earnings exceed the limit on income or wealth? One option is to allow the person to set up a foundation, like the Bill and Melinda Gates Foundation, and thus have some influence on how the extra wealth will be distributed. Once a person's basic needs are satisfied and one has achieved a certain level of wealth, they may gain deep satisfaction from giving to causes they believe in. Naturally, these foundations need to be monitored by the government to make sure they actually serve a social need and are not used for personal gain.

A Three-Tiered Economic System

Today, economic centralization is achieved primarily through corporate structures. As corporations can own other corporations, complex webs of ownership are created that not only centralize wealth but also obscure the real owners.

Corporations all over the world not only have the status and rights of natural persons, but they also have further rights—such as deducting certain expenses from their taxes, including legal costs, and material and labor costs, as well as the depreciation of assets—rights that an individual does not have.

Corporations were originally created to gather resources for projects too big for individual undertakings, such as building a factory or damming a river. At the time, however, strict restrictions were imposed on their undertakings. Corporations were not legal persons, and they could only operate within a limited range of activities to serve the specific public purpose they were created for.

Since corporations concentrated money under individual control, they became very powerful, both economically and politically. Their economic power was effectively used to influence politicians to change laws and regulations that restricted their economic activities. But even though corporations are the main source of financial control in the world today, there is nothing sacrosanct about them. There is no God-given law which says that the corporate system must remain in place forever. Corporations are effective entities for controlling complex organizations and concentrating wealth, but they are far from ideal institutions for distributing wealth rationally.

An alternative to unrestricted private ownership through corporations has been the state-ownership system developed in the Soviet Union and other communist countries during a large part of the twentieth century. This system of collective ownership was an extremely centralized form of ownership where a small clique of bureaucrats and politicians controlled the majority of the national wealth.

While unlimited private accumulation of wealth is problematic, the near-total elimination of private property is far worse. The purpose of limiting the personal accumulation of wealth is to ensure that everybody has enough income and wealth to be comfortable. Whether we ban personal property altogether or allow unrestricted accumulation of individual wealth, in both cases the majority of people will be deprived.

The solution to wealth concentration is therefore not to ban private property, but to ensure that everyone has a chance to own enough to lead a comfortable life. This is the essence of economic democracy.

Tier One: Private Small-Scale Businesses

Let us take a closer look at how we can restructure the economy and thus spread the ownership of wealth more equitably. A radical approach would be to ban corporations altogether and only allow privately owned companies that must adhere to a wealth ceiling. This would effectively distribute wealth widely, but it would also make it difficult to operate large-scale ventures requiring huge amounts of capital, such as car manufacturing and oil exploration. Such a capitalist economy would not be practical, since a modern economy cannot be made up solely of hundreds of millions of small-scale private enterprises. While small private companies are an essential part of the economy, they have to be supplemented with other, larger forms of businesses that can more effectively serve vital functions in society.

How then do we accommodate large-scale enterprises without having wealth concentrated in the hands of the few? One approach would be to continue with the corporate structure, but to set a limit on the total value of shares one person can own. This would resolve the problem of wealth accumulation while allowing corporations of the size that are needed to exist in a modern economy. Unfortunately, this may not be an ideal solution either. In his book *Small is Beautiful*, E.F. Schumacher points out that there are two types of ownership: "(a) property that is an aid to creative work and (b) property that is an alternative to it."[3] Schumacher continues, "There is something natural and healthy about the former — the private property of the working proprietor; and there is something unnatural and unhealthy about the latter — the private property of the passive owner who lives parasitically on the works of others."[4]

Simply putting restrictions on the total value of shares people can buy does not address this problem. If we want a system that discourages passive ownership, we need to limit ownership to ventures where an individual actively participates. (Naturally, small children; old or retired people; and the chronically sick or mentally challenged have to be excluded from this principle.) One way to achieve this is to limit shareholdings in companies to those who work in the company. Another way is to turn large-scale companies into cooperatives.

Tier Two: Cooperatives

While the main purpose of a corporation is short-term profit for its shareholders, in a cooperative or any type of company structure owned by the employees, the owners are likely to have a more balanced view of operating a business. They are likely to care about long-term employment, working conditions, the impact of the company on the environment where they live, the long-term sustainability of the community where they work, environmental issues, etc. In short, if ownership, and by extension power, is vested in the people who work in the company, we can expect more balanced and farsighted business decisions.

Adam Smith remarked that the interest of the factory owners goes against the interest of society as a whole, while the interest of the laborers is aligned with the interests of society. When the workers become owners, this dichotomy will vanish, or at least be greatly reduced.

Cooperative enterprises are actually more widespread than is generally known. There are worker owned industries, banks, farmers markets, local work-exchange programs, agricultural processing plants, service projects, and health clinics in most countries of the world. Around 15 percent of the world's population, or about one billion people, are members of cooperatives. The turnover of cooperatives in the ten largest economies is 5 percent of the GDP of this group, slightly smaller than the GDP of Italy, the world's seventh-largest economy. In Europe, cooperatives directly employ 4.7 million individuals. Twenty countries in Europe have networks of cooperative banks, and there is evidence that these fared much better during the recent economic crisis than commercial banks. As of today, 1478 cooperative banks and other businesses across forty-six countries had a turnover of over $100 million each. In addition, there are thousands of smaller coops in virtually every country in the world.

One of the most successful cooperatives in the world is the Mondragon cooperative established in the Basque region of Spain by Father Jose Maria Arizmendi in 1959. Mondragon has grown to comprise 256 enterprises employing nearly 84,000 workers.

According to Jaroslav Vanek, one of the world's foremost authorities on economic-democracy institutions, once these "democratic firms are organized… they work far better than capitalist enterprises."[5] For poor regions of the world, where there is little industrial development, Vanek maintains that coops are the most effective way to develop local industry:

There are existing enterprises already in place. These can be leased to the workers [in poor areas] at a reasonable price. It could be in the form of a fixed lease contract that would give an incentive to the workers to earn extra income. The lease money would have to be efficiently allocated to those who need it for start-up costs. The best use of finance is to develop second level co-ops. If we have mining in an area, we should also have local production facilities. Rather than ship copper to Moscow for smelting, they could build a smelter and factories for the production of copper commodities for sale in their local market as well as for export.[6]

Finally, Professor Vanek also emphasizes that coops are more efficient and satisfying workplaces than capitalist firms:

One of the greatest advantages of economic democracy in well-organized coops is mutual supervision. In French construction coops, capital productivity is double the norm. The democratic firm can produce two buildings while the capitalist firm produces only one. The reason for this increased productivity is that in a democratic firm the workers supervise each other while in capitalist firms they cover each other's theft or poor work. Then there is the savings of materials. Capitalist firms invest in a lot of unnecessary machinery. They replicate the inclination of the average Americans buying things they don't need. The democratic firm can adjust to the optimum level of intensity. Productivity is not measured only in dollars and output but also in happiness and job security. [7]

Not only are cooperatives more efficient, they promote solidarity and a sense of individual worth. On the one hand, one's effort in the workplace is experienced as a valued contribution to society, and on the other hand, one is working as a part of a team and has a direct democratic influence over one's life situation. This connection generates happiness, and the more a nation or a region increases its happiness, the dependency on overconsumption decreases. Hence a local economic base leads to a more balanced use and allocation of resources and a "demonstrated capacity to innovate, since [people] can react to external challenges and meet new needs arising at the local level."[8] In Canada it is well known that cooperatively run hospitals provide better and cheaper healthcare because the cooperative spirit fosters an active ability of the workers to care about their patients. As economist and Nobel Laureate Joseph Stiglitz writes:

> On the one hand, more socially oriented enterprises are less inclined to exploit those with whom they interact: their workers, their customers, and their suppliers. Systems in which there is more participation, more openness, and more transparent management can also be important in spreading an entrepreneurial culture, where everybody in the firm is part of the decision-making process, which can increase efficiency in the enterprise. Job satisfaction, as I mentioned before, is an important part of the quality of life. An important study showed that a higher quality workplace, including larger participation in decision-making, leads to greater job satisfaction, even for low-wage jobs.... There are also some fundamental psychological aspects of this that have been well studied: better performance increases the sense of satisfaction, from what I call intrinsic rewards more than from extrinsic or monitoring rewards. The problem is that the for-profit sector relies almost exclusively on extrinsic rewards. [9]

Cooperatives can exist within a capitalistic environment and tend to prove more efficient. They have proven their strength and resilience, and there is nothing to suggest that a larger proportion of cooperatives, or indeed having cooperative structures completely replacing corporations, would have a negative impact on productivity or on the economy as a whole. Rather the opposite is true.

In addition, since cooperatives can have other objectives than simply profit maximization, they are more flexible. For example, if the economy is slow, cooperatives can reduce working hours for its members rather than firing people, and in some instances people can be paid in kind rather than in cash.

Tier Three: State-Run Enterprises

Some projects are too large and too vital for the economy to be run as cooperatives. Traditionally, these types of enterprises were run and controlled by the state, the region, or city government. In recent years, this trend has been reversed and there has been a rush toward privatization of state companies. State ownership has almost become a dirty word. State enterprises are assumed to be inefficient, corrupt, inept, and a drain on the coffers of the state.

The main argument for privatizing state-owned companies is the idea that people do not care for things that are not their own property. The problem with that argument is that most large companies are not run by their owners but by a board of hired executives. Therefore, the same problem you find in state enterprises you also find in Coca Cola, Exxon, Halliburton, ABB, and the majority of large global corporations, but no economist has ever argued that these corporations should be sold to a single shareholder who would manage the business himself.

There are numerous examples of efficient and profitable state-owned companies. Norwegian Statoil is a state-owned oil company with revenues in 2012 of 705 billion Norwegian kroner (about $115 billion). Statoil is certainly not losing money and is in part responsible for Norway being one of the wealthiest countries in the world, with the least economic inequality. The average skilled worker earns three times more than his British contemporary, and the CEO of Statoil earns "only" about two million dollars. The Norwegian state also owns a large part of Telenor, the country's biggest telephone operator; Norsk Hydro, its biggest aluminum producer; Yara, its biggest fertilizer maker; and DnBNor, the nation's biggest bank. Singapore Airlines is one of the most successful airlines in the world, and it is also state owned. It has not had a financial loss in thirty-five years. In fact, Singapore, which is regarded as a leading example of a free-market economy, has a very large state sector. According to Ha-Joon Chang: "[Singapore's government-linked companies] do not just operate in the usual public 'utility' industries, such as telecommunications, power and transport. They also operate in areas that are owned by the private sector in most other countries, such as semiconductors, shipbuilding, engineering, shipping and banking." [10]

A recent article in the Harvard International Review argues that a new, efficient form of state-owned enterprises (SOE) seems to be emerging in the twenty-first century, and these new enterprises are likely to be much more efficient than those common in the 1980s, having learned from past failures. [11]

In an economic democracy, state-owned enterprises can play a crucial role by complementing private and cooperative industries. An economy where ownership is divided between private, cooperative, state-run, or publicly owned by a region or city, we may term a "three-tiered" economic structure. [12]

A Decentralized Economy

"Save the Local Economy" and "Buy Local" campaigns are very popular these days, but these slogans and the movements behind them are not sufficient to create a viable local economy. Corporations will not change their business practices voluntarily. Even with a ceiling on wealth and widespread ownership of businesses by the workers, economic democracy will not take hold as long as economic activity is limited to certain geographical areas, neglecting others and leaving them economically backward and deprived. Likewise, as long as there is drainage of wealth from one area or country to another, economic democracy will remain a pipedream. A decentralized economic structure, instituted by law, is therefore essential for the success of economic democracy.

In the present economic system, economic activity is centralized in growth poles that generally exploit the surrounding areas.[13] To counteract this tendency, a concerted effort through public campaigns, governmental laws, and voluntary change by businesses will be required. The change will not take place automatically. This need for political and economic pressure, however, is not in itself an indication that a decentralized economy is unsound. In reality, all efforts to organize change in society require concerted effort.

This is especially true of "free markets." As Polanyi, Chang, Reinert, and others have pointed out, there is nothing inherently natural about free markets. Recent history has proven that without government intervention and coercion the market will not function optimally, neither for people nor for the environment. One reason for this is that today's market has been placed outside democratic control through the imposition of international trade agreements such as the Trans-Pacific Partnership (TPP) between the US and eleven other countries. Negotiated behind closed doors, this trade agreement, like the North American Free Trade Agreement (NAFTA), will not only enforce free trade and intellectual property rights but also continue creating job losses, a downward spiral in wages, and inefficient environmental regulations. These agreements, favored by corporations and regulated by treaties, are often outside the jurisdiction of individual governments and thus democratic processes. A decentralized economic structure would thus require concerted government intervention and the necessary legal framework to function. Just as it requires efforts to enforce a "free market," it will also require effort to enforce a societal structure that supports economic democracy. The difference is that the capitalist market increases inequality while a more democratic market structure promotes more equality.

In some cases, a decentralized economy may not maximize economic profit, but decentralization is a necessary foundation for economic democracy, since a localized economy will maximize the use of resources, reduce environmental degradation, and increase income equality.

Economic decentralization does not have to mean a reduction in technology and know-how. Rather, the most advanced technology still ought to be used. In a capitalist market economy this poses a serious dilemma, since efficiency and advanced technology are associated with corporate centralization. With the birth of the Internet this has changed. Know-how and technology can immediately be transferred geographically to any point in the world, and many decentralized production units can easily coordinate their activities through joint communication channels. This being said, if there is an abundance of unskilled labor, it is better in a transition period to promote labor-intensive industries to ensure that everyone is employed, even if these industries are less efficient than mechanized industries. By simultaneously working on skills training for staff, more advanced industries can gradually be established.

The reverse situation exists when we find skilled, educated people in a region but no job opportunities to utilize their skills. In this case, people emigrate causing a brain drain, making it even harder for the region to progress. To avoid this, labor-intensive industries need to be established in the short term, and enterprises that use advanced technology utilizing people's technical skills and education remain the long-term focus of development. If this point is neglected, the long-term economic outlook for the local economy will be bleak.

Self-sufficient Economic Zones

An integral aspect of a decentralized economy is to introduce self-sufficient economic zones. The term self-sufficient economic zones does not imply isolation and inefficiency, such as in the case of the North Korean Juche idea, developed by Kim Il-Sung as a form of political and economic self-reliance, a battered system that has impoverished and isolated the country. On the contrary, a self-sufficient economy means that economic activities within or across the borders of a country are maximized and well balanced, and that the exchange of goods and services between various regions takes place in mutually beneficial ways, without draining wealth from either region.

An economic zone is an area with sufficient factors in common to create economic self-sufficiency and self-reliance. These factors can be both economic and psychological. Among the economic factors are economic viability, common economic problems, natural resources to make the zone self-sufficient, etc. Among the psychological factors are linguistic and cultural similarities. The common economic factors are necessary to ensure that the economic zone is viable, and the psychological factors are necessary to ensure that there are sufficient unifying sentiments so that the people will work unitedly toward a common goal.

In a self-sufficient economic zone, it is imperative that both the cultural heritage and the productive resources are under the control of local people so that no Walmart or McDonald's, for example, can have free license to set up shop and compete with local stores and restaurants. It is also important that the local language is encouraged and that all economic decisions are administered by the people living in the area. Another vital objective of an economic zone is full employment for the people, and thus the local population is given priority in this regard. As the movement of people will not be restricted, people from outside the zone will be free to move in, as long as they chose to settle in the area and become part of its economy. It is best not to encourage migrant guest workers, on the other hand, since they may cause problems for both local workers and for their own families that they have left behind. In general, migrant workers and illegal immigration are signs of an imbalanced economy, often the result of free-trade agreements between developed and less developed regions or countries—such as NAFTA, the free-trade agreement between Mexico, the US ,and Canada that devastated the Mexican small-farm economy and resulted in millions of poor Mexicans migrating illegally to the US.

While a common language and a common culture bring people together, it is essential that humanist, color-blind sentiments prevail, so that discrimination based on color, language, ethnicity, or other narrow sentiments does not arise. Thus the criteria for who will be part of an economic zone is not based on ethnicity but rather on whether people have merged their individual interests with the interests of the economic zone they live and work in. As we mentioned before, a common problem all over the world is that resources are drained from poor to rich areas. Therefore, drainage of wealth from one economic zone to other economic zones will have to be checked. In particular, the repatriation of profits from one zone to another should be tightly controlled. In this way, profits made in one region can be ploughed back into the same area—which is an important feature of economic democracy.

Economic zones of this nature can develop areas that otherwise would be considered "uneconomic" or "inefficient." Even if some zones initially are much less efficient than others, it is still more beneficial for society as a whole to encourage economic activity rather allowing less developed areas to be put out of business through free trade and global competition. In many places, natural and human resources are extremely underutilized because they cannot compete with the highest producing areas of the world. As a consequence, a wealth of human and natural potential is left untapped. From both a global and local perspective, it is not efficient and balanced when only the high-producing areas are developed and the less developed regions are kept impoverished. It is much better for the economy, society, and the environment to maximize the potentials of all regions of the world; to make them all sustainable and self-sufficient.

In free-trade zones the strongest producers and nations take advantage of the weaker ones, reaping high profits while reducing the welfare of people of the poorer nations. This is evidenced in large economic systems such as the EU, which is engaged in EU-centric trade with poor countries, as well as in national economies such as the US, where corporations like Walmart and Lowe's often wipe out the local competition. In golf, the handicap system enables weaker players to compete with stronger players, and nobody thinks this is unfair. Similarly, economically struggling nations can be allowed to compete with stronger nations by introducing customs barriers and tariffs. Such protectionism is an important and effective system to improve slow economies. As we illustrated earlier, that is how the rich nations got rich. Due to current free-trade deals that favor the already powerful, protections for the weak are often absent in the world economy.

While centralization is efficient in certain ways, such as in maximizing output with less manpower, a centralized economy is very inefficient in other ways, since it often leaves vast areas undeveloped and many people unemployed. The development of local sources of energy whenever possible is also important. Economic independence is augmented by energy independence. Finally, most of the arguments presented in the chapter *Making Poor Countries Rich* also apply to economic zones and regions as well as to countries. Even if a region is currently backward, and it would be easier for people to move to richer, more populous urban areas, or to sell their local raw materials to industrial areas, such a strategy, or lack thereof, will leave the area undeveloped and poor, and its many human, economic, environmental, and cultural potentials largely unfulfilled. Only when an area's potentials are fully developed, with a balanced mix of sustainable, economic activities, will the area prosper. In the beginning it is costly to industrialize an undeveloped area, but in the long run it is the best and most sustainable way to spread development broadly. As the economy develops and communication improves, economic zones will over time grow and merge into larger units.

A Balanced Economy

Agriculture has been the foundation of human civilization for thousands of years. Without agriculture, most of humanity would die of famine within a short time. In spite of this, those countries that dedicate a majority of their resources to agriculture are generally poor. In order to become wealthier, countries traditionally concentrated on manufacturing, with its more stable and higher value-added prices. In recent years, increasing profits have moved from manufacturing to the service sector, which now makes up the biggest part of the economy in economically advanced countries. But without an industrial base, there would be no service economy, and without an agricultural base there would be no industry. One part of the economy derives value from the other; one part siphons off some of the value from the underlying base and turns it into profits. In other words, the reason the service industry is profitable is because of the strong industrial and agricultural foundation it is based on.

To succeed, it is important that a balanced economy, as we have defined it above, is introduced in each economic zone. Instead of some areas specializing in one part of the economy, it is economically more sustainable if there is a balanced mix of agriculture, industry, and services within each economic zone.

Countries and economic zones are best served by concentrating on areas of the economy that will be most profitable in the future, rather than on what makes a quick profit now. Initially, these countries and areas may have to pay higher prices for inferior goods by producing them locally, but later on, when they are able to produce better products themselves and are thus able to compete with other economic zones, they will prosper and become more sustainable.

Such strategic planning only applies to areas of the economy undergoing change, including industrial infrastructure, education, and other areas through which a nation can improve. There are some areas impacting the economy, however, that never change. Climate, natural resources, geographical location, etc., remain relatively unchanged over time. Therefore, all economic zones must consider such regional peculiarities in their planning. In spite of all zones attempting to develop all aspects of the economy, the final mix will naturally differ between the various zones.

Due to the variability in agricultural, industrial, and raw-material potential in each zone, trade between them is beneficial and necessary. While free trade, taken to its most extreme, will prevent any developing country to build up the skills and know-how needed to bring it out of poverty, no trade at all would be even worse. What is needed is dynamic balance. Free trade should be encouraged between nations and areas that have reached comparative levels of development. Trade between developed and developing nations can also be beneficial, as long as the development interest of the poorer area is taken care of and a transfer of skills and knowledge is part of the trade agreement.

Decentralized Planning

There are strong sentiments these days against centrally planned economies in contrast to the supposed decentralized nature of decision-making in free-market economies. This categorization is not quite correct, for all economies have some elements of centralized planning. In the words of economy professor Michael Hudson:

> In practice, every market is planned and organized by some parties or others, ever since the Neolithic rhythms of agricultural planting and harvesting. The euphemism "free market" means central planning by the banks and high finance — by Wall Street, the City of London, Frankfurt, the Paris Bourse and centers further eastward... This shifts the allocation of capital and policy planning out of the hands of government into those of the banking sector. This financialization of the economy (and

indeed of the political system) is more centralized than public planning by elected officials. [14]

Everybody attempting to succeed will make sure to plan ahead. This is equally true for individuals, companies, and states. The better the planning, the better the results. Singapore, South Korea, Taiwan, and Japan very deliberately planned their economies, and that is why they are prosperous countries today. China is currently doing he same.

The difference between this type of central planning and the type exercised in Maoist China or the Soviet Union is that the latter tried to centrally make detailed plans for each and every factory, farm, educational institution—in short, for nearly every economic or political issue in society. As history has shown, this over-centralized and micromanaged system failed miserably. Successful central planning outlines the broad features and policies of the economy but allows the details of the economy to be drafted and managed in a decentralized manner by individuals, companies, states, counties, and cities.

In free-market economies, the broad rules of the macroeconomy are decided in a centralized manner by international treaties and organizations such as the World Trade Organization. The next level of planning is handled by large financial institutions and big corporations. On the microeconomic level, individuals and smaller corporations do the planning. However, this type of top-down, bank- and corporate-friendly planning is not aimed at promoting universal welfare, true sustainability, or economic democracy. Quite the opposite. On the global level, current free-market policies promote inequality, income disparity, resource depletion, and environmental destruction. On the local level, we have too many parties scheming to promote their own personal interests at the expense of other parties, the community, and the environment.

The idea behind Adam Smith's invisible hand, at least the way it has been adopted by contemporary economists, is that maximum benefit will be reached by everyone individually pursuing their own self-interest. But this is not how it works in the real world. Economic development occurs when people cooperate with each other, not when they fight each other. Just think about it—why does a large corporation out-compete small businesses? Because in a large corporation there are more people cooperating and acting in a preplanned manner and with access to more resources. We may investigate this on any level we want—the result will still be the same. A big country can impose its will on small countries because it has more people cooperating and more resources. A well-trained army of a few hundred can easily defeat thousands of untrained and unorganized fighters. Furthermore, a coordinated football team will easily defeat an uncoordinated team, regardless of the individual skill of the players.

To make economic democracy a reality, decentralized economic planning is essential, not only for a country or an economic zone, but also in much smaller areas. If local businesses, cooperatives, local governments, and social boards representing the people in each locality sit down and discuss how best to build their community, they will be far more successful, and far more satisfied, rather than if a central planner or a corporate entity situated in a foreign country makes the decisions for them. But in the current corporate economy the latter is most often the case. Consequently, the corporations become the winners and the local economies the losers.

Local planning is thus more advantageous than no planning. Local planning must naturally take many factors into consideration, such as the economic realities of the country, available infrastructure, available raw materials, supply of skilled labor, markets, etc.

As communication improves and the economy becomes larger and more developed, the area of planning can gradually increase, since wider and wider areas can work as cohesive units without neglecting parts of its population.

Summary of Policy Suggestions

- Introduce an enterprise structure that discourages passive ownership and spreads the ownership among the population. We recommend that the economic structure consists of three tiers:
- Private, small-scale enterprises. These consist of family businesses or any business employing less than twenty-five people.
- Small, medium, and large-scale cooperatives where the workers participate in the ownership of the business.
- Efficient, state-owned enterprises. These are for very large scale-operations, such as road and bridge infrastructures, and those that are of vital importance to society as a whole, such as the oil industry, military, electric plants for conventional and renewable energy, water plants, and the health and education industry.
- Decentralized economic activity.
- Decentralization will spread employment and ownership and stimulate the entire economy.

- While decentralization may not maximize profit, it will minimize hoarding and speculation, which is far more important. Most of the profits will be circulated back into the economy.
- Introduce new, sustainable, efficient, and appropriate technology.
- Self-sufficient economic zones.
- Put all resources in the area to work in an environment-friendly and sustainable manner.
- Reduce the amount of idle resources while spreading the wealth.
- Regional food self-sufficiency by maximizing local agricultural output.
- Develop local industry, as mentioned in the previous chapter. It is better to have local industries, even if they are not the most efficient, than to have unutilized productive resources. With know-how and training, efficiency will increase and the industries will eventually become competitive.
- Encourage trade with other economic zones but protect budding industries until they can compete with other zones to prevent them from being outcompeted.
- Since there is a link between agriculture, manufacturing, and the service industry, it is important that a balanced economy is developed where all three are adequately represented.
- Develop alternative energy sources such as wind, geo-thermal, solar, and others.
- Decentralized economic planning.
- Centralized planning is good for providing overall guidelines and general policies, but to centrally micromanage a detailed plan for the whole country, including its cities and villages, is wasteful and inefficient. History has shown that it will not work.
- As far as possible, local people should be part of planning their own economy. When planning, keep in mind the overall economic conditions of the country, available infrastructure, raw materials, markets, resources, skills, etc. If certain skills and know-how is lacking, then efforts should be made to increase these. Meanwhile, fledgling industries may need protection.
- As communication and trade increases, the planned-for area can be expanded.

Chapter Thirteen

Environmental Solutions: Beyond Green Capitalism

We do need a 'new economy,' but one that is founded on thrift and care, on saving and conserving, not on excess and waste. An economy based on waste is inherently and hopelessly violent, and war is its inevitable by-product. We need a peaceable economy.

—Wendell Berry

O NE OF THE MAIN gifts of the green movement has been to show that "prosperity transcends material concerns,"[1] that true wealth resides in the quality of our lives, in vibrant communities and a healthy environment, and that true wealth has little to do with profit. The greens have also managed to present a new macroeconomic vision where sustainability trumps growth and consumption for real needs and not mindless consumerism guides economic planning. Most importantly, they have emphasized the need to establish environmental and resource limits on economic activity. What the greens have overlooked, however, is the power of the profit motive, the structurally inbuilt growth impulse in capitalism, which will trump all other visions unless we restructure the macroeconomic system itself.

The profit motive in capitalism makes the market undemocratic and monopolistic. Capitalism is fundamentally based on property rights, while democracy is based on personal rights. As economist Jaroslav Vanek says, "The most important aspect of capitalism, its objective function, is to maximize profit."[2] In other words, capitalist firms do not like regulation. They do not like to be told to add costs, including environmental costs, to the profit equation. They will fight that possibility at every turn in the road. It is for this reason that greenwashing—when companies advertise being more environmentally responsible than they actually are—is so common. The powerful drive of the profit motive trumps all other interests—be they the interests of the employees, the community, or the environment—is also the main reason why an unregulated capitalist economy and a democratic and sustainable economy are incompatible.

We Need Systems Change

We have two choices: we can, as we do today, make incremental or half-hearted changes through consumer choices and painstakingly slow legislation, or we can make more fundamental changes by facilitating the democratic evolution of the economy toward an economy whose objective is not to maximize profit but to maximize the welfare of people and the environment through better participation and planning. The main difference between our suggestions and most green policy suggestions, then, is that they emphasize consumer choice and legislation, while we maintain that this is not good enough, since it will not curb the profit motive of the capitalist economy. We also need economic restructuring; we need to grow a new economic structure to take the place of the old one.

Without such a systems change the old economic vision will continue to drive economic concerns; we will continue to look at nature as a free lunch and a sinkhole to dump our waste in. Rhetoric aside, the main problem with the old economy is the capitalist market's inevitable nature to concentrate wealth and compromise human and environmental concerns. This fundamental issue has not been compellingly addressed by the green parties, the green writers, or the environmental movement in general.

The capitalist economy is best suited for smaller-scale private enterprises, the way Adam Smith originally intended it. If not broken up or restructured through governmental policy, the corporate giants will grow the capitalist market to unsustainable levels, no matter how many checks and balances society sets in place; no matter how ethical our leaders are. Just like today. Therefore the capitalist market economy must be restructured so that it only comprises small private businesses such as restaurants, farms, shops, artisan breweries, and bakeries. Sustainability is incompatible with capitalism in an economy of scale. In other words, sustainability is incompatible with corporate capitalism.

If capitalism is left structurally unchanged—that is, without reducing the size and power of the corporations—the profit motive will eventually dominate the economic and cultural esprit of society, no matter how much legislation is imposed. More importantly, it will delay the inevitable emergence of the new economy, an economy built not only on healthy competition but on worker cooperation and entrepreneurial collaboration.

We Need Deep Structural Changes in the Economy

Political democracy—a single vote every two to four years—is not enough. We also need economic democracy, people's ability to create and manage their own economic destiny on a day-to-day basis and from the grassroots up. In addition, we need an economy that is need based not greed based, an economy that measures its economic health on how well it delivers people's basic needs, how high their purchasing capacity and real income is, not on how high the GDP is. Economic health should be measured by growth and sustainability from the bottom up rather than from the top down. The GDP says nothing about the economic health of the average citizen, or about the sustainability of an economy; it simply measures the total output of the economy, even if those outputs lead to negative growth: more crime or more industrial pollution. These structural economic changes are the greatest need in today's economy, and they will take place either through popular pressure and eventual legislation or through economic and environmental crises—most likely both.

Today, perhaps more than at any other time in the history of capitalism, businesses favor the short term over the long term. Corporations have no qualms about producing an appliance that will break down or need to be replaced in a few years, rather than producing a product that will last. Short-term outcomes win the day in most every case, and there is no sector more keenly attuned to this than the financial sector. This sector, which today is one of the main drivers of our profit-based economy, is the largest stumbling block to a sustainable world. The financial market has the shortest planning horizon of any part of the economy: it measures progress in nothing but profit. In a matter of seconds, financial speculators can change their balance-sheet wealth by the billions. Hence, we cannot just patiently wait until this part of the economy responds more ethically, more sustainably—it has to be controlled and changed by legislation and by restructuring. A profit-based, sustainable economy is therefore an oxymoron—it has never existed and never will.

The power in today's society lies with the large corporations and those individuals who have accumulated the most wealth. Therefore, until the distribution of wealth changes and real power is transferred into the hands of the people, the chance of any meaningful reform in environmental policies taking place is unlikely. This is the primary reason that we have placed this chapter on Green Solutions after that of Economic Democracy. For long-term sustainability to take hold in society, the reforms suggested in the Economic Democracy section will first have to be implemented. This kind of deep systems change is imperative. Its absence is the main stumbling block to long-term sustainability.

We Need Decentralized, Long-term Planning

Once we have a decentralized economy where no entity is so large that it can singlehandedly impose its will on the rest of the people, new considerations can be introduced in economic planning. Profit does not need to be the sole motive any longer. Quality-of-life issues, cultural development, and the preservation of the environment in the interest of future generations will then become obvious considerations. We can then, as the Native Americans used to say, "make plans for seven generations." We can then much more easily implement large-scale ecological industrial-design programs, such as the cradle-to-cradle designs mentioned earlier in the book, advocated by cutting-edge scientists and planners such as William McDonough and Michael Braungart. Industry will then become a reflection of and partner with nature rather than being its enemy.

Economic democracy and a network of decentralized local economies will by themselves have many positive effects on the environment, including a huge reduction in energy for transport and production, and in pollution, but there will still be environmental challenges, even in an economic democracy. Hence, we will have to always be vigilant in pursuing policies that minimize pollution and utilize resources in a sustainable manner.

Beyond Green Capitalism

It is an understatement to say that our economy is dependent on nature for its survival and continued growth—the economy is part of a living environment, and it can only thrive if nature and humanity thrives. As humans we thrive best when living in harmony with nature, and human culture thrives best when it expresses its reverence for nature. But if these qualities are lacking in society, then humans suffer another form of poverty—spiritual poverty. With the right economic and environmental policies, it is possible to create an economy that thrives, both culturally and economically, coevolving with nature herself, in virtual perpetuity. Such an economy will be decentralized, restructured, democratic, culturally rich, and circular. Here are, in a short summary, a set of comprehensive recommendations we think can form the basis of a green economy that is more democratic, equitable, and sustainable:

Individual Lifestyle Change: Creating a lifestyle based on a more plant-based diet, solar panels on the house, biking or walking to work, recycling, organic fair-trade food, and other green choices has an important role to play in creating sustainability. If our values are not reflected in our lifestyle, they will not be reflected in the society we wish to create; we will not have the moral strength to protest injustice or to create constructive environmental change.

Political Mobilization: When our green lifestyle—our walking the talk—is combined with political activism, such as forming transition towns, practicing permaculture, buying from local farmers, industries, and businesses, protesting unsustainable business practices, and voting for political parties with green policies, we can have an even greater impact on creating a greener world.

Economic Democracy: The forces against sustainability—the corporate capitalist system and its economic machinery of production and finance—are formidable, and until it is dismantled and restructured into a more democratically controlled economy, we cannot expect to see a truly sustainable economy.

Maximum Utilization: All natural resources need to be utilized in the most efficient and ecological way possible. We need to create affluence from effluence. And we need the humility to proceed with caution and respect for life when introducing new technology.

No exploitation: No one has the right to exploit another; no one should be used as an end to someone else. There are hidden geniuses working in sweatshops. The best way to end exploitation is by developing human potential. This not only increases the wealth of human ability, but also when individual potential is developed there is a corresponding decrease in negative personality characteristics—a corresponding decrease in social problems.

Rational Distribution of Money and Resources: So many of our resources are wasted before, during, and after the production cycle of a product. This negative cycle must be broken. Moreover, money and resources are unequally distributed, dividing the world into rich and poor countries. This growing trend needs to be altered.

Decentralization: The corporate economy is an economy of centralization of money and power. Political change is necessary, but real life and change happens in the real economy—where we live and work. People, not corporate shareholders, need to control the economy through political and economic democracy, and the economy needs to be localized in order to be democratic, just, and sustainable.

Circular Economics: The newly restructured economy needs to be rooted in ecological wisdom and practices—it needs to be a cradle-to-cradle, circular economy in which all its byproducts circle back into production, just as they do in nature. The economy needs to be guided by an ecological ethics that is inspired by ancient wisdom as well as the latest in the ecological and technological sciences. The economy will then be an extension of nature, not its destroyer and exploiter.

Specific Policy Suggestions for Solving the Environmental Crisis

Economic Restructuring

- Implement all policy suggestions in the previous chapters, including economic democracy.

Legal Reforms

- Follow Ecuador's example by giving constitutional legal rights to ecosystems.
- Allow people to sue on behalf of rivers, lakes, mountains, etc.

- Require the government, businesses, and corporations to remedy violations of these rights.
- Require corporations to prove that their new inventions are not harmful to the environment before marketing them.
- Legislate general standards for true cost pricing.
- Pass governmental and nongovernmental legislation to label products according to their sustainability level, as a first step in the right direction.
- Pass stricter governmental legislation to ban products that are not environmentally friendly, as a next step in the right direction.

Policies

- Shift planning away from profit concerns toward economic democracy and social and environmental responsibility.
- Encourage development of local industrial and agricultural markets—this will also maintain market competition but from the bottom-up, which is an important key to economic democracy, better wages, and a better local and global environment.
- Institute an effective global carbon tax to reduce global CO_2 emissions—today individual countries have such taxes, but corporations, such as those in the EU, are lobbying to stop or reduce them. This must not be allowed.
- Divest from the fossil-fuel economy and invest in a fossil-fuel-free economy for the future.
- Move toward zero emission technologies.
- Increase research and development of environmentally friendly products.
- Enact economic policies based on ethics and sustainability, not profit.
- Curb consumerism by promoting better lifestyles and nonmaterial sources of happiness through education and community development. Studies have shown that once people have a good standard of living, increased consumption decreases people's happiness.
- Enact short- and long-term legislation to make farming practices organic within ten to twenty years.
- Reduce farming subsidies so that prices reflect real cost, thus creating a localized agriculture based on real consumer needs.
- Reduce meat production for sustainability and health—meat

production, unless based on free-range, grass-fed fowl and animal production, is the most wasteful and environmentally unfriendly agricultural method. Its overconsumption has also been proven to be the main cause of heart disease, cancer, and diabetes.

- Educate people on a national level about the importance of a plant-based diet as per the latest science on nutrition and health.
- Increase the production, processing. and distribution of fruits, vegetables, herbs, plant oils, and grains for maximum local, regional, and national food sovereignty.

Part V:
The New Economy

Chapter Fourteen

Economic Systems Change: A New Economy for a New Era

You never change things by fighting the existing reality. To change something, build a new model that makes the existing model obsolete.

—R. Buckminster Fuller

WE HAVE TRIED REFORMING capitalism for decades, and a growing number of people have come to realize that it is too late to reform our economy. We need to grow an entirely new economy with a new structure, an economy beyond capitalism. But what will this economy look like?

Economics is a part of the social sciences. Economics is not just an objective study of what is—it is an expression of what we wish reality to look like. We have to decide what type of society we want to live in, then set up laws and structures to bring that world into being. We have to decide what the underlying philosophy of our economy ought to be. Should the economy be based on personal, selfish needs, or on sharing and cooperation? Should the economy be based on exploiting the environment, or on utilizing the environment in a rational and sustainable way? Capitalism is mainly based on satisfying selfish human needs, and look where that economic philosophy has brought us—to the brink of an economic and environmental disaster, into the clutches of a perfect storm. The economy of tomorrow must be different; it must be based on the needs of everyone, both individual and collective needs, including the needs of the environment, the needs of our animals and plants.

Economics is a subsection of nature. It is a human-made system meant to facilitate the utilization and distribution of natural resources. In order to actualize the changes recommended in this book, which would dramatically alter the way capitalism utilizes and distributes resources, there must be a change in outlook, a rethink of the world we want to live in. Purely tinkering with capitalism, an economic system that reflects values different than those we want to promote, will not work.

If our social goals are mainly financial, our economy will resemble classical and neoclassical economics. If our goals for society, however, are broader, such as enhancing the well-being of all people and utilizing properly all of nature's gifts, our economy will have much wider concerns. Such concerns lie beyond the scope of present-day economics.

What Kind of World Do We Want?

The choice before us is clear. We either aim for a world where everyone has equal rights, a fair share of the world's resources, and the opportunity to develop their full potential, or we aim for a world where certain people's interests are promoted while others are suppressed and exploited.

If our goal is a world where everyone is guaranteed basic rights and a dignified life, those who have a larger share of the economic pie will have to sacrifice some of their wealth. They can either voluntarily choose to curtail their excess accumulation, or society will have to compel them.

In principle, there is no difference between forcing rich people to reduce their share of the wealth and the present system where society decides to abide by the rules of free markets and thus unfairly privilege the rich to the disadvantage of the poor. In one, the rich benefit, and in the other, the people at large benefit. Enforcing rules that benefit the majority of the people cannot be considered any more unjust than enforcing rules that privilege the minority.

A New Economic System

Many writers and philosophers have wanted to develop a more just society, but very few have taken the time to mold these ideas into a coherent political and economic system. Even the prolific writer and thinker Karl Marx left a large gap between his communist ideals and the means to achieve them. In Marx's books, there is a remarkable absence of information about the future socialist or communist economy. Most of his writings criticize capitalism, but he wrote little about what the communist state would look like or how the transition would take place. It was as if Marx concluded that as soon as the ills of capitalism are understood, then a new and better system will arise by historical necessity. But history has proven Marx wrong.

But what about contemporary critics? After studying the most important critics of modern capitalism and the best writings on green capitalism and socialism, from the bestselling writings of academic Thomas Piketty to global-economy critics Eric S. Reinert and Ha-Joon Chang, from green economists E. F. Schumacher to Herman Daly, from classical economists Adam Smith to macroeconomic reformer John Maynard Keynes to Marxist economist Thomas Wolfe and many more, we have become familiar with most of the critical theories and alternative ideas. It has been striking to see the strong consensus about what is wrong with capitalism and what reforms are needed, but it has been equally striking to learn that few economic models have been proposed to replace the current economic system. One of those rare models has been developed by the Indian philosopher P. R. Sarkar. His Progressive Utilization Theory (PROUT), more than any other we have come across, combines the best of capitalism with the best of socialism while defining a new value base and many new economic features that go beyond both systems. Most of the recommendations in the previous chapters have been directly or indirectly derived from Sarkar's economic theory.

The Progressive Utilization Theory

To grow a new economy, we must start with a vision of the society we want to live in. Holding that vision before us, we proceed by creating mechanisms, policies, and regulations to build the new society. Sarkar's vision of society is distinct and clear: a place of mutual cooperation where each individual is given the opportunity to develop his or her maximum potential in all spheres of existence—physical, mental and spiritual. He envisioned a world where everyone's physical needs are guaranteed by society, but in exchange each individual is required to cooperate, compete, and contribute according to their capacity to build and defend this world.

Discrimination, intolerance, intellectual suppression, dogmas, and economic exploitation are a few of the issues Sarkar opposes. Instead, he favors pluralism, allowing each culture to flourish and grow into a beautiful flower in the garden of humanity. But not only are human beings important—nature also needs protection. Since we human beings are more intelligent and powerful than any other species on our planet, it is our responsibility to protect the environment and other species from exploitation and destruction. We are a part of nature and we have a responsibility to protect it.

Spirituality is high on Sarkar's list of priorities. Not religion or dogma but spirituality as a form of personal development—the human attempt to achieve inner peace and happiness. Free intellectual and artistic expression is another integral aspect of his vision of a new society. When people are encouraged to develop their inner talents, from acquiring scientific knowledge to the study of literature, art, and music, society benefits by being able to draw on a pool of educated and creative citizens.

However important spiritual, intellectual, and artistic development is for individuals as well as for society, these cultural advancements are not possible without an appropriate material base. Hence it is fundamental that all human beings are guaranteed the minimum necessities of life, including food, clothing, shelter, medical care, and education. With these provisions, however, come responsibilities, and the individual is given these privileges through guaranteed work that pays a living wage rather than by welfare or hand-outs. This new economic system thus provide the framework for an economy where creating a dynamic balance between cultural and economic values and between economic and ecological needs is possible.

An Expanded Social Contract

By guaranteeing the minimum necessities of life to all, this new economic system expands the contract society has with each of its citizens. Providing the minimum necessities of life for all should be part of the constitution of all nations. In other words, everyone who is willing and able to work should be guaranteed employment with a living wage. These goals might seem utopian in a world where the main problem is scarcity. But scarcity is actually not the problem facing us: our problem is unfair wealth distribution. Providing everyone with minimum necessities is easily achievable if we institute the necessary policies and garner enough political support.

When discussing the provision of minimum necessities for all, what matters is not the monetary value of our salary but the amount of goods our money can buy. Hence the guarantees of minimum necessities means a guaranteed job that provide sufficient purchasing capacity to afford food, clothing, and housing. Medical care and education should be free of charge, as they already are in Sweden, Norway, Denmark, and many other European states. Educating the population is not charity. It is an investment in the future. Education is an integral part of a prosperous and culturally rich society. If only the rich can afford to educate their children, we neglect an enormous pool of human potential. It is in the interest of society that all individuals receive a fair chance to develop their potentials. Since there is no link between wealth and intelligence, the most brilliant people can come from families with modest means. It is therefore imperative that all children are given an equal chance to develop their talents.

In addition, all individuals, depending on their merit, should have an opportunity to earn salaries greater than what is required for their basic requirements. Capitalism provides incentives for hard work and entrepreneurship, but unfortunately the present incentive system is unjust and counterproductive. It awards huge benefits to people who harm the common interest, such as giving bonuses to bank managers who bankrupt the banks and impoverish the depositors. Secondly, as economist Thomas Piketty has shown, the greatest rewards go to those who possess vast amounts of capital, regardless of whether these individuals contribute anything at all to society.

Economic rewards should be tied to an individual's social and environmental contribution. People who perform activities that benefit society should be rewarded, while those who harm society, or who contributes nothing, should not. Extra amenities can also be rewarded to those who have special needs, such as the handicapped. Basic amenities for all is not a fixed concept. An economy's ability to increase these amenities over time is the real measurement of society's vitality.

Fundamental Principles of the New Economy

While the decision to provide the minimum requirements to all members of society may be considered an ethical or political concept, the ability to deliver on these promises comes under the umbrella of economics. The economic system Sarkar proposes has been crystallized into five fundamental principles. These principles are both simple and profound. They may even appear self-evident to many readers; yet not a single principle is presently applied in the world of economics. The following section is a short overview of these principles. For people interested in a more comprehensive study, please refer to the book *Principles of a Balanced Economy*.[1]

These fundamental principles are basic rules for society to live by. They lay out the general ideas needed for a balanced economy, but they are not policies, since policies change. Rather, they are general economic formulas, principles from whose broad vision concrete economic policies will emerge, and at various times and conditions, these principles may be implemented differently. Most of the policies we have suggested and discussed in earlier chapters are direct applications of one or more of these principles.

Principle 1: There should be no accumulation of wealth without the approval of society.

Since one of the fundamental objectives of the new economy is to guarantee everyone the minimum necessities of life, this first principle is a logical necessity. If someone is allowed to accumulate unlimited wealth, the rest of society will be deprived and the primary objective of the good society—contentment and plenty for all—will be thwarted.

There are two aspects to the limitation of wealth. One is to set a ceiling on income; the other is to set a ceiling on the amount of wealth a person may accumulate. While these concepts are related, they are not necessarily the same. Likewise, when we consider a ceiling on income, there are again two distinct categories: income from work and passive income from various forms of capital. This first principle concerns all these forms of wealth.

Apart from the truism that if one or more persons accumulate excess wealth there won't be enough to go around for the rest of us, there are other problems associated with inequality. Over-accumulated wealth is rarely used productively; it most often ends up in economic ventures involving speculation or gambling. If the majority of a country's population is poor and illiterate, their potential will be wasted and the whole of humanity will be poorer for it. Spreading the wealth more equitably is the best way to make society prosperous and people happy, and this can only be accomplished if the accumulation of wealth is managed in a more balanced manner.

It should be noted that wealth, in this context, is not necessarily limited to physical wealth. For example, what we now call "intellectual property rights" is another type of wealth that needs to be controlled. If someone accumulates patents and other IP and prevents other people from using it, it can have the same negative effects as the accumulation of physical wealth. The basic guideline is that any hoarded wealth that restricts other people's ability to use it should be controlled. In addition, there may be legitimate reasons for society to limit the spread of certain types of information. For example, teaching people how to make bombs from items one can buy in a grocery store is a type of intellectual wealth society has an interest in restricting. Another example is the nonmaterial wealth invested in symbols that represent negative sentiments, such as the Confederate flag, which to many in the US represents racism and slavery. Due to its tattered and unflattering history, the Confederate flag was recently removed from the state capital in South Carolina, a restriction of intellectual and symbolic value put in place by state law. The necessity of controlling the accumulation of wealth is a principle, but the way to control this accumulation is a matter of policy and legislation. Possible ways to institute this principle is through wealth caps, a maximum wage, and other related policies discussed in previous chapters.

Principle 2: There should be maximum utilization and rational distribution of crude, subtle, and causal resources.

Limiting the accumulation of wealth is vital to ensuring that everyone can be guaranteed the minimum requirements of life. But unless sufficient wealth is created to satisfy everyone's needs, limiting accumulation will not be sufficient. The second principle addresses this issue. First it establishes the necessity of the maximum utilization of resources, and then it states that these resources have to be rationally distributed.

Presently, economists claim that economic growth is the best way to solve poverty. But if inequality rises as the economy grows, the rich will receive the largest portion of the economic benefits. Piketty demonstrates with comprehensive historical data that for the past two hundred years the return on capital has been much higher than the growth of the economy, something he expresses in the formula $r > g$.[2] The only exception to this rule, according to Piketty's research, was seen during the first and second world wars, a time that effectively reduced inequality due to the destruction of the assets of the rich. This means that even though the economy is growing, inequality is also growing, and the poor end up with only a small part of the total growth. If the portion of the economy's wealth allotted to the poor is lower than the population growth, then the poor will actually be worse off than before, despite the economic growth. The Philippines is a typical example of an economy that has grown rapidly in recent years without any reduction in poverty.

Due to this reason, the second principle does not only discuss maximum utilization but also rational distribution of resources. Since high concentration of wealth is associated with speculation and unproductive investments, as well as many other social ills discussed earlier, rational distribution implies a drive toward equality. We could thus consider the first principle to be encompassed and fulfilled by the second, but the importance of limitations to wealth accumulation is so central to a healthy economy that it has been made into a separate principle.

Maximum utilization, however, goes beyond the issue of economic growth. In modern economics, rebuilding houses destroyed by a natural disaster contribute to economic growth, ignoring the fact that we are only replacing something that was already there. Similarly, any activity designed to clean up environmental pollution is also considered economic growth. Somehow economists fail to account for destruction and disaster in economic activity, but when destroyed assets are rebuilt they readily add it as a plus. With that logic, destroying and rebuilding a house over and over again would contribute to economic growth.

Naturally, this would be a very poor utilization of available resources, and here is where the difference between these new economic principles and classical economics become very clear. This new economy is not concerned merely with GDP but with the maximum utilization of resources. Looking at the GDP of a country is not sufficient to establish how efficiently resources are being utilized. Thus to measure utilization of the type considered here, new indices will have to be developed.

As mentioned earlier, the new economy outlined here acknowledges other types of resources besides the physical or material. Material resources include land, water, minerals, agricultural products, wind, wave, and solar energy, and all other natural resources, in whatever form, as well as the human body's capacity for work. Material resources also include all natural resources that have been transformed by human intervention, such as factories, farms, ships, cars, etc. The second principle states that all these are to be maximally utilized. This would mean, among other things, that minerals must be extracted efficiently and transformed into useful articles with a minimum of wastage; that productive capacities are not kept idle, and so on. During the utilization of resources, the latest appropriate technology should be used.

Subtle or intellectual resources are ideas, knowledge, and know-how. They also include artistic expressions, such as music, poetry, literature, and film. In fact, the human mind itself is a subtle resource. Software could also be considered an intellectual resource. Without intellectual resources, it is impossible to utilize material resources, since the very process of utilization is an intellectual concept. Intellectual resources are different than physical resources in that they do not diminish when they are used. The more intellectual resources are distributed, the more value they give. The more educated people a society has, the greater its potential social, cultural, and economic prosperity.

Finally, this principle also recognizes spiritual resources. All cultures and religions recognize a spiritual reality as a source of strength, inspiration, and solace to individuals. Spirituality is therefore an important part of society's culture and should not be neglected or suppressed. Spiritual practices, such as meditation, increase one's enjoyment of the inner world and deserve to be encouraged and recognized as a valuable source of inspiration for humanity. Spiritual resources include uplifting scriptures, moral education, spiritual practices of various kinds, contact with saintly people, attendance at spiritual functions, and learning from holy and saintly persons. The spiritual and cultural contributions of mystics such as Rumi in Iran, Kabir in India, and Saint Teresa of Avilla in Spain, for example, are of immense value to both society and individuals.

Maximum utilization is closely related to rational distribution. It is impossible to maximally utilize something if it is not properly distributed. Rational distribution means to:

- Set aside enough resources for future production, such as reinvestment, infrastructure, education, healthcare, and future research.
- Provide everybody with the minimum requirements by producing sufficient quantities of basic necessities at affordable prices.
- Provide special amenities to people who have contributed greatly to society.

Maximum utilization is also related to the concept of efficient usage. If something is inefficiently used, there will by definition be wastage and hence less than maximum utilization.[3] Consequently, all resources have to be used as efficiently as possible. Unfortunately, this principle is rarely followed in the world today. The success of individual corporations generally comes at an enormous cost to the planet as a whole. The more wasteful a society is, the higher the corporate profit.[4] This may seem paradoxical, since large corporations, with all their wealth and resources, clearly are able to invest in more efficient, environmentally friendly operations. But when we examine their corporate goals, the paradox vanishes: the main objective of corporations is to produce short-term profits for its owners and shareholders; and this goal, more often than not, stands in direct contrast to the maximum utilization of the world's resources and the interests of the environment. Corporate managers are even often legally bound to maximize profits for their shareholders and could be sued if they had other priorities, such as the welfare of their staff, prevention of pollution, or more efficient use of raw materials. Their highest priority is to maximize profits, and in the current economy, it is unfortunately more profitable to underpay the employees, pollute the environment, and waste natural resources.

Since a company is only concerned with its own costs, the tendency will naturally be to transfer as much as possible of its costs to society. Economists generally consider these costs, or externalities, to be unimportant. If an individual company can dump toxic waste in rivers and let society be burdened with cleaning it up, then it is in the best economic interest of the company to do so. Unfortunately, the cost of cleaning up pollution is normally far higher than preventing the pollution in the first place, thus the total cost to society increases many times just so a few individuals can maximize their profits. This is just one of many examples of how the interests of an individual company often are at odds with the interests of society.

Competing corporations also duplicate efforts and waste resources. Take car production, for example. Many US cars made in Detroit are exported to Japan, while the Japanese make cars near Tokyo and then export them to the US. Such duplicitous industrial and economic activities, while profitable to corporations, waste enormous amounts of resources in fuel and shipping costs, as well as in increased pollution. Alumina produced in Jamaica is shipped to Ghana to be smelted into aluminum, just to be shipped back across the Atlantic to be sold in the US. The maximization of profits for individual corporations is therefore not consistent with the efficient utilization of resources for the world as a whole.

The inefficiencies of the current economy go much deeper, however. Not satisfied with the profits made through normal business activity, most investors speculate rather than make productive investments. As was mentioned earlier, 95 percent of all investments today are speculative, and only 5 percent go into productive ventures. Speculation does not add any value or produce anything. It is a parasitic economy that feeds off the real, productive economy. Hence 95 percent of all investments that should have been the source of economic growth are completely wasted.[5]

It is not only material resources that are underutilized in the present economic system but intellectual resources as well. In today's world, where the underlying motive of most everything is profit, anyone with a new invention will keep that idea from others and even have it legally sanctioned as intellectual property so that it cannot be used by anyone else, except through a license or other agreement. This increases the profits of the intellectual property owners while in turn reducing the collective wealth of humanity as a whole, since it reduces the total good that potentially could be produced.

The notion of intellectual property asserts that someone can own ideas. Had that been a fact, had someone actually developed new ideas or inventions from scratch, private ownership of intellectual property might be justified. However, all present-day ideas are the result of generations of human progress, and their developments and distribution are often funded by the general public. The idea that someone came up with a new invention in isolation, or outside the framework of contemporary scientific thought, makes little sense. As Sir Isaac Newton said, "I stand on the shoulders of giants." Many specific discoveries are based upon the works of inventors and thinkers who came before us. Their inventions are often funded by the government, which is to say that the taxpayers helped them by subsidizing their research. But once a useful invention is made, a private person or company patents it and is thus allowed to reap all the profits of an invention that came from a concerted effort of many scientists and institutions funded by taxpayers' money. As an example, Bill Gates, the founder of Microsoft and one of the world's wealthiest men, would not have been able to create his company's computer programs had it not been for his near-unlimited access to a computer lab purchased by the Mother's Club at his private college, Lakeside. It was not just talent and hard work that made Bill Gates who he is today but an intricate series of opportunities such as these. In his own words, "I had a better exposure to software development at a young age than I think anyone did at that period of time, and all because of an incredible series of lucky events." [6] As Malcolm Gladwell demonstrates in his popular book *Outliers: The Story of Success*, through this story and numerous others, the idea of the self-made genius is a myth. Without the cooperation and support of other individuals and institutions, from the past and the present, the success of every genius would be impossible to achieve.

There are also problems with the way contemporary research is beholden to institutions of economic and political power. In the US, the military-industrial complex often sponsors research into computer technology, aircraft, etc. Even when there are spinoffs to civilian applications, the whole process is extremely wasteful and is specifically geared toward the destruction of resources. Indeed, war, and by extension the arms industry, is one of the most wasteful of human activities. We invest enormous resources into designing gadgets that are literally made to self-destruct, and while destroying themselves, they cause maximum damage to other productive assets. While some war efforts may be driven by the need for self-defense, a large portion is driven by financial interests profiting from the arms industry. After all, if there were no wars, what would be the use of weapons?

Research is also deliberately restricted in areas where large corporations have a vested interest in not seeing any progress. Oil companies, for example, have little interest in developing alternative, renewable energy since it is more difficult to monopolize. And because electric cars, for example, are not yet as profitable as gasoline-guzzling cars, car manufacturers and dealerships are not so interested in selling them.[7] Maximum utilization of physical and mental resources would imply solving such economic anomalies. Evidently, our resources are not maximally utilized today. And regarding rational distribution, the situation is even worse, as we have already shown earlier in this book.

Poverty does not only deprive people of material needs; it also prevents them from developing their own potentials. Without adequate education and health, they become burdens rather than assets, and the maximum utilization of their potentials becomes difficult to realize. If all human beings had access to education, healthcare, food, and other resources to develop their innate potentials, they would be able to contribute immensely to society and indeed increase the collective wealth over and beyond what they consume. Keeping the majority of the world in poverty, while a minority lives in luxury, is both morally bankrupt and extremely wasteful.

Although this second principle may seem self-evident in contemporary society, it is being systematically violated due to the profit motive, capitalism's principle of self-interest being the main driver of economic growth.

Principle 3: There should be maximum utilization of the physical, mental, and spiritual potentialities of the individual and the collective.

While the second principle recognizes the need for the maximum utilization of all resources, the third principle acknowledges that it is individuals who make these utilizations possible.

The third principle is concerned with the utilization of human resources without which any other utilizations would be impossible. There are two aspects to this principle. The first is the maximum utilization of the physical, mental, and spiritual resources of both individuals and groups, and the second is the interconnectivity between the individual and the group, the recognition that individual welfare is an integral part of collective welfare and that collective welfare is an integral part of individual welfare. To sacrifice individual welfare for the sake of an impersonal "collective" benefit, such as was done in communist countries, does not properly promote economic or social benefits for anyone. What is the collective except a collection of individuals? How can we even talk about collective benefit if the individuals that make up the collective are being abused or deprived of the minimum necessities? At the same time, if individual interests are allowed to take precedence over collective interest, then a small interest group will soon live a life of privilege, far above the possibilities of the rest. Neither situation is desirable.

The development of the maximum potentials of individuals requires an adequate economic base, good education, and opportunities to develop in all spheres of life. Countries such as Finland and Singapore keep up their international competiveness by investing in education. It is a policy that pays off, both in terms of individual prosperity as well as for society as a whole. Unfortunately, most countries in the world take a much shorter view of the problem. Considering free education and decent living conditions as "costs" and "subsidies," they try to cut costs to reduce deficits by curtailing public healthcare, education, and housing, while they cut taxes on the rich to "stimulate growth." This is indeed very shortsighted. Investing in educational resources is what makes human culture flourish. An educated and intelligent work force is also the foundation of high labor productivity and prosperity.

This principle pertains to all physical, mental, and spiritual potentialities. Increasing the physical potentialities of a person can be done by physical training, so that the person is stronger and healthier and more physically able, but also by providing mechanical tools such as tractors, trucks, bulldozers, computers, etc., which extend the physical capabilities of an individual.

In the mental sphere, education develops the innate potentialities of each individual, and job opportunities allow them to use the knowledge they have gained to creatively serve their families and communities. Without such development, individuals will be little more than cogs in the machine. Also, it is the mind that enjoys and suffers, so mental development is important in its own right. By expanding the mind, individuals experience happiness and peace.

Finally, we have spiritual development. Far from being something mystical or alien to human beings, spirituality is the subtle inner core of every individual, what author and psychologist Mihaly Csikszentmihalyi calls the "happiness of flow" and what popular philosopher Eckhart Tolle simply calls "being." [8] It is the experience of inner fulfillment and ultimately the stillness beyond our thoughts and feelings. This inner experience of spiritual peace is an important dimension of human beings and the only permanent asset we have. True peace and happiness can never be realized if we neglect this inner part of ourselves. The popularity of yoga and meditation in modern society is a response to the innate human realization that it is not money that makes us happy; rather happiness comes from the ability to flow with the inner desire for peace and awe, from the state of mind beyond stress and the acquisition of material things.

As the saying goes, the whole is greater than the sum of its parts. To truly develop our potentials, we need to learn how to develop not only individually but also collectively. Many tasks are impossible for individuals alone to accomplish. In our modern society so many tasks require cooperation between individuals and between groups of people and institutions. It is not only competition that sets us apart and drives society forward, but more often our ability to cooperate and be creative and efficient by working together. Therefore, individual development must not be at the expense of collective development, and one of society's most important tasks is to help to bring everyone along in their all-round development. No group of people, whether an army, a football team, or a company, can successfully develop unless the individual members of the group work together.

The development of individual and collective potentials is therefore an integral requisite for the optimum functioning of the second principle, the maximum utilization and rational distribution of external resources.

Principle 4: There should be a well-balanced adjustment among the crude, subtle, and causal utilizations.

Principles two and three discussed the necessity of maximally utilizing resources and potentialities. These principles of maximum utilization contain several inherent contradictions. It is not possible to maximally utilize everything in all possible ways: for example, the choice to utilize a certain resource often makes it impossible to utilize other resources. If we choose to cut down a forest for timber, it will not be possible to maximally utilize the green foliage of the forest to reduce carbon dioxide and support wildlife. As the proverbial saying goes: we cannot have our cake and eat it, too!

From an ecological perspective, this conundrum is addressed by this fourth principle, which advocates a well-balanced adjustment between the various utilizations. Yes, we can harvest timber, but in a sustainable manner so that the forest can continue to grow, thus helping to reduce carbon dioxide, providing shelter for numerous plant and animal species, and serving us with medicinal plants, water, and as a sanctuary for recreation. To achieve such a well-balanced adjustment requires analysis, prioritizing, and clear decision making, which is the function of political management and leadership. The fourth principle, by extension, thus concerns itself with ecological management and the role of political legislation to safeguard the environment from overfishing, overharvesting of herbs, clear-cutting, and pollution—in short, from one-sided over-utilization.

From another perspective, a well-balanced adjustment between utilizations means to prioritize rarity and subtlety. If we have an abundance of a certain resource, say energy, and a shortage of another, say food, then further development of resources should be directed toward increasing food production rather than energy production. In this situation, it would be wise to utilize the abundant energy to produce more food, such as building heated greenhouses to grow food in the off-season. This could be a viable option for Iceland and Norway, both countries who are exactly in this predicament: high on energy but short on domestic food production. If the situation is reversed—an abundance of food but a shortage of energy—biofuel production could be a viable option.

While such political and economic considerations seem quite obvious from a holistic-economy perspective, they are often not followed. In the current global market, the determining factor for resource allocation is often maximum profitability rather than developing a balanced economy.

Prioritizing subtle resources is also an important general consideration. Physical resources are important, but their utilization is not possible without adequate planning. Ideas and inventions guide our development of physical resources. A well-developed knowledge industry is important for the utilization of the physical sphere. Therefore, a high priority has to be given to developing subtle resources, such as education in science, and especially in the integration of the various sciences and humanities.

In poor and developing countries, it is better to educate children rather than force them to do manual labor at an early age, and it is important to allocate resources to scientific discoveries and industrial development to properly utilize physical resources such as soil, minerals, water, and so on. It is through the development of science and rationality that we have harnessed electricity, grown food, made cars, and invented many of the electronic gadgets we take for granted. It is also through a more holistic educational integration of the sciences and the humanities that we will be able to use humanity's intellectual resources for economic development in a more sustainable fashion.

This fourth principle applies to both natural resources and human resources. During Mao Zedong's Great Leap Forward, from 1958 to 1961, plans were executed for localized steel production and the collectivization of peasant farms. This action was taken without proper analysis or understanding and gave negligible returns compared to the immense resources that were expended in the program. It is estimated that as many as 45 million people may have died during this period, all due to Mao's misguided utilization policy. In addition, China lost valuable intellectual and cultural resources by under-employing the country's teachers, writers, professors, and scientists. Properly employed and utilized, this vast pool of intellectual talent could not only have saved millions from starvation but could have truly created an economic and cultural leap forward.

Causal or spiritual resources are even more subtle than intellectual ones. The deep balance and strength that comes from the spiritual realm, the silent peace acquired in meditation by accessing the deep awareness behind the mind's activities, is vital to all human beings and gives us the ability to direct, harmonize, and control the mind's activities. While spiritual resources are less obvious than intellectual resources, they are vital for our existence. By developing this inner resource—not to be mistaken with a particular religious doctrine, but rather with the perennial wisdom at the heart of all religions—great spiritual teachers like St. Teresa of Avilla and the Buddha have taught the world about social harmony, inner strength, and peace. An individual's spiritual balance, peace, and compassion, enhanced by study, prayer, and meditation, can have a positive effect on millions. This personal yet universal spirituality, which has no conflict with science, is a great cultural resource that society needs to enhance and prioritize.

How and when we utilize these various resources is an ongoing task for political, social, and economic leaders to determine. Broadly speaking, we need to emphasize with equal importance the development of both material as well as human resources. Each and every individual should therefore be encouraged to utilize their full potential. To turn people into mindless automatons at an assembly line is a waste of their potential. Continuous development in education, creativity, art, music, and spirituality is vitally important for the welfare of both individuals and society.

The question of prioritizing resources leads us directly to the question of decision-making. Who makes the decisions?

The burden of decision-making ultimately falls on individuals, regardless of what governmental system is in place. The prevalent system in the world today is representative democracy. Unfortunately, in most cases money directly or indirectly wins elections. For example, in the United States Congress, 95 percent of the seats are won by the candidate who spends most on the electoral campaign. Perhaps most importantly, 65 percent of this funding comes from 1 percent of the American population. A "democratic" system where the leaders are bought is not that democratic after all. This is one of the reasons why economic democracy is far more important than political democracy. When economic power is widely distributed, people's control over their daily lives automatically increases. Special-interest groups that favor small groups at the expense of society and the environment will have a much harder time hijacking the decision-making process. Economic democracy coupled with political democracy will create a comprehensive shift in how and why decisions are made.

Regardless of government reforms, personal power can be abused for personal ends; thus spiritual and moral values in leaders are as important as political and economic expertise. Without a spiritual and moral foundation, a person may make selfish decisions or promote the goals of special-interest groups. Therefore, the need for spiritual and moral leaders cannot be underestimated. Unfortunately, there is no simple way to measure these qualities. A person can, like Machiavelli advises, pretend to be good and show a saintly face while he or she acts in selfish and destructive ways. There is therefore no scope for complacency. Concerned people will have to remain alert and monitor the activities of their leaders to make sure that they serve with the best interests of society in mind. Whenever a political system becomes corrupt and self-seeking, people will have to exercise their right to change either their leaders or the system, and if necessary both.

Principle 5: Utilizations vary in accordance with changes in time, space, and person; the utilizations should be progressive.

The final principle recognizes that change is inevitable in this world. Hence the utilizations of resources and potentials will likewise change. This is an inevitable law of nature.

Some changes are caused by the environment, such as weather patterns and the long-range patterns of global warming and cooling. The weather changes regularly during a year. If we do not adjust with these changes, agricultural production on a large scale would be difficult. Sometimes natural disasters, such as an earthquake, can wipe out a whole city, and we have no choice but to deal with the damage, the deaths, and the suffering. Some changes, such as global warming, may be long-term and lasting. These will require adaptation in other ways, since inaction will be catastrophic for the environment and for humanity.

Some changes are due to demographic shifts. As populations grow, the ability to live off the land changes and a once-prosperous area may no longer be able to support a growing population unless there are changes in the production of food and essential commodities.

Other changes are due to the increased scientific knowledge and new technological developments. Technological advancements will continue to bring progress as well as challenges. It is the nature of human beings to try to understand, utilize, and mitigate this progress. Technology will continue to advance as long as the human race is alive, but it is up to us to learn how to use it appropriately.

Since time and place are always changing, we will have to adjust to these historical changes. The basic principles of the new economy may not change, but the timely application of the new economy will have to adjust with the changing circumstances. Human beings must move forward by recognizing and adjusting with changes in time and place. Adjustment and flexibility are essential for human progress. [9]

While change is inevitable, progressive change is not. For example, people often try to resist environmental pressures rather than adapt to them. Such resistance results in a static society that relies on systems and policies ill adapted to handle the inevitable problems. This is not progressive change. Progressive change implies changes made in the utilization of resources and potentialities in harmony with existing conditions. If populations increase, production methods will have to adapt and become more efficient. Food may have to be grown in greenhouses, urban areas, or on previously nonfertile land. If the climate changes, adjustments have to be made in the way we live. When technology changes, we need to utilize it for everybody's welfare while simultaneously ensuring that the side effects of the technology do not destroy our environment and quality of life.

True progress is development in all spheres of existence, culminating in spiritual realization and peace. This Eastern concept, which differs radically from the Western notion of progress as material growth, reflects the new economy's roots in the nonmaterial notion that human happiness is relative to our state of mind and not to how much wealth we have. To achieve this inner state, however, each citizen needs the basic necessities of life and opportunities for optimum growth on all levels—physically, mentally, and spiritually. This will require a gradual increase in the standard of living while maintaining ecological balance. Progress then becomes a quality-of-life indicator rather than solely a material-progress indicator. Over the long term, people can gradually reduce their dependency on material products—they can opt to work less and give more importance to tourism, sports, art, and other cultural pursuits. The more these subtle cultural and spiritual resources are developed, the more opportunity there will be for sustainable balance between all of society's resource utilizations.

Implications of the Principles on Economic Policies

These five fundamental principles may seem self-evident to some readers, since they reflect basic realities of ecological and economic life. Still, these principles—which encourage us to live and flourish within our means—are constantly and systematically violated around the globe. The global corporate forces driving economic growth take no account of these basic realities. If they did, the very foundation of our economic system would have been reassessed, and a new base for economic development would have been established.

The reason we left the deliberation of these principles to the last chapter of the book is that they are still way ahead of the economic curve. Any serious and comprehensive attempt to implement them would be next to impossible within the framework of current free-market policies. If we accept the validity of these principles, it compels us to design a radically different economic system based on economic democracy, decentralization, economic justice, and the progressive and balanced use of all material and human resources for the benefit of all humans, animals, and plants on the planet. Unfortunately, these fundamental aspects of the new economy barely register in the agenda of today's corporate-driven economic climate.

Most of the policies discussed in previous chapters are concepts directly or indirectly drawn from the principles we have discussed above. The principles themselves, however, form a solid foundation that is more than a collection of policies. They inspire us to look at the world, the markets, and economics in general in a fresh light. Let us therefore briefly review the policy suggestions we have presented so far in light of these fundamental principles.

Financial Reforms to Resolve the Immediate Crisis

The effort to limit rampant inequality while still giving incentives to people who contribute more to society through hard work, innovation and service is inherent in these fundamental principles. In addition, the principle of maximum utilization of resources and human potentialities put these ideas at odds with economic speculation, wealth creation through passive ownership, and any other arrangement that rewards those who do not contribute to the growth and welfare of the economy as a whole.

So, while the policy suggestions of high taxation on wealth, transaction taxes on speculation, and so on, are good steps to take to reduce inequality, they are only intermediate steps toward economic democracy. In a market based on economic democracy, economic power is decentralized among private business owners and corporate worker-owners, as well as among geographic regions. In addition, there will be ceilings on wealth accumulation, so the need for punitive taxes will not arise. Speculative markets would also be restricted by legislation, hence no speculation taxes will be required. The many financial reform measures we have suggested will thus gradually fall away once there is an economic-system's shift, once the economy is transformed through three-tiered restructuring, economic democracy, and decentralization.

Making Poor Countries Rich

Exploitation of resources and labor in one area for the benefit of another has been an integral feature of the history of capitalism, from colonial rule to the present free-trade agreements. This systemic economic trend continues to increase profits for individuals, companies, and rich nations, but it is in clear conflict with the second principle—it does not promote the maximum utilization and rational distribution of resources. The proposals given in this section of the book are directly aligned with these new economic principles and policies, including the initial protection of local industries and the gradual opening up to international trade. In addition, priority is given to local labor and migrant labor is discouraged, since the latter is most often a direct result of increased inequality between unequal trading partners, between rich and poor countries. Furthermore, there will be strict controls on the movement of capital. Profits from any service, industrial, or agricultural operation in a particular country or economic zone should be reinvested in the area, not drained away from it. Intellectual property legislation must also be carefully reviewed, with patents only being granted when it is in the public interest to do so.

Economic Democracy

Economic democracy, which enables private citizens and local areas to be more self-sufficient and empowered, is a new and groundbreaking concept. The policy suggestion to place a ceiling on private wealth accumulation is a direct adaptation of the first principle. The three-tiered economic system, with small private enterprises, cooperatives, and state-run key industries, as well as the concept of a decentralized economy with local planning, are two of the central building blocks to implement the second and third principles. The economic restructuring needed to create economic democracy—including small-scale private enterprises, large-scale worker-owned cooperatives, decentralized planning, economic zones, and balanced economy—are central features in restructuring a new economy beyond the current forms of both socialism and capitalism.

Green Solutions

In the chapter on green solutions, we observed that we already have many of the technical and scientific skills needed to develop a sustainable world. What we lack is the political will to oppose special-interest groups, such as the big oil companies and the auto industry, companies whose short-term profit interests undermine the urgent need for developing alternative fuels. This is not surprising, since political power to a large extent rests with the same special-interest groups, those who profit from the economic practices destroying the planet.

In an economy based on the five fundamental principles, the concentration of wealth that empowers these special-interest groups will gradually seize to exist. This will remove the few real obstacles to implementing the necessary economic and environmental changes.

Maximally utilizing our resources with a well-balanced adjustment between priorities naturally requires good stewardship of our environment and the preservation of the inherent life-giving gifts of the ecosystem. As planetary stewards, it is our human responsibility to safeguard all living things, in fact, to constitutionally protect the rights of both animals and plants.

Expanding the Scope of Economics

These new concepts expand the purview of economics beyond those discussed in present-day economics. This newly restructured system further divides economics into four major parts, which are termed the quadri-dimensional economy: the general economy, the commercial economy, the people's economy, and the psycho-economy.[10] According to

Sarkar, "Most economists today understand only a little of the principles of general economy and of commercial economy, but both of these parts are still in an undeveloped stage. People's economy and psycho-economy are totally overlooked by modern economists, and as such could find no place in the present mode of economic thinking." [11]

General Economy

The general economy comes closest to what could be considered economics as we know it today. It concerns itself with the workings of the economy as a whole and the organization and structure of agriculture, service, and industry. That is, the general economy concerns itself in particular with the three-tiered structure of the new economy and the "coordination of economic planning at all levels to ensure collective welfare." [12]

Commercial Economy

The commercial economy is closest to what is presently taught in business schools but extends its scope much further. Instead of focusing on how production can be made more profitable for an individual company, the core of the commercial economy is to ensure the maximum utilization and rational distribution of all resources. Naturally, all economic activities, in order to be sustainable, have to be profitable, but profit cannot be the sole criteria of a successful business. By introducing the concept of maximum utilization on a global scale and disallowing externalities, a new idea of commerce emerges that works in dynamic balance with all living and material things.

People's Economy

The people's economy is concerned with providing people's essential needs, such as food, clothing, education, shelter, and medical care. Presently it is assumed—in spite of ample proof to the contrary—that people's needs are always met by market forces. However, as we have seen in innumerable examples in this book, that is not always the case. It is not always profitable to care for the needs of the poor, since they have little purchasing capacity. Hence, the provision for people's basic needs is often neglected. In the present economic climate, except perhaps for a few European countries, these needs are not met by the general and commercial economy. Thus the need for a people's economy.

The people's economy ensures that the needs of ordinary citizens are prioritized, even at the expense of more profitable but less useful economic projects. In times of war and disasters, people often forego the normal business models and focus on providing basic necessities for the country. In doing so, the extreme concentration of wealth usually dwindles and equality rises. Indeed, wars and disasters have, according to Piketty, been the main equalizer of economic forces in the last century.[13] To make the people's economy a permanent feature of the economy is to permanently secure a role for providing the basic needs for people before expanding the production of luxury goods and services. This means that the purchasing capacity of basic necessities is to be guaranteed to all under the constitution. While freedom of expression and the formation of parties are important features of democracy, freedom from want is even more essential. Nobody who is forced to go hungry or who is unemployed can be considered free.

Adam Smith, the so-called father of capitalism himself, apparently agreed that the profit motive should not be the driving force of an economy; rather it should be the production of commodities for consumption. Hence, profits must be subordinated to this more important goal. In *Wealth of Nations*, Smith writes, "Consumption is the sole end and purpose of all production; and the interest of the producer ought to be attended to, only so far as it may be necessary for promoting that of the consumer. The maxim is so perfectly self-evident, that it would be absurd to attempt to prove it." [14]

It is interesting to note that Sarkar also includes education as a basic necessity. Apart from upheavals through wars and disaster, the wide availability of education and knowledge has, according to Picketty, been one of the most important factors in counteracting inequality.

Psycho-economy

The psycho-economy pertains to the relationship between human psychology and economics. Economic exploitation is often accompanied by psychological and cultural exploitation. This dual impact is a near-universal phenomenon in the advertising industry, where artificial needs are created in order to drive sales profits. Yes, there is a need to supply breakfast cereals, but we do not need 4945 different types—which was the number of cereals produced in the US in 2012—in order to satisfy those needs, the majority of them advertised to impressionable kids watching television.[15] Children are thus lured to eat these "low fat" cereals containing large amounts of sugar.

In this way, the advertising industry creates an artificial need, fooling kids and parents into thinking these foods are good for health when in fact they are not, when in fact they make kids unhealthy and obese from the consumption of too much sugar. This kind of business marketing Sarkar termed "psycho-economic exploitation": to make people think that a certain product is needed to be healthy and happy when in fact it is not true. Another form of psycho-economic exploitation takes place in underdeveloped countries today, namely the myth that free trade is a panacea for economic growth in developing countries.

The second area of psycho-economics concerns our intellectual assets. This may include, but is not limited to, intellectual-property rights, which are limited to ideas that by law cannot be utilized by everyone without a license. Intellectual assets, on the other hand, are all valuable ideas in areas such as art, philosophy, and science that are essential for advancing human creativity and knowledge.

In the past, intellectual ideas have been one of the main drivers behind the evolution of human civilization and have been the foundation for many commercial or economic developments. By making psycho-economics an integral part of economics, this fundamental truism is recognized, and giving value to these important human assets becomes a viable economic possibility.

Some Features of the New Economy

- The new economy is not a utopian vision but a series of policy doctrines validated by practice. It acknowledges that today's policies must be proactively altered in response to the changing social and economic conditions of tomorrow.
- The new economy expands the concept of humanism beyond a concern for human welfare to the concern for the welfare of all living beings.
- The new economy is a holistic alternative to materialist philosophies such as communism and capitalism.
- The new economy is designed to serve the whole expression of human nature—humanity's physical, mental, and spiritual needs—in a balanced and integrated way.

- The new economy does not favor material development over cultural development, as in modern capitalism, nor cultural development above material development, as in traditional societies, but recognizes their interdependent contributions to nurturing a balanced and thriving human society.
- The new economy transcends the left-right political spectrum and acknowledges the positive contribution of many social philosophies.
- In the new economy the idea of progress is not solely based on material and technological change but on improving the integrated welfare of human beings.
- The new economy affirms that the well-being of individuals lies in the development of the collective, and that collective well-being lies in the development of individuals.
- The new economy supports a decentralized economy and proposes a fundamental shift in the locus of economic, social, and cultural power from transnational corporations and nation-states to local and regional levels.
- The new economy rejects profit as the core motive for economic activity. While important in operating enterprises, when profit supersedes consumer needs, sustainability, environmental health, and worker fulfilment, it leads to materialism and a dog-eat-dog capitalist economy.
- The new economy supports a deep sustainability that maintains balance at all levels of material, mental, and spiritual development in society.
- The new economy is rooted in and informed by ecology.
- The new economy is neither a free-market nor a command economy; it advocates a regulated and planned market economy.

Epilogue

The central message of this book—that the economy cannot just be reformed but needs to be restructured in order to save us from a perfect storm of economic and environmental crisis—is an urgent insight that needs to be spread far and wide. And the main reason we need economic-systems change, we have argued, is because the current capitalist economy is largely based on a myth: the perception that selfishness is both an essential and benign human drive, and that if our economy is based on this primitive urge, we will not only succeed as individuals but also as a society.

As we have shown in the previous chapters, capitalist selfishness has instead driven us to the brink of economic disaster expressed as four major global problems: inequality; unsustainable debt, resource depletion, and environmental destruction. We have also shown that by reforming the current market economy, we can prolong the system's viability for some time longer. But we have also argued that capitalism ultimately cannot be reformed—it must be replaced. Hence our call for a new economy beyond both capitalism and socialism. Such a need has been expressed by founder of the Capital Institute and former Wall Street trader John Fullerton, as well as by some environmentalists. Fullerton says we need a more holistic economy, and some environmentalists warn that we cannot simply "shop ourselves into a better world," that our real leverage for creating change lies "with our policies, not with our purchases."[1]

The economic principles we have outlined above represent these kinds of holistic economic policies. This new economy integrates small-scale private enterprise with worker-owned industries and large-scale government institutions, and yet goes beyond both left and right ideologies; an economy that speaks to the heart of humanity's urgent need for an economic system that distributes our financial resources more equitably and our environmental resources more sustainably.

Even if we all agree that such an economy is desirable in order to save ourselves from an unsustainable future, how will a more humane and planet-friendly economy come about? How will we be able to reduce inequality, increase purchasing capacity for the poor, and save the environment at the same time? The answer is simple: by creating a political movement that is dynamic and powerful enough to influence groundbreaking changes in governmental policies.

For this change to take place, however, two vital conditions are required: 1) a critical mass of people dissatisfied with the current economic system, and 2) large-scale support for a new economic theory capable of replacing the old one.

This movement has already begun. In his book *Blessed Unrest*, Paul Hawken estimates there are over 3 million people worldwide working in over one hundred thousand organizations who are advocating economic, environmental, and social change. When the inevitable global crisis reaches a critical stage, this movement's influence—which includes labor activists, environmentalists, and social-justice activists—will increase in power many times over.

The global economic and environmental crisis is already here. This crisis can be reduced by instituting the reforms we have suggested in this book, but nevertheless, it is a crisis that is inevitable due to the inherent problems within capitalism itself. Thus the urgent need to grow an entirely new economy. This new postcapitalist economy will also be market based, but it will be regulated, not by profit-driven corporations and their lackey governments but by the ethics of a law-abiding society upholding the best interests of both people and the environment.

Notes

Part I: The Perfect Storm

1. Erik Reinert, "Dette kan være begynnelsen på Europas fall," *Nettavisen No 24*, 12 January, 2014, http://www.na24.no/article3738548.ece.

Chapter One: The Financial Crisis: A Question of Life and Debt

1. *The U.S. Financial Tsunami Slams the World*, as quoted in article from www.theorybiz.com

2. Reuters, *Update 2-Greek Economy to Contract in 2013, Recover Next Year— Cenbank*, February 25, 2013. http://www.reuters.com/article/2013/02,26/greece-economy-cenbank—id

3. Carmen Reinhart and Kenneth Rogof, *This Time is Different* (Princeton, 2009), pp 12-13

4. Source: Eurostat, June 1, 2013

5. These figures only look at people who are willing and able to work; students are not counted. They do not reflect the number of young people who looked at the job market and decided to stay at school and gain a more advanced degree. Nor do they reflect those who left the country to look for work elsewhere. Further, in the months between November 2011 and November 2012, a reported 323,808 people lost their jobs — an astounding 887 people per day. Unemployment figures also don't count discouraged workers — only those who actively apply for jobs during a given period are counted. As high unemployment rates continue over time, the proportion of discouraged and thus uncounted unemployed rises, so the figures could actually be much worse than those stated.

6. New York Times, "Money Troubles Take Personal Toll in Greece", May 15, 2011, http://www.nytimes.com/2011/05/16/business/global/16drachma.html?_r=2&ref=business&

7. New York Times, Dec 13, 2012 — Source not found online

8. Helena Smith, 'Greek debt crisis far from over', *The Guardian*, January 2, 2013, *http://www.theguardian.com/world/2013/jan/02/greek-crisis-far-from-over*

9.   In particular, see chapters 5, "From Mercantilism to Green Capitalism," 6, "European Integration," 9, "Critique of the Neo-Classical Economic Theory," and 11, "Making Poor Countries Rich."

10. Juan Ignacio Sanz, a professor of banking at the Esade business school in Barcelona, New York Times, November 29 2011, http://www.nytimes.com/2012/11/29/business/global/european-commission-approves-bailout-of-four-spanish-banks.html

11. There are several credit rating institutes that rate companies and countries to indicate to lenders how likely the party is in repaying its debts. The scale varies slightly between the different agencies, but Standard and Poor has a scale ranging from AAA, indicating "Prime" to D, which indicates "in default." The rating of B is classified as "highly speculative," which means that there is a good chance that the lender won't get his or her money back. Statistically, a country rated B has a one in three probability to default on the loan—that is, it is unlikely to ever pay the loan back.

12. The accuracy of GDP and GDP per capita as a measurement of level or prosperity is highly contested, both in regards what economic activity goes into measuring GDP, and whether economic activity is in itself a sufficient indicator. There are also several other competing indices that try to measure human well-being, such as the Human Development Index of the UNDP. However, in spite of its limitation, GDP and GDP per capita are still useful tools in economics.

13. Peter Spiegel 'Euro deal over bank bailout in doubt', Financial Times, September 25, 2013 http://www.ft.com/intl/cms/s/0/5798ec4e-0730-11e2-b148-00144feabdc0.html#axzz2MahDiMX5

14. Nouriel Rounbini, 'Too Big To Bail Out?', CBS News, November 22, 2010, http://www.cbsnews.com/news/too-big-to-bail-out-ireland-gm-and-the-fate-of-americas-banks/

15. The Economist, 'Taking Europe's Pulse', January 1, 2014, http://www.economist.com/blogs/graphicdetail/2014/03/european-economy-guide

16. RT Business, '2013: Lucky or unlucky for the world economy?', January 3, 2013, http://rt.com/business/russia-world-economy-2013-997/

17. Alex Hern, "Unemployment up and inflation down", The Statesman, April 30, 2013. http://www.ifrc.org/PageFiles/134339/1260300-Economic%20crisis%20Report_EN_LR.pdf

18. See for example Chapter 5, "From Mercantilism to Green Capitalism, " Chapter 9, "A Critique of Neo Classical Economic Theory" and Chapter 11, "Making Poor Countries Rich."

19. For more information, see http://www.nytimes.com/2011/04/23/business/global/23charts.html

20. Although the euro was introduced as an accounting currency in 1999, bank notes and coins were not introduced until 2002, when the older currencies went out of circulation.

21. The source for the trade-balance graphs is the OECD statistical database.

22. Roger Cohen in the International Herald Tribune, November 11 2010. No online source found.

23. U. S. Debt Clock as of 4 July 2013, http://www.usdebtclock.org/. Source: Federal Reserve Bank. The unfunded liabilities are not debts due at the moment, but rough estimates of what future liabilities might be. The figures are based on a variety of assumptions, and could vary greatly due depending on future demographic trends. Nevertheless, they do serve as a reminder that even if the budget was balanced at this time, there are still potential difficulties ahead in the future.

24. The Dow Jones Industrial Average is a commonly used index to measure the performance of the New York Stock Exchange. If the Dow goes up, it indicates that stock prices in general are increasing, and if it goes down, it indicates that stock prices are declining.

25. Source: United States Census Bureau, http://www.census.gov/hhes/www/poverty/data/historical/people.html

26. Charles A. S. Hall and Kent Klitgaard, *Energy and the Wealth of Nations: Understanding The Biophysical Economy*, Spring, New York, 2012

27. Actually, the only countries with rapid economic growth are those that are not heavily indebted such as China.

28. For details on this and other energy-related issues touched upon here, the reader should refer to the third part of this chapter, which deals with the issue in more detail.

29. Michael Hudson. *The Bubble and Beyond: Fictitious Capital, Debt Deflation and Global Crisis* (Islet, Dresden, 2012) Amazon Kindle Edition, Location 126.

30. Erik Reinert, *Ibid.*

31. Thomas Piketty, *Capital in the Twenty-First Century*, Harvard University Press, London, 2014

32. Ibid

33. World Bank, "Bangladesh Reduced Number of Poor by 16 Million in a Decade", Press release, June 20 2013, http://www.worldbank.org/en/news/press-release/2013/06/20/bangladesh-reduced-number-of-poor-by-16-million-in-a-decade.

34. Jayati Gosh, "Poverty reduction in China and India: Policy implications and recent trends," in DESA Working Paper No. 92, January 2010

35. For detailed sources, see Noam Chomsky, *Understanding Power: The Indispensable Chomsky* (The New Press: New York, 2002), Chapter 5, Note 8, www. understandingpower.com

36. Noam Chomsky, *Understanding Power: The Essential Chomsky* (New Press: New York, 2002) p.378

37. Vaughan Gunson, "Why We Need To Tax Financial Speculation", *Converge,* http://www.converge.org.nz/watchdog/24/05.htm

38. Michael Hudson, Overview: The Bubble and Beyond', 10 August, 2012, http://www.michael-hudson.com

39. Michael Hudson, *The Bubble and Beyond: Fictitious Capital, Debt Deflation and Global Crisis,* Islet, Dresden, 2012, Amazon Kindle Edition, Location 476.

40. Investopedia, Definition of 'rent seeking', 2013, http://www.investopedia.com/terms/r/rentseeking.asp

41. Global Research, "Financial Implosion: Global Derivatives Market at $1,200 Trillion Dollars … 20 Times the World Economy", May 20, 2012, http://www.globalresearch.ca/financial-implosion-global-derivatives-market-at-1-200-trillion-dollars-20-times-the-world-economy/30944

42. Warren Buffet, Berkshire Hathaway Inc, Annual Report, 2002, http://www.berkshirehathaway.com/2002ar/2002ar.pdf

43. See: Too Big Has Failed, "9 Reasons to Change Your Bank", May 25, 2013, http://www.switchyourbank.org/why_switch_blog_page and Matt Philips, "Why Having a Lot of Bankers is Dangerous for Any Economy, March 4, 2013,

http://qz.com/58091/why-having-a-lot-of-bankers-is-dangerous-for-any-economy/

44. Professor Morgan from UCL makes an interesting parallel between neurology and economics, highlighting the similarities between an epileptic brain and the modern global financial system. He suggests that the emergence of a few highly connected and powerful banking hubs has made the system more prone to periodic fits and seizures.

45. Richard Price, "Appeal to the Public on the Subject of the National Debt.", London, 1772, as quoted in Michael Hudson, *The Bubble and Beyond: Fictitious Capital, Debt Deflation and the Global Crisis*, Islet, Dredsen, 2012.

46. Michael Hudson, *The Bubble and Beyond: Fictitious Capital, Debt Deflation and Global Crisis*, Islet, Dresden, 2012, Amazon Kindle Edition, Location 557.

47. *Ibid.*, Loc.718.

48. Paul Krugman, *The Return of Depression Economics and the Crisis of 2008*, Norton, W. W. & Company, Inc, 2009, p. 165

49. Ravi Batra, *End Unemployment Now: How to Eliminate Joblessness, Debt, and Poverty Despite Congress*, Palgrave McMillan, 2015

Chapter Two: The Inequality Crisis: Poverty in the Land of Plenty

1. Credit Suisse, "Global Wealth Report 2013", Zurich: Credit Suisse, 2013, https://publications.credit-suisse.com/tasks/render/file/?fileID=BCDB1364-A105-0560-1332EC9100FF5C83

2. Luisa Kroll, "Inside the 2013 Billionaires List: Facts and Figures," *Forbes*, 4 march, 2013, http://www.forbes.com/sites/luisakroll/2013/03/04/inside-the-2013-billionaires-list-facts-and-figures/

3. International Federation of Red Cross and Red Crescent Societies (ICRC), "Think differently: humanitarian impacts of the economic crisis in Europe", 2013, http://www.ifrc.org/PageFiles/134339/1260300-Economic%20crisis%20Report_EN_LR.pdf

4. OECD, "Crisis squeezes income and puts pressure on inequality and poverty", Paris: OECD, 2013, http://www.oecd.org/els/soc/OECD2013-Inequality-and-Poverty-8p.pdf

5. In fact, as reported by Oxfam (2013), the combined wealth of Europe's ten richest people exceeds the total cost of austerity measures implemented across the European Union (EU) between 2008 and 2010 (€217bn compared with €200bn) and (total $283.2bn, equivalent to €217.3bn (as at July 2013). EU-stimulus measures over 2008—ten totaled €200bn, see "Today's ranking of the world's richest people", *Bloomberg*, 12 July, 2013, http://www.bloomberg.com/billionaires/2013-07-12/aaa

6. Michael Hudson, *The Bubble and Beyond: Fictitious Capital, Debt Deflation and the Global Crisis*, Islet, Dresden, 2012, Amazon Kindle Edition Loc. 238

7. Ibid., Loc. Based on data from Thomas Piketty and Emmanuel Saez,

"The Evolution of Top Incomes: A Historical and International Perspective," http://elsa.berkley.edu/~saez/piketty-saezAEAPP06.pdf.

8. Branko Milanovic, *The Haves and Have-nots: A Brief and Idiosyncratic History of Global Inequality,* New York: Basic Books, 2012

9. IMF. "Globalization and Income Equality: an international perspective", IMF Working Paper, 09, 2007, http://www.imf.org/external/pubs/ft/wp/2007/wp07169.pdf

10. Thomas Piketty, *Capital in the Twenty-First Century*, Harvard University Press, London, 2014

11. Ibid

12. Ibid

13. Ibid

14. Some of the following arguments have been taken from the works of economist Dr. Ravi Batra, especially from his books *Commonsense Macro Economics*, Liberty Press, 2002, and *End Unemployment Now*, Op. Cit.

15. US Bureau of Labor Statistics

16. Ibid

17. Warren Buffet, "Stop Coddling the Super-Rich," *The New York Times,* August 14, 2011. http://www.nytimes.com/2011/08/15/opinion/stop-coddling-the-super-rich.html

18. Warren Buffet, "A Minimum Tax for the Wealthy," *The New York Times,* November 25, 2012, http://www.nytimes.com/2012/11/26/opinion/buffett-a-minimum-tax-for-the-wealthy.html?_r=0

19. Source: http://usdebtclock.org/ as of 19 December 2013.

20. *End Unemployment Now, Op. Cit.*, Kindle Edition Loc. 864-866

21. Ibid. Loc. 868

22. Richard Wilkinson and Kate Pickett, *The Spirit Level: Why Equality is better for Everyone* (Penguin, 2010)

23. Erik Reinert, "Dette kan være begynnelsen på Europas fall," in *Nettavisen No24*, 12 January 2014, http://www.na24.no/article3738548.ece.

Chapter Three: The Resource Crisis: Depleting Nature's Bank Account

1. The idea for the illustrations are taken from Charles A. S. Hall and

Kent A. Klitgaard, *Energy and the Wealth of Nations: Understanding the Biophysical Economy*, Springer, New York, 2012

2. World Wildlife Fund (WWF), "The Living Planet Report 2012," http://awsassets.panda.org/downloads/1_lpr_2012_online_full_size_single_pages_final_120516.pdf

3. WWF, "Living Planet Report 2008," http://wwf.panda.org/about_our_earth/all_publications/living_planet_report/living_planet_report_timeline/lpr_2008/

4. ttp://www.scientificamerican.com/article.cfm?id=forget-peak-oil-were-at-peak-everyt-2013-03.

5. Michael T. Klare, *The Race for What's Left: The Global Scramble for the World's Last Resources*, Metropolitan Books, New York, 2012

6. Charles A. S. Hall and Kent A. Klitgaard, *Energy and the Wealth of Nations: Understanding the Biophysical Economy*, Springer, New York, 2012, Amazon Kindle Edition Location 8026

7. The only sources of energy presently available to human beings that do not directly or indirectly come from the sun are nuclear and geothermal energy.

8. Michael T. Klare, *The Race for What's Left: The Global Scramble for the World's Last Resources,* New York: Metropolitan Books, 2012, Kindle Edition Loc. 143-45

9. *Ibid*, Loc. 149-66

10. NRK, " Tidligere Hydro-sjef: — Dropp oljeleting i Lofoten", April 2, 2013,

11. See Colin Campbell's website, http://peak-oil.org.

12. David J. Murphy and Charles A. S. Hall, "Year in review: EROI or energy return on (energy) invested" in *Annals of the New York Academy of Sciences* 1185 (2010), pp. 102-118

13. Association for the Study of Peak Oil and Gas USA (ASPO), "Peak Oil Review", December 2, 2013, http://peak-oil.org/2013/12/peak-oil-review-02-december-2013/

14. U.S. Energy Administration Information, 2014, http://www.eia.gov/forecasts/steo/

15. Charles. E. Mann, "What if We Never Run Out of Oil?," *The Atlantic*, April 24 2013, http://www.theatlantic.com/magazine/archive/2013/05/what-if-we-never-run-out-of-oil/309294/2/

16. Table 1: EROI of Various Fuels. Source: Murphy and Hall, "Year in Review: EROI or Energy Return on (Energy) Invested," in *Annals of the New York Academy of Sciences 1185*, 2010, p.109.

17. International Energy Agency, "World Energy Outlook 2012", p. 98, http://www.iea.org/publications/freepublications/publication/English.pdf

18. *Ibid*, p. 105.

19. International Energy Agency, "World Energy Outlook 2013", p. 25, http://www.worldenergyoutlook.org/publications/weo-2013/

20. *Ibid*, p. 72

21. See for example: Terry Macalister, "Key Oil figures were Distorted by US Pressure, says Whistleblower" in The Guardian, November 11, 2009, http://www.theguardian.com/environment/2009/nov/09/peak-oil-international-energy-agency Retrieved 2014-01-01. Other major ciritcs include Kjell Aleklett, Professor in Physics at Uppsala University, Sweden. See http://www.peakoil.net/headline-news/the-iea-raises-a-little-warning-flag-on-future-oil-production-world-energy-outlook-201.

22. Maria van der Hoeven, Executive Director of the International Energy Agency, Opening remarks for launch of World Energy Outlook 2013, 12 November 2013, London, http://www.iea.org/newsroomandevents/speeches/131107_WEO2013_ED_OpeningRemarks.pdf

23. Elizabeth Ridlington and John Rumpler, "Fracking by the Numbers: Key Impacts of Dirty Drilling at the State and National Level", *Environment America*, October 2013, http://www.environmentamerica.org/sites/environment/files/reports/EA_FrackingNumbers_scrn.pdf

24. *Ibid.*

25. Office of the Director of National Intelligence, "Global Water Security," U.S. Intelligence Community Assessment, February 2, 2012, http://www.fas.org/irp/nic/water.pdf

26. Fred Pearce, *When the Rivers Run Dry - The Defining Crisis of the 21st Century*, Beacon Press, 2006, Kindle Edition Loc. 145

27. Steven Solomon, *Water: The Epic Struggle for Wealth, Power, and Civilization*, Harper Collins, 2009

28. Maude Barlow, *Blue Covenant: The Global Water Crisis and the Coming Battle for the Right to Water*, The New Press, 2009

29. Gabriella Zanzanaini, quoted in "EU Commission Forces Crisis-Hit Countries to Privatise Water", *Food And Water Watch,* October

17   2012,   http://www.foodandwaterwatch.org/pressreleases/
eu-commission-forces-crisis-hit-countries-to-privatise-water/

30. European Environment Agency, "Observed Drought Episodes in Europe
(1971-2011), November 28, 2012, http://www.eea.europa.eu/data-and-maps/
figures/observed-drought-episodes-in-europe-197120132011

31. Peter Hall, *Lumberjacks in Eden*, (London: Privately published, 2007),
Electronic version available at http://www.populationmedia.org/
wp-content/uploads/2009/06/lumberjacks_in_eden1.pdf.

32. Donella H. Meadows, Dennis L. Meadows, Jørgen Randers, and William
W. Behrens III, *The Limits to Growth: A report for the Club of Rome's Project
on the Predicament of Mankind*, (New York: New American Library,1972)

33. Donella H. Meadows, Dennis L. Meadows, Jørgen Randers, and William
W. Behrens III, *Limits to Growth: The 30-Year Update*, (Chelsea Green
Publishing Company, 2004)

34. Charles A. S. Hall and John W. Day, Jr. "Revisiting the Limits of Growth
After Peak Oil," *American Scientist*, 230-237, 2009, http://www.esf.edu/
efb/hall/2009-05Hall0327.pdf

Chapter Four: The Environmental Crisis: No Nature, No Economy

1. Living Planet Report, 2012, produced by The WWF International and
other organizations.

2. http://www.guardian.co.uk/science/2005/mar/30/environment.research

3. George Monbiot , *Op. Cit.*

4. The Millennium Ecosystem Assessment Report, the UN, 2005

5. http://www.naturalcapitalforum.com/programme

6. Georg Monbiot, The Great Impostors, from article in the *Guardian*,
London, August 7, 2012

7. Vandana Shiva, Water Wars, New York: South End Press, 2002

8. George Monbiot, from article in the *Guardian*, London

9. Ibid.

10. "Dodelig Hav" (Deadly Oceans), article in the Norwegian newspaper
Morgenbladet, 13-19 December, 2013

11. From an article at:: www.therightsofnature.org

12. From an article at www.earthtimes.org

13. Vandana Shiva, *Water Wars*, South End Press, 2004, page 15

Chapter Five: From Mercantilism to Green Capitalism: Economic History with a Twist

1. Ekelund, Robert B., Jr.; Hébert, Robert F., A History of Economic Theory and Method (4th ed.),(Waveland Press, Long Grove, 1997) pp. 40-41, as quoted in Wikipedia http://en.wikipedia.org/wiki/Mercantilism.

2. N. Brisco, The Economic Policy of Robert Walpole, (New York: The University of Colombia Press,, 1907).

3. Alavi, H. , "India: The Transition to Colonial Capitalism," in H. Alavi et al. (eds), *Capitalism and Colonial Production* (London: Croom Helm, 1982) p. 56.

4. Adam Smith, *An Inquiry into the Nature and Causes of the Wealth of Nations*, University of Chicago Press, 1976, Originally published in 1776) Book IV, Chapter 2, "Of Restraints upon Importation from Foreign Countries of Such Goods as Can Be Produced at Home."

5. Ha-Joon Chang, Bad Samaritans, The Myth of Free Trade and the Secret History of Capitalism, New York: Bloomsbury Press, 2008.

6. *Ibid*, Amazon Kindle Edition, Loc. 908

7. *Ibid.*, Loc. 912

8. *Ibid.*, Loc. 914. For a technical critique of Ricardo's theory of comparative advantage, see Erik Reinert, *How Rich Countries Got Rich ... And Poor Countries Stay Poor* (London: Constable & Robinson Ltd., 2007) Appendix I, "David Ricardo's Theory of Comparative Advantage in International Trade."

9. Adam Smith, *Op. Cit.*, Book 1, page 18.

10. Adam Smith, *The Theory of Moral Sentiments*, London: Prometheus, 2000, originally published 1759.

11. *Ibid.*, Amazon Kindle Edition, Loc. 3579

12. *Ibid*, Book 1, p. 477

13. Erik S. Reinert, *How Rich Countries Got Rich and Why Poor Countries Stay Poor*, London: Constable, 2007, page 54

14. Kaldor, Nicolas, *The Review of Economic Studies*, Vol. 23, No. 2 (1955

- 1956), pp. 83-100

15. The Economist, from the article "The Next Supermodel", February 2, 2013

16. Karl Marx, *Capital: A Critique of Political Economy, Volume I* (Penguin Classics, 1992, Originally published 1867) Book I, Chapter 1, Section 4, "The Fetishism of the Commodity and its Secret." Amazon Kindle Edition, Loc. 2844.

17. Friedrich List, *The National System of Political Economy* (1841, translated by Sampson S. Lloyd M.P., 1885 edition, Fourth Book, "The Politics.") Chapter 33, as quoted on Wikipedia. http://en.wikipedia.org/wiki/Friedrich_List.

18. Two of his main works were *A Tract on Monetary Reform* (1923) and *Treatise on Money* (1930)

19. Say's Law basically states that supply creates its own demand, since the person who is supplying a product will not do so unless he intends to buy something with the money he makes from supplying that product.

20. Joseph Schumpeter as quoted in Erik Reinert, *How Rich Countries Got Rich ... And Poor Countries Stay Poor* (London: Constable & Robinson Ltd., 2007) Kindle Edition Loc. 465.

21. Karl Polanyi, *The Great Transformation: The Political and Economic Origins of Our Times* (Beacon Press, 2001, originally published 1946)

22. Karl Polanyi, *The Great Transformation*, Beacon Press, 2001, page 43

23. *Ibid*, p. 3.

24. *Ibid*, p. 75.

25. *Ibid*, p. 76.

26. Ibid.

27. Ibid.

28. Ibid.

29. Ibid., from Foreword by Joseph E. Stiglitz

30. http://grecof2.econ.univpm.it/esposti/wiki/lib/exe/fetch.php?media=didattica:coase_jle1960.pdf. jj

31. Needs full citation http://www.pbs.org/wgbh/commandingheights/shared/minitextlo/int_miltonfriedman.html.

32. Robert P. Murphy in an article on the website of the Ludwig von Mises Institute, http://mises.org/daily/5390/.

33. Milton Friedman interview with Richard Heffner on "The Open Mind" (December 7, 1975)

34. Michael Hudson, *The Bubble and Beyond: Fictitious Capital, Debt Deflation and Global Crisis*, Dresden: ISLET-Verlag, 2012, Amazon Kindle Edition Loc. 238.

35. *Ibid*, Loc. 476. cite

36. *Ibid*, Loc. 183. cite

37. *Ibid*, Loc. 190

38. Erik S. Reinert, *Why Rich Countries Become Rich and Why Poor Countries Stay Poor*, (London: Constable, 2007).

39. Erik S. Reinert, *Why Rich Countries Become Rich and Why Poor Countries Stay Poor*, London: Constable, 2007.

40. Paul Hawken, as quoted in E. F. Schumacher's *Small is Beautiful*, 25th Anniversary Edition, Point Roberts, WA: Hartley and Marks, 1999, p. 5

41. E.F. Schumacher, *Small is Beautiful*, Point Roberts, WA: Hartley and Marks, 25th Anniversary, , 1999

42. Vandana Shiva, "Real Wealth-Real Poverty—How Economic Globalization is Robbing the Poor of Wealth," a speech given at Scripps College in Claremont, California on Dec. 2, 2003.

43. Ibid

Chapter Six: The European Union: The Future of the World or the End of an Era?

1. Merkel, Angela, as quoted in *Spiegel.de* on October 26, 2011, http://www.spiegel.de/international/europe/german-parliamentary-vote-merkel-says-future-peace-and-prosperity-at-stake-in-crisis-talks-a-794141.html

2. Alan Woods, "A Socialist Alternative to the European Union", article on "In Defence of Marxism", http://www.marxist.com/Europe-old/socialisteurope.html

3. Treaty of Versailles, Section 231, https://en.wikisource.org/wiki/Treaty_of_S%C3%A8vres/Part_VIII

4. John Maynard Keynes, *The Economic Consequences of the Peace*, New York: Skyhorse Publishing, 2007, originally published by McMillan in 1919, p. 100

5. Erik S. Reinert, *How Rich Countries Got Rich... and Why Poor Countries Stay Poor*, London: Constable , 2007, Amazon Kindle Edition, Loc 1951

6. Ha-Joon Chang, *Bad Samaritans: The Guilty Secrets of Rich Nations and the Threat to Global Prosperity*, New York: Random House, 2008, p.31.

7. Vandana Shiva, "The Suicide Economy of Global Corporations," article published on *Countercurrent*, April 5 2004, http://www.countercurrents. org/glo-shiva050404.htm

8. Rudiyard Griffiths,(Ed.), *The Munk Debates, Has the European Experiment Failed?*, Toronto: Anansi, 2012

9. Erik S. Reinert, "The Only Way Out: Organized Debt Default, interview on Geopolitika", No. 63, May 2013, http://www.geopolitika. rs/index.php/en/drutvo/209-srpski/2013-06-12-18-05-45/english/ interview/538-erik-s-reinert

10. The Maastricht Treaty, http://www.eurotreaties.com/maastrichtext.html.

11. "A Lesson for Great Britain," article on www.tfa.net The Freedom Association's website.

12. "EU Subsidies Linked To Overfishing", *Ecologist* Magazine, 31 March 2010

13. Tvzetina Borizova, "Small Farming in South East Europe at a Crossroads", article in *Osservatorio Balcani e Caucaso*, on November 19, 2013, http:// www.balcanicaucaso.org/eng/Regions-and-countries/Balkans/ Small-farming-in-South-East-Europe-at-a-crossroads-144134

14. Eirik Grasaas-Stavenes, "WTO Conducts War on Resources (WTO fører ressurskrig)", Klassekampen, November 13, 2013, http://www. klassekampen.no/article/20131113/ARTICLE/131119983

15. Niall Ferguson, "Has the European Experiment Failed", in Rudyard Griffith (Ed.), *The Munk Debates*, Ontario: House of Ananasi Press, 2012

16. Johan van Overtveldt, *The End of the Euro*, Chicago: B2 Books, 2011

17. Richard Swift, "Dictatorship of No Alternatives", article in *New Internationalist*, October 2006, Issue 394, http://newint.org/ features/2006/10/01/european-union/

18. Dawidow, Bill, "The Euro is Doomed," *Atlantic Monthly, December, 2011*

19. Alam, Gazi Mahabubul and Hoque, Kazi Enamul, "Who gains from 'brain and body drain' business -developing/developed world or individuals: A comparative study between skilled and semi/unskilled emigrants", *African Journal of Business Management*, 4(4), 2010, 534—548,

http://www.academicjournals.org/article/article1380710374_Alam%20 and%20Hoque.pdf

20. Mogstad, Eadvard, lecture given at EU workshop, Vig, Denmark, Summer 2012

21. Information from http://www.oecd-library.org

22. John Hilary, quoted in "Is the European Union Damaging to Democratic Rights?" *New Internationalist*, issue 449, January 1, 2012, http://www.alter-eu.org/media-coverage/2012/01/01/eu-damaging-democratic-rights

23. Sterling, Bruce, "The Prospect of Western Europe Collapsing Like Eastern Europe," *Wired*, May, 2012

24. Krugman, Paul, "America Has a Currency Union that Works" *New York Times*, January 12, 2011

25. All information from the Norwegian "Nei til EU" ("No to EU") organization's website www.neitileu.no

26. Ibid.

27. "Free Trade: The Facts", *The New Internationalist,* No. 374

28. Mark Mardell, "Winds of Change Shake Romanian Farms", BBC News, September 4, 2007, http://news.bbc.co.uk/2/hi/europe/6977597.stm.

Chapter Seven: Free Markets: Fictitious Commodities and False Promises

1. Ha-Joon Chang, *23 Things They Don't Tell You about Capitalism*, Penguin, 2010

2. Karl Polanyi, *The Great Transformation*, New York: Farrar & Rinehart, 1944

3. Karl Polanyi, *The Great Transformation: The Political and Economic Origins of Our Time*, Boston: Beacon Books, 2001. Originally published 1949

4. Ibid, Amazon Kindle Edition Loc. 409.

5. Ibid, Loc. 2231

6. Ibid, Loc. 2253

7. Ibid, Loc. 2272

8. Ibid, Loc. 2274

9. Ibid, Loc. 2275

10. Ibid, Loc. 2278

11. Schwartz, Judith D, Should We Put A Dollar Value On Nature?, *Time*, March 6, 2010

12. An attempt to introduce some principles for such an economic system is developed in Chapter 12.

13. The one exception to this is intellectual property rights, which actually do the opposite. It is a way to legalize rent-seeking and protect intellectual property from the effects of a perfect market, in the way that tariffs and quotas are trying to protect a geographical area.

14. Eric Reinert, , Chapter 5, in *How Rich Countries Got Rich... .... and Why Poor Countries Stay Poor*, London: Constable & Robinson Ltd, 2007, Kindle Edition.

15. Ibid., *Loc.* 2180

16. The source of the figures is Bairoch, P. *Victoires et déboires: Histoire économique et sociale du monde du XVIe siècle à nos jours*, (Paris: Gallimard, 1997)

17. H. Alavi, "India: The Transition to Colonial Capitalism," in H. Alavi et al. (eds), *Capitalism and Colonial Production* (London: Croom Helm, 1982), 56.

18. Eric Reinert, *How Rich Countries Got Rich... ..... and Why Poor Countries Stay Poor*, (London: Constable & Robinson Ltd, 2007), Kindle Edition, Loc. 166.

19. Joseph Alois Schumpeter, Austrian-American economist, 1932, as quoted in *How Rich Countries Got Rich...*, Op. Cit.

20. Victor Norman as quoted in *How Rich Countries Got Rich...*, Op. Cit., Loc. 593

21. *How Rich Countries Got Rich...*, Op. Cit., Loc. 600 - 605

22. Ibid, loc. 371-72

23. Ibid, loc. 754

24. Ibid, loc. 754 -59

25. Ibid., Loc. 1227-30

Chapter Eight: Neoclassical Economics: A Grand Theory on Shaky Grounds

1. See for example: Michael Hudson, "How Economic Theory Came to Ignore the Role of Debt", in *Real-World Economics Review*, no. 57, 6 September 2011, 2-24

2. The Century Foundation, http://tcf.org/blog/detail/graph-how-the-financial-sector-consumed-americas-economic-growth.

3. Benoit Mandelbrot and Richard Hudson, *The Misbehavior of Markets*, Basic Books, 2004.

4. Karl Polanyi, *The Great Transformation*

5. Charles A.S. Hall and Kent A. Klitgaard, *Energy and the Wealth of Nations: Understanding the Biophysical Economy*, New York: Springer, 2012, Amazon Kindle Edition, Loc. 4345.

6. Duncan K. Foley, *Adam's Fallacy: A Guide to Economic Theology*, Kindle Edition Loc. 86-89

7. Attributed by Sir George Schuster, *Christianity and Human Relations in Industry* (Epworth, 1951), p. 109

8. Adam Smith, *The Theory of Moral Sentiments*, Prometheus, 2000. Originally published by Richard Griffin in 1854, p.195.

9. Daniel Kahneman, *Thinking, Fast and Slow*, New York: Farrar, Straus and Giroux, 2011, Amazon Kindle Edition, Loc. 329.

10. *Energy and the Wealth of Nations*, Op. Cit., Loc. 4584-87

11. Ibid, Loc. 4922-25

12. The market only presents prices and superficial knowledge about products. Information about who made it, how it was made, the community impact, the conditions in the factory, etc., is very seldom available to consumers unless they are willing to research it for themselves.

13. There is also a cost that goes beyond what can be calculated in money. By trying to calculate everything in money, we are putting the financial system above all else in the universe. This obviously does not make any sense. Money and economics are a tiny part of nature, and nature would manage well without them. However, money would be meaningless without nature. Therefore, to set a dollar value on the ecological system is, in a sense, a gross logical error, since the unit of measurement is incapable of measuring what we are trying to measure. Without photosynthesis and plants binding solar energy into carbohydrates, life would not exist on the planet. How can you put a price on this? Also, how can you put a price on beauty, love, and spiritual enlightenment? Although for the sake of the discussion we put prices on the services of nature, it should be understood that the value of life on earth and the ecosystem as a whole is limitless and cannot be measured in money.

14. http://www.nbcphiladelphia.com/news/local/Three-Mile-Island-221665871.html.

15. Léon Walras, *Elements of Pure Economics,* (Psychology Press, 2003, originally published as *Éléments d'Economie Politique Pure,* 1874-1877).

16. Factor-price equalization is an economic theory by Paul A. Samuelson (1948) that states that the prices of identical factors of production, such as the wage rate, or the return on capital, will be equalized across countries as a result of international trade in commodities. Samuelson assumes that there are two goods and two factors of production, for example capital and labor. Other key assumptions of the theory are that each country faces the same commodity prices because of free trade in commodities, uses the same technology for production, and produces both goods. Crucially, these assumptions result in factor prices being equalized across countries without the need for factor mobility, such as the migration of labor or capital flows. http://en.wikipedia.org/wiki/Factor_price_equalization

17. James Buchanan, *What Should Economists Do?* (Indianapolis, 1979) p. 236, as quoted in Erik Reinert, *Op. Cit.*

18. Edward S. Herman, *Triumph of the Market: Essays on Economics, Politics, and the Media* (South End Press, 1994), p.19.

19. Karl Polanyi, *The Great Transformation,* Beacon Press, 2001

20. Redlich and J. Hirst, *Local Government in England,* Vol. II, p. 240, quoted Dicey, A. V., *Law and Opinion in England,* p. 305.

21. Noam Chomksy, *Year 501: The Conquest Continues,* Verso Books, 1993

22. Ryutaro Komiya, et al., *Industry Policy of Japan,* Tokyo: Academic Press, 1984; 1988.

23. David Francis, as quoted in Noam Chomsky's, *Year 501: The Conquest Continues,* Beacon Press, 2001

24. Dertouzos et al: *Economist,* May 23, 1992, *Made in America.*

25. Paul Kuznet,, *The East Asian Miracle: Economic Growth and Public Policy,* Vol 4, No 44, July 1996.

26. Philip Mirowski, *More Heat Than Light: Economics as Social Physics: Physics as Nature's Economics.* This book is recommended for anyone who wants to understand the historical relationship between physics and the development of economics.

27. Léon Walras, Elements d'Economie Pure, Théorie de la Richesse Sociale, 1874. As quoted in *Wikipedia* article on Léon Walras.

28. J. A. Schumpeter, *History of Economic Analyses*, Oxford University Press, 1996

29. Philip Mirowski, *More Heat Than Light: Economics as Social Physics: Physics as Nature's Economics.*

30. www.economitricsociety.org/society.asp#constitution

31. Rodger Backhouse, *The Puzzle of Modern Economics.* (Cambridge University Press. 2010)

32. Ibid

33. Philip Mirowski, Op. Cit.

34. In a letter from Laurent to Walras. Quoted in Ivan Moscati: *Were Jevons, Menger and Walras Really Cardinalists? On the notion of measurement in utility theory, psychology, mathematics and other disciplines, ca. 1870–1910.* (2010) Note that "measurable" has a specific mathematical meaning and is important to establish the integrability of the function.

35. Ibid.

36. Léon,Walras, *Elements of Pure Economics*, Psychology Press, 2003, originally published as *Éléments d'économie politique pure*, 1874-1877

37. Paul Davidson, *Is Economics a Science? Should Economics be Rigorous? Real-World Economics Review*, no. 59

38. Ibid.

39. Keuzenkamp and Magnus. "On Tests and Significance in Econometrics". *Journal of Econometrics* 67 (1995) 5-24

40. Robert F Engle, , *Handbook of Econometrics, Vol. II.*, 1984. As quoted in Keuzenkamp and Magnus.

41. Infinite variance does not mean that the variables are infinite, only that variance grows unpredictable and without bound with increasing sample size.

42. Charles A. S. Hall and Kent A. Klitgaard, *Energy and the Wealth of Nations*, Op. Cit., Loc. 9438-42.

43. Charles A. S. Hall and Kent A. Klitgaard, *Energy and the Wealth of Nations*, Op. Cit., Loc. 9523-35.

Chapter Nine: Green Capitalism: Why it is not as Green as They Say

1. Bellona, "UN Climate Panel Says Emissions Quotas Insufficient—Focus

Should Lie on Industry," May 13, 2007, http://www.bellona.org/articles/
articles_2007/UN_Climate

2. Erik Martiniussen, Drivhuseffekten—Klimapolitikken som forsvant
    [translation from Norwegian: The Greenhouse Effect—The Climate
    Politics That Disappeared], Forlaget Manifest, 2013

3. Heather Rogers, *Green Gone Wrong: Dispatches From The Front Lines of
    Eco-capitalism*, London, Verso Books, 2013

4. Ibid.

5. Emily Knapp, "Organic Farming: the New Frontier, in Wall Street Cheat
    Sheet," *Wall Street Cheat Sheet*, February15, 2012,http://wallstcheatsheet.
    com/politics/economy/organic-farming-the-new-frontier.html/

6. Heather Rogers, *Green Gone Wrong: Dispatches From the Front Lines of
    Eco-capitalism*, London: Verso Books, , 2013

7. Robert and Edward Skidelsky, *How Much Is Enough?* New York: Other
    Press, , 2013

8. Greenpeace, "The Baia Mare Gold Mine Cyanide Spill: Causes, Impacts
    and Liabilities", April 12, 2002, http://reliefweb.int/report/hungary/baia-
    mare-gold-mine-cyanide-sp ill-causes-impacts-and-liability

9. Ibid.

10. Ibid.

11. Ibid.

12. Charles Eisenstein, *Sacred Economics*, Berkeley: Evolver Editions, , 2011

13. Riane Eisler, as quoted in *Sex, Ecology, Spirituality* by Ken Wilber, Boston:
    Shambhala, , 1996, page 167

14. Theodore Roszak, *Voice of the Earth*, Phanes Press, 2001

15. Charles C. Mann, *1491 New Revelations of the Americas Before Columbus*,
    New York: Vintage, , 2006

16. From *Wikipedia*: 'Steady State Economy,' http://en.wikipedia.org/wiki/
    Steady_state_economy

17. William McDonough and Michael Braungart, *The Upcycle*, New York:
    North Point Press, , 2013, page 14

18. Robert Reich, from his documentary film *Inequality for All*, 2013, see http://
    inequalityforall.com/

19. Tom Bawden, "*IPCC Report: The Financial Markets are the oO hope in the Race to Stop Global Warming*," *The Independent*, September 27, 2013, http://www.independent.co.uk/environment/climate-change/ipcc-report-the-financial-markets-are-the-only-hope-in-the-race-to-stop-global-warming-8843573.html

20. Heather Rogers, *Green Gone Wrong: Dispatches From the Front Lines of Eco-capitalism*, London: Verso Books, , 2013

21. Ibid.

22. E. F. Schumacher, *Small is Beautiful*, Vancouver, BC: Hartley and Marks, 1999

23. Paul Hawken, *Blessed Unrest*, New York Penguin Books , 2008

24. World Watch Institute, "Vital Signs 2012," Washington DC, http://www.worldwatch.org/vitalsigns2012

Chapter Ten: Resolving the Financial Crisis: Short-term Reforms That Will Work

1. Thomas Piketty, Capital in the Twenty-First Century (London: Harvard University Press, , 2014), Chapter 5.

2. Ravi Batra, *End Unemployment Now*, Pallgrave Macmillan, 2015

3. The doctrine of eminent domain says that the government has the power to force a purchase of any land to a fair price set by the government if it is in the public interest.

4. A Credit Default Swap (CDS) is an insurance against losses when a debtor fails to repay a loan. What makes it different from insurance is that you can take out CDSs on debts that do not belong to you, so if someone else cannot repay his debts, the person holding the CDS gets paid! Not only that, but you can insure the debt for many times its real value. It is insurance on steroids, and is presently not regulated.

5. Short selling is a process where party A borrows shares in a company from Party B and sells them at market value. If the price of the shares goes down before Party A has to give the shares back, Party A can buy back the shares at the present lower price and return them to Party B. The difference between the selling price and the buying price is the profit. Naked short selling is selling securities without first having borrowed them. The idea is to buy them back at a later time so that the only money that changes hands is the difference of price between the shares that were supposedly sold when they were bought back.

6. Options are promises to buy or sell a commodity at a certain price at a certain time. A legitimate way of using an option could be as follows: a manufacturer needs silver for its production but is worried about the fluctuation in the silver prices. By buying a call option on silver, the manufacturer can make sure that if the price of silver gets too high, he can still buy it at a reasonable price. For this insurance, the manufacturer pays a fee. But what if you do not have any manufacturing, and you still buy options? In this case, it is gambling. You gamble that the price of silver will go up, and if it does, you make money. There is no productive use for this type of gambling.

7. As noted earlier, one of the most eloquent critiques of the free market was written by Karl Polanyi in his book *The Great Transformation: The Political and Economic Origins of Our Time*, (Boston: Beacon Books, , 2001. Originally published 1949), in which Polanyi argues that the consequences of free markets are disastrous to society, since the government always has to intervene by forming policies and regulations to undo the negative effects of the market on society and the environment.

Chapter Eleven: Making Poor Countries Rich: Economics from Free to Fair Trade

1. See *Chapter 5: A Critique of Neo Classical Economic Theory* in the section, "Neo Classical Theory Disproved by History."

2. Ha-Joon Chang, *Bad Samaritans: The Guilty Secrets of Rich Nations and the Threat to Global Prosperity* (London: Random House, 2007) p.109.

3. Ibid, p. 110.

4. Erik Reinert, *How Rich Countries Got Rich... and Why Poor Countries Stay Poor* (London: Constable, 2008) Amazon Kindle Edition, Loc. 2983.

5. See Chapters 5, 8 and 9.

6. Many of the following points are paraphrased from the work of economist Erik Reinert.

7. This approach to a gradual transition to free trade was originally proposed by Friedrich List in 1840. For details, see Erik Reinert, Op. Cit., Loc. 2055.

8. Ha-Joon Chang, Op. Cit., p. 142.

9. Ibid., p. 130.

10. Ibid., p 134.

11. Ibid, p. 126.

Chapter Twelve: Economic Democracy: Changing the Economic Ground Rules

1. Working for the Few, Oxfam Briefing Paper, from www.oxfam.org

2. Adam Smith, An *Inquiry into the Nature and Causes of the Wealth of Nations* (Chicago: University of Chicago Press, 1976. Originally published in 1776.), Book 2, p. 279

3. E. F. Schumacher, *Small is Beautiful: A Study of Economics as if People Mattered* (New York: Harper, 2010; London: Blond and Briggs, , 1973) p. 222

4. Ibid.

5. Anthony Perkins, "Cooperative Economics: An Interview with Jaroslav Vanek," *New Renaissance Magazine*, Vol. 5, No. 1

6. Ibid.

7. Ibid.

8. Wim Van Opstal and Caroline Gijselinckx, *The Cooperative Provision of Public Services in an Evolving Welfare State*, 2009. EMES Conferences, Selected Papers Series.

9. J. Stiglitz, *Moving Beyond Market Fundamentalism*. Annals of Public and Cooperative Economics, 2009

10. Ha-Joon Chang, *Bad Samaritans: The Myth of Free Trade and the Secret History of Capitalism,* Bloomsbury, 2008

11. Aldo Musacchio and Francisco Flores-Macias, "The Return of State Owned Enterprises" in *Harvard International Review* (April 9, 2009). http://hir.harvard.edu/the-return-of-state-owned-enterprises accessed on 15 March 2014.

12. P. R. Sarkar, "Socio-Economic Movements" in *Prout in a Nutshell, Volume 3* (Kolkata: A. M. Publications, 1984)

13. Michael Lipton, *WhyPoor People Stay Poor: Urban Bias in World Development* (London: Maurice T. Smith, 1977)

14. Michael Hudson, *The Bubble and Beyond: Fictitious Capital, Debt Deflation and Global Crisis* (Dresden: Islet, 2012), Amazon Kindle Version, Loc. 190.

Chapter Thirteen: Environmental Solutions: Beyond Green Capitalism

1. Tim Jackson, as quoted in the *Resilience Imperative: Cooperative Transitions to a Steady-state Economy*, by Michael Lewis and Pat Conaty

2. Jaroslav Vanek, interview first published in *Prout Journal*, then republished in *New Renaissance Magazine*, please see: http://www.ru.org/51cooper.html

Chapter Fourteen: Economic Systems Change: A New Economy for a New Era

1. Roar Bjonnes, *Principles for a Balanced Economy: An Introduction to the Progressive Utilization Theory* (Prout) Research Institute, Copenhagen, 2012)

2. Thomas Piketty, *Capital in the 21st Century* (London: Harvard University Press, 2014)

3. "Efficient" is defined in the *Oxford Advanced Learners Dictionary* as "able to work well and without wasting time or resources."

4. Marxist economists have since long pointed out these inefficiencies. They point out that within each corporation, activities are carefully planned to reach desired results, while in the capitalist economy as a whole, everything is left to chance without any planning whatsoever. From this developed the idea of centrally planned economies that unfortunately never functioned in reality. However, the basic criticism of the capitalist system was correct, even if the cure was wrong.

Adam Smith also noted:

[Profit] is naturally low in rich, and high in poor countries, and it is always highest in the countries which are going fastest to ruin. *Wealth of Nations*, Op. Cit., Book 1, p 278.

5. The root of the financial crisis that broke in 2008 was unrestrained speculation and an unprecedented growth in fictitious financial assets that had no real representation in the physical world.

6. Malcolm Gladwell, *Outliers: The Story of Success* (Back Bay Books, 2008), 62

7. The film *Who Killed the Electric Car* describes how manufacturers managed to produce and market a very successful electric car as a response to California legislation for cleaner cars but then withdrew the cars from

the market and got California to reverse the legislation. (Available at Amazon: http://www.amazon.com/Who-Killed-Electric-Martin-Sheen/dp/B000I5Y8FU)

8. Eckhart Tolle, *The Power of Now: A Guide to Spiritual Enlightenment* (Vancouver: Namaste Publishing, 1999)

9. P. R. Sarkar, "The Specialty of the Fifth Fundamental Principle of Prout," discourse given on March 16, 1988 and published in *A Few Problems Solved, Part 9* (Ananda Marga Publications).

10. P.R Sarkar, "Quadri-Dimensional Economy," in *The Electronic Version of the Works of P.R. Sarkar*, Version 7.5 (Calcutta: Ananda Marga Publications, 1986)

11. Ibid.

12. P. R. Sarkar, *Proutist Economics: Discourses on Economic Liberation* (Calcutta: Ananda Marga Publications, 1992, page 45)

13. Thomas Piketty, *Capital in the 21st Century* (London: Harvard University Press, , 2014)

14. Adam Smith, *An Enquiry Into the Nature and Causes of The Wealth of Nations* (Chicago: University of Chicago Press, 1976, originally published 1776), Book 2, 279

15. "Breakfast Cereals Market Report - Market Research Reports - Research and Markets". Key Note Publications Ltd. Retrieved 2008-04-20.

Epilogue

1. Michael Hobbes, "The Myth of the Ethical Shopper," article in the *Huffington Post*, 2015

Acknowledgments

Even though writing most often is a solitary job, the ideas and concepts presented in this book have taken many years to develop into maturity in collaboration with many other people. We are especially indebted to our study of the great fathers of modern economics, Adam Smith and Karl Marx. Without them, capitalism and socialism would not exist; neither would many of the economic concepts we today take for granted—concepts such as markets, mixed economics, the welfare state, and economic justice. The book's many ideas have also evolved in private conversations, at retreats and workshops, during lectures at universities, while reading alone at home, and especially while working on this manuscript for the past three years. In addition to the two of us, there has been a large group of people, too many to mention here, who have been very helpful in discussing and contributing to the main points in our book. Some of them have also helped us to shape it into a more logical and readable form. For that we are especially grateful to these folks:

Devashish Donald Acosta, editor and writer, for his wonderful editing skills, valuable comments, and for his patience while the final deadline was approaching.

Bruce Dyer, banker and political activist, for reading the manuscript and providing important comments at a crucial stage in the text's development.

Dada Devajinana, yogi and activist, for his diligent help with research and his astute contributions to various chapters, especially those on economic history and neoclassical economics.

Edward McKenna, professor of economics, for his valuable feedback, especially on the chapter about neoclassical economics.

Mirra Price, copyeditor, for her excellent copyediting, feedback, and her work on correcting and organizing the long trail of footnotes.

James P. Quilligan, political economist, for reading hundreds of pages on short notice and for saying that the solutions we have summarized, especially those from P. R. Sarkar, contain the main outlines for the future economy.

Last but not least, we want to express our gratitude to our families and loved ones, whose nurturing and encouragement made even the most tedious parts of this project feel inspiring.

Index

F

Ferguson, Niall 147, 155, 345
finance capitalism 44
finance sector 297
financial crisis vi, vii, 7, 8, 11, 239, 333, 352
financial economy 7, 44, 49, 114
financial markets 201, 352
financial system 41, 42, 48, 250
Financial Times 21, 334
Foley, Duncan K. 191, 348
food crisis 49, 84, 85, 88, 89, 94, 101, 102, 154, 218, 323, 340
fossil-fuel economy 301
four freedoms, in the EU 148, 149, 150, 152
fracking 76, 77, 80, 83, 84
France 22, 23, 28, 29, 30, 49, 53, 116, 117, 146, 147, 151, 153, 155, 162, 181, 259, 260, 268
Franklin Roosevelt 149
free markets 18, 26, 123, 131, 139, 145, 151, 154, 156, 166, 171, 172, 187, 204, 287, 291, 353
free trade 8, 109, 110, 111, 112, 114, 119, 123, 127, 130, 131, 132, 134, 143, 144, 146, 148, 149, 152, 153, 156, 158, 163, 165, 166, 174, 179, 181, 182, 184, 185, 186, 201, 236, 248, 262, 265, 266, 267, 268, 286, 289, 291, 329, 349, 353
fresh water 9, 65, 85, 92, 93
Friedman, Milton 61, 126, 129, 189

G

gas reserves 72, 85
Gates, Bill 197, 277, 315
GATT 131, 142, 144, 194, 269
GDP 12, 14, 17, 19, 21, 22, 31, 32, 34, 35, 41, 44, 45, 62, 77, 83, 93, 94, 177, 180, 188, 225, 282, 297, 312, 334
General Agreement on Tariffs and Trade (GATT) 131, 144, 269
general economy 327
General Equilibrium Theory 200, 211
General Mills 218
general policies 260
Genetically Modified Food (GMO) 218
German Green Party 137
Germany 18, 22, 26, 27, 28, 37, 115, 120, 137, 141, 142, 146, 147, 151, 155, 156, 157, 158, 162, 166, 179, 181, 206, 268
global debt 30
global economy 1, 7, 18, 38, 49, 68, 97, 143, 145, 243, 272
global oil production 73, 76

Rogers, Heather 218, 227, 230, 351, 352
Roszak, Theodore 223, 351
Russia 74, 117, 180

S

Sarkar, P. R. 3, 274, 307, 354, 356, 357
Scandinavia 11, 12, 55, 97, 117, 151, 255, 260
Scandinavian Monetary Union 30, 155
scarcity 68, 101
Schumacher, E. F. 135
Second World War 34, 58, 120, 124, 125, 126, 130, 140, 141, 142, 181, 182, 205, 279
self-regulating markets 119, 120, 122, 174, 202
self-sufficient economic zones 287
shale oil 75, 77
Shell 77, 137, 194, 230
Shiva, Vandana 96, 136, 146, 341, 342, 344, 345
Singapore 125, 206, 258, 259, 260, 285, 292, 317
Singapore Airlines 259, 285
Smith, Adam 93, 106, 109, 116, 133, 138, 182, 270, 279, 328, 342, 348, 354, 356
socialism 115
Social Security 40
Soros, George 201
South Korea 125, 180, 206, 258, 264, 268, 279, 292
Spain 18, 19, 20, 21, 22, 23, 24, 26, 27, 28, 29, 38, 133, 153, 156, 157, 162, 164, 182, 240, 282, 313
speculative bubbles 27, 43
spiritual resources 313, 317, 321, 323
Structural Adjustment Programs 47, 131
supply-side economics 61, 130
sustainability 15, 95, 102, 135, 150, 153, 156, 206, 226, 227, 228, 230, 231, 237, 258, 261, 262, 282, 292, 295, 297, 298, 299, 301, 330
sustainable capitalism 218
Sweden 52, 55, 75, 152, 155, 156, 158, 160, 164, 179, 181, 309, 340

T

Taiwan 125, 132, 180, 206, 258, 259, 264, 268, 279, 292
tar sands 78, 79, 80
taxation 40, 56, 58, 60, 61, 125, 150, 159, 244, 246, 247, 255, 276, 325
taxes 20, 27, 39, 47, 56, 58, 59, 60, 61, 124, 125, 127, 129, 130, 150, 159, 174,

Organizations and Institutes

Here is a partial list of organizations, magazines, newsletters, and movements we believe are working toward a new economy and a more people- and earth-friendly world:

New Economy Organizations and Institutes

The Capital Institute
www.capitalinstitute.org
Economic Democracy Advocates
www.economicdemocracyadvocates.org
E. F. Schumacher Foundation
www.centerforneweconomics.org
Institute for New Economic Thinking
www.ineteconomics.org
New Economy Coalition
www.neweconomy.net
The Next Systems Project
www.thenextsystem.org
The Other Canon
www.othercanon.org
PROUT Economics
www.proutglobe.org and www.proutcollege.org

Magazines and Newsletters

Ecovillages Newsletter
www.ecovillagenews.org
New Internationalist
www.newint.org
Resilience
www.resilience.org
Resurgence and Ecologist
www.resurgence.org
Yes! Magazine
www.yesmagazine.org

Environmental Organizations

Climate Change

www.350.org
Friends of the Earth
www.foe.org
Work that Reconnects Network
www.workthatreconnects.org

Communities and Eco-villages

Transition Towns
www.transitionnetwork.org
Global Ecovillage Network
www.ecovillage.org

Cooperatives

International Co-operative Alliance
www.ica.coop
Mondragon
www.mondragon-corporation.com

The Commons

P2P/Commons Movement
www.p2pfoundation.net
The Commons Network
www.commonsnetwork.eu

Social Service Organizations

www.amurt.net and www.amurthaiti.org

Keep In Touch With the Authors

If you would like to communicate with the authors, purchase copies of *Growing a New Economy*, read their blogs, and be part of the growing movement for a new economy, please visit: www.growinganeweconomy.com or www.facebook.com/growinganeweconomy/

www.ingramcontent.com/pod-product-compliance
Lightning Source LLC
Chambersburg PA
CBHW021027210326
41598CB00016B/930